PATTERNS OF COMPETITIVE COEXISTENCE: USA vs. USSR

Patterns
of Competitive
Coexistence:
USA *vs.* USSR

EDITED BY
Young Hum Kim

ASSOCIATE PROFESSOR OF POLITICAL SCIENCE
CALIFORNIA WESTERN UNIVERSITY

G. P. PUTNAM'S SONS   NEW YORK

TO SUSAN

We cannot hope to escape a prolonged and powerful competition with Soviet power—a competition which demands that we act from enlightened impulses but never act impulsively.

—JOHN F. KENNEDY

1

Preface

Soviet foreign and domestic policies began to take a new course—from "zig" to "zag"—after the death of Stalin in March, 1953. Within the context of this "new look," Soviet foreign policy was tailored to fit into the general strategy toward the attainment of its long-term objectives.

Although the Soviets envisaged the worldwide triumph of Communism, which they believed was guaranteed by both the dialectic process of history and their own superior power and strategy, they came to realize their failure in hastening the global process of political, social, and economic transformation toward Communism through the crude, rigid, and direct "cold war" tactics of the Stalin era. Hence, the "collective leadership," which was established immediately after Stalin's death, shifted to the subtle, flexible, and long-term strategy of what was called "peaceful coexistence." Its nature and context was gradually intensified and transformed into "peaceful competition." In late 1955, Nikita Khrushchev challenged the leaders of Western democracies in the following words: "Let us prove in practice whose system is better; this is our appeal to the statesmen of capitalist countries. Let us compete without war. . . . Our proposals are for peaceful competition in raising the living standards of all peoples." To all intents and purposes, the "peaceful competition" developed into the "competitive coexistence" of today.

The implication is that coexistence between the free world and the Communist camp in general, and between the United States and the Soviet Union in particular, should be described as "competitive." The recession of the threat of nuclear war has created an excellent opportunity for the rival camps to compete on economic, social, political, cultural, and ideological—all but military—battlefields in demonstrating which of the two—democracy or Communism—could more effectively eliminate human misery and poverty. Such phenomenal competition and the concomitant conflict in which the two superpowers are now engaged manifest themselves in various patterns: strengthening of national power, vying for superiority, competing for allies, and, above all, struggling for survival.

The anarchic state of the contemporary international society compels a sovereign nation to enhance its capacity to wage war, not only as a means of self-defense, but also as an instrument of national policy. From the standpoint of the United States, America's stepped-up military preparedness is necessitated and justified by the militant policy of Soviet Russia and other Communist states, who are determined to undermine and ultimately bring about the final demise of the capitalist system. By the same token, the Soviet Union regards the United States and other democracies as bent upon the destruction of the Communist system. Military planning of both countries is, therefore, designed equally to render physical support to national policy, to deter aggression, and to defeat aggression when deterrence fails.

At the present time the incomprehensible destructive power of the thermonuclear weapons in the hands of both nations has made an all-out war a highly volatile and conceivably self-defeating instrument of policy. As a result, it has created a power equilibrium between the two countries that enables them to pursue their competing interests and objectives with a certain sense of guarded optimism concerning their basic security needs. Consequently, the competition in other areas of national strength such as economic growth, better education, higher national morale, and improved international position continues to be waged by nonmilitary means within the framework of a military setting.

For victory in the "competition" with the United States, the Soviets rely heavily on what they believe to be the ideological supremacy of Communism. Marxist-Leninist doctrine is the fundamental source of their commitment to dialectic or economic determinism. Their persistent conviction in the inevitable triumph of Communism is based on this "scientific" law of history. Khrushchev's terse remark to Americans that "your grandchildren shall live under Communism" is but a succinct manifestation of this conviction. In contrast, Americans place their confidence in a constitutional democracy that guarantees the political principles of individual freedom. They are convinced that history has shown, and will continue to prove, the triumph of individual liberty in the long struggle against tyranny since the early beginnings of human civilization. In this view, Communist dictatorship is but a passing phenomenon, destined to collapse.

The struggle for ideological supremacy has taken the concrete forms of competition in the area of economic productivity, advancement in the field of science and technology, and exploration in the vastness of space. The growing Soviet prestige due to industrial progress, military accomplishment, and scientific achievement has further added an appearance of respectability and responsibility to the naked fact of power. The United States is cognizant of the fact that it was Soviet science and technology that first launched the artificial satellite and first took pictures of the other side of the moon. What makes the United States apprehensive is the possibility that many of the emerging nations of the world will believe that they should obtain assistance and advice from the Soviets, whose significant technological achievements might seem inherent in the Soviet political system.

Many of the emerging nations have attained their political freedom and national independence since World War II, and they are now seeking to achieve economic progress, which is of great importance to the maintenance of lasting peace and security in the world. The peoples of these nations, however, cannot lift themselves up by their own bootstraps; they need help from the industrially and technologically advanced countries. In a message to Congress, President Eisenhower stated in 1957: "Lacking outside help these new nations cannot advance economically as they must to maintain their independence. Their moderate leaders must be able to obtain sufficient help from the free world to offer convincing hope of progress. Otherwise their people will surely turn elsewhere." The President added: "Our helping hand in their struggle is dictated by more than our own self-interest. It is also a mirror of the character and highest ideals of the people who have built and preserved this nation." United States foreign aid, technical assistance, the International Development Act, and the Peace Corps are various agencies designed to implement the basic process of people helping people.

After the death of Stalin, the Soviet Union cast off its economic isolationism and launched a program of aid and trade directed primarily toward the underdeveloped countries on the fringe of the Communist bloc, and the following year the Soviets offered to make a financial contribution to the United Nations Expanded Program. The Soviet aid program, which has steadily accelerated in scope and scale, is designed for political, psychological, and propaganda effects rather than sheer economic and technical advancement. Thus, the aid programs have come to constitute one of the permanent features of "competitive coexistence."

A considerable number of experts and laymen believe that for the first time in human history, mankind is confronted with the possibility of total self-destruction. The all-out use of nuclear weapons in total war, triggered by either accident, misunderstanding, miscalculation, irrational act, or escalation, is equated with automatic mutual annihilation. Under such a "balance of terror" condition, leaders of both the United States and the Soviet Union seem to realize the inherent threat subsisting in nuclear policies, not only to the survival of their own peoples, but to that of humanity as a whole. They therefore avoid pursuing ambitious policies that might set in motion a chain reaction that could bring about their own doomsday.

The alternative to mutual annihilation is the accommodation whereby nations endeavor to eliminate, or at least to reduce, the means of destruction, thus enhancing the chances for peace. Disarmament negotiations, the Test-Ban Treaty, and other measures in the improvement of American-Soviet relations are steps taken in this direction. Meanwhile, leaders of the United States need be neither "dead" nor "red"; only through bold and imaginative national determination and character will they ultimately triumph over Soviet Communists. They must neither embrace the spirit of appeasement nor neglect a courageous response to this Soviet challenge in the "competition."

The purpose of this book is to provide students of international politics, especially those engaged in the study of American-Soviet relations, with comprehensive reading materials that will enable them to better understand the complex nature and scope of "competitive coexistence" between the United States and the Soviet Union.

Acknowledgments

I wish to express my profound gratitude to the following persons who have granted me permission to reproduce their works: Vice-President Hubert H. Humphrey; Senator James W. Fulbright; Senator Henry M. Jackson; Dr. W. W. Rostow, Counselor and Chairman of the Policy Planning Council; Professor C. P. FitzGerald of the Australian National University; Dr. Robert A. Kilmarx of the Department of Defense; Professor Richard Lowenthal of the Free University of Berlin; Mr. Clarence B. Randall of Inland Steel Company; Professor Alvin Z. Rubenstein of the University of Pennsylvania; and Dr. Barbara Ward.

I am also indebted to the following organizations and publishers whose generous permissions to reprint their copyright publications made this volume possible: the American Academy of Arts and Sciences; the American Academy of Political and Social Science; George Braziller, Inc.; *Current History*; the Council on Foreign Relations, Inc.; Forschungsinstitut, Munich, Germany; the International Arts and Sciences Press; the Joint Committee on Slavic Studies, Columbia University; the *New Republic*; McGraw-Hill, Inc.; *The New York Times*; Frederick A. Praeger, Publishers; the Princeton University Press; Saturday Review, Inc.; the UNESCO Publication Center; the United States Information Agency; the University of Virginia; and *Vital Speeches*.

Finally, I am extremely grateful to my colleague, Professor Stanley Newcomb, for his advice and suggestions; to Dr. Hazel Pulling, Miss Elizabeth Armstrong, and their Ryan Library staff for their assistance in search of materials; to Miss Leila Tvedt and Mrs. Rachel Schwartz for their unselfish help in the preparation of the manuscript; and to my wife, Susan, for her constant encouragement and infinite patience.

Contents

Part Four:

ACCOMMODATION—ALTERNATIVE TO ANNIHILATION

Part One

Struggle for Strength

CHAPTER I

Military Preparedness

*Our strategic retaliatory forces are fully capable of destroying the
Soviet target system, even after absorbing an initial surprise attack.*
                                                        —ROBERT S. MCNAMARA

*The Communist Party and the Soviet people show constant concern
for the further strengthening of the military might of the Soviet
state and for arming the Army and Navy with the most modern
weapons of warfare.*
                                                        —RODION Y. MALINOVSKY

*At the top of essential requirements for safeguarding na-
tional interest is military preparedness, the physical capability to deter
possible aggression from without and to repulse and retaliate against
an enemy attack if it should occur. Inasmuch as no nation feels
absolutely secure from the threat of potential adversaries, military
preparedness becomes competitive as each nation attempts to achieve
relative superiority of its armed forces over those of others who
threaten its security implicitly or explicitly.*

*Some of the issues confronting military planners are formulation
of effective tactics and strategy; maximum utilization of manpower
and material resources, with minimum waste; organizational and
operational efficiency in military establishments; scientific and technological advancement in weaponry; budgetary appropriations and
arms production; and military alliances and foreign bases.*

*All told, this competition, in the case of the United States vis-à-vis
the Soviet Union, seems to have culminated in the military capability
of either side to "overkill" the other.*

*This chapter is devoted to an illustration of some aspects of this
military competition between the United States and the Soviet Union.*

Nikolai Galay, Editor of the Bulletin *of the Institute for the Study
of the USSR, Munich, Germany, analyzes the Soviet military program*

3

adopted at the Twenty-Second Party Congress in October, 1961, in terms of the principle of increasing party influence in the Army, the doctrinal basis of armed forces, and the pressure of Sino-Soviet ideological competition relevant to military policy.

Matthew P. Gallagher, an expert on Soviet military affairs, discusses the scope and character of Soviet military-political interactions in the policy sphere by tracing the course of a single issue—military manpower, i.e., Malinovsky's concept of "mass, multimillion" man armies vs. Khrushchev's notion of a troop-cut.

Robert S. McNamara, Secretary of Defense, in his testimony before the House Armed Services Committee, presents a detailed exposition of the problems and principles involved in the formulation of an effective defense policy for the United States in the strategic nuclear field.

1. SOVIET ARMED FORCES AND THE PROGRAMME*

BY NIKOLAI GALAY

In 1958, when the Soviet Army celebrated the fortieth anniversary of its founding, Marshal Bagramyan marked the occasion with an article in the party organ *Kommunist* in which he said:[1]

. . . creation of the Red Army was complicated by the fact that we were the first in the world to have to establish such a body without any kind of practical experience whatsoever. To make matters worse, this question had not been decided even on a theoretical level in Marxist literature.

This assertion was supported with a quotation from Lenin,[2] from which Bagramyan extracted an allusion to the poverty of Marxist

---

* From *The U.S.S.R. and The Future*, Leonard Schapiro, ed. (New York: Praeger, 1963), pp. 222–231. Copyright © 1962 by Forschungsinstitut, Munich, Germany; reprinted by their permission.

[1] I. Bagramyan, "Slavny boyevoi put" (The Glorious Fighting Road), *Kommunist*, 1958, No. 2, p. 35.

[2] V. I. Lenin, *Sochineniya* (Collected Works), Fourth Edition, Vol. XXIX, p. 132.

literature concerning the working out in theory of the question of the formation and organisation of the armies of "victorious revolution." The significance of Lenin for Soviet military theory and organisation, Bagramyan continued, was his contribution of the principle of "proletarian" military organisation. He asserted that Lenin worked out this principle purely by the empirical method, the characteristic feature of which is "creative development, not barren dogmatisation."[3]

The position taken by Bagramyan in 1958 was a repetition of one of the basic postulates of the Soviet military theory which was then still known as "Stalinist military science," despite the fact that this "science" had undergone substantial revision in the 1953–56 period and had lost the label "Stalinist." About the only change made by Bagramyan and Soviet military theoreticians after Stalin's death was to transfer credit from Stalin to Lenin for having worked out Soviet military theory and principles of army organisation. Thus, even in the wake of de-Stalinisation, the statements of Bagramyan reflected awareness of the absence of a military-theory "heritage" among the founders of Marxism.

It is hardly relevant to a discussion of the new Party Programme to go into the question of who made the greater contribution to Soviet military theory and practice: Lenin, who died 38 years ago, or Stalin, who was not only nominal but actual commander-in-chief during the USSR's major military test—World War Two. Nor is there anything to be gained by exploring the correct observation of Bagramyan— leaving aside the indisputable contribution of Marxism to the general theory of war—that the founders of Marxism, meaning Marx and his military specialist Engels, contributed nothing of substance to the working out of an organisational system for "proletarian" armies. (It would be too much to expect that calculations in the mid-nineteenth century would in any event fit the technical requirements for the armies of "victorious revolution" in the twentieth century.) What is significant for the present analysis, however, is the question of what is the contribution of the present heirs of Marxism and their military specialists to the theory of organisation of armed forces and the connection this may have with the publication of a new Party Programme designed to carry the USSR straight into communism.

The new Programme comes after lengthy preliminary preparation and after more than forty years of existence of the armed forces, a

[3] Bagramyan, *op. cit.*

period in which its troops have experienced battle duty. One might have expected, therefore, that the oversight of the founders of Marxism would be corrected at last by the setting forth in the new Programme of the principles, the system and the rôle of armed forces in a communist society, or that at least the new Programme would give some indication as to the general fate of the armed forces upon establishment of a communist society.

However, even a quick glance at the section of the Programme devoted to the armed forces impresses one with its brevity. Of the 54 pages of small print used for the text of the Programme in the appendix to this volume, less than one full page is devoted to the armed forces. And this despite the fact that the Soviet armed forces constitute not only an important branch of the Soviet state apparatus but also a very important segment of the party apparatus. The several hundred thousand officers (at least 300,000) represent a very large part of all the executive personnel in the service of the state. Servicemen also constitute fully 7 per cent of the party (about 700,000 members and candidates) and more than 10 per cent of the Komsomol (some 2,000,000) membership. Furthermore, 31 high-ranking officers are in the CPSU Central Committee (almost 10 per cent). In view of this, and the complexity of the political and military problems facing the Soviet armed forces in the atomic age, the brevity of the section of the Programme devoted to the armed forces would seem to be not only paradoxical but also intentional. In comparison with the 1919 Programme (see below), the military section of the new Programme is inserted for the sake of form alone. The present analysis cannot be confined, therefore, to the contents of this part of the new Programme but must also seek the reasons for the omission from the Programme of the basic problems of the Soviet armed forces today.

The military section of the Programme is part of the chapter dealing with the general problems of governmental organisation during the construction of communism. It is a chapter which discusses the "withering away" of the state during the transition to communism and a corresponding increase in the rôle of social organisations. The new Programme preserves the theoretical Marxist postulate about the disappearance of the state under the influence of the objective historical process.[4] The Programme does say, it is true, that full withering

[4] On this topic see the essay by Solomon Schwarz in *The U.S.S.R. and the Future.*

away of the state can occur only after the building of "a developed communist society" and the "victory and consolidation of socialism in the world arena." Nevertheless, this qualification does not alter the essence of the Programme's principal postulate about the tendency for part of the functions of the state to atrophy at an early stage in the building of communism. In connection with this it would be logical to expect that the section devoted to one of the most important organs of state—the armed forces—would reflect this allegedly existing tendency. However, there is nothing in the Programme even remotely hinting at such a process applying to the armed forces. The section confines itself entirely to delineating the tasks for the present and the near future:

. . . the CPSU considers it necessary to maintain the defensive power of the Soviet state and the combat preparedness of its Armed Forces at a level ensuring the decisive and complete defeat of any enemy who dares to encroach upon the Soviet Union.

To this duty is added an "internationalist duty to guarantee, together with the socialist countries, the reliable defence and security of the entire socialist camp."

The Programme is silent about the forms of military organisation in which this task is to be met by the armed forces as part of a state which is in the process of partial dying away. Attention is directed instead solely to technical details of the ways and means for ensuring the "decisive and complete defeat of any enemy."

The Soviet state will see to it that its Armed Forces are powerful, that they have the most up-to-date means of defending the country—atomic and thermonuclear weapons, rockets of every range and that they keep all types of military equipment and all weapons up to standard.

Among the measures intended to ensure "a high standard of organisation and discipline" (i.e., fighting capacity) of the forces, the Programme mentions two basic principles:

One-man leadership (*yedinonachaliye*) is a major principle of the organisation of the Soviet Armed Forces.

Party leadership of the Armed Forces, and the increasing rôle and influence of the party organisations in the Army, Air Force and the Navy . . .

With this the Programme's statements on the principles, the system and the methods of army organisation in a land of "socialism achieved" are virtually exhausted. The Programme does not mention a number of those problems, the absence of an answer to which compelled Lenin (and Bagramyan) to admit the silence of the Marxist classics on questions of military organisation under socialism. These problems include: establishment of permanent troops or a militia army; territorial or non-territorial formation of the armed forces; methods of overcoming internal contradictions between the national and international tasks of the Soviet armed forces—none of which receive mention in the Programme.

Even the principle of *yedinonachaliye*, the extreme importance of which the Programme stresses, is merely stated without reasons for its acceptance as the final, unique and immutable form of organisation for the Soviet armed forces. The principle of *yedinonachaliye* is, of course, not the only possible basis for the organisation of command in the armies of communist countries. The 1919 Programme carried the principle of *dvunachaliye* (two-man command, comprising commander and commissar). In practice the principles of *yedinonachaliye* and *dvunachaliye* have been resorted to in alternation. From 1918 to 1925 the system of *dvunachaliye* prevailed; from 1925 to 1937 a combined system of *dvunachaliye* and *yedinonachaliye* (the latter for commanders who were party members of long standing) was in force; from 1937 to August 1940 *dvunachaliye* was introduced; from July 1941 to October 1942—*dvunachaliye*. From the end of 1942 up to the present time the principle of *yedinonachaliye* has again been in force, at least officially.[5] However, as this analysis will reveal, while the Soviet armed forces have retained the principle of *yedinonachaliye*, it has been the practice since 1957 to limit the scope of the commander's functions by a collective: the commander, the political deputy, and the secretaries of the unit's party and Komsomol committees. Thus, during its 40-year existence the Red Army has spent eleven years under the system of *dvunachaliye*, twelve years under a mixed system, sixteen years under *yedinonachaliye* and the last four years under a new system—*yedinonachaliye* in principle with deviations in practice.[6]

[5] N. Galay, "Principles of Command in the Soviet Armed Forces," *Bulletin*, Munich, 1955, No. 6, pp. 11–15.
[6] N. Galay, "The Soviet Army and Domestic Policy" in *Problems of Soviet Internal Policy* (A Symposium of the Institute for the Study of the USSR), Munich, 1960.

Of even greater importance is the fact that Red China is building her armed forces on entirely different principles—principles which she loudly proclaims to be purely Marxist. Although Mao Tse-tung nominally heads the Chinese army, his deputy and the actual head, Marshal Chu Teh, has described the Chinese system of military organisation as follows:[7]

The Communist Party of China . . . has created a whole complex of systems of party leadership of the army; namely, a system of personal responsibility of every officer corresponding to the division of duties (as determined) under the collective leadership of the party committees, a system of commissars, a system of political work in the army, etc.

This system is not even one of *dvunachaliye,* but a complex of various collective organs of party leadership. Speaking of the need to draw on Soviet military experience Chu Teh suggests that this has to be done not "dogmatically" (i.e., fully) but "selectively" (i.e., partially), but he makes no reference to *yedinonachaliye,* and it would seem that the Chinese have rejected this principle.

The new Party Programme avoids the issue entirely, not even mentioning the deviation from *yedinonachaliye* which has been observable in the Soviet armed forces since the end of 1957. Although *yedinonachaliye* has been retained with regard to operational problems (training, mobilisation and administration), restriction of, and departure from, this principle may be observed in problems relating to political work, troop education, supplies and feeding, discipline, etc., where it has been virtually replaced by the principle of collective leadership—a fact which is obvious in the new Regulations of the Soviet Armed Forces, which were introduced in 1960. Although the Regulations try to conceal the deviation from *yedinonachaliye* by stressing its preservation, the Soviet leaders, who have long experience with both systems of command, cannot but be aware that deviation from *yedinonachaliye* in any one field will weaken its effectiveness in the operational, mobilisation and training spheres. The Programme's silence on this situation well may be an indication that the present departure from *yedinonachaliye* is only temporary. By examining the Programme's omissions also in handling the second principle of organisation of the Soviet armed forces—the principle of *increasing*

[7] Chu Teh, "The People's Army and the People's War," *Pravda,* 3 August 1958.

the rôle and influence of party organisation in the armed forces—
it is possible to obtain a better idea of the reasons for the departure
from *yedinonachaliye* in practice.

Increasing the rôle and influence of party organisations is proclaimed as the "principle of principles" in military organisation; its
aim, which is not mentioned in the Programme, is that of reform.
This desired reform is part and parcel of the Soviet leadership's
design to change the social face of the armed forces. Despite every
effort, the army has remained an anomaly in the socialist state, an
organism with a sharp social division between officers and enlisted
men, and with social distinctions within these groups; an organism
with "government service" traditions which predominate over any
artificial duties imposed by the party.

The intention to subject the social face of the armed forces to
drastic reform is perhaps most clearly set forth in the speeches of
the law of 15 January 1960 on "new large-scale reduction of the
the Soviet leaders at the USSR Supreme Soviet session which passed
Soviet armed forces."[8] The methods proposed for reshaping the
army's social structure were: a "cold" purge of the officers corps by
release from service of more than 250,000 officers, together with a
deliberate declassification—to lower rankings—in order to increase
political pressure on those officers who had been retained,[9] as well
as departure from the principle of *yedinonachaliye* already noted so
as to transfer a number of control functions to commanders of the
political apparatus and to secretaries of party and Komsomol committees in the armed forces.

Both measures are merely disguised by the so-called principle of
increasing party influence in the army, a principle the official purpose
of which is "to rally the servicemen round the Communist Party and
the Soviet Government." This could be interpreted as an obvious
inadequacy, in attempting to communise the army, of saturating its
personnel with party and Komsomol members. In fact this practice
has already reached almost the upper limits of saturation (90 per
cent of all officers).

---

[8] See report by Khrushchev in *Pravda,* 15 January 1960. Also the speech of
Defence Minister of the USSR R. Ya. Malinovsky, *Krasnaya Zvezda,* 20
January 1960.

[9] N. Galay, "Social Problems in the Reorganization of the Soviet Armed
Forces," *Bulletin,* Munich, 1960, No. 4.

The future will show to what extent the new methods of pressure on and education of the army will be capable of improving radically the *quality* of the army's communist stratum; however, almost half a century of experience in such work with the army has yet to produce the desired results. And in connection with this problem it should be noted that all the internal contradictions and difficulties of organising the Soviet armed forces along communist lines do not find expression in the new Party Programme. The same Eighth Party Congress which proclaimed the 1919 Party Programme also adopted a lengthy resolution "On the Military Question" which gave detailed consideration to the problems of the social, political, and military organisation of the army and attempted not only to provide a concrete solution meeting the conditions of the time but also to establish a theoretical postulate for the army of the "proletarian dictatorship."[10] Thus, in comparison with the documents of 1919 (however naïve and pragmatic they may have been) the new Programme can only be described as exceedingly empty and intentionally vague.

Finally, the military section of the new Programme is completely void of statements about future forms of military organisation as the Soviet Union approaches the frontiers of communism. The new Programme says nothing about the possibilities for structural changes in the direction of greater democratisation of military organisation—and this despite the fact that a whole chapter of the Programme is devoted to the democratisation of the principles of state administration. The 1919 Programme had also discussed this problem with specific reference to the army. In forming a standing army as opposed to the earlier Marxist principle of a people's socialist militia, the 1919 Programme described the standing Red Army as a transitional form to be followed by a territorial militia system "armed for defence of the people's revolution." (See footnote 10.)

Oddly enough, the declarations of early Bolshevism on the abolition of standing armies were, despite their archaic nature in this highly technical age, repeated by Khrushchev as recently as January 1960 on the occasion of the adoption of the new military law:[11]

---

[10] For the Russian text see *KPSS v rezolyutsiyakh i resheniyakh syezdov, konferentsii i plenumov TsK* (The CPSU in Resolutions and Decisions of Congresses, Conferences and Plenums of the Central Committee), Seventh Edition, Moscow, 1954, Part I (1898–1924), pp. 430–441.

[11] *Pravda*, 15 January 1960.

The government and the Central Committee of our party are now considering and studying the problem of a later transition to a territorial system in the organisation of the armed forces . . . We think that the territorial system can provide the necessary cadres and contingents of the population trained in military matters and able to use modern weapons . . .

The same thoughts were repeated also much later by Marshal Malinovsky.[12] However, these statements, which could be useful for Soviet propaganda, find no echo in the new Programme.

Nor does the Programme mention what will happen with the Soviet public security forces (the KGB, the frontier guards and other internal security organs) during the transition to, and under conditions of communism. These forces, which even after postwar reductions in their strength still number 350,000 to 400,000 persons organised in regiments and divisions and equipped with tanks, artillery and aircraft, are numerically greater than the fighting forces of, for example, Great Britain.

The new Programme declares in one single sentence that: "In terms of internal conditions, the Soviet Union needs no army." However, the Programme is not definite about whether such powerful police forces as those of the present will continue to be required.

Having stressed in the foregoing points so many omissions, it now becomes necessary to pose the question: What are the reasons for the new Programme's silences and lack of content?

It would be wrong to seek the answer in subjective causes, i.e., in the probable influence on the content and form of the Party Programme of Khrushchev's primitive approach to theory, his ideological instability, and perhaps that of his influential colleagues. He has, no doubt, enough educated and politically trained specialists (probably more than Lenin had), and this must partly compensate for his own theoretical shortcomings. It might be thought that Khrushchev's undoubted technical skill would have been enough to make him show a certain restraint in the military section of the Programme, especially in view of the circumstances influencing the Soviet government. Among these are two basic factors:

1) the presence of ideological competition from China, and
2) the use by the Soviet government of a so-called modern "military revolution" to develop and equip its armed forces.

[12] R. Ya. Malinovsky, "On Guard for Peace," *Pravda,* 23 September 1960.

Chinese competition consists in the possibility that this country might create structural forms in its army which are primitive, but close to the ideas of early Marxism, this possibility being predetermined by the industrial and technical backwardness of the Chinese state. The technical Soviet army cannot permit itself such ventures, for it has been a regular standing army since the middle of the 1920s, a form of military organisation condemned by the founders of Marxism. This forces the Soviet leaders to a certain restraint in their pronouncements in the Programme concerning their armed forces. The Soviet leaders have no opportunity, like the Chinese, to give their army the task of regular participation in the "production process," or to introduce into their forces the principles of "economic and social democracy," as Marshal Chu Teh calls the absence of any sharp difference in the pay, food and clothing of officers and men. The industrial character of Soviet society and the complex equipment of the Soviet army do not permit such experiments as the Chinese can still undertake.

The second factor—the influence of the "military revolution" (that is, of nuclear bombs and missiles) on Soviet ideology, policy and military doctrine—is reflected in a *toning-down* of the ideological content of communist policy. For instance, this de-emphasis of ideological bases is seen in the threats addressed to the USA and her allies to wipe whole countries from the face of the earth with Soviet missiles. Even if Soviet fears of aggression from any particular country were justified, threats to "wipe from the face of the earth" not only capitalist governments and their supporters but also whole populations, including the workers and the proletariat (those to whom the Programme promises liberation from the capitalist yoke) is an expression of militarism gone rampant.

The 1919 resolution on military matters adopted by the Eighth Congress pointed to a number of measures for the establishment of the "mightiest army the world has ever known" and stated:

It [that is, the communist army of the RSFSR–N.G.] will not only be a weapon to defend the socialist community against possible attacks from the still existing imperialist states, but will also permit the rendering of decisive support to the proletariat of these states in their fight against imperialism.[13]

[13] *KPSS v rezolyutsiyakh . . ., op. cit.,* p. 439.

The new Programme not only reckons with the presence of an army as powerful as the one of which the 1919 Programme dreamed, but it also tries to create a strong impression that the Soviet armed forces are super-powerful and can solve all the political and theoretical problems of the building of an army in a socialist state. The Soviet leaders need such forces not so much to render "decisive support to the proletariat of imperialist states," since the proletariat is virtually disappearing as a revolutionary class in the industrial countries of the West, as to serve as a weapon of Soviet imperialist aggression or, at the very least, as a means for a "missile" policy under the cover of which the USSR can pursue economic and psychological expansion.

Furthermore, the Soviet leaders need a powerful army to deal with the problems involved in the existence of other socialist states. As the present frictions within the communist bloc testify, the problem of coexistence of communist states is an acute one even when they are confronted by the common "capitalist enemy." This problem would be even more acute if communism were to prevail throughout the world and communist states of different ideological *Anschauungen* had to "coexist."

For all these reasons the Soviet leaders found it necessary to say as little as possible in the military section of the new Party Programme which might well be designated the section of eloquent silence.

2. SOVIET MILITARY MANPOWER—
A CASE STUDY*

BY MATTHEW P. GALLAGHER

The principal line of stress in Soviet military-political relations over the past three years has occurred along what might be called the missiles-*vs.*-ground forces split in Soviet strategic thinking. Running through the complex disputes over strategy and force struc-

* From *Problems of Communism,* Vol. 13 (May–June, 1964), pp. 53–62. Reprinted by permission of United States Information Agency.

ture which have attended this split, and which have divided military theorists against each other, a persistent tug-of-war has been waged between Khrushchev and the Ministry of Defense over a seemingly subsidiary point—the size of the ground forces.

This tug-of-war should not be thought of as a purely institutional conflict: many military leaders have spoken out on behalf of Khrushchev's policies; on the other hand, some of Khrushchev's colleagues in the political leadership may be assumed to have supported contrary views advocated by the Ministry of Defense. Neither should it be thought of as a purely personal conflict—an aberrant phenomenon entirely tied to Khrushchev's idiosyncracies. Any Soviet leader occupying the post of party first secretary might have provoked a similar conflict: as the initiator of national policy he would have had to face the same choices that Khrushchev has had to face; as the spokesman for the general, as opposed to the special, interests of Soviet society, he could hardly have avoided conflicts with such a powerful special interest group as the military establishment. Thus, the conflict between Khrushchev and the Ministry of Defense over the manpower issue may be regarded as a natural product of the Soviet political system and, in particular, of the relationship between the political and the military interests within that system.

The manpower issue concerns more than just officers' jobs. Tangible economic stakes are involved: repeatedly throughout the past three years Khrushchev has indicated that his programs for consumer welfare have been dependent upon diverting resources from defense commitments; and while manpower may not be the largest item in the military budget, it is the most vulnerable. In addition, a conflict of strategic concepts is involved. The significance of the strategic issue fluctuates more or less sharply depending upon the scale and character of any troop-cut contemplated. It would be relatively less important, for example, should force reductions be aimed, as well they may be, primarily at low-efficiency cadre divisions in the interior of the country. Yet the fate of even these divisions might largely decide such vitally significant questions as whether the country could carry out a large-scale mobilization quickly, or whether the military could establish semiautonomous centers of civil control in the event of attack. If large force reductions were involved, the specter of 1941 would be evoked—for no lesson of that traumatic experience has left a deeper impression on Soviet military minds than the importance of large and ready reserves.[1] Even though all military men might not agree in their assessments of the course and character of a future war, they would be likely to rally together on such a point of policy conflict, recognizing that military interests as a whole stood to gain or lose by the outcome.

In sum, the manpower issue is a touchstone which has served over the past three years to distinguish two quite different approaches to the problem of national defense: the one, sanguine about the possibilities of peace, confident that short-cuts to national security can be found; and the other, preoccupied with the possibilities of war, insistent that all the means that might possibly be needed to fight and win a war should be retained.

The issue was first posed by Khrushchev in a speech of January 14, 1960, to the Supreme Soviet.[2] In it, he not only announced that a troop-cut of 1.2 million men had, in fact, been decided on, but he presented a rationalization of the measure which seemed calculated to cut the ground from under any known or potential opposition. He argued that conventional armaments, including surface ships and aircraft, as well as large standing armies, had become or were rapidly becoming obsolete—and hence could be dispensed with in the Soviet Union's defense establishment. The strength of a state today, he added, is measured not by the number of men that it maintains in "army greatcoats" but by the amount of "firepower" at its disposal. Finally, in an allusion that must have sent shivers of apprehension up military spines, he recalled with approval the territorial-militia system that had preceded the regular professional army in Soviet history, suggesting that a reconstitution of the system might be appropriate after disarmament had been achieved.

The echoes of his speech had scarcely died away before intimations of the military opposition it would evoke were heard. Speaking in

---

[1] A curious but by no means untypical illustration of the pervasive effects of this lesson is afforded by several retrospective analyses of the war of 1812 published in the Soviet press during the sesquicentennial year 1962. An article by Malinovski, which appeared in *Pravda,* Sept. 7, 1962, laid such stress on the importance of numbers in the shifting fortunes of the two armies as virtually to ascribe to this factor the decisive significance in the outcome of the war. Another article, in *Kommunist,* No. 12, 1962, co-authored by the military historian P. Zhilin, pointed out that among Kutuzov's virtues as a commander was his profound understanding of the importance of the "numerical size of armies."

[2] *Pravda,* Jan. 15, 1962.

the same hall, on the same day, Marshal Malinovski reiterated—in the midst of an otherwise dutiful gloss on Khrushchev's speech—the classic military formula that victory in war depends upon the combined action of all arms and services.[3] The contrast with the tone and implication of Khrushchev's words on this point was sharp. Where Khrushchev had told the Supreme Soviet that the USSR could completely annihilate any enemy with existing strategic firepower, Malinovski countered with the declaration that "it is not possible to solve all the tasks of war by one branch of the armed forces." And where Khrushchev had avoided any mention of the need to develop the conventional branches of the armed forces, and had even called for the replacement of the surface fleet and most of the air force by rocket forces, Malinovski asserted that "the successful carrying out of military actions in a modern war is possible only on the basis of a unified use of all types of armed forces. . . ."

In the weeks and months that followed, military spokesmen lined up to profess loyalty to Khrushchev's strategic wisdom—but a surprising number of them managed at the same time to register professional demurrals to key aspects of his program. Reservations were most apparent regarding Khrushchev's evident intention to relegate conventional arms and the standing army to the limbo of military antiquities. The cachet of these reservations was the "combined arms" formula. A Colonel F. Sverdlov, writing in *Red Star* on January 21, 1960, argued that it was necessary to develop all branches of service in order to provide the "greatest harmony and unity in the armed forces as a whole." A Colonel Grudinin, writing in the same paper on February 16, stated:

. . . our military science assumes that strategic rocket troops alone, as the main type of our armed forces, cannot fulfill all the tasks of war. The successful conduct of military operations in a rocket-nuclear war is possible only on the basis of the coordinated use of all means of armed combat, and on the unity of effort of all types of armed forces. This implies that all types of armed forces are and will be preserved in given proportions.

Not surprisingly, top officers of the branches of service most threatened by Khrushchev's reorganization plans found ways of stressing the continued importance of the forces under their command

[3] *Ibid.*

while professing overall agreement with Khrushchev's principles. Admiral Gorshkov, writing in *Soviet Fleet* on Armed Forces Day, acknowledged that rocket forces had become the "main type" of forces.[4] But he went on to argue that "it does not at all follow that the need for other types of armed forces has passed." Marshal Vershinin, speaking to an officers' *aktiv* meeting on January 19, 1960, achieved a somewhat similar effect by pointing out that, despite decreases in the size of the air forces, "new, more perfect" aircraft were being introduced as standard equipment.[5] Some officers indicated disapproval by faint praise or silence. Marshal Konev, commander of the Warsaw Treaty forces, was conspicuously restrained in his comment on the troop-cut, treating the measure as though its major significance lay in the field of disarmament negotiations rather than in the field of military strategy;[6] Marshal Sokolovski, chief of the general staff, disdained comment entirely. Both of these officers were retired from active duty within a few months after Khrushchev's speech—almost certainly because of their opposition on this issue.

International events intervened at this point to modify for a time the terms of the conflict. The U-2 incident and the collapse of the Paris summit meeting undermined the philosophical underpinnings of Khrushchev's program and led to corresponding modifications in his defense prospectus. The last occasion on which Khrushchev publicly disparaged the effectiveness of military aircraft was on July 12, 1960[7]—and a week later, in a speech to the Soviet intelligentsia, he referred approvingly, if indirectly, to the "combined arms" concept.[8] Military spokesmen, in the meantime, were pushing ahead to find additional doctrinal supports for their concept of the ground forces' role in a future war. In November, *Red Star* introduced a new formula to the armory of arguments appropriate to this purpose— the assertion that "mass, multi-million" man armies would be required.[9] And some months later, a military author was arguing—in flagrant, if unacknowledged, opposition to Khrushchev—that "the

[4] *Sovetski flot,* Feb. 23, 1960.

[5] *Krasnaià zvezda,* Jan. 20, 1960.

[6] *Sovetskaia Rossiia,* Feb. 23, 1960.

[7] *Pravda,* July 13, 1960.

[8] Khrushchev's speech to the intelligentsia on July 17 was withheld from publication for ten months, appearing finally in abbreviated form in the May 1961 issue of *Kommunist,* No. 7.

[9] Lieutenant General Krasilnikov, *Krasnaia zvezda,* Nov. 18, 1960.

might and variety of equipment technology does not entail a sharp reduction of troops."[10]

The gap between Khrushchev and the military was narrowed further by the events of the spring and summer of 1961. As a result of the new crisis that built up over Berlin, the troop-cut policy was officially suspended, appropriations for defense were increased by one-third, the regular release of servicemen into the reserves was deferred, and the resumption of nuclear testing was announced. This confluence of policy with military views on the practical level was accompanied by moves by Khrushchev on the psychological level evidently calculated to conciliate military opinion. Appearing in a Lieutenant General's uniform for the first time in three years, on the occasion of the 20th anniversary of the Nazi invasion (June 22, 1961), Khrushchev announced a formal concession to the military on the missiles-*vs*.-ground forces issue. Addressing the armed forces directly, he said:

The strengthening of the defense of the Soviet Union depends on the perfection of all services of our armed forces—infantry and artillery, engineering corps and signal corps, armored tank divisions and the navy, the air force, and the missile forces.[11]

But to interpret these policy shifts and political moves as signifying a basic change of views would be to accept the credibility of a complete about-face by Khrushchev in the space of a year and a half on a matter of vital national significance—a matter in which, moreover, he had heavily invested his personal prestige. To do so would be to ascribe to him a softness of character and inconstancy of purpose which seem out of line not only with the office he holds but with the record of persistence he has demonstrated in the pursuit of his basic goals. Khrushchev's own statements at the time suggest that he regarded the steps being taken as a temporary turn rather than as a decisive reversal of his policies. In a speech to military graduates on July 8, 1961, he carefully explained that the measures were "temporary" only and purely responsive in nature.[12] He seemed concerned to stress the notion that the measures would be rescinded as soon as evidence of a corresponding willingness to relax tensions was offered by the United States. And in a radio-television speech of August 7,

[10] Colonel S. Kozlov, *Kommunist vooruzhennykh sil,* No. 11, 1961.
[11] *Pravda,* June 22, 1961.
[12] *Ibid.,* July 9, 1961.

he was even more explicit in defining the political purpose behind the regime's action:

Why does the Soviet government consider such measures? These are measures in the nature of a reply. . . . The experience of history teaches: When an aggressor sees that no rebuff is given to him he grows more brazen, and, conversely, when he is given a rebuff he calms down. It is this historic experience that should guide us in our actions.[13]

Since the summer of 1961 there have been recurrent signs of controversy centering around the ground forces issue, indicating at the least that, however far Khrushchev may have retreated for a time from his original conceptions, he did not abandon his goal of seeking manpower economies—and that the military did not cease to resist.

· · · ·

The most striking indication of this sensitivity was Marshal Malinovski's article in the May issue of *Kommunist,* No. 7, 1962. Stressing the danger of aggression from the West and the need for continuing development of Soviet military capabilities, Malinovski vigorously defended the cost of Soviet defense programs. Arguing that Soviet defense expenditures should not be compared with the policy of "militarization" pursued by the Western powers, Malinovski asserted that while the latter consumed the budget, enriched the monopolists, and impoverished the workers, Soviet expenditures were dictated by legitimate state needs. The situation in the world was such, he said, that expenditures for defense were "absolutely necessary," and the Soviet people welcomed them. He then stated:

To this one must add that, with us, military expenditures are strictly regulated. In the Soviet government there is not and cannot be an exaggeration of military expenditures; our government carries out all measures for strengthening defense might within the limits called forth by the actual requirements for defense of the USSR and the fraternal socialist countries from capitalist aggression.

This excursis on the rationale of Soviet military spending had no known precedent in Soviet public utterances. That it was argumentative seemed evident from the content. The notion that defense expenditures might be "exaggerated" would hardly be raised—even if only to deny it—unless there was a compelling reason to do so. A

[13] *Izvestia,* Aug. 9, 1961.

good guess as to what this reason was could be deduced from Malinovski's stress elsewhere in his article on the need for maintaining
a large standing army.

In discussing current Soviet military doctrine, Malinovski placed
unusual emphasis on the notion that a future war will require mass
armies. The notion had been expressed in virtually the same terms in
his 22d party congress speech, but there he had placed it in the
context of a balanced presentation of other elements of the doctrine.
By contrast, in the *Kommunist* article, it was the only element of the
doctrine that he emphasized. Moreover, the substance of the argument was reiterated in another passage where Malinovski asserted
that in constructing the armed forces

. . . the party is forced . . . to adhere to the principle of maintaining a
cadre regular army which by virtue of its composition, numerical scale,
and degree of preparation would be able from the beginning of a war to
repulse an attack and destroy the aggressor.

. . . .

Evidence of tensions over the missiles-*vs.*-ground forces issue
appeared again in the wake of the Cuban crisis. The first sign that
some move was underway to revive the issue was the appearance of
a pamphlet attributed to Malinovski, entitled *Vigilantly Stand Guard
Over the Peace*.[18] Whether Malinovski was in fact the author of this
work is subject to some doubt, as Mr. Wolfe has discussed in the
preceding article.[19] In any event, though published late in November
1962, the pamphlet was given to the printers before the Cuban crisis
so that its contents cannot easily be interpreted as a mere reflection
of the lessons derived from that confrontation. It seems more likely
that the pamphlet represented the military aspect of a broad policy

[18] *Bditelno stoiat na strazhe mira,* Moscow, 1962.
[19] The writer shares Mr. Wolfe's view that this pamphlet is not typical of
Malinovski. Whether or not he was the author, the pamphlet should not be
taken as indicative of Malinovski's personal position on the question at issue
or in the policy debate which evidently followed. It is quite conceivable that
Malinovski could have accepted the broad outlines of a Khrushchev reform
proposal without conceding all points of his previous reservations and without
relinquishing his option to renew opposition when the opportunity presented
itself. Malinovski's ability to oppose Khrushchev was presumably much weaker
in the period before Cuba than in the period after it. Special advocacy in the
Soviet Union must adjust to the opportunities presented by the shifting fortunes
of the political leader.

initiative that Khrushchev was evidently preparing for the November plenum in anticipation of the successful outcome of his Cuban gamble. The pamphlet's confident claims of Soviet missile superiority, and its merely perfunctory bow to the "mass, multi-million-man" armies thesis, seem compatible with this hypothesis. Moreover, its stress on "qualitative" criteria, in speaking of the Soviet Union's commitment to maintain missile superiority, seemed to reflect a respect for the economic realities of defense which would be harmonious with Khrushchev's known objectives in the welfare aspects of his program.

A notable sign that the ground forces issue was centrally involved in post-Cuban policy debates was the publication in *Red Star,* on January 11, 1963, of a full page of articles defending the role of the ground forces in contemporary war. The demonstrative nature of this action was unmistakable. Other articles in the military press, both before and after this action, gave more evidence that a squabble around the missiles-*vs.*-ground forces issue was in progress.[20]

An interim resolution of the conflict was registered in Khrushchev's February 27 speech to the Supreme Soviet. In it he announced, in strikingly defensive terms, that the realization of the welfare goals that he had raised would be deferred due to the implacable demands posed by defense requirements. Khrushchev's capitulation proved to be temporary, but the fact that it occurred at all seemed due, in large part, to the strength of the internal political forces arrayed against him.[21]

. . . .

Whatever Khrushchev's reaction may have been to the affront over Stalingrad, several months intervened before there was a significant new confrontation over the manpower issue. That came last December when Khrushchev, in his concluding speech to a plenum of the CPSU Central Committee, announced that the regime was "contemplating" a new troop-cut. The indefinite character of the announcement, the ambiguity of subsequent regime references to the proposal,

[20] For examples of the reformist side of the argument, see editorial in *Kommunist vooruzhennykh sil,* No. 24, 1962, and Colonel General S. Shtemenko, *ibid.,* No. 3, 1963. For the conservative side, see Marshal P. Rotmistrov, *ibid.,* No. 2, 1963, and Colonel Skidro, *ibid.,* No. 5, 1963.

[21] Evidence of such opposition is presented in Mr. Carl Linden's article, "Khrushchev and the Party Battle," *Problems of Communism,* Sept.–Oct. 1963.

and the conspicuously inhospitable reception accorded the announcement by the military press indicated that a new phase of policy conflict was developing along traditional lines.

The first indication of military resistance to the proposed measure appeared in an article by Marshal Chuikov, published in the December 22 issue of *Izvestia*. Chuikov reiterated the doctrinal thesis regarding the role of ground forces in a future war with a forcefulness that had not been seen in the Soviet press in some time. He declared:

Soviet military science considers that victory in a future nuclear war . . . can be achieved only by means of the joint action of all types of armed forces.

And one sentence later:

Therefore, in modern conditions the ground forces continue to be not only a mandatory but also a most important integral part of the armed forces.

In between these two propositions in Chuikov's text was a sentence which appears to have been inserted arbitrarily, since it destroys the logical and grammatical sequence of the paragraph. The sentence reads: "There is no doubt that a decisive part in achieving the main aims of war will be played by the strategic rocket troops." The suggestion of tampering conveyed by this sentence adds to the impression that Chuikov's article represented a move in intra-regime politics.

Military resistance to the notion of a troop-cut seemed to be registered also in a major two-part article on doctrine by military theorist Colonel General N. Lomov which was published in *Red Star* on January 7 and 10, 1964. The article added up to a comprehensive restatement of Soviet military requirements and seemed contrived to emphasize the undiminished scope and priority of the defense establishment's claim on national resources. On the issue of ground forces, the article restated the traditional "combined arms" postulate with a bluntness that betrayed a fine disregard for the political proprieties of the moment:

Winning the victory in a clash with a strong adversary requires the efforts of a multi-million-man modern army. This determines the contents of one of the most important principled theses of Soviet military doctrine, which is that to win a final victory over the aggressor the combined efforts of all types of armed forces, which rely on the decisive role of rocket nuclear weapons, will be needed.

Since the turn of the year negative evidence of the military's attitude has been even more impressive. It seems clear that the military has been staging a demonstration of resistance which rivals in boldness the "feats of silence" performed by other professional groups, on other occasions, when government policy clashed with professional interests. At the time of this writing—some three months after Khrushchev's announcement of the proposal for a further troop-cut—not a single Soviet marshal has yet mentioned the subject in any article in the Soviet domestic press.[26] And not a single reference to the subject has been made by *Red Star* since its one and only mention of Khrushchev's proposal on December 25, 1963. Whatever the outcome of the most recent troop-cut issue, this campaign of silence again demonstrates the Soviet military's readiness to protest decisions in the policy area in defense of its institutional interests.

3. UNITED STATES STRATEGIC PROBLEMS*

BY ROBERT S. MCNAMARA

In the event of general nuclear war, attacks might be directed against military targets only, against cities only, or against both types of targets, either simultaneously or with a delay. They might be selective in terms of specific targets or they might be general. In this regard, it is important to bear in mind that the types of situations I shall be discussing are illustrative. They reflect the way we go

---

[26] Two references have appeared in statements addressed to foreign audiences. One was in an article by Marshal Yeremenko, published in the English language *Moscow News*, Jan. 8, 1964. The other was in an article signed by Marshal Malinovski, published in *Zolnierz Wolnosci* (Warsaw), Feb. 22, 1964, and *Neues Deutschland* (East Berlin), Feb. 23. Both references were noncommittal, expressing neither approval nor disapproval. Malinovski's was, however, contradictory to Khrushchev's most recent, February 14 statement on the subject, since the Marshal referred to the measure as merely "contemplated," whereas Khrushchev had implied that it was much closer to implementation.

* From *Aviation Week and Space Technology*, Vol. 82 (March 1, 1965), pp. 62–66. Reprinted by permission of McGraw-Hill Publishing Co.

about determining our requirements. They do not necessarily reflect all the ways in which a general nuclear war might be fought.

In such a war, the following types of U. S. strategic forces would be involved:

1—Strategic Offensive Forces.

● Manned bombers, strategic reconnaissance aircraft, intercontinental ballistic missiles and submarine-launched missiles and their associated support forces and command and control systems.

2—Strategic Defense Forces.

● Anti-aircraft defenses: Manned interceptors; surface-to-air missiles, and their associated warning and control systems (including a capability against air breathing missiles).

● Anti-ballistic missile defenses: Anti-missile missiles together with the associated sensing, data processing and communications system, and the anti-submarine warfare forces directed against enemy missile launching submarines, together with the associated ground surveillance systems.

● Anti-satellite defenses: Interceptor missiles and the space detection and tracking systems.

3—Civil Defense Programs.

● Fallout shelters, warning, etc.

The strategic objectives of our general nuclear war forces are:

1—To deter a deliberate nuclear attack upon the U. S. and its allies by maintaining a clear and convincing capability to inflict unacceptable damage on an attacker, even were that attacker to strike first.

2—In the event such a war should nevertheless occur, to limit damage to our populations and industrial capacities.

The first of these capabilities (required to deter potential aggressors) we call "Assured Destruction," i.e., the capability to destroy the aggressor as a viable society, even after a well planned and executed surprise attack on our forces. The second capability we call "Damage Limitation," i.e., the capability to reduce the weight of the enemy attack by both offensive and defensive measures and to provide a degree of protection for the population against the effects of nuclear detonations.

While, for the most part, I will be discussing general nuclear war from the point of view of the U. S., it is important to note that we are actually dealing here with a two-sided problem. Assuming that both sides have the same general strategic objectives, which I believe to be the case, our assured destruction problem is the other side's damage limiting problem, and our damage limiting problem is their assured destruction problem. The significance of this point will become more apparent when we discuss the possible interactions between the U. S. and the Soviet offensive-defensive programs later in this section.

Viewed in this light, our assured destruction forces would include a portion of the ICBMs, the submarine-launched ballistic missiles (SLBMs) and the manned bombers. The damage limiting forces would include the remainder of the strategic offensive forces (ICBMs, SLBMs and manned bombers), as well as area defense forces (manned interceptors and anti-submarine warfare forces), terminal defense forces (anti-bomber surface-to-air missiles and anti-ballistic missile missiles) and passive defenses (fallout shelters, warning, etc.). The strategic offensive forces can contribute to the damage limiting objective by attacking enemy delivery vehicles on their bases or launch sites, provided that our forces can reach them before the vehicles are launched at our cities. Area defense forces can destroy enemy vehicles enroute to their targets before they reach the target areas. Terminal defenses can destroy enemy weapons or delivery vehicles within the target areas before they impact. Passive defense measures can reduce the vulnerability of our population to the weapons that do impact.

It is generally agreed that a vital first objective, to be met in full by our strategic nuclear forces, is the capability for assured destruction. Such a capability would, with a high degree of confidence, ensure that we could deter under all foreseeable conditions a calculated, deliberate nuclear attack upon the U.S. What kinds and amounts of destruction we would have to be able to inflict in order to provide this assurance cannot be answered precisely. But, it seems reasonable to assume that the destruction of, say, one-quarter to one-third of its population and about two-thirds of its industrial capacity would mean the elimination of the aggressor as a major power for many years. Such a level of destruction would certainly represent intolerable punishment to any industrialized nation and thus should serve as an effective deterrent.

Once high confidence of an assured destruction capability has been provided, any further increase in the strategic offensive forces must be justified on the basis of its contribution to the damage limiting objective.

Here, certain basic principles should be noted.

First, against the forces we expect the Soviets to have during the next decade, it would be virtually impossible for us to be able to provide anything approaching perfect protection for our population no matter how large the general nuclear war forces we were to provide, including even the hypothetical possibility of striking first. Of course, the number of fatalities would depend on the size and character of the attack as well as on our own forces. But the Soviets have it within their technical and economic capacity to prevent us from achieving a posture that would keep our immediate fatalities below some level. They can do this, for example, by offsetting any increases in our defenses by increases in their missile forces. In other words, if we were to try to assure survival of a very high per cent of our population, and if the Soviets were to choose to frustrate this attempt because they viewed it as a threat to their assured destruction capability, the extra cost to them would appear to be substantially less than the extra cost to us.

Second, since each of the three types of Soviet strategic offensive systems (land-based missiles, submarine-launched missiles and manned bombers) could, by itself, inflict severe damage on the U.S., even a "very good" defense against only one type of system has limited value. A "very good" defense against bombers, for example, could be outflanked by targeting missiles against those areas defended solely by anti-bomber systems. This is the principal reason why, in the absence of an effective defense against missiles, the large outlays for manned bomber defenses made during the 1950s now contribute disproportionately little to our damage limiting capabilities. A meaningful capability to limit the damage of a determined enemy attack, therefore, requires an integrated, balanced combination of strategic offensive forces, area defense forces, terminal defense forces and passive defenses. Such a structure would provide a "defense in depth," with each type of force taking its toll of the incoming weapons, operating like a series of filters or sieves, progressively reducing the destructive potential of the attack.

Third, for any given level of enemy offensive capability, successive additions to each of our various systems have diminishing marginal value. While it is true that in general the more forces we have, the better we can do, beyond a certain point each increment added to the existing forces results in less and less additional effectiveness. Thus, we should not expand one element of our damage limiting forces to a point at which the extra survivors it yields per billion dollars spent are fewer than for other elements. Rather, any given amount of resources we apply to the damage limiting objective should be allocated among the various elements of our defense forces in such a way as to maximize the population surviving an enemy attack. This is what we mean by a "balanced" damage limiting force structure.

The same principle holds for the damage limiting force as a whole; as additional forces are added, the incremental gain in effectiveness diminishes. When related to our other national needs, both military and non-military, this tendency for diminishing marginal returns sets a practical limit on how much we should spend for damage limiting problems. Accordingly, the question of how much we should spend on damage limiting programs can be decided only by carefully weighing the costs against expected benefits.

Pervading the entire damage limiting problem is the factor of uncertainty, of which there are at least three major types—technical, operational and strategic. Technical uncertainties stem from the question of whether a given system can be developed with the performance characteristics specified. Operational uncertainties stem from the question of whether a given system will actually perform as planned in the operational environment.

The third type, strategic uncertainty, is perhaps the most troublesome since it stems from the question of what our opponent or opponents will actually do—what kind of force they will actually build, what kind of attack they will actually launch, and how effective their weapons will actually be. What may be an optimum defense against one kind of attack may not be an optimum defense against a different kind of attack. For example, within a given budget, a Nike-X defense optimized for an attack by ICBMs with simple penetration aids would include fewer high cost radars than one optimized against an attack by ICBMs with more advanced penetration aids. Thus, for a given cost, the efficiency of our defenses depends upon the correctness of the assumptions we make during the design of these defenses about the size and character of enemy attacks.

In the same way, the effectiveness of our strategic offensive forces in the damage limiting role would be critically dependent on the timing of an enemy attack on U.S. urban targets. Our missile forces would be most effective against the enemy bombers and ICBMs if the attack on our urban centers were withheld for an hour or more after an attack on U.S. military targets—an unlikely contingency. Our manned bomber forces would be effective in the damage limiting role only if the enemy attack on our urban centers were withheld for several hours.

To reduce the technical uncertainties, we rely on painstaking studies and research and development tests; and to hedge against the risks of technical failure, we support parallel development approaches. We try to cope with the operational uncertainties by repeated testing in a simulated operational environment. We hedge against the strategic uncertainties by accepting a less than optimum defense against any one form of attack in order to provide some defense against several forms of attack, and by purchasing "insurance," i.e., keeping open various options—to develop and deploy, for example, a new bomber, a new interceptor, or an anti-missile defense system.

How far we should go in hedging against these various uncertainties is one of the most difficult judgments which have to be made. Analytical techniques can focus the issue but no mechanical rule can substitute for such judgments.

With these factors in mind, we can now examine the capabilities of the planned general nuclear war forces in the light of our two strategic objectives—assured destruction and damage limitation.

In order to assess the capabilities of our general nuclear war forces over the next several years, we must take into account the size and character of the forces the potential aggressors are likely to have during the same period. . . . Such long range projections of enemy capabilities are, at best, only informed estimates, particularly since they deal with a period beyond the production and deployment lead times of the weapon systems involved. Nevertheless, certain development and deployment patterns which have already become apparent make it possible to identify likely future trends, at least in their broad outline. . . . I would now like to discuss the adequacy of the Strategic Offensive-Defensive Forces we propose to build and maintain through Fiscal 1970.

In evaluating the adequacy of our forces from the standpoint of convincing others that the initiation of general nuclear war would inevitably bring about their own destruction, it is helpful to recall that in all industrialized (or industrializing) societies, population and industry tend to be clustered in a relatively limited number of urban areas.

The degree of concentration, of course, varies from country to country. Thus, for example, if we look ahead to the 1970s, we find that the concentration of population in the U.S. will continue to be greater than that in the Soviet Union. However, in both countries, about three-fourths of the industrial capacity will be concentrated in the 200 largest urban areas. Parenthetically, I might note that although much of Communist China's large population is distributed outside of major urban areas, Communist China remains vulnerable since most of its industrial capacity, its key governmental, technical and managerial personnel, and its skilled workers are concentrated in far fewer urban areas than is the case with the U.S. and the Soviet Union.

Beyond the 200 largest urban areas, the amount of population and industrial capacity located in each additional increment of 200 cities falls off at a rapidly declining rate, and small and smaller percentages of the total population and industrial capacity would be destroyed in the event that such areas were subjected to attack. It is apparent, then, that a point of diminishing returns is soon encountered, insofar as requirements for assured destruction forces are concerned. The ability to destroy smaller and smaller urban areas would add little to our ability to deter attack.

Based on the projected threat for the early 1970s and the most likely planning factors for that time period, our calculations show that even after absorbing a first strike, our already authorized strategic missile force, if it were directed against the aggressor's urban areas, could cause more than 100 million fatalities and destroy about 80% of his industrial capacity. If our manned bombers were then to mount a follow-on attack against urban areas, fatalities would be increased by 10 to 15 million and industrial destruction by another per cent or two.

I believe it is clear that only a portion of our total programed ICBM and Polaris force and none of the strategic bombers would be required to inflict on an aggressor unacceptably high levels of destruction. The remaining elements of the strategic offensive forces are being procured because it is believed they, along with air defense forces, will limit damage in the event deterrence fails. The requirement for strategic offensive forces for this purpose and their relationship to the defensive forces (aircraft and missile defenses, fallout shelters, etc.) will be discussed later.

The fact that the programed missile force alone should provide more than adequate deterrent capability does not, in and of itself, mean that the assured destruction job might not be done more efficiently by bombers alone or with higher assurance by a mix of bombers and missiles. To test the first possibility, i.e., using bombers alone, we have examined the comparative cost and effectiveness of four alternative strategic offensive systems which could be available by the early 1970s—Minuteman, Polaris, B-52/SRAM and AMSA/SRAM (SRAM is a new short range air-to-ground missile; AMSA is the new bomber proposed by the Air Force). Each system was examined in terms of its effectiveness against a given urban/industrial complex. Using the operational factors expected for the early 1970s, any one of the four forces could, with a high degree of confidence, destroy this complex even after absorbing a surprise attack.

However, a comparison of the approximate incremental costs of the four alternative forces makes it clear that AMSA would be the most expensive way of accomplishing this particular task. Indeed, against improved defenses, which might be available by the 1970s, the cost of AMSA would be roughly four times the cost of Minuteman, the least expensive of the four systems examined.

This leaves the second question to be answered—would a mixed force of bombers and missiles provide greater confidence that we could achieve our assured destruction objective? There are two principal arguments usually advanced to support the case for a mixed missile and bomber force.

• Complicating the enemy's defensive problem—It is clear that as long as we have strategic aircraft the enemy cannot effectively defend himself against ballistic missiles without concurrently defending himself against the aircraft and their air-to-surface missiles. Conversely, defense against aircraft without concurrent defense against ballistic missiles also leaves him vulnerable. In the absence of a bomber threat, a potential enemy could re-allocate his resources to strategic offensive forces, or to anti-missile defenses or some other military program.

This fact, however, does not necessarily argue for a large bomber force. Most of the major elements of cost in an anti-aircraft defense system (e.g., the ground environment and part of the interceptor force) are quite insensitive to the size of the opposing bomber force. The requirement for air defense is more a function of the number of targets to be defended than of the number of attacking bombers. Since the enemy would not know in advance which targets our bombers would attack, he would have to continue to defend all of the targets. Accordingly, his expenditures for air defense are likely to be about the same regardless of whether we have a relatively small bomber force or a large one.

• Hedging uncertainties in the dependability of our strategic offensive forces—The percentage of the "unit equipment" of a particular system which can be depended upon to penetrate to the target is termed the system dependability rate. There are four major factors which determine this rate: readiness, survivability, reliability and penetration. The readiness (alert) rate is the proportion of the operational force which can immediately respond to an execution order; the pre-launch survival rate is the proportion of the alert operational force which is expected to survive an enemy attack in operating condition; the reliability rate is the probability that the surviving "alert" missiles or aircraft will operate successfully, exclusive of enemy defensive action; the penetration rate is the probability that a reliable system will survive enemy defenses to detonate its warhead.

The readiness and reliability rates of Minuteman and Polaris, which constitute the bulk of our missile forces, are excellent. We are providing substantial amounts of money for extensive testing programs. There can be no reasonable doubt that, for the time period in question, the readiness and reliability of these systems will be fully satisfactory.

With regard to survival, it is highly unlikely that an enemy, even by the early 1970s, would be able to destroy any significant number of Polaris submarines at sea.

Since the enemy's intercontinental missile force will face over 1,000 hardened and dispersed U.S. ICBMs, I believe that our land-based missiles also have high survival potential.

I am not as confident of the survival potential of our aircraft. If, for any of a number of reasons, they are not airborne within the BMEW's warning time, they could be caught on their home bases by an enemy ICBM or SLBM attack.

With regard to penetration, if and when the enemy deploys anti-ballistic missile defenses, our penetration aids and other measures should keep the "entry price" of missile attacks against the defended targets within tolerable limits. ("Price" is defined as the number of missiles that must be placed over the defended target area to ensure that the target is destroyed.)

Aircraft also will face penetration difficulties. Our studies have shown that an effective anti-bomber defense is a necessary complement to an anti-missile defense and that the two should have an "inter-locked" deployment to avoid obvious vulnerabilities. The cost of an effective anti-bomber defense appears to be much less than the cost of a comparably effective anti-missile defense.

In summary, I see little merit to the argument that bombers are needed in the assured destruction role because our missiles are not dependable. But I do recognize that presently unforeseeable changes in the situation may occur against which a bomber force might possibly provide a hedge. Therefore, as will be discussed later, I propose to retain the option to maintain indefinitely bomber units in our strategic offensive forces.

CHAPTER II

Economic Growth

The material foundation of our national safety is a strong and expanding economy. This we have—and this we must maintain.
—DWIGHT D. EISENHOWER

Economics is the main field in which the peaceful competition of socialism and capitalism is taking place, and we are interested in winning this competition in a historically brief period of time.
—NIKITA S. KHRUSHCHEV

One of the most important areas of US-Soviet competition is the expansion of national economy. The increase in Gross National Product (GNP) and the growth of per capita income represent not only a barometer of the extent of improvement in material well-being of the people generally, but also may be a reflection of the comparative degree of superiority of one economic system over the other, e.g., the American free enterprise system vs. the Soviet regimented economy.

As an economic system is inextricably enmeshed with a political system, economic policies cannot be formulated separately from political factors. They are, therefore, partial reflections of overall national endeavors with special emphasis on farm programs, capital formation, employment problems, technological progress, population growth, price control, industrial output, distribution, consumption, and others.

This chapter is intended to illustrate national economic goals and achievements of the United States and the Soviet Union.

Gregory Grossman, Professor of Economics at the University of California (Berkeley), in his investigation of Soviet economic growth, discusses various reforms in agriculture such as the cultivation of "virgin lands" and the abolition of machine tractor stations (MTS). He points out the problems and difficulties in the execution of the

Seven-Year Plan for 1959–1965 and organizational and institutional weaknesses in the Soviet economic system.

Rush V. Greenslade, an American specialist in Soviet economy, maintains that it is wrong to assume, as many Soviet economists seem to do, that "some modification of or partial approach to 'market socialism'" is "consistent with Khrushchev's outlook." Greenslade explains the practical incompatibility between Soviet economists' rules and Party authority.

W. W. Rostow, Counselor and Chairman of the Policy Planning Council, presents a brief history of American response to the "great" challenges in the nation's life and sets forth greater future tasks to help build an orderly and peaceful world community in competition with Communism.

1. THE SOVIET ECONOMY*

BY GREGORY GROSSMAN

While the time perspective is still short for reliable judgment, the post-Stalin decade seems to break up fairly well into two periods. The dividing point is not the 20th Party Congress in February 1956, as it is in the realm of economic thought and in the political and cultural fields, but rather the second half of 1958. The first period therefore embraces somewhat over five years (or just five years if it is dated from the launching of the "new course" in the summer of 1953), while the second period encompasses some four and one-half years to the end of 1962 (when these lines are being written). Whether the important reforms introduced by the Central Committee Plenum in November 1962 constitute in some real sense the end of the second period and the start of another phase cannot yet be told.

The first period, 1953–58, can be most succinctly characterized as a vast, if not always very profound or radical, rescue operation that resulted in rapid expansion of the Soviet economy along a broad

* From *Problems of Communism*, Vol. 12 (March–April, 1963), pp. 32–41. Reprinted by permission of United States Information Agency.

front. This was a time devoted to redressing with haste the most serious imbalances inherited from Stalin, righting some of the worst injustices and inequities in the society, salvaging incentives, eliminating the grossest organizational inefficiencies of the economy, and directing resources to areas where they were most urgently needed.

The reforms in agriculture which began in earnest in September 1953 launched a long series of remedial measures in this sector, the end of which is not yet in sight. At the very first, the emphasis was on various incentive elements—prices, taxes, and delivery obligations; at the same time, controls over the peasants were also tightened, on the assumption that a larger carrot not only serves its own purpose but also makes the bigger stick more effective. But the two measures that received most publicity and attention, especially from Mr. Khrushchev himself, were the plowing up of the semi-arid and arid "virgin lands," begun in 1954, and the expansion of acreage under corn, started in 1955. Both were designed primarily to augment, radically and swiftly, the feed-grain base of livestock husbandry— the latter directly, the former largely by shifting bread-grain production to the new lands and thereby releasing some of the old areas for feed grains, including corn. The magnitude of the virgin lands campaign is vividly indicated by the fact that the land newly brought under the plow there since 1954, about 100 million acres, is equivalent to almost one third the *total* cropland currently harvested in the United States.

These measures, and many others that cannot be discussed here for lack of space, contributed in varying degree to a quick and large increase in agricultural output—about 50 percent overall—during 1953–1958. On the other hand, attempts to free local initiative by decentralizing planning and management in agriculture, especially through a decree published in May 1955, remained almost entirely on paper. "Campaign" methods, constant pressure for large deliveries to the state, inadequate incentives on the farm (especially in animal husbandry), ingrained habits of the high and petty bureaucracy, daily intervention by party officials, and all the other modes of operating carried over from the past, combined to thwart any extension of meaningful autonomy for the individual collective farms. Moreover, towards the end of this first period the authorities began to tighten the squeeze on the collective farmers' private plots. The last are of considerable significance not only for the welfare of the farmers but also as a source of food supply: in 1958, together with certain other small forms of private cultivation, they accounted for one-third of the agricultural output of the USSR, although covering less than four percent of the total sown areas.[1]

One of the most important structural reforms in post-Stalin Soviet agriculture took place toward the very end of the first period, in mid-1958. This was the abolition of machine and tractor stations (MTS), the sale of most of their equipment to collective farms, and the attendant thorough revamping of the farm price structure. The MTS had been virtually the sole source of large-scale machinery for collective farming: moreover they had played a very significant role in ensuring procurements and enforcing political control in the countryside. They were also quite wasteful and inefficient. The reform of mid-1958 eliminated dual authority on the land, did away with much of the above-mentioned waste and inefficiency, and largely abolished the baneful multiple-price system. It happened that the same year witnessed extraordinarily favorable weather conditions. As agricultural production rose sharply, so did the incomes of peasants, and particularly their earnings from working for the collective farms.[2]

. . . .

The actual rationalization of Soviet economic policies and planning that has ensued from these developments should not be exaggerated. Nevertheless, toward the end of the first period under examination the erstwhile neglect of the chemical industries was reversed (May 1958), the stress on gigantic hydroelectric projects was seriously

---

[1] These figures derive from official data, which however may not be very firm. See J. A. Newth, "Soviet Agriculture: The Private Sector, 1950–1959," *Soviet Studies,* October 1961, pp. 160–71. Note that the enormous discrepancy between output and area in this instance is explained in part by much higher yields in the private sector as compared to the socialist sector, and in part by the former's concentration on livestock products, to an extent utilizing feed obtained from the socialist sector.

[2] Jasny estimates the rise in per capita peasant incomes from all sources between 1952 and 1958 to have been as much as 55 percent, but it must be borne in mind that 1952 incomes were catastrophically low. Naum Jasny, *Essays on the Soviet Economy* (New York: Frederick A. Praeger, Inc., 1962), p. 155. *Cf.* Alec Nove, "The Incomes of Soviet Peasants," *The Slavonic and East European Review,* June 1960, pp. 314–33. For discussions of the various post-Stalin measures in agriculture see Lazar Volin, "Reform in Agriculture," *Problems of Communism,* Jan.–Feb. 1959; see also Volin's and Nancy Nimitz's contributions to *Comparisons,* Part I, and this author's article, "Soviet Agriculture since Stalin," *The Annals,* January 1956.

questioned (August 1958), the development of petroleum and natural gas was given emphatic priority over coal, the dieselization and electrification of railroads was sharply speeded up, and a much heightened sense of urgency was ascribed to automation. Soviet industry seemed to be heading away from the 1920's and 1930's and adopting an aspect more consonant with the 1950's and 1960's.

In sum, as the last of the 1958 harvest reached the government's collection points and the year waned, Mr. Khrushchev and his lieutenants had reasons for satisfaction and even self-congratulation. Under the Premier's personal tutelage, agriculture had increased its total output by half over five years, and the revision of Stalin's agricultural policies seemed to be paying off handsomely (although extremely favorable weather in the new lands in 1956 and 1958 also had much to do with successes). Per capita incomes in both town and village had risen sharply. Industry—buoyed by the success in agriculture and by a continued large inflow of resources (in part unlocked by the 1957 reorganization)—was also expanding its output rapidly. Finally, the regime's new technological and investment policies, coupled with prospects of rapidly growing capital formation, bore promise of further vast gains in the productivity and efficiency of industry and of other economic sectors.

The optimism that prevailed was fully reflected in the Seven-Year Plan for 1959–1965, adopted by the 21st Party Congress in January–February 1959.[3] The Plan was said to inaugurate the period of "the full construction of communist society"—that ideal society of economic abundance and full social harmony envisioned by Marx as the ultimate stage of human history. Supposedly the Plan would boost the Soviet economy most of the way toward the goal of overtaking and surpassing the United States in per capita production and consumption—a point which would finally be reached around 1970, clinching the "historic victory of socialism over capitalism" on our planet.

---

[3] Mr. Khrushchev's "Draft Theses" for the Seven-Year Plan were first published in the Soviet press on November 14, 1958. For the English translation of the final text of the "Directives for the SYP" see *Current Digest of the Soviet Press*, April 1, 1959. For analyses of the Plan see Oleg Hoeffding, "Substance and Shadow in the Soviet Seven-Year Plan," *Foreign Affairs*, April 1959; Leon Herman, "The Seven-Year Haul," *Problems of Communism*, March–April 1959; and Naum Jasny, "The Soviet Seven-Year Plan: Is It Realistic?," *Bulletin*, Institute for the Study of USSR (Munich), May 1959.

These grand claims have since been somewhat modified: at the 22nd Party Congress in October 1961—perhaps best remembered for its "de-Albanization"—a new Party Program was adopted which called for the "building of the foundations of communism," over the next two decades and outlined certain major production targets for 1970 and 1980. The Program, however, carefully avoided stating that communist society would come into existence in the USSR by 1980.[4]

From the latter part of 1958 on, the upward momentum of the Soviet economy began to slacken: some of the "single-shot" benefits (such as those stemming from the industrial reorganization of 1957, or from the mass release of prisoners) began to exhaust themselves; the labor supply became much less favorable for demographic reasons; the new plans and investment policies, as well as various international and scientific commitments, placed additional pressure on resources; and various institutions and operations created by Khrushchev's reforms began to spawn new difficulties and problems. Compared with the first post-Stalin period, the four years from 1959 through 1962 have therefore been marked by reduced rates of growth and a more moderate rise in living standards, remedial measures of a patchwork nature aimed at closing loopholes, steps to safeguard or bolster incentives, and other steps to tighten—and especially to recentralize—the organizational structure.

The retardation is especially noticeable in agriculture, where total output has been marking time, fluctuating with the weather, and at best keeping up with the population increase. The extraordinarily favorable weather conditions of 1958 have not recurred, indeed could hardly be expected to over the short run. Weather apart, the chief reasons for the very limited progress (if any) in agriculture seem to be: (a) continued imposition of overly ambitious plans, which often operate perversely; (b) unwillingness or inability to allot sufficient resources to this sector and its supporting activities (fertilizer production, roads, distribution facilities); (c) continuing ineptness in planning, management, distribution, supply, *etc.*; and (d) a possible sag

---

[4] A liberally annotated English translation of the Program is to be found in Herbert Ritvo, ed., *The New Soviet Society* (New York: The New Leader, 1962). Translation of the preliminary text appears in *Current Digest of the Soviet Press,* August 9, 16, and 23, 1961. For an extensive discussion of the Program see *Survey* (London), October 1961.

in incentives. Concerning the last point, it should be noted that peasant incomes apparently dropped significantly after 1957, continuing low at least to 1960, owing to a renewed squeeze on the peasants' private plots and livestock and to the financial burden that fell on the collective farms for tractor and machinery purchases following the dissolution of the MTS.[5]

The rate of growth of industrial production, though still high, declined substantially after 1957.[6] Given this fall-off and the failure of agricultural output to rise significantly after 1958, it is not surprising to discern a substantial reduction in the rate of growth of the national product as a whole and of urban real income.[7] Changes in defense expenditures further complicated the problem of achieving planned goals. In mid-1961, the budgeted outlays on defense were sharply raised, so that by 1962 and 1963 the nominal appropriations for this purpose increased some 50 percent over the level of early 1961. However, it is not certain that in real terms defense outlay rose as much as the budget figures would have one believe.[8]

As the Seven-Year Plan progressed, it also became increasingly apparent that the various reforms and reorganizations of the preceding five years had not been sufficient to improve fundamentally the "qualitative" aspects of the economy's operations, such as adherence to plans ("plan discipline"), the articulation of supply and demand, the quality of manufactured articles, the speed and effectiveness of construction, the meeting of consumer needs, and, last but definitely not least, the propensity to innovate. In some of these regards, such as industrial innovation, the new institutions seem to have aggravated rather than ameliorated the economy's chronic problems and defects.

On the organizational plane, remedial steps generally have been of two sorts: the elaboration of the administrative hierarchy in the economic sphere, and the recentralization of planning and economic

[5] See Arcadius Kahan, "Recent Trends in Soviet Farm Incomes," *Problems of Communism,* Nov.–Dec. 1961, pp. 54–57. The writer has also consulted on this subject with Professor Jerzy F. Karcz.

[6] According to the Greenslade-Wallace index, the average annual increase of civilian industrial output was 10.7 percent in 1952–57 and 7.7 percent in 1957–61 (*Dimensions,* p. 120).

[7] *Cf. Dimensions,* p. 75, with regard to national income, and the calculations by Rachel E. Golden on p. 354 with regard to real disposable wages.

[8] On the magnitude of the Soviet defense effort see the contribution of J. G. Godaire in *Dimensions,* pp. 33 ff.

administration. Neither development is surprising: they constitute the natural response of any formal organization which is faced with serious problems of operational effectiveness and which—for reasons good or bad—is not ready for a more fundamental overhaul. In this sense, as well as in some others, the recent organizational changes have been essentially conservative.[9]

To mention the most important of these: In June and July of 1960, republic-wide economic councils (sovnarkhozes) were created in the three largest republics (Russian, Ukrainian, and Kazakh) to administer the many smaller sovnarkhozes of 1957 vintage. In November 1962, it was announced that an all-union sovnarkhoz (SNKh SSSR) would be established, apparently on the organizational ruins of the old State Planning Commission (Gosplan), suddenly charged with policy errors and bungling by Mr. Khrushchev at the Central Committee Plenum. Among other related trends, the main all-union supply administrations, attached to Gosplan following the 1957 reorganization, have steadily acquired greater powers. At the same time, by all signs, the (lower) sovnarkhozes have steadily lost power to the various republican and all-union bodies. The sovnarkhozes themselves are being reduced, at this writing, to somewhat less than half their previous number by a process of amalgamation, following a resolution of the November 1962 Plenum. (In the RSFSR the reduction is particularly sharp—from 67 to 24 sovnarkhozes.) The same Plenum also decreed the vertical cleavage of the party structure into two parallel hierarchies, one concerned primarily with industry and related branches, the other with agriculture.

In agriculture, the major organizational innovations during the period since 1958—that is, following the abolition of the MTS—have been: (a) the establishment in early 1961 of a separate organization to supply agriculture with equipment, spare parts, and various essential materials (Selkhoztekhnika); and (b) the creation of a full-fledged hierarchy of territorial production and procurement administrations to which both collective and state farms are subordinate, paralleled by a structure of territorial councils and (at higher levels) agricultural boards. The latter measure is notable, *inter alia,* for

[9] They are discussed at some length in Alec Nove, "The Industrial Planning System: Reforms in Prospect," *Soviet Studies,* July 1962, pp. 1–15, Herbert S. Levine's essay in *Dimensions,* pp. 47–65, and my article, "The Structure and Organization of the Soviet Economy," *Slavic Review,* June 1962, pp. 203–22.

setting up a definite administrative machinery responsible for agricultural production, and for virtually abolishing the distinction between state and collective farms in this regard.

On the planning side the changes have been equally substantial. The product-line ("branch") State Boards,[10] established primarily in the defense industries at the time of the 1957 reorganization, have been gradually increased in number until they now cover construction and nearly all branches of industry. They are responsible for planning and implementing policy on technical progress and investment in their respective branches. But planning must be coordinated territorially as well as within individual industries. Hence, in May 1961 the country was divided into 17 so-called large economic regions, each on the average comprising six sovnarkhozes, and each with a "coordinating and planning council." These, however, never had much of an active existence and were apparently abolished (though this is not entirely clear) when the sovnarkhozes were consolidated at the end of 1962. At that time also (November 1962), the USSR State Scientific-Economic Council, concerned with long-term planning, was transformed into (or renamed?) the USSR Gosplan. (On March 13, 1963, it was announced that a USSR Supreme National Economic Council was being created within the Council of Ministers to supervise and coordinate the activities of Gosplan and the product-line state boards. The erection of a logical but highly complex and cumbersome structure for planning and management of the Soviet economy seems thus to have been completed—at least for a while.—Ed.)

The cumulative effect of these reorganizations of the past four years, as well as of various other changes, has been to further centralize planning, management, and administration. Agriculture and investment are two good examples. In the final analysis this "creeping" recentralization has come about primarily because of two underlying factors: the chronic overcommitment of resources (*i.e.,* the haste of Soviet economic development, in historical terms), and the divergence between the goals, values, and interests of the regime and those of individuals and groups within Soviet society. The conception, widespread in the West, that the Soviet economy today is in some general sense less centralized than at the end of Stalin's regime, is of very dubious worth; indeed, the opposite could probably be convincingly argued. Certainly, with regard to one of the most crucial

[10] Often and less exactly rendered into English as "State Committees."

criteria of decentralization—the enhancement of the autonomy of the individual enterprise—the changes in the past decade have been minute. The Soviet enterprise is still closely and continuously directed and controlled from above. In fact, this virtual lack of autonomy at the enterprise level—with its attendant problems of irritating and often incompetent "petty tutelage" from above, frequent changes in plans, continuing and even growing supply difficulties, and, more recently, the multiplication of superordinate authorities, each with its directives and audits—has prompted increasingly frequent and vocal complaints, sometimes bordering on cries of desperation, on the part of managers and some economists.[11]

A related problem that has been of special concern to the Soviet leaders in recent years is the sluggishness of efforts at innovation, despite constant and heavy pressure from above—a phenomenon that derives from a powerful combination of "conservatism" in management, which often stands to lose financially by upsetting production routines, and the cumbersomeness of the bureaucratic apparatus.[12] This particularly complicated and thorny matter is intimately connected with the various problems of institutional and organizational structuring, planning and performance criteria ("success indicators"), and the price pattern.

Nearly double in size (in terms of the national product), far more advanced technologically, and somewhat reformed organizationally, the Soviet economy today has left the grim and bleak days of the winter of 1953 far behind. But its most pressing problems still bear a striking resemblance to those of a decade ago. They are four, in sum:

(a) The constant pressure on the economy's resources created by the regime's continued drive for its "world-historic" goals, by the internal problems of the "socialist camp," by the cold war and the scientific and technical race with the West, and by the ever-rising economic aspirations of a fairly rapidly growing population.

---

[11] The Soviet press has been increasingly candid on these matters in recent years. An especially valuable source of such information, including sensible analyses and proposals for remedial action, is the weekly *Ekonomicheskaia gazeta* (Economic Journal), organ of the Central Committee of the Soviet Communist Party.

[12] Some of these problems are discussed more fully in the writer's "Soviet Growth: Routine, Inertia, and Pressure," *American Economic Review,* May 1960, pp. 62–72.

(b) The very slow increase (if any) in agricultural production since 1958, severely retarding overall economic growth as well as the rise in living standards.

(c) In other sectors, the welter of problems consisting of poor planning, widespread and large-scale waste of resources, all-too-frequent production of the wrong things at the wrong time, resistance to innovation, and so forth. Construction is faring particularly badly in these respects, with the volume of so-called uncompleted construction (due to inefficient planning and management) rising every year.[13]

(d) The Soviet man's imperfect tractability in "remolding" himself to accord with "communist morality." Even if he is more abiding of moral and juridical laws than his prerevolutionary grandfather, as Soviet ideologists would have us believe, there are today many more laws to break at every turn. There is no doubt a good deal of dedication and idealism in the populace at large, especially among the young; but cynicism toward communist ideals also prevails, and a callous disregard of regulations is encouraged both by the possibility of handsome material rewards and by the inefficiencies and disequilibrium of the economy. If the Soviet press is to be believed, economic crimes and transgressions of all sorts and degrees—from petty pilferage of state property, through systematic deception of superiors, to large-scale "speculation" and bribery—are widespread and may be on the increase. Time will tell whether the new series of severe penalties enacted in the past two years, including capital punishment, will turn the tide.

With all its ills and problems, the Soviet economy could undoubtedly continue for a good time under present conditions. Certainly neither paralysis nor explosion is to be expected, and no serious student of the Soviet economy predicts such catastrophe. But this is not the issue, of course. The significant facts are that the limits of patching over the essentially Stalinist structure of the economy are being approached; that this situation is increasingly recognized by many persons in various positions and walks of life; and that a great deal of rethinking in all areas, from abstract political economy down

---

[13] It may be worth dispelling here the myth that "at least" the Soviet economy fully utilizes its productive capacity. In point of fact, this is not so. While no general statistics on the subject are available, the Soviet press frequently reports idle capacity, including whole factories, major underutilization of nominally employed assets, and a large and growing backlog of equipment awaiting installation or repair, sometimes for many years.

to practical everyday operations, is underway. "Anyone who is at all familiar with planning and economic reality [in the USSR] can see that it is presently undergoing an important if not a crucial stage— a time of profound thinking, of re-examination of habitual concepts, of the appearance of new problems which only yesterday raised no thoughts, and of the seeming disappearance of other problems which only yesterday looked very important." Thus *Ekonomicheskaia gazeta* commented editorially in October 1962.[14] It is difficult to believe that Mr. Khrushchev's tinkering with the economic-administrative structure and his reshuffling of planning bodies a month later offers a fundamental and durable solution. On the other hand, the simultaneous splitting of the party into parallel industrial and agricultural pyramids is a radical step that has more of a ring of desperation than a tone of conviction to it.

In brief, the Soviet economy today faces an enormous organizational and institutional problem, the problem of finding a workable degree of centralization (or decentralization) under new and changing conditions. Unlike the difficulties in agriculture, which at least bear reasonable hope of alleviation as the economy grows richer and can afford to pour in more resources to rescue that sector, the organizational problem promises to grow worse by dint of the economy's very successes. The sheer bulk of the planning job, as it is now carried on in the Soviet Union, can be mathematically likened to the square of the number of commodities plus the square of the number of economic units. As both products and producing units multiply with the economy's growth, the task of planning swells much faster. The top-heavy Soviet economic structure is costly not just in the resources it engages, but eminently more so in its inimical effects on adaptation to demand and to changing technology, and on efficiency and morale.

One possible way out is to preserve or even enhance the degree of centralization, but to render its operation more supple and swift with the aid of mathematical economics and electronic computers. An ideologically and politically palatable course, especially after the purging of the worst dogmas from Soviet economics, this approach is now attracting great attention on the part of Soviet economists, mathematicians, and planners. Another possible course, with politically and ideologically opposite implications, is a thorough decentralization, which in its extreme form would amount to some sort of a

14 October 13, 1962, p. 6.

socialist market economy. However, the bars to full-scale decentralization are formidable both from an ideological and from a practical point of view. Given the present severe pressure on the economy's capacities, and the consequent need to mobilize resources and enforce priorities, it seems safe to predict that the regime will exhaust the possibilities of the first approach before experimenting to any meaningful degree with the second.

2. KHRUSHCHEV AND THE ECONOMISTS*

BY RUSH V. GREENSLADE

Current speculation about the future evolution of the Soviet economy usually includes the suggestion that the leaders in Moscow may increasingly adopt capitalist techniques in order to improve economic efficiency. In the last few months, as if in confirmation of this suggestion, some Soviet economists have proposed that profitability be the aim and the success indicator of enterprise management. They have also proposed that the price system be reformed and prices more explicitly recognized as guideposts in enterprise decision-making. The proposals are very reminiscent of "market socialism," the version of socialism which most resembles capitalism and which is practiced—imperfectly—in Yugoslavia.

Indeed, it is tempting to assume—and the Soviet economists appear to be making just this assumption—that some modification of or partial approach to "market socialism" would also be consistent with Khrushchev's outlook. In the past he has gone to some pains to build a reputation for "liberalism," and his often-repeated organizational preferences include implacable opposition to bureaucratic rigidities, emphasis on the creative initiative of workers and production managers, a continuing demand for efficient use of resources, and an unashamed admiration for the beneficial effect of competition on the productivity of the individual farm and firm in the United States.

The purpose of this article is to argue that the assumption is wrong

* From *Problems of Communism,* Vol. 12 (May–June, 1963), pp. 27–32. Reprinted by permission of United States Information Agency.

and that Khrushchev's approach to economic management is basically incompatible with the proposals of the economists. This is not to say that the economists' proposals may not be adopted in part or in whole but that, even if they are adopted, they will not work as intended.

The demands for more decentralized economic management come from a small group of Soviet economists and from some, if not all, enterprise managers. The recent proposals of these economists and industrial managers represent the convergence of two streams of thought which closely resemble the two basic ideas of market socialism as expounded by the Polish economist, Oskar Lange.[1] These two ideas are that the socialist state should (1) set market (or transfer) prices which equate supply and demand and (2) enjoin production managers to seek maximum profit—at the prices set under (1)—but otherwise not interfere in enterprise management.

The first stream of thought was set in motion in 1959 by the Leningrad mathematical economist, L. V. Kantorovich. Kantorovich was one of the original inventors of linear programing, a generalized mathematical method for solving problems of choice under complicated technical restraints.[2] In 1959 he published a book which applied linear programing to the problem of general economic planning. One feature of his proposal that attracted widespread interest among economists was the notion that the calculations necessary to operate his system could be programed on electronic computers. The idea that mathematical methods and electronic computers could be applied to economic planning had by then been under investigation by other Soviet economists, and Kantorovich's proposals fell on many receptive ears and added momentum to a movement which was already underway. Several special institutes for the development of mathematical techniques of planning are now in existence, and research is being actively pushed.

The other main feature of Kantorovich's proposal was the proposition that the correct solution of any economic planning problem required the calculation of prices of inputs and outputs which, in effect, equated supply and demand. Prices that are generated by a linear programing model are referred to as "shadow prices." Kantoro-

[1] *On the Economic Theory of Socialism,* University of Minnesota Press, 1938, pp. 57–142.

[2] For example—to find the optimum routing of ships between several ports of call, the quantities of freight to be hauled between each pair of ports being given.

vich did not say that they had to be used in actual transactions but only in the calculation of the plan. The idea of shadow prices immediately evoked vigorous controversy among economists: some, such as Academician Nemchinov and B. Belkin, supported Kantorovich; others denounced him for adopting Western economic concepts. But whether or not they agreed with Kantorovich's proposals, almost all Soviet economists are in agreement that prices in the Soviet economy badly need reform.

A separate stream of thought has been generated by the wide concern about the system of economic incentives for enterprise managers. The question of the index of performance on which managers' bonuses should be based has preoccupied political leaders, including Khrushchev, and enterprise managers as well as economists. General dissatisfaction with Gross Value of Production (gross output expressed in rubles) as an index of enterprise performance led to a revision of the system of bonuses in 1959; the new system tied the managers' rewards to cost reduction and several other indexes in a very complicated formula. The chief results of this bonus revision were renewed controversy and a lengthened list of press complaints about bad industrial practices. In fact, there is no evidence that the new system was ever widely implemented.

In September 1962, *Pravda* unveiled Professor Ye. Liberman's now famous proposal to use profitability as the primary index of enterprise performance. Since this plan is discussed in greater detail by Professor Harry Shaffer elsewhere in this issue, it is enough to note in the present context that Liberman also suggested that some prices might need to be adjusted (upward) so as to make sure that all necessary goods are produced. Shortly thereafter came the proposal of Professor Berg that industrial prices be drastically revised and made to cover full costs.[3] Berg's proposal was essentially a revival of Kantorovich's ideas, except that neither Kantorovich nor the principle of scarcity (supply and demand) were mentioned in his public statement.[4] Finally, in the wake of Khrushchev's criticism of industrial planning and performance at the November 1962 Central Committee Plenum, economists I. Birman and B. Belkin wedded the

[3] *Pravda*, Oct. 24, 1962.

[4] The distinction between full cost pricing and pricing by supply and demand is crucial to Marxists and in practice. Even if the price of a product covers the full cost, including capital charges, production either may exceed or may fall short of demand, in the short run.

Liberman and Berg proposals, advocating a revision of prices as a necessary condition for the success of Liberman's profitability criterion.[5] Like Berg, they, too, called for prices determined by full costs, including capital cost, and, going a little further than Berg, they noted that prices must take account of the scarcity of some types of goods and of different rent. (Enterprise managers, who worry less about prices and more about the confusion and lack of coordination in the enterprise output and supply plans, have, in general, endorsed simplifications—although not necessarily Liberman's—which promised to reduce the quantity of supervision and petty tutelage over the enterprise.)

These latest proposals of the economists are only one step short of the principle of Lange's market socialism—that is, that prices should be set so as to clear the market. In his favorable comment on Liberman's proposal, V. S. Nemchinov clearly advocated the use of price incentives by the state to guide production, i.e. raising the price of a good of which the state wants a greater supply. If the economists were to say that prices should be deliberately used to transmute the demands of buyers into the production patterns of the suppliers, they would have taken the last step toward Lange's concept.

Soviet economists are familiar with Western economics and with Lange's writing. The Soviet press is filled with complaints by buyers against suppliers. Liberman has denied, to be sure, that he wished to undermine central planning—and indeed his proposal as it now stands does not do so—but the logic of economic calculation is inexorable. One cannot avoid the conclusion that supply-demand pricing would be the next objective of some "liberal" economists, if the present proposals were adopted. This small logical step, however, would be enormous ideologically: the economists would be proposing, in effect, to substitute for central planning of enterprise outputs Adam Smith's "invisible hand."

Whether or not this is true, the common characteristic of all the economists' and enterprise managers' proposals is the search for impersonal and automatic rules to substitute for arbitrary or bureaucratic decision-making; a profitability rule for enterprises, a full cost rule for prices, or linear programing rules for central planning.

Nikita Sergeyevich Khrushchev has been called a shrewd Russian peasant who believes in communism and common sense and sees no

[5] *Isvestia*, Nov. 29, p. 3.

inconsistency between the two. He has spent a lifetime promoting the Communist Party and its historic mission, but the niceties of ideological theory mean little to him. Nor has he any use for impersonal logic or administrative theory. His guide is his personal experience, and he perceives national economic problems as simple multiples of the difficulties that he personally solved in this mine or that farm in the Ukraine many years ago.

Khrushchev's model for solving economic problems is as follows. The party man (Khrushchev) sees the problem (output must be raised). He goes directly to the worker, explains the goal and its importance, and wins his confidence and enthusiasm. The worker then reveals a secret trick that can double output—a trick which he will adopt provided that certain government bureaucrats leave him alone. The party man chases away the bureaucrats, and the problem is solved. This model was perfectly illustrated in an anecdote from his earlier days that Khrushchev related in his speech of November 29, 1962, to the Party Central Committee:

. . . This happened at the Petrovsky Mine. During the revision of norms I went to the smithy, where I met an old smith.

He asked me: "Look, Khrushchev, why do you send a girl who stands beside my forge clicking a stop watch? I know why she came, she decided to check the output norm. Listen: You come and ask me whatever you need to know. Then I will tell you what my norm is now and how it should be raised. Only take away this girl. . . ."

Then he said: "Listen to what I did. I saw that she was measuring the time it took to finish a part. I deliberately kept the fire low in the forge." (He was making insulator brackets.) "I took a rod, cut it, put it in the furnace, heated it, shaped it, put in another rod. She stood there, timing everything. Then having marked down the time, she calculated the norm and left. When she had gone, I took and built up a big flame in the furnace and put in not one rod but several, and heated them. I have a press; I don't shape the brackets by hand, as I did in front of the girl, but under a machine hammer—bang! And the bracket is finished. So much for the stopwatch record and the norm the girl figured."

Khrushchev concluded:

Talk with the workers, tell them what has to be done, and they will understand you correctly. But for this you have to go to the worker not as some bureaucratic administrator, but as a comrade of this worker; then he will open up his soul and show the possibilities he possesses for raising labor productivity and reducing production costs.[6]

All of Khrushchev's reorganizations in both industry and agriculture have been merely generalizations of this model. He sees the problems of the economy as a list of specific bad practices—in enterprises, farms and administrative organs—and he recites them endlessly in his speeches. But he gives few general rules for correcting them. On the contrary, he sees administration as a kind of continuous troubleshooting.

This view of administration is most apparent in the agricultural reorganizations. Discussing the proposed production administrations in his March 5, 1962, speech to the Central Committee, he said:

The production administrations must keep accounting for control in their hands, apply their efforts where organizational and production weakness arises, and reinforce lagging sectors. And reinforcement should proceed not through directives, letters and orders but by sending out inspectors to the state and collective farms, directly to the brigades and state farm divisions, with a view to deciding production questions on the spot.[7]

Khrushchev's violent opposition to bureaucrats and bureaucracy has been the most conspicuous feature of his administrative approach. Beginning with his attacks on the ministries in 1957, and continuing to the chastisement of Gosplan in November 1962, bureaucratic rigidities, compartmentalization, and red tape have been the villains of the long drama. The hero of the drama, of course, is Khrushchev, the inspired party man who sees the goal; discovers a means; and acts immediately, disregarding procedures, channels, jurisdictions, and vested interests. He has steadily reduced or eliminated government bureaucracies—the industrial ministries, the Ministry of Agriculture, the machine tractor stations—and replaced them with party organs or lower-level government agencies under the supervision of party organs.

This procedure does not mean the replacement of a government bureaucracy by a party bureaucracy. The essence of a bureaucracy (which is to say, any administration) is the performance of specified routine functions by a hierarchy of authority, each level operating

[6] *Pravda,* Nov. 20, 1962.
[7] *Ibid.,* March 6, 1962.

under a clear and unduplicating set of rules and responsibilities. A bureaucrat is a functionary; a party man is or is supposed to be an *activist*. The good bureaucrat fulfills his assigned function faithfully according to the rules. The good party man achieves an overriding goal, assigned or not, regardless of rules. Khrushchev is profoundly *anti-rule*.

Khrushchev's reorganizations have weakened or abolished government administrative chains of command with their bureaucratic rules, and increased party participation in decision-making at all levels. This has meant duplicating and unclear lines of authority, petty tutelage, and arbitrary intervention into the affairs of enterprises and kolkhozes by any number of uncoordinated authorities at local, oblast, republic, or all-union levels.

The latest reorganization, which was announced in November 1962, does not correct these weaknesses. The party organization at each level has been divided into parallel industry and agriculture committees or bureaus in order to monitor the two parts of the economy more closely and more continuously. The party industry committee at the oblast level appears to be the direct and immediate supervisor of enterprises, since the sovnarkhozes were amalgamated into larger units with jurisdiction over two or more oblasts in most cases.

At the same time, the functions of Gosplan were dispersed among several agencies. Gosplan itself is to concentrate narrowly on planning; the newly established all-union sovnarkhoz (Sovnarkhoz SSSR) is to take over Gosplan's former administrative and supervisory responsibilities; and the state committees for various branches of the economy have an increased but undefined responsibility for introducing new technology and guiding new investment. The general instruction to all is to innovate, introduce new technology, and uncover hidden reserves.

In March of this year the obvious need to coordinate this gaggle of overlapping agencies led to the establishment of a Supreme Economic Council capping the whole economic pyramid. Gosplan, the all-union sovnarkhoz and Gosstroi were subordinated to the Supreme Council, and each of the various state committees was subordinated to one of these four organs. One would suppose that the Supreme Council would now be establishing broad policy lines and general rules of administration and jurisdiction so as to bring order out of chaos. It is more likely, however, that it will simply be one more troubleshooting agency. The agenda for its first meeting revealed Khrushchev's fine administrative hand all too clearly. The items up for discussion were: (1) organizing the production of silicate material; (2) increasing the production of tire cord; and (3) improving the productivity of machinery manufactured at the Novo-Kramatorsk machine-building plant.[8]

The arguments of the two preceding sections clarify the positions of Khrushchev and the economists. Both are against the same thing— rigid bureaucratic administration of the economy. But what each is *for* could not be more different. The economists would replace bureaucratic rules by the impersonal rules of profit maximization, prices set by full cost (or supply and demand), or planning by mathematically programed electronic computers. Khrushchev wishes party supervision of the economy to be bound by no rules whatsoever.

In this respect he differs little from other party members. Arbitrary intervention into economic administration has been a chronic feature of the Soviet economy for a long time, and, given a party organization that parallels the government organization, this is inevitable. The party, to be sure, has been intent on maintaining its unrestricted authority, but Khrushchev has now made continuous party participation a central principle of Soviet administration.

The economists' rules and party authority are mutually incompatible in practice. This does not mean that both cannot be formally accepted—only that both cannot operate simultaneously. Khrushchev presumably will have his reorganization, and some parts of the economists' proposals also may be adopted. But there is small chance that the party *activists* would accept the operation and results of profit maximization as being in the "best interest of the state." Profit maximization would on occasion call for reducing output, for turning down the delivery of a machine if it had defects, for refusing to adopt a new technology if it was dubious or unproved, or for reducing output of a high-priority commodity in favor of a low-priority one. The liberal economists would say that each of these developments could and should be corrected by adjusting some price. The party *activist,* out of patience, would denounce the enterprise managers in question for commercialism, and operation would be restored to the condition intuitively preferred by the party man. In short, the effect

8 *Pravda,* March 27, 1963.

of a profit-maximizing rule is likely to be nil, just as the effect of the cost-reduction rule in 1959 was nil.

Nevertheless, the economic pressure for better management of resources is more likely to grow than to diminish. This is probable not because of the increasing complexity of the economy, as many observers have claimed, but because of something rather different. Recent evidence indicates that the return on investments in the Soviet economy is declining—a situation that has come about partly as a penalty of success. The level of technology of new plant and equipment generally exceeds the average level of technology in use. In the case of the Soviet Union, the rapid growth of its economy has been due to the large gap between the low level of technology in use and the high level in the West available for borrowing. As a result of 15 years of massive investment in the postwar period, the gap has narrowed, and gains from new technology are not coming as easily as before. In consequence, gains from organizational change appear to be more attractive than before.

If, as it now appears, party troubleshooting should prove to be an inadequate answer to increasingly subtle economic problems, some successor of Khrushchev's may decide that the interests of the party as a whole are better served by limiting the authority of lower party levels through stricter rules. There appear to be only two choices in rules for economic administration: (1) a systematic administrative hierarchy with appropriate definitions of mission and function, or (2) the rules of the market place, with profit maximization and prices equating supply and demand. These two possible directions of evolution are an interesting dilemma for the party of the October Revolution—bureaucratization or creeping capitalism.

3. PERSPECTIVE OF THE TASKS OF THE 1960'S*

BY W. W. ROSTOW

The world of government, as you know, is a world of practical, concrete tasks. Every step taken in foreign policy, in mili-

* Address by W. W. Rostow at Kenyon College, Gambier, Ohio, *Department of State Bulletin,* Vol. 50 (June 1, 1964), pp. 864–867.

tary policy, or in policy here at home requires that an enormous number of factors be taken into account. Legitimate interests, domestic and foreign; the limits and possibilities of our democratic procedures; a wide array of hard, technical facts—all this and more must be woven into the making of national policy or the design and passage of a piece of legislation.

The tasks of government lie, as it were, in the domain of engineering and art, not pure science or abstract ideas, although, as with engineering and art, science and ideas are a fundamental part of government.

It was with some awareness of this inescapable characteristic of government—derived from an experience reaching back to the summer of 1941—that I pasted in the back of one of the two books I brought with me to Washington in January 1961 the following quotation from John Maynard Keynes:

Words ought to be a little wild, for they are an assault of thought upon the unthinking. But when the seats of power and authority have been attained, there should be no more poetic licence. . . . When a doctrinaire proceeds to action, he must, so to speak, forget his doctrine. For those who in action remember the letter will probably lose what they are seeking.

On the other hand, there is another dictum from an even more relevant British source—these words of Winston Churchill:

Those who are possessed of a definite body of doctrine and of deeply rooted convictions upon it will be in a much better position to deal with the shifts and surprises of daily affairs than those who are merely taking short views, and indulging their natural impulses as they are evoked by what they read from day to day.

I do not intend this morning to arbitrate between a great academic's warning against doctrinaires in government and a great statesman's plea for doctrine in the making of public policy, but I should like to talk—not about a doctrine—but about a perspective on the period through which we are passing, which, I believe, does illuminate a little where we are in the sweep of history, the character of our tasks, and the way we are most likely to succeed in prosecuting them. While the tasks we face are complex and their unfolding may be irregular— or even erratic—there is a broad shape in them and a clear-cut sense of direction which derives not merely from the character of the problems themselves but from the very roots of our society, its history, and its ultimate objectives on the world scene.

The perspective I would suggest on the 1960's differs from that which has governed some of our judgments of the past.

American historians and political scientists have tended to rate as "great" periods in our political life the administrations of Lincoln, Theodore Roosevelt, Wilson, and Franklin Roosevelt. Closer still, and perhaps somewhat more debatable, I would add the administration of President Truman.

Lincoln's period inevitably falls in this category. He saw us through a civil war which maintained the unity of this nation and overcame the tragic divisions which boiled up in the 1850's and which Buchanan could not master.

In this century we generally think of "great" periods under two sets of circumstances.

The first were intervals in domestic policy when there occurred a sudden outpouring of major new legislation, with permanent consequences for the organization of our society. Since 1900 there were two such intervals: the legislative execution of Wilson's concept of the "New Freedom" during his first term, and the vast flow of New Deal legislation in Franklin Roosevelt's first term.

Theodore Roosevelt's administrations belong, I believe, on the list of great periods, although new legislation actually passed in his time was limited and there were no great international crises to be overcome. He nevertheless laid the groundwork for new attitudes and policies, at home and abroad, which foreshadowed many fundamental later developments.

The second phases of greatness in the 20th century were occasions of desperate crisis on the international scene. Theodore Roosevelt's effort to educate the Nation to the vistas of world power and responsibility had not sufficiently succeeded. In 1917 the United States had to go to war to avoid the passage of power in Western Europe and in the Atlantic to forces hostile to the United States and its way of life. Thus we undid our previous commitment to isolationism.

In 1941, with the passage of lend-lease and then our full engagement after Pearl Harbor, we again had to salvage vital American interests by engaging in a world conflict, undoing a prior, costly return to isolationism.

In 1947 we had to reverse the course of immediate postwar policy in order to salvage and protect Western Europe and the balance of world power, having weakened our position by hasty and drastic demobilization. In June 1950 we had to go to war in Korea to meet a major act of Communist aggression and repair the weakness of our conventional military establishment in the Far East, which, in turn, resulted from our relatively low postwar military budgets.

The great periods in executive leadership in this century have, thus, been periods where radical action was taken at home to correct previous distortions in our domestic affairs or to cope with desperate crises abroad.

In the 1960's it is clear that we have faced and still face both at home and abroad issues and challenges which, by any standard of the past, are great. Basic characteristics of our domestic society are at stake as well as life-and-death issues on the world scene.

By any standards of the past they require of us great performance, both in our government and in our society at large. But there is a difference. In a nuclear age we cannot afford to let matters slide away from us—as they did in the years before 1917, 1941, and even 1947—to the point where a massive, convulsive response is required to overcome the danger and redress the balance.

At home we face—in race relations, in our balance-of-payments position, in the need to achieve and maintain the full and regular use of our human and material resources, in overcoming serious margins of poverty in our society, in developing an educational system adequate to the needs of our society, and in other directions as well—truly great tasks. But here, too, it would be unwise for us to permit any of these problems to become so massive that they yielded a domestic crisis of the kind which in the past was generally required to yield national concensus and a massive, vigorous response.

My theme today is, then, simply this: The task of American leadership in the 1960's—and the task of our society at large—is to bring about movement toward large objectives by small increments over considerable periods of time. It is no longer safe for public policy in the United States to oscillate in the classic rhythm of our past: between periods of relative passivity, in the face of mounting problems, and periods of heroic but convulsive and sometimes bloody endeavor. To protect the Nation's essential values and interests, our style in public life must be steadier, more regularly active and forward-moving, than it has tended to be in the long sweep of our history.

It is something like this vision which has governed national policy since President Kennedy's inaugural in January 1961. In the wake of a narrow victory at the polls, he, nevertheless, called on the Nation to "begin anew."

In domestic policy he set out to lead the Nation toward higher but steadily maintained levels of employment and overall growth; toward the correction of our balance-of-payments deficits; toward a new justice in race relations; toward the reduction of the margins of poverty in our society; toward a strengthening through Federal action of the educational foundations of our society; toward the acceptance of collective responsibility for the medical care of the aged. None of these were problems which yielded, either technically or politically, to immediate definitive solution. But all of them were moved forward in his time in a series of limited steps. Each step required clarity and determination about the objective, but it also required realism, care, and often caution about the extent to which progress was possible as of the moment of forward movement. For example, historians will, I believe, find fascinating and perhaps somewhat surprising the intimacy with which President Kennedy personally guided the delicate but essential effort to move simultaneously toward sustained business expansion and toward balance-of-payments equilibrium.

Picking up from the day he assumed responsibility, President Johnson in 6 months has moved forward on all these fronts with the vigor which is his mark, leaving already his strong imprint on the march down these long roads of domestic progress.

In foreign policy, where I am more directly involved, much the same is true.

In 1961 President Kennedy faced two massive tasks.

First, he had to deal with a series of dangerous and degenerative crises. These took their origins from the period after the first Sputnik was launched in October 1957. The Communist world was swept by a wave of confidence and aggressive enterprise. It was in 1958 that Khrushchev laid down his ultimatum on Berlin and the Communists began to press hard in Southeast Asia, Africa, and Latin America.

Second, President Kennedy had to define a set of long-run positive objectives and begin to devise policies which would move toward them, step by step.

With respect to Western Europe and Japan, he held up the vision of a partnership in world affairs that would replace the acute dependence on the United States, which had marked the early postwar years. With respect to Latin America—and the other developing areas—he aligned the United States firmly with those who were committed to reshape their societies so as to reconcile economic growth, social equity, and the development of democratic political institutions.

With respect to the Communist world, he radically increased our military strength but simultaneously set the Government to work with a new intensity to find the means to start—even in small ways— down the long road to arms control and disarmament.

This is not the occasion to detail how these enterprises were carried forward. But between May 1961 and October 1962 Khrushchev's post-Sputnik offensive was painstakingly defused. This was done not by war. It was accomplished by a series of military and political moves, each difficult and protracted, each involving moments of hazard, climaxed, of course, by the Cuba missile crisis.

As President Johnson has underlined, from his State of the Union message on, our cold-war problems have by no means ended. We face, in particular, the task of dealing in Southeast Asia and the Caribbean with those who would foment Communist insurrection by the illegal infiltration of arms and men across international frontiers.

But we have seen in these 3 years one of the most dramatic shifts in the balance of power in modern history.

From the latter days of January 1961, however—amidst the unrelenting pressure of multiple crises—the constructive enterprises were nevertheless launched and carried forward.

The arrival of Ambassador [Edwin O.] Reischauer in Japan and the visit of Prime Minister [Hayato] Ikeda to Washington launched a new phase of more profound association in our relations with Japan and also set in motion forces which have drawn Japan deeply into the nonmilitary affairs of the North Atlantic community.

In the fields of trade, monetary affairs, political consultation, and nuclear cooperation, enterprises were launched which moved the Atlantic community forward on new lines, despite some evident frustration and even setback. Above all, the Atlantic community proved its essential vitality and unity in the Berlin and Cuban crises.

We set out on the Alliance for Progress with a decade as the initial working horizon, and despite what may appear a slow start, substantial progress has been made. Elsewhere, in the developing areas—in Africa, the Middle East, and Asia—new efforts were launched both to help protect the independence of the developing societies and to strengthen the underpinnings of that independence by programs of development assistance.

And, choosing his moment in the wake of the Cuban missile crisis, President Kennedy, in his American University speech of June 1963, found the occasion to begin to move forward on the path of arms control he had defined so vividly in his inaugural more than 2 years earlier. The atmospheric test ban agreement and President Johnson's initiative in cutting back production of fissionable material are first steps along the way.

Behind all these ventures is a vision of our ultimate task on the world scene. That task is to help build an orderly and peaceful world community to supplant the world system which was shattered in 1914 and never replaced. This is the grand purpose which suffuses the effort to build a great partnership in the north stretching from Tokyo east to Berlin, to build a new north-south relationship between the more developed and developing nations of the free world. This is our ultimate objective in East-West relations, where we aim not merely to frustrate Communist aggression but to draw the nations now under Communist rule into an orderly and peaceful world community, for the struggle with communism is ultimately a struggle about how this small planet shall be organized.

In talking about our foreign policy we are talking about the biggest piece of architecture ever undertaken at a time of peace. None of the lines of action we have launched is yet complete. But, while final results have not been reached, these have not been paper programs nor policies of rhetoric. We have moved some distance down long roads: toward a binding up into partnership of the more advanced nations of the free world, across the Atlantic and the Pacific; toward new relations of dignity and collaboration within the free world between the advanced nations of the north and the developing nations to the south; toward a definitive frustration of the Communist thrust; and toward controlling the dangers posed for humanity by the existence of nuclear weapons.

What is required both within the Government and in our country as a whole is the will and the capacity to persist. We need steadiness, patience, and a stubborn sense of direction. In all conscience, the world is complicated and dangerous enough to insure that crises will arise. But our objectives will prove attainable if we bring to them the mood of the old schoolyard game of Indian wrestling, where victory went to him who summoned the extra moment of endurance.

The frontiers of the past were probed, explored, and consolidated by stubborn, protracted enterprise, not by the convulsive reaction to crisis; and this is the way it is—and should be—with the new frontiers of the 1960's.

I am deeply convinced that, if we in the United States do a job that lies wholly within our capacity and if the free world maintains a reasonable degree of unity and common purpose, the events, decisions, and initiatives launched in recent years could mark the beginning of the end of the cold war.

The Cuba missile crisis of 1962 could emerge as the Gettysburg of that global civil conflict. We owe it to all free men to labor to make it so.

CHAPTER III

Education and National Morale

In the life of the individual, education is always an unfinished task. And in the life of his nation, the advancement of education is a continuing challenge.

—LYNDON B. JOHNSON

Let anyone try to name any other country, apart from the Soviet Union, where the higher schools graduate so many specialists as we do in the Soviet Union. Today the U.S.A. is setting the task of overtaking the Soviet Union in science and in the training of specialists.

—NIKITA S. KHRUSHCHEV

"Nothing matters more to the future of our country: not military preparedness—for armed might is worthless if we lack the brain power to build a world of peace; not our productive economy— for we cannot sustain growth without trained manpower; not our democratic system of government—for freedom is fragile if citizens are ignorant. We must demand that our schools increase not only the quantity but the quality of America's education." Thus declared President Johnson in his message to Congress, January 12, 1965. If the words, "democratic," "freedom," and "America's" are replaced by "Communistic," "Marxism," and "Soviet" respectively, the message could well be adopted by Soviet leaders as their own educational policy declaration.

Education has long been regarded as the very foundation of, and the vital investment in, a nation's future. The fundamental difference in the objective of education between the United States and the Soviet Union is that the former aims at the individual's highest moral, spiritual, and intellectual development, the latter at the "moulding of harmoniously developed members of Communist society." Critics of the American educational system and performance deplore its mass production of "well-adjusted idiots"; they warn that the United States

62

is losing a battle against the Soviets in the educational field and lament that America's national morale and vitality are proportionately eroding.

This chapter focuses on a comparative discussion of educational goals, national character, and morale of the United States and the Soviet Union.

President Kennedy, in his special message to Congress in January, 1963, affirming that the quality and opportunity of education is vital to national security and well-being, recommended prompt legislation of a program to assist public as well as private institutions of higher education through scholarships and the construction of urgently needed academic facilities such as classrooms, laboratories, libraries, dormitories, etc.

S. V. Utechin, a research fellow at St. Antony's College, Oxford, presents a critical and penetrating analysis of the Soviet educational program outlined at the Twenty-Second Party Congress in October, 1961.

Klaus Mehnert, a German historian and political commentator, discusses the strong patriotism and dynamic energy of the Russian people, basing his observation on his personal contact with Russians from all walks of life.

1. THE URGENCY OF BETTER EDUCATION*

BY JOHN F. KENNEDY

For the nation, increasing the quality and availability of education is vital to both our national security and our domestic well-being. A free nation can rise no higher than the standard of excellence set in its schools and colleges. Ignorance and illiteracy, unskilled workers and school drop-outs—these and other failures of our educational system breed failures in our social and economic system: delinquency, unemployment, chronic dependence, a waste of human resources, a loss of productive power and purchasing power and an increase in tax-supported benefits. The loss of only one year's

* Special Message to Congress, January 29, 1963.

income due to unemployment is more than the total cost of twelve years of education through high school. Failure to improve educational performance is thus not only poor social policy, it is poor economics.

At the turn of the century, only 10 percent of our adults had a high school or college education. Today such an education has become a requirement for an increasing number of jobs. Yet nearly 40 percent of our youths are dropping out before graduating from high school; only 43 percent of our adults have completed high school; only 8 percent of our adults have completed college; and only 16 percent of our young people are presently completing college. As my Science Advisory Committee has reported, one of our most serious manpower shortages is the lack of Ph.D.'s in engineering, science and mathematics; only about one-half of 1 percent of our school-age generation is achieving Ph.D. degrees in all fields.

I do not say that the federal government should take over responsibility for education. That is neither desirable nor feasible. Instead, its participation should be selective, stimulative and, where possible, transitional.

A century of experience with land-grant colleges has demonstrated that federal financial participation can assist educational progress and growth without federal control. In the last decade, experience with the National Science Foundation, with the National Defense Education Act, and with programs for assisting federally affected school districts has demonstrated that federal support can benefit education without leading to federal control. The proper federal role is to identify national education goals and to help local, state and private authorities build the necessary roads to reach those goals. Federal aid will enable our schools, colleges and universities to be more stable financially and therefore more independent.

These goals include the following:

First, we must improve the quality of instruction provided in all of our schools and colleges. We must stimulate interest in learning in order to reduce the alarming number of students who now drop out of school or who do not continue into higher levels of education. This requires more and better teachers—teachers who can be attracted to and retained in schools and colleges only if pay levels reflect more adequately the value of the services they render. It also requires that our teachers and instructors be equipped with the best possible teaching materials and curricula. They must have at their command methods of instruction proven by thorough scientific research into the learning process and by careful experimentation.

Second, our educational system faces a major problem of quantity —of coping with the needs of our expanding population and of the rising educational expectations for our children which all of us share as parents. Nearly 50 million people were enrolled in our schools and colleges in 1962—an increase of more than 50 percent since 1950. By 1970, college enrollment will nearly double, and secondary schools will increase enrollment by 50 percent—categories in which the cost of education, including facilities, is several times higher than in elementary schools.

Third, we must give special attention to increasing the opportunities and incentives for all Americans to develop their talents to the utmost—to complete their education and to continue their self-development throughout life. This means preventing school drop-outs, improving and expanding special educational services, and providing better education in slum, distressed and rural areas where the educational attainment of students is far below par. It means increased opportunities for those students both willing and intellectually able to advance their education at the college and graduate levels. It means increased attention to vocational and technical education, which have long been underdeveloped in both effectiveness and scope, to the detriment of our workers and our technological progress.

In support of these three basic goals, I am proposing today a comprehensive, balanced program to enlarge the federal government's investment in the education of its citizens—a program aimed at increasing the educational opportunities of potentially every American citizen, regardless of age, race, religion, income and educational achievement.

This program has been shaped to meet our goals on the basis of three fundamental guidelines:

An appraisal of the entire range of educational problems, viewing educational opportunity as a continuous lifelong process, starting with preschool training and extending through elementary and secondary schools, college, graduate education, vocational education, job training and retraining, adult education, and such general community educational resources as the public library;

A selective application of federal aid—aimed at strengthening, not weakening, the independence of existing school systems and aimed at meeting our most urgent education problems and objectives, including quality improvement; teacher training; special problems of slums, depressed and rural areas; needy students; manpower shortage areas such as science and engineering; and shortages of educational facilities; and

More effective implementation of existing laws, as reflected in my recent budget recommendations.

To enable the full range of educational needs to be considered as a whole, I am transmitting to the Congress with this message a single, comprehensive education bill—the National Education Improvement Act of 1963. For education cannot easily or wisely be divided into separate parts. Each part is linked to the other. The colleges depend on the work of the schools; the schools depend on the colleges for teachers; vocational and technical education is not separate from general education. This bill recalls the posture of Jefferson: "Nobody can doubt my zeal for the general instruction of the people. I never have proposed a sacrifice of the primary to the ultimate grade of instruction. Let us keep our eye steadily on the whole system."

In order that its full relation to economic growth, to the new age of science, to the national security and to human and institutional freedom may be analyzed in proper perspective, this bill should be considered as a whole, as a combination of elements designed to solve problems that have no single solution.

This is not a partisan measure—and it neither includes nor rejects all of the features which have long been sought by the various educational groups and organizations. It is instead an attempt to launch a prudent and balanced program drawing upon the efforts of many past Congresses and the proposals of many members of both houses and both political parties. It is solely an educational program, without trying to solve all other difficult domestic problems. It is clearly realistic in terms of its cost—and it is clearly essential to the growth and security of this country.

Our present American educational system was founded on the principle that opportunity for education in this country should be available to all—not merely to those who have the ability to pay. In the past, this has meant free public elementary and secondary schools in every community, thereafter, land-grant, state and municipal colleges, and vocational education, and more recently, job retraining and specialized teachers for students with special educational problems.

Now a veritable tidal wave of students is advancing inexorably on our institutions of higher education, where the annual costs per student are several times as high as the cost of a high school education, and where these costs must be borne in large part by the student or his parents. Five years ago the graduating class of the secondary schools was 1.5 million; five years from now it will be 2.5 million. The future of these young people and the nation rests in large part on their access to college and graduate education. For this country reserves its highest honors for only one kind of aristocracy—that which the Founding Fathers called "an aristocracy of achievement arising out of a democracy of opportunity."

Well over half of all parents with school-age children expect them to attend college. But only one-third do so. Some 40 percent of those who enter college do not graduate, and only a small number continue into graduate and professional study. The lack of adequate aid to students plays a large part in this disturbing record.

Federal aid to college students is not new. More than 3 million World War II and Korean conflict veterans have received $6 billion in federal funds since 1944 to assist them to attend college. Additionally, the National Defense Education Act college student loan program has aided more than 300,000 students in more than 1,500 institutions who have borrowed nearly $220 million. In four years of operations, defaults have totaled only $700 while repayment rates are more than twice that required by law.

But as effective as this program has been, it has not fulfilled its original objective of assuring that "no student of ability will be denied an opportunity for higher education because of financial need." The institutional ceiling of $250,000 per year on the federal contribution limits loan funds in at least ninety-eight of the presently participating institutions. The annual statutory ceiling of $90 million on federal appropriations restricts the size of the program. As a result, only about 5 percent of the students enrolled in participating colleges are assisted. Additionally, the forgiveness feature for teachers is rendered less attractive as well as less meaningful by excluding those who go on to teach in colleges, in private schools or on overseas military posts. This proven program must be enlarged and strengthened.

Other types of assistance are needed. For students who cannot meet the financial criteria under the NDEA loan program, a loan insurance program—drawing on techniques well established by the FHA and other federal programs—would encourage banks and other institutions to loan more money for educational purposes.

Moreover, many students from families with limited incomes cannot and should not carry a heavy burden of debt. They must rely largely on income from employment while in college. For these students, the federal government should—as it did in the days of the National Youth Administration—help colleges provide additional student work opportunities of an educational character.

A serious barrier to increased graduate study is the lack of adequate financial aid for graduate students. Only 1,500 fellowships are permitted annually under the National Defense Education Act program, upon which we are dependent for urgently needed increases in the number of college teachers and the number of graduate students pursuing other courses essential to the nation's advancement and security. The National Science Foundation has broad authority for fellowships and training grants, but its program, too, has been restricted by limited appropriations. The President's Science Advisory Committee has predicted that the dramatically increasing demand for engineers, mathematicians and physical scientists will require that the output of Ph.D.'s in these fields alone be increased two and one-half times, to a total of 7,500 annually by 1970, and that the number of master's degrees awarded annually be substantially increased. In all fields the need exceeds the supply of doctoral recipients. The shortage is particularly acute in college teaching, where at present rates the nation will lack 90,000 doctoral degree holders by 1970. It is clearly contrary to the national interest to have the number of graduate students limited by the financial ability of those able and interested in pursuing advanced degrees. Fellowship programs can ease much of the financial burden and, most importantly, encourage and stimulate a fuller realization and utilization of our human resources.

The welfare and security of the nation require that we increase our investment in financial assistance for college students both at undergraduate and graduate levels. In keeping with present needs and our traditions of maximum self-help, I recommend that the Congress enact legislation to:

1. Extend the National Defense Education Act student loan pro-

gram, liberalize the repayment forgiveness for teachers, raise the ceiling on total appropriations and eliminate the limitation on amounts available to individual institutions.

2. Authorize a supplementary new program of federal insurance for commercial loans made by banks and other institutions to college students for educational purposes.

3. Establish a new work-study program for needy college students unable to carry too heavy a loan burden, providing up to half the pay for students employed by the colleges in work of an educational character—as, for example, laboratory, library or research assistants.

4. Increase the number of National Defense Education Act fellowships to be awarded by the Office of Education from 1,500 to 12,000, including summer session awards.

5. Authorize a thorough survey and evaluation of the need for scholarships or additional financial assistance to undergraduate students so that any further action needed in this area can be considered by the next Congress.

In addition, as part of this program to increase financial assistance to students, the 1964 budget recommendations for the National Science Foundation, which are already before the Congress, include a proposed increase of $35 million to expand the number of fellowships and new teaching grants for graduate study from 2,800 in 1963 to 8,700 in fiscal 1964.

Aid to college students will be to no avail if there are insufficient college classrooms. The long-predicted crisis in higher education facilities is now at hand. For the next fifteen years, even without additional student aid, enrollment increases in colleges will average 340,000 each year. If we are to accommodate the projected enrollment of more than 7 million college students by 1970—a doubling during the decade—$23 billion of new facilities will be needed, more than three times the quantity built during the preceding decade. This means that, unless we are to deny higher education opportunities to our youth, American colleges and universities must expand their academic facilities at a rate much faster than their present resources will permit.

In many colleges, students with adequate modern dormitories and living quarters—thanks to the College Housing Act—are crammed in outmoded, overcrowded classrooms, laboratories and libraries. Even now it is too late to provide these facilities to meet the sharp increases in college enrollment expected during the next two years. Further delay will aggravate an already critical situation. I recommend, therefore, the prompt enactment of a program to provide loans to public and nonprofit private institutions of higher education for construction of urgently needed academic facilities.

The opportunity for a college education is severely limited for hundreds of thousands of young people because there is no college in their own community. Studies indicate that the likelihood of going to college on the part of a high school graduate who lives within twenty to twenty-five miles of a college is 50 percent greater than it is for the student who lives beyond commuting distance. This absence of college facilities in many communities causes an unfortunate waste of some of our most promising youthful talent. A demonstrated method of meeting this particular problem effectively is the creation of two-year community colleges—a program that should be undertaken without delay and which will require federal assistance for the construction of adequate facilities. I recommend, therefore, a program of grants to states for construction of public community junior colleges.

There is an especially urgent need for college level training of technicians to assist scientists, engineers and doctors. Although ideally one scientist or engineer should have the backing of two or three technicians, our institutions today are not producing even one technician for each three science and engineering graduates. This shortage results in an inefficient use of professional manpower—the occupation of critically needed time and talent to perform tasks which could be performed by others—an extravagance which cannot be tolerated when the nation's demand for scientists, engineers and doctors continues to grow. Failure to give attention to this matter will impede the objectives of the graduate and postgraduate training programs mentioned below. I recommend, therefore, a program of grants to aid public and private nonprofit institutions in the training of scientific, engineering and medical technicians in two-year college-level programs, covering up to 50 percent of the cost of constructing and equipping as well as operating the necessary academic facilities.

Special urgency exists for expanding the capacity for the graduate training of engineers, scientists and mathematicians. The President's Science Advisory Committee has recently reported that an unprecedented acceleration in the production of advanced degrees is immediately necessary to increase our national capability in these fields. Added facilities, larger faculties and new institutions are needed. I have recommended, therefore, in the proposed 1964 budget already before the Congress, a strengthening of the National Science Foundation matching grant program for institutions of higher education to expand and improve graduate and undergraduate science facilities.

Because today's trend in colleges and universities is toward less lecturing and more independent study, the college and university library becomes even more essential in the life of our students. Today, as reported by the American Library Association, nearly all college libraries are urgently in need of additional books, periodicals, scientific reports and similar materials to accommodate the growing number of students and faculty. Additionally, they need buildings, equipment and publications to serve their academic communities, whether public or private. I recommend the authorization of federal grants to institutions of higher education for library materials and construction, on a broad geographic basis, with priority to those most urgently requiring expansion and improvement.

Expansion of high-quality graduate education and research in all fields is essential to national security and economic growth. Means of increasing our supply of highly trained professional personnel to match the rapidly growing demands of teaching, industry, government and research warrants our interest and support.

We need many more graduate centers, and they should be better distributed geographically. Three-quarters of all doctoral degrees are granted by a handful of universities located in twelve states. The remaining states with half our population produce only one-fourth of the Ph.D.'s.

New industries increasingly gravitate to or are innovated by strong centers of learning and research. The distressed area of the future may well be one which lacks centers of graduate education and research. It is in the national interest to encourage establishment of these critically needed centers of advanced learning, especially in parts of the nation now lacking them.

I recommend enactment of a federal grant program administered by the Department of Health, Education and Welfare for the development and expansion of new graduate centers. I also urge appropriation of the increased funds requested in my 1964 budget for expansion of the National Science Foundation program of science development grants, which will also contribute to strengthening of graduate education.

Our experience under the National Defense Education Act with respect to modern language and area centers has demonstrated that federal aid can spur development of intellectual talent. They deserve our continuing support, with assurance that resources will be available for orderly expansion in keeping with availability of teaching talent. I recommend that the current Modern Foreign Language program aiding public and private institutions of higher learning be extended and expanded.

A basic source of knowledge is research. Industry has long realized this truth. Health and agriculture have established the worth of systematic research and development. But research in education has been astonishingly meager and frequently ignored. A fraction of 1 percent of this nation's total expenditures for education is now devoted to such research. It is appalling that so little is known about the level of performance, comparative value of alternative investments and specialized problems of our educational system—and that it lags behind, sometimes by as much as twenty or even fifty years, in utilizing the results of research and keeping abreast of man's knowledge in all fields, including education itself.

Highest priority must be given to strengthening our educational research efforts, including a substantial expansion of the course content improvement programs which the government has supported, particularly through the National Science Foundation. Two interrelated actions are necessary.

I have recommended appropriations in the 1964 budget for substantially expanding the National Science Foundation science and mathematics course materials program and the Office of Education educational research program.

I recommended legislation to broaden the Cooperative Research Act to authorize support of centers for multipurpose educational research and for development and demonstration programs; and to broaden the types of educational agencies eligible to conduct research.

The second step to improvement of educational quality is teacher training. The quality of education is determined primarily by the quality of the teacher. Yet one out of every five teachers in the United States has either not been certified by his state as qualified to teach or failed to complete four years of college study. In the field of

English, between 40 and 60 percent of the secondary school teachers lack even the minimum requirement of a college major in that subject. Thus it is not surprising that, largely because of unsatisfactory elementary and secondary school instruction, our colleges and universities are now required to spend over $10 million annually on remedial English courses.

The lack of teacher quality and preparation in other fields is equally disturbing. More than two-thirds of our 1.6 million teachers completed their degree work more than five years ago. Yet within the past five years major advances have been made—not only in the physical, biological, engineering and mathematical sciences, but also in specialized branches of the social sciences, the arts and humanities, and in the art of teaching itself.

In addition, we lack sufficient trained teachers for 6 million handicapped children and youth, including 1.5 million mentally retarded and another 1.5 million with very serious social and emotional problems. Only through special classes, taught by specially trained teachers, can these children prepare for rehabilitation, employment and community participation. Yet less than one-fourth of these children now have access to the special education they require, primarily because of the lack of qualified special teachers, college instructors, research personnel and supervisors. It is estimated that 75,000 special teachers—55,000 more than presently available—are needed for the mentally retarded alone.

The teacher training support programs of the National Science Foundation and the Office of Education have demonstrated their value. I recommend, therefore: that the National Science Foundation program for training institutes for teachers in the natural sciences, mathematics, engineering and social sciences be expanded to provide for upgrading the knowledge and skills of 46,000 teachers, as provided in my 1964 budget recommendations. . . .

2. SOVIET EDUCATION AND THE PROGRAMME*

BY S. V. UTECHIN

"The transition to communism," states the subsection of the new Party Programme devoted to education, "implies training that will make people communist-minded and highly-cultured, people fitted for both physical and mental labour, for active work in various social, governmental, scientific, and cultural spheres." Public education is to further the "moulding of harmoniously developed members of communist society," and make for "solution of a cardinal social problem, namely, the elimination of substantial distinctions between mental and physical labour." The system of public education having these aims must, according to the Programme, "ensure that the instruction and education of the rising generation are closely bound up with life and productive labour, and that the adult population can combine work in the sphere of production with further training and education in keeping with their vocations and the requirements of society."

The practical tasks of the party in furthering the stated aims for education are set out in the Programme under four headings: (a) introduction of universal compulsory secondary education; (b) the public (*obshchestvennoye*) upbringing of children of pre-school and school age; (c) creation of conditions for high-standard instruction and education of the rising generation; and (d) higher and secondary special education.

The main task under the first heading is to realise, in the course of the next ten years, compulsory secondary general and polytechnical eleven-year education for all children of school age, and education corresponding to eight classes for young people occupied in the national economy who have not had appropriate schooling; in the subsequent ten years "everyone will have the opportunity to receive a

* From *The U.S.S.R. and the Future,* Leonard Schapiro, ed. (New York: Praeger, 1963), pp. 212–221. Copyright © 1962 by Forschungsinstitut, Munich, Germany; reprinted by their permission.

complete secondary education." This represents a reversal of the policy pursued by Khrushchev since 1956. Universal education up to the age of 18 (that is, some kind of secondary education) was included in the Party Programme of 1919. In fact, primary education (four classes) was made compulsory in 1930/31 and incomplete secondary (seven classes) in 1949. The Nineteenth Party Congress in 1952 restated the goal of universal secondary education (ten classes), which was to be realised by 1960. But the 1958 law on school reform dropped this goal and reduced compulsory schooling to eight classes. A policy of expanding secondary education was in fact vigorously pursued between 1949 and 1956. As is usual in communist practice, the reversal in policy which actually took place from 1956 and was made official in 1958 was carried out without making any mention of the previous policy of expansion. The present return to the pre-Khrushchev policy (perhaps it should be called the Malenkov policy, since it coincided with Malenkov's ascendancy after the death of Zhdanov) is thus represented as a great advance (which of course it is over the present situation) and no reference is made to the 1952 decision to achieve universal secondary education by 1960. Another departure from Khrushchev's policy hitherto is also involved in the aim of universal general secondary education. The 1952 decision was to have *general* secondary education; in 1956 this was modified by Khrushchev at the Twentieth Party Congress to general *or* specialised secondary education, and in his Memorandum on school reform in 1958 he expressed himself definitely against universal general secondary education; now, however, it is once again general secondary education that is to become compulsory during the next ten years.

The reasons for this change can only be guessed at, though one of them is obvious. The Communist Party has always claimed that socialism inevitably means a great advance over capitalism in educational facilities, and the stage of the "transition to communism" would logically imply a further forward move in this direction. Besides, the 1919 Party Programme had proclaimed universal education up to the age of 18, and it must have been an embarrassment that this not only remained unrealised after forty-two years but that until recently it had not even been the official policy. The struggle against the "Anti-Party Group" also demanded that Khrushchev should show himself to be no less concerned with the welfare of the country than Malenkov had been (there is a close parallel here with the consumer goods policy). Another possible reason is that with all the talk of overtaking the United States, the Soviet Union should go one step further and make secondary education compulsory, since in the United States it is already generally available. It also seems probable that the scientists and technologists have succeeded in persuading Khrushchev that outstanding achievements are only likely to be forthcoming if the general educational level is high. And finally, since people in Russia are highly education-conscious, it is conceivable that this is yet another concession made by Khrushchev to popular sentiment, although there is a considerable dissatisfaction with the present curriculum in the upper forms of the 11-year school and the authorities are concerned about the numbers of those who leave it before finishing.

On the types of schooling, the Programme says that "universal secondary education is guaranteed by the development of general and polytechnical education, professional training combined with socially useful labour of school children to the extent of their physical capacity, and a considerable expansion of the network of all types of general schools, including evening schools, which provide a secondary education in off-work hours." The final text of this passage differs from the original draft published in July, and the changes reflect the diverse tendencies that are now shaping educational policy. One of the changes was the insertion in the final text of the reference to "professional," i.e. vocational, training. Vocational training was introduced as part of the curriculum of the general secondary school during the late 1950s and the insistence on a reference to it in the Programme must have come from those who are anxious that it should not be swept away by the renewed emphasis on universal general secondary education. On the other hand, the insertion of the reference to "all types of general schools," which was also missing in the draft, must be due to the influence of those who do not share Khrushchev's preference for evening schools. Evening schools have in fact been expanding rapidly since 1958, and more than half of all those who completed general secondary education in 1961 had passed through at least their last class in evening school.

As far as the content of schooling is concerned, the Programme says that "secondary education must furnish a solid knowledge of the fundamentals of the basic sciences, an understanding of the principles of the communist world outlook, and a labour and polytechnical training in accordance with the rising level of science and engineering, with due regard to the needs of society and to the abilities and inclinations of the students, as well as the moral, aesthetic and physical education of a healthy rising generation."

Here again we find tasks that are mutually contradictory. The first task, the acquisition of knowledge of the fundamentals of the sciences (the term "sciences" includes the humanities as well as the natural sciences) and the last one concerning the moral, aesthetic and physical upbringing, are the traditional tasks of the secondary school, especially as understood on the European continent. It is questionable whether they are compatible with the task of polytechnical and vocational training, at least as this is conceived in Russia now; and they are certainly incompatible with the assimilation of the principles of the communist view of the world. The communist view of the world includes the scientific outlook of a century ago, an equally antiquated approach to the humanities, and a utilitarian view of morals and aesthetics. It is obvious, therefore, that in trying to inculcate the communist view of the world, the authorities will have to withhold knowledge of much of the methodology of modern science, the methodology as well as some of the factual content of history and the modern social sciences, and to favour a rather one-sided moral and aesthetic development. Thus, a leading authority on the subject, discussing the content of education in the light of the new Party Programme, says: "The content of school education is directed towards the upbringing of pupils in the spirit of communist consciousness, i.e. towards forming their scientific world view and communist attitude to work, towards the assimilation by them of the moral code of a builder of communism and towards overcoming the survivals of the past in the consciousness and behaviour of some youths and girls. The realisation of these tasks must be facilitated by the selection of appropriate facts, concepts, laws, scientific theories and the utilisation of materials which depict the successes of communist construction in the USSR and the crisis of world capitalism."[1] On the other hand, those teachers who may try to acquaint their pupils with the fundamentals of modern sciences and the modern views in the field of the humanities will thereby inevitably be undermining the communist view of the world.

The wording of the Programme does not suggest that any changes in the curriculum are intended beyond those made during the last

[1] *Sovetskaya Pedagogika*, October 1961, p. 29.

two or three years. These include the introduction of compulsory vocational training in the upper forms of secondary schools and of a new subject, Fundamentals of Political Knowledge, a re-orientation in the teaching of history and literature to make them to an even greater extent into vehicles of political propaganda, and a reorganisation for the better in the methods of teaching foreign languages. But it is possible that the aim of universal secondary education will make it easier to achieve some diversity in the curriculum. Only vocational training is diversified at present, while the other subjects follow a rigidly prescribed syllabus. Diversification has been advocated in recent years by some educationalists, and one of them[2] raised the issue in connection with the new Party Programme. It is on these lines that a solution might be found to the problem of how universal secondary education can cater for the different abilities of children.[3]

The last paragraph under the heading (a) is concerned with the need for a constant perfection of the system of vocational technical training and the training of workers at places of employment in order that the skills of the workers should be combined with raising their general educational level and with the acquisition of engineering, agricultural, medical or other specialised knowledge. Vocational Technical Schools now cater, according to the reform law of 1958, for people who have finished an incomplete secondary (eight-year) school, though in fact some of them admit pupils with only primary (four-year) education, and it is not clear from the Programme what is meant to happen to them after universal general secondary education has been achieved; the vast majority of Vocational Technical Schools do not teach general subjects and cannot, therefore, be considered as a form of full secondary education.

Under heading (b)—the public upbringing of children of school and pre-school age—the Programme states that "the communist system of public education is based on the public upbringing of children. The educational influence which the family exerts on children, must be brought into ever greater harmony with their public upbringing." This might be taken as an indication of renewed emphasis on the communal upbringing of children and as indicating the intention to weaken the family once again, as happened in the 1920s

[2] M. A. Melnikov, in *Sovetskaya Pedagogika,* September 1961, p. 15.
[3] This question is discussed in more detail in my article "Educating the New Man" in *Survey,* No. 38, October 1961.

and early 1930s. But in fact, this does not seem to be the case. Khrushchev, in his report on the Party Programme at the Congress, said precisely in regard to this point that those who maintain that the significance of the family will diminish with the transition to communism, and that with the passing of time the family would completely disappear, were altogether wrong. In reality, Khrushchev said, the family would be strengthened under communism. The only definite point put forward under this heading is that the development of the network of preschool institutions and of boarding-schools of various types will guarantee the full satisfaction of the needs of the toilers for the communal upbringing of children of pre-school and school age according to the wishes of the parents. Some boarding-school enthusiasts in Russia maintain that the boarding-schools will be the main, and perhaps the only, form of school in the future, and the insertion of the clause about the wishes of the parents seems to be designed to allay the legitimate apprehensions of those parents and others who do not favour such an exclusive influence of the authorities on the upbringing of children. On the other hand, the parents' wishes clause makes this task quite realistic, since there is no reason to expect a significant rise in the demand for boarding-school education.[4] It is not quite clear what meaning is to be attached to the statement that "the importance of the school, which is to cultivate love of labour and knowledge in children and to raise the younger generation in the spirit of communist consciousness and morality, will increase." As the Programme does not say in relation to what other institutions the importance of the school should be heightened, the whole passage is perhaps intended simply to affirm the rôle of the school, possibly in anticipation of a revival of the earlier communist view that the school was to "wither away" as society approached communism. A similar conservative tendency may perhaps be deduced from the slight change in the phrase which in the draft had read "in all this an exalted, honourable and responsible rôle belongs to the teacher, the Komsomol and Pioneer organisations"; in the final text this reads ". . . to the teacher, and also to the Komsomol and Pioneer organisations." This, at first sight mere stylistic change, may in fact have been made in order to put the Komsomol and Pioneer organisations into a somewhat lower, rather auxiliary, position as compared to the teacher.

Under heading (c)—creation of conditions for higher-standard

[4] Cf. my article referred to earlier.

instruction and education of the rising generation—the Programme deals with school buildings and equipment as well as sports grounds, etc. "The party plans to carry out an extensive programme for the construction of schools and cultural-education establishments to meet fully the needs of education and instruction. All schools will be housed in good buildings and will go over to a one-shift time-table. They will all have study workshops and chemical, physical and other laboratories; rural schools will also have their own farming plots; large factories will have production training shops for school children. Modern facilities—cinema, radio, and television—will be widely used in schools. For physical training and aesthetic education, all schools and extra-scholastic establishments will have gymnasiums, sports grounds and facilities for the creative endeavour of children in music, painting, sculpture, etc. The network of sports schools, sports grounds, tourist camps, skiing centres, aquatic stations, swimming pools, and other sports facilities will be expanded in town and countryside." There is nothing in all this that is new, either for the Soviet Union or for non-communist countries, except the promise to build enough schools to eliminate the need for two-shift classes. It is very unlikely that the latter will be achieved, unless a much higher priority is given to school-building than has been the case hitherto.

Under heading (d)—Higher and Secondary Special Education— the Programme says that the "shorter working hours and a considerable improvement in the standard of living of the entire population will provide everyone with an opportunity to receive higher or secondary special education if he so desires," and promises that the numbers of those admitted to higher and specialised secondary educational institutions will "considerably increase every year." In his report to the Twenty-Second Congress on the Programme, Khrushchev specified that the number of students (including evening and correspondence students) receiving higher education, which now stands at 2,600,000, will rise to 8,000,000 by 1980. This signifies a break with the traditional European and Russian view of higher education as an instrument for creating an intellectual élite (a view that was abandoned by the communist authorities in 1917 but re-asserted itself in the mid-1930s), and an adoption of the American practice of mass education on the post-secondary level. It is also another instance of the reversal in the Programme of the views so far professed by Khrushchev, who stated in one of his speeches in 1957 that there would be no expansion of higher education in the years to come. His remedy for the "divorce of the higher school from life" was not to increase the numbers of students, but to change the composition of the student body through the institution of an obligatory two-year period of employment after completion of secondary school and the requiring of certificates of worthiness issued by the employers and the party, Komsomol and trade union organisations to be presented by those seeking admission to higher educational establishments. This change in the admission requirements, shifting the emphasis from ability and academic achievements to efficiency in manual work and political conformity, left intact the idea that the purpose of higher education was to produce an élite, though the élite itself was to be semi-intellectual and semi-political. The results of entrance examinations in the last two years have shown that the academic standards of applicants have fallen heavily, and there have been cases of higher educational institutions where the majority of applicants failed to achieve the minimum requirements, the result being an insufficiency of successful candidates to fill the vacancies. The way out has been found in "Americanising" the concept of higher education, though this is not of course stated explicitly in the Programme.

It is not clear how the policy of expansion is going to be implemented, but it is hard to see how its effects can fail to be beneficial. Even if the present system of admission depending on a certificate of political reliability remains, the greater numbers will inevitably lead to less exacting standards in this respect. At the same time the expansion of full secondary education will increase the number of people qualified for admission from the academic point of view and make competition keener. The stress in the Programme is laid, as it has been in practice in the last few years, on the expansion of higher education through evening and correspondence courses, and the authorities may intend to continue restricting the numbers of full-time students. In this case, the operation of the political test can seriously affect the composition of the student body (57 per cent of those who were admitted to full-time study in 1960 were applicants with two or more years of work experience and were therefore holders of satisfactory political certificates). The authorities may also continue to encourage the practice (re-introduced in 1959 after a break of 25 years) of seconding employees or *kolkhoz* members for full-time study on the condition that they afterwards return to their place of work.

The selection of such people is likely to be almost entirely in the hands of the party organisations. In 1960, 8.7 per cent of those admitted to full-time higher education came from this category (and even as many as 19.8 per cent in the Ukraine). This practice would reinforce the effect of the general political test to produce a situation in which full-time students would to a considerable extent constitute a privileged political élite. However, in such a situation the political conformity of many students would be likely to be purely formal, and, more important, with the simultaneous expansion of part-time study, an able and determined person could choose to forego the advantages of full-time education and nevertheless compete successfully with full-time students.

As for the genuinely "American" result of the policy of mass education on the post-secondary level—the lowering of academic standards—this is presumably inevitable for the majority of institutions, but, as in the U.S.A., the competition for entry into the best establishments (owing to the expanded secondary education) is likely to enable these at least to maintain their standards. And the pressure from the influential scientific community for facilitating the best and most appropriate training for outstanding students, already strong, is if anything, likely to increase.

The prospects for secondary specialised education, which is treated in the Party Programme in the same paragraph as higher education, are not clearly stated. On the one hand, it is meant to expand rapidly alongside higher education; on the other hand, the growth of general secondary education will increasingly restrict the field from which candidates for specialised secondary education can be drawn. Faced with a similar situation in the 1950s, the technicums and other specialised secondary schools reacted by going over to the admission for shortened courses of people with completed general secondary education; yet this was possible mainly because at that time entry to higher education was severely restricted. There would seem to be two feasible ways out of this dilemma: some people, if denied the chance of full-time higher education, might prefer full-time secondary specialised to part-time higher education; and the secondary specialised schools themselves might look for candidates among older people who for one reason or another have not received full general secondary education.

Since those who are to receive education in Russia during the next twenty years will, it is professed by the Communist Party, live thereafter in a fully communist society, it is legitimate to ask whether the educational system outlined in the new Programme will produce suitable people to live in the kind of communist society that is envisaged by Khrushchev—that is, a society presided over by the Communist Party enjoying a monopoly of power and influence. The aims, forms and content of education are essentially to remain as they are now—an uneasy mixture of disparate and mutually contradictory, traditional and communist, elements. Neither of the two extremes, the intellectual élite-ism of the European tradition or the radical communist idea of the withering away of school and family, have found a place in the Programme. Having abandoned the anti-intellectual radicalism of Khrushchev's 1958 Memorandum, the new Programme does not revert to Zhdanov's traditionalism, but to Malenkov's policy of progressive "Americanisation" of the educational system. What distinguishes the educational system outlined in the Programme from genuine "Americanism" is the implied rigidity of syllabus and above all the all-pervading political element designed to inculcate the acceptance of domination by the Communist Party. While the rigidity of syllabus may to some extent be overcome, it is unthinkable that the party, at least as long as it is led by the generation now in power, should abandon its claim to control all spheres of life in the country, and it will continue to use education as one of its main tools to this end. But how effective is the tool likely to be? The educational policies of the 1920s, inspired by communist enthusiasm and modernist pedagogical theories, failed to produce a generation of dedicated communists—had it done so there would, for example, have been no need to appeal to patriotism when the war came. The systematic restoration of traditional forms and discipline coupled with the permeation of all teaching by the "party spirit" during the 1930s and 1940s equally failed to produce a generation of true conformists—hence the intellectual ferment when once the preventive terror was removed after Stalin's death and Beria's fall. And what one knows of the present generation of students and other young people suggests that the jumble of educational prescriptions tried out in the 1950s has not been conducive to forming the kind of people who will blindly accept the word of authority. Khrushchev and those who now support his brand of fundamentalism-cum-opportunism evidently hope that this approach may succeed where others failed.

* * * * * * * * * * * *

THE 1961 PARTY PROGRAMME IN THE FIELD OF PUBLIC EDUCATION*

The transition to communism implies training that will make people communist-minded and highly-cultured, people fitted for both physical and mental labour, for active work in various social, governmental, scientific, and cultural spheres.

The system of public education is so organised as to ensure that the instruction and education of the rising generation are closely bound up with life and productive labour, and that the adult population can combine work in the sphere of production with further training and education in keeping with their vocations and the requirements of society. Public education along these lines will make for the moulding of harmoniously developed members of communist society and for the solution of a cardinal social problem, namely, the elimination of substantial distinctions between mental and physical labour.

The main tasks in the field of instruction and education are:

(a) *Introduction of Universal Compulsory Secondary Education.* In the next decade compulsory secondary general and polytechnical eleven-year education is to be introduced for all children of school age, and eight-year education for young people engaged in the national economy who have not had appropriate schooling; in the subsequent decade every one will have the opportunity to receive a complete secondary education. Universal secondary education is guaranteed by the development of general and polytechnical education, professional training combined with socially useful labour of school children to the extent of their physical capacity, and a considerable expansion of the network of all types of general schools, including evening schools, which provide a secondary education in off-work hours.

Secondary education must furnish a solid knowledge of the fundamentals of the basic sciences, an understanding of the principles of the communist world outlook, and a labour and polytechnical training in accordance with the rising level of science and engineering, with

* *Ibid.,* pp. 305–306. Reprinted by permission.

due regard to the needs of society and to the abilities and inclinations of the students, as well as the moral, aesthetic and physical education of a healthy rising generation.

In view of the rapid progress of science and engineering, the system of industrial, professional and vocational training should be improved continuously, so that the skills of those engaged in production may develop together with their better general education in the social and natural sciences and with the acquisition of specialised knowledge in engineering, agronomy, medicine, and other fields.

(*b*) *The Public Upbringing of Children of Pre-School and School Age.* The communist system of public education is based on the public upbringing of children. The educational influence which the family exerts on children must be brought into ever greater harmony with their public upbringing.

The growing number of pre-school institutions and boarding-schools of different types will fully meet the requirements of all working people who wish to give their children of pre-school and school age a public upbringing. The importance of the school, which is to cultivate love of labour and knowledge in children and to raise the younger generation in the spirit of communist consciousness and morality, will increase. An honourable and responsible role in this respect falls to teachers, and to the Komsomol and Young Pioneer organisations.

(*c*) *Creation of Conditions for High-Standard Instruction and Education of the Rising Generation.* The Party plans to carry out an extensive programme for the construction of schools and cultural-education establishments to meet fully the needs of education and instruction. All schools will be housed in good buildings and will go over to a one-shift time-table. They will all have study workshops and chemical, physical and other laboratories; rural schools will also have their own farming plots; large factories will have production training shops for school children. Modern facilities—cinema, radio, and television—will be widely used in schools.

For physical training and aesthetic education, all schools and extra-scholastic establishments will have gymnasiums, sports grounds and facilities for the creative endeavour of children in music, painting, sculpture, etc. The network of sports schools, sports grounds, tourist camps, skiing centers, aquatic stations, swimming pools, and other sports facilities will be expanded in town and countryside.

(d) *Higher and Secondary Special Education.* In step with scientific and technical progress, higher and secondary special education, which must train highly-skilled specialists with a broad theoretical and political background, will be expanded.

Shorter working hours and a considerable improvement in the standard of living of the entire population will provide everyone with an opportunity to receive a higher or secondary special education if he so desires. The number of higher and secondary specialised schools, evening and correspondence schools in particular, as well as higher schools at factories, agricultural institutes (on large state farms), studios, conservatories, etc., must be increased in all areas of the country with the support of factories and trade unions and other social organisations. The plan is to considerably increase every year the number of students at higher and secondary specialised schools; special education will be afforded to tens of millions of people.

3. SOVIETS' FATHERLAND*

BY KLAUS MEHNERT

Of all the pillars that support the Soviet regime, the strongest, I think, is the patriotism of the Russian people. It is a kind of love for the mother country peculiar to the Russians, a natural phenomenon that existed ages before the Bolsheviks were ever heard of, and which their long years of attack have failed to shake. It is the love of little mother Russia—her vast expanse, her language, her songs, and her proverbs—and although in bygone days Tsar and Church were also important elements in it, Russian patriotism has survived both the extinction of the monarchy and the state's bitter war against the church.

I still remember the first time I came across this particular form of patriotism. It was in the summer of 1930, when I spent two months in Russia. Among the people I met was a Russian girl of my own age.

* From *Soviet Man and His World* by Klaus Mehnert (New York: Praeger, 1962), pp. 202–209. Reprinted by permission of the publisher.

She came from a middle-class family, had lost her parents in the upheavals of the revolution and civil war, had herself experienced much suffering and injustice, and was now just barely managing to eke out an existence. At first our conversations were confined to generalities, but later we began to talk politics. 'We talked' is perhaps not quite accurate, for she did all the talking, and she complained bitterly against the Bolshevik regime, its cruelty and malevolence, its complete disregard for happiness and human dignity. It was obviously a great relief to her to be able to pour out her woes to a foreigner who could have no possible reason for denouncing her later. It was only after she had unburdened her heart that I was able to get a word in.

I had no difficulty in sympathizing with her complaints or, for that matter, in pointing out further abuses which she had not mentioned and which seemed to me particularly evil. But then a complete change came over her. She began to contradict me sharply, explaining the necessity of the Party measures I had criticized. The more I said, the more heated she became, and she ended by defending Bolshevism. Later I often came across similar, though perhaps not quite so violent, examples of sudden shifts from criticism of the regime to vindication of it—switches inspired purely by patriotism.

The significance of Russian patriotism first became clear to the outside world during World War II. In the beginning, the Red Army was fighting for the Soviet state and Stalinism. But was the whole of the Red Army really fighting? Hundreds of thousands laid down their arms at the first opportunity. Stalin had reduced a patriotic people to such a condition that their love of the homeland was overshadowed by their hatred of the regime, by the hope of a change for the better with the help of the Germans. Then Stalin himself changed course; the slogan of an anti-fascist war for the advancement of socialism was transformed into an appeal for the 'great patriotic war,' the 'great war for the defence of the fatherland.' And it was this that in the end led the Red armies from Stalingrad to the Brandenburg Gate.

In the eyes of Soviet citizens the fact that the Soviet state survived the onslaught of the German divisions which had swept without much apparent effort across the rest of Europe, and that the Red Army eventually surged forward from the Volga to the Elbe, provided the most convincing proof of the might of the Soviet Union. Not everybody will agree with Soviet propaganda claims about the manner in which victory was achieved, the part played by Russia's allies, and the causes that led to the final collapse of Germany; but that does not alter the salient fact that victory was won.

The senseless and appalling atrocities committed, on Hitler's orders, against Russian prisoners-of-war and civilians in occupied territories made it easier for Stalin to push this change of line. But it had started long before. As early as spring, 1934, Stalin had issued a decree about the teaching of history, which was no longer to be approached from the international viewpoint but primarily on a national basis; as a result Russian history was rewritten for the second time in a single generation. After the Revolution Soviet historians had spent years denigrating the Russia of the Tsars as one vast and bloody prison, painting a sombre, terrible background against which the Bolshevik state would shine all the brighter. But with the change introduced in 1934, the Soviet historian was to portray Russian history from its very beginnings to the present day as a single and logical entity.

I have described in detail elsewhere this reversal of policy and its development since 1934. Here we are concerned not with Stalin's decrees but with the reaction of the people. Their patriotism, affronted first by Stalin and then by Hitler, rallied again to Stalin the moment he presented himself as the symbol of Russia and of resistance to the foreign invader. I think the Bolsheviks have succeeded in representing the Soviet state as the heir to Russia's past, and in drawing to it that love of the homeland innate in all Russians. Throne and church, music and literature, the conquests of Siberia and of the Caucasus— all have been blended harmoniously like the elements of a great propaganda film.

One day I joined a group of Russian sightseers touring the Kremlin. The guide spoke of the treasures of the imperial armouries and of the churches converted into museums as normal features of the Russo-Soviet historical picture. As we were being conducted through the Uspenskaya, the Cathedral of the Assumption, he said: 'And over there in the corner, comrades, you see the tomb of a great Russian patriot.' We all turned our heads towards the tomb, and I wondered to whom he was referring. I already knew that Tsarist generals had been transformed into heroes of the Soviet Union. But neither Kutuzov nor Suvorov was buried there.

'There lie the remains of the patriarch Hermogen,' the guide went on, 'who was murdered after gallantly resisting the Polish invaders.' He did not mention that this prince of the church had played a prominent part in suppressing the peasant revolt of 1606.

There was certainly a ludicrous side to the official encouragement of patriotism in Stalin's day, when everything from aircraft to the electric bulb was claimed as a Soviet invention. It was only after Stalin's death that this mania subsided; but the tendency is beginning to appear again—for example, it is now asserted that colour television is based on an invention of a Russian, Mikhaíl Lomonósov (1711–1765). The successes of Soviet science are presented as results both of Russian genius and Communist leadership; thus not only Gagarin was decorated after he orbited the earth but also—Khrushchev!

During the de-Stalinization phase of 1956 I had an interesting conversation. The woman I talked to was in her late thirties, simply dressed, and a professional of some kind, probably a teacher. We had met in a bookshop, where my attention was first drawn to her by her look of disappointment when, in response to her request for four or five books, she received the same reply 'No.' I invited her to have tea with me in one of Moscow's few cafés.

The general excitement over the sudden denunciation of Stalin had loosened her tongue, and it had, indeed, loosened the tongues of a great many of her compatriots; during this period Soviet citizens were able to speak more frankly, perhaps, than ever before. One thing she said remains vividly in my memory:

'Do you know what I particularly hate about the whole business? I never liked Stalin—I knew too much about him, and some of my own family were unjustly condemned; but after all he was the regime, and you can't spend all your life hating the regime you have to live under. You can't go on forever bemoaning your fate day in and day out. So you try to convince yourself that things are not so bad after all. I don't know if you see what I mean. But there is such a thing as a feeling of being at peace with your fate, even when your life is bitter and joyless. You can either rebel against fate—but who does?— or you can come to terms with it, and the best way of doing that is to touch up all the drab pictures of the daily round with a little bright colour.'

She put into words the things which, I felt, others were also thinking, but which I had never before heard so clearly expressed.

There are, apparently, opponents of Bolshevism who create their own picture of the world they live in, because it makes life easier. The daily lot is hard enough as it is. If, in addition, you feel compelled to say to yourself that everything you have been through is pointless anyway or, even worse, that it has perhaps served only evil ends, then life becomes intolerable. Soldiers who believe in what they are fighting for will endure the hardships of war better than those who feel they are battling and suffering in an unworthy cause.

Knowing that many Soviet citizens give themselves up to wishful thinking of this sort, I sometimes found it difficult, in conversation with them, to attack and expose the weakness of their positions. But whenever I talk to Party officials or representatives of the Soviet state, I never pull my punches, and I never hesitate to tell them bluntly about the antipathy I feel towards the system they represent. With the ordinary citizen it is a different matter. Who, from the safe haven of immunity, would wish to rob people of the consolation that makes life bearable—even when one knows that it is mere illusion?

An episode that occurred in 1955 comes to mind. I went for a drive in the country near Moscow with a group of Russians I had met quite casually. The conversation was lively and dealt mainly with contemporary literature, in which we were all interested. Then we reached the moment that comes in any conversation with Soviet citizens, and which I knew so well—the moment when their outward self-confidence and their inner uncertainty clash and when this produces a compulsion in them to elicit from the foreigner an assurance that all is well in the Soviet Union. As we drove past long blocks of new buildings I heard nothing but exaggerated expressions of self-congratulation—'A year ago there wasn't a sign of that huge block!' and so on, with pauses to give me an opportunity to exclaim 'How wonderful! The world has never seen anything like it before!' But I said nothing. And eventually came the question, in a rather obviously casual tone: 'Have you built any houses in Germany since the war?'

'Oh yes,' I replied, in an equally off-hand tone, 'we've been building about half a million apartments a year.'

There was a moment of silent consternation. Then one of the women in the group broke the silence. 'With American money!' she said scornfully.

'Immediately after the war,' I replied, 'we had the good fortune to receive brotherly help from the Americans.' I used the word 'brotherly' deliberately, because it is one the Soviets themselves are so fond of using when speaking of their aid to other countries. 'But for many years we've needed no help from anybody.'

This reply spoilt the friendly atmosphere of the outing, and soon afterwards my Russian companions took leave of me with some formality. Instead of bolstering their self-assurance, I had shattered it. I felt sorry for them.

The Communists have not forgotten the lessons of World War II, and they have encouraged patriotism ever since. Apart from the family, patriotism and devotion to the regime are the only loyalties they tolerate. They can go on doing this only so long as they can point to successes which support their claim to be the rightful custodians of the Russian heritage. But a series of national failures could make things very dangerous for them. From what we have seen so far, it is not very likely that the Soviet people will rebel if things go badly for them personally; but they might well rebel if they were convinced as Russian patriots that they could no longer support a Bolshevik policy that was proving catastrophic. We must, however, be clear on one point; the situation would have to be unmistakably disastrous, not merely a run of setbacks.

Another great asset of the regime is the dynamic energy of the Soviet people, which every visitor becomes aware of as soon as he enters the country. This drive is by no means self-explanatory, for the Soviet citizen himself derives only limited personal benefit from it. The modest improvement in living standards bears little relation to the demands which have been made on the people decade after decade. New factories, mines, dams, and canals are being built all the time, but they seem to have a life of their own, to be beneficial only to each other, rather than improving the living standards of the public. Where, then, did the Russians' enthusiasm for work stem from, since for a long time it did not lead to any appreciable improvement in their living conditions?

The goad of the 'plan' and the production norm; the draconian discipline imposed on the workers; the severe penalties for failing in a given task; the absence of any logical relation between wages and prices, which compels people to work extremely hard in order to raise their living standards even a little—all these things offer only a partial explanation of the dynamic force that undoubtedly exists. The impressive reconstruction and expansion of the Soviet Union could not have been brought about by these factors alone; the pressure imposed from above must be reciprocated by a drive from below. What, then, are the reasons for this drive? As I have shown elsewhere, the great discrepancy between the poverty of the population and the vast riches of the country must have inspired a powerful urge to overcome this poverty by exploiting the natural wealth that lies dormant.

The determination of the Soviet people, and particularly of the younger generation, is very different from that which existed during the First Five-Year Plan or during the Revolution itself. It is not political or ideological, but is like the drive shown by other nations at times of great economic expansion—by the Americans, for example, in the pioneer spirit that drove them irresistibly onward to conquer and open up the American West.

Closely linked with the urge for economic expansion is the belief that technology is a panacea. The mystic light in which the Russians are inclined to see something which the rest of us have come to regard with unemotional sobriety can be understood only when their psychology is taken into account. A deeply religious people whose emotional fervour has been deprived of its expression within the framework of its church is now seeking new forms and objects of faith. People who have laboriously plodded, step by step, through the process of technical development regard technology with a far more sceptical eye than the Russians, who, in the beginning, simply adopted its formulas and achievements. The suddenness of their leap into complex modern technology—the construction, for example, of a modern steelmill or even an atomic energy plant—blinds them to everything but the positive aspects. The reserve with which automation is regarded in the West, where its drawbacks as well as its advantages are recognized, is something as yet unknown in the Soviet Union.

But there is a limit to all things. The unceasing torrent of invariably optimistic Soviet propaganda is fraying the nerves not only of foreign visitors but also of the Soviet people themselves. No note of pessimism is allowed to creep into anything concerning the Soviet Union or its officially sanctioned interpretation of history.

On one of the main boulevards of Moscow there stood for many years a statue of Gogol. When I was a child I never passed it without stopping to gaze at it. Gogol, who died insane, was shown seated in an armchair, brooding, melancholy, his chin sunk on his chest. During the 1930's it was still there. But on my first post-war visit in 1955 I found that it had been replaced by a new Gogol, standing with head erect, gazing into the future, and radiating optimism.

Even Chekhov, that master of tender melancholy, has been re-modelled as an optimist by Soviet literary historians. No one has been praised more for his faith in the future or been held up more frequently as an example of a good Communist than Mayakovsky, the young poet of the Revolution, who committed suicide in 1930 in despair at the direction the Soviet regime was taking.

However the people may react to official optimism, it seems to me that on the whole they now regard the future with more confidence than they did in the 1930's. Although reconstruction and expansion have brought only minor benefits to the people as a whole, the national advance has given rise to a feeling that things are progressing, that eventually the man in the street will also reap the benefit.

One final thought on this subject. The imperial mission—the urge to expand and the desire for power that have existed in the Russian people for centuries—is now proving of great value to the Bolsheviks. The dynamic force which extended the boundaries of the once insignificant state of Moscow to the shores of the Pacific is still an active and potent factor. The incorporation of half of Europe, the swift spread of Communism to some 600 million Chinese, its thrust into Korea and Vietnam, the influence exerted by Moscow on the former colonial world—all these things have increased the self-assurance and the sense of mission that received their first great impetus from the winning of World War II.

The dynamic urge of this imperial mission is to be found primarily, of course, among those in the Soviet Union who feel themselves to be masters in their own home—the Great Russians. It is much less prevalent among the many non-Russian elements in the U.S.S.R., and even less so in the East European states that have fallen under the domination of Moscow. The drive there, as the events of the autumn of 1956 proved, is not towards Bolshevism but away from it.

Chapter IV

National Interests and International Organizations

> We are striving unceasingly to make the UN a more effective instrument for making and keeping peace and serving the welfare of mankind.
>
> —Dean Rusk

> We call for strengthening the United Nations in the interests of peace and the security of the peoples.
>
> —Leonid I. Brezhnev

The United Nations, instituted on the basis of the principle of "sovereign equality," is a world forum for debate and diplomacy. The organization, initially with 51 member-states, has grown to more than double that size, shifting the balance of power from the Western bloc to the Afro-Asian bloc, which now enjoys a clear majority in the General Assembly. Despite some apprehensions about the ebbing of the Western position in general, and of the United States' influence in particular, an analysis of the voting record of member nations points to an optimistic conclusion that the United Nations will continue to support vital American policies. In the US-Soviet contest for leadership, the United Nations rendered support for the United States position on such crucial issues as the Berlin Blockade, the Korean problem, Chinese Communist aggression in Tibet and India, the Middle East crisis, the Congo, the Cuban missile crisis, and UN financing.

With its hopes and despair, the United Nations is at present in serious financial difficulties stemming primarily from the refusal of the Soviet Union and France to pay their assessments for UN peacekeeping operations in the Congo. The future of the United Nations is *uncertain; what is certain, however, is the continued US-Soviet com-petition—each attempting to make the organization a valuable asset in its arsenal of diplomacy to serve its national interest.*

This chapter deals with the policies and actions of the United States and the Soviet Union at the United Nations.

President Eisenhower, in his two addresses to the nation in 1956 and 1957, expressed his conviction that "the United Nations repre-sents the soundest hope for peace in the world" and pledged to pursue the policy of securing international peace and justice within the framework of the United Nations.

Alexander Dallin, Professor of International Relations at Columbia University's Russian Institute, examines Soviet objectives, tactics, and strategy at the United Nations, and discusses Soviet maneuvers under-taken to effect a change in the structure, functions, and duties of the Secretariat of the organization.

Henry M. Jackson, Senator from the State of Washington, recog-nizes the importance of the United Nations as a useful avenue of American foreign policy, but he declares that the United States must neither lose sight of the UN's limitations, nor regard the organization as a substitute for national programs carefully formulated by the policy-planners in the American Government.

1. THE UNITED NATIONS AND THE MIDDLE EASTERN CRISIS

BY DWIGHT D. EISENHOWER

(1) ADDRESS TO THE NATION, OCTOBER 31, 1956.*

My fellow Americans:

Tonight I report to you as your President.

We all realize that the full and free debate of a political campaign surrounds us. But the events and issues I wish to place before you this evening have no connection whatsoever with matters of partisan-

---

* From *The New York Times* (November 1, 1956), p. 14. Reprinted by their permission.

ship. They are concerns of every American—his present and his future.

I wish, therefore, to give you a report of essential facts so that you—whether belonging to either one of our two great parties, or to neither—may give thoughtful and informed consideration to this swiftly changing world scene.

The changes of which I speak have come in two areas of the world—Eastern Europe and the Mideast. . . .

The Middle East . . . was, as we all know, an area long subject to colonial rule. This rule ended after World War II when all countries there won full independence.

Out of the Palestinian mandated territory was born the new State of Israel.

These historic changes could not, however, instantly banish animosities born of the ages. Israel and her Arab neighbors soon found themselves at war with one another. And the Arab nations showed continuing anger toward their former rulers, notably France and Great Britain.

The United States, through all the years since the close of World War II, has labored tirelessly to bring peace and stability to this area.

We have considered it a basic matter of United States policy to support the new State of Israel and, at the same time, to strengthen our bonds both with Israel and with the Arab countries. But, unfortunately, through all these years, passion in the area threatened to prevail over peaceful purpose, and, in one form or another, there has been almost continuous fighting.

This situation recently was aggravated by Egyptian policy including rearmament with Communist weapons. We felt this to be a misguided policy on the part of the Government of Egypt. The State of Israel, at the same time, felt increasing anxiety for its safety. And Great Britain and France feared more and more that Egyptian policies threatened their life line of the Suez Canal.

These matters came to a crisis on July 26 of this year when the Egyptian Government seized the Universal Suez Canal Company. For ninety years, ever since the inauguration of the canal, that company has operated the canal—largely under British and French technical supervision.

Now, there were some among our allies who urged an immediate reaction to this event by use of force. We insistently urged otherwise, and our wish prevailed, through a long succession of conferences and negotiations, for weeks—even months—with participation by the United Nations.

And there, in the United Nations, only a short while ago, on the basis of agreed principles, it seemed that an acceptable accord was within our reach.

But the direct relations of Egypt with both Israel and France kept worsening to a point at which first Israel, then France—and Great Britain also—determined that, in their judgment, there could be no protection of their vital interests without resort to force.

Upon this decision events followed swiftly.

On Sunday, the Israeli Government ordered total mobilization.

On Monday, their armed forces penetrated deeply into Egypt and to the vicinity of the Suez Canal—nearly 100 miles away.

And on Tuesday the British and French Governments delivered a twelve-hour ultimatum to Israel and Egypt, now followed up by armed attack against Egypt.

The United States was not consulted in any way about any phase of these actions. Nor were we informed of them in advance.

As it is the manifest right of any of these nations to take such decisions and actions, it is likewise our right if our judgment so dictates, to dissent.

We believe these actions to have been taken in error, for we do not accept the use of force as a wise or proper instrument for the settlement of international disputes.

To say this, in this particular instance, is in no way to minimize our friendship with these nations, nor our determination to maintain those friendships.

And we are fully aware of the grave anxieties of Israel, of Britain and France. We know that they have been subjected to grave and repeated provocations.

The present fact nonetheless seems clear. This action taken can scarcely be reconciled with the principles and purposes of the United Nations to which we have all subscribed. And beyond this we are forced to doubt that resort to force and war will for long serve the permanent interests of the attacking nations.

Now we must look to the future. . . .

It is—and it will remain—the dedicated purpose of your Government to do all in its power to localize the fighting and to end the conflict.

We took our first measure in this action yesterday. We went to the United Nations with a request that the forces of Israel return to their own line and that hostilities in the area be brought to a close.

This proposal was not adopted because it was vetoed by Great Britain and by France.

It is our hope and intent that this matter will be brought before the United Nations General Assembly. There, with no veto operating, the opinion of the world can be brought to bear in our quest for a just end to this tormenting problem.

In the past the United Nations has proved able to find a way to end bloodshed. We believe it can and that it will do so again.

My fellow citizens, as I review the march of world events in recent years I am ever more deeply convinced that the United Nations represents the soundest hope for peace in the world. For this very reason I believe that the processes of the United Nations need further to be developed and strengthened.

I speak particularly of increasing its ability to secure justice under international law.

In all the recent troubles in the Middle East there have, indeed, been injustices suffered by all nations involved. But I do not believe that another instrument of injustice—war—is a remedy for these wrongs.

There can be no peace without law. And there can be no law if we work to invoke one code of international conduct for those who oppose, and another for our friends.

The society of nations has been slow in developing means to apply this truth. But the passionate longing for peace on the part of all peoples of the earth compels us to speed our search for new and more effective instruments of justice.

The peace we seek and need means much more than mere absence of war. It means the acceptance of law and the fostering of justice in all the world.

To our principles guiding us in this quest we must stand fast. In so doing, we can honor the hopes of all men for a world in which peace will truly and justly reign.

I thank you, and goodnight.

(2) ADDRESS TO THE NATION, FEBRUARY 20, 1957.*

I come to you again to talk about the situation in the Middle East. The future of the United Nations and peace in the Middle East may be at stake.

In the 4 months since I talked to you about the crisis in that area, the United Nations has made considerable progress in resolving some of the difficult problems. We are now, however, faced with a fateful moment as the result of the failure of Israel to withdraw its forces behind the armistice lines, as contemplated by the United Nations resolutions on this subject. . . .

When I talked to you last October, I pointed out that the United States fully realized that military action against Egypt resulted from grave and repeated provocations. But I said also that the use of military force to solve international disputes could not be reconciled with the principles and purposes of the United Nations. I added that our country could not believe that resort to force and war would for long serve the permanent interests of the attacking nations, which were Britain, France, and Israel.

So I pledged that the United States would seek through the United Nations to end the conflict. We would strive to bring about a recall of the forces of invasion and then make a renewed and earnest effort through that organization to secure justice, under international law, for all the parties concerned.

Since that time much has been achieved and many of the dangers implicit in the situation have been avoided. The Governments of Britain and France have withdrawn their forces from Egypt. Thereby they showed respect for the opinions of mankind as expressed almost unanimously by the 80 nation members of the United Nations General Assembly.

I want to pay tribute to the wisdom of this action of our friends and allies. They made an immense contribution to world order. Also they put the other nations of the world under a heavy obligation to see to it that these two nations do not suffer by reason of their compliance with the United Nations resolutions. . . .

We are approaching a fateful moment when either we must recognize that the United Nations is unable to restore peace in this area

* From *The Department of State Bulletin,* March 11, 1957.

or the United Nations must renew with increased vigor its efforts to bring about Israeli withdrawal.

Repeated, but, so far, unsuccessful, efforts have been made to bring about a voluntary withdrawal by Israel. These efforts have been made both by the United Nations and by the United States and other member states.

Equally serious efforts have been made to bring about conditions designed to assure that, if Israel will withdraw in response to the repeated requests of the United Nations, there will then be achieved a greater security and tranquillity for that nation. This means that the United Nations would assert a determination to see that in the Middle East there will be a greater degree of justice and compliance with international law than was the case prior to the events of last October-November.

A United Nations Emergency Force, with Egypt's consent, entered that nation's territory in order to help maintain the cease-fire which the United Nations called for on November 2. . . .

Israel seeks something more. It insists on firm guaranties as a condition to withdrawing its forces of invasion.

This raises a basic question of principle. Should a nation which attacks and occupies foreign territory in the face of United Nations disapproval be allowed to impose conditions on its own withdrawal?

If we agree that armed attack can properly achieve the purposes of the assailant, then I fear we will have turned back the clock of international order. We will, in effect, have countenanced the use of force as a means of settling international differences and through this gaining national advantages.

I do not, myself, see how this could be reconciled with the Charter of the United Nations. The basic pledge of all the members of the United Nations is that they will settle their international disputes by peaceful means and will not use force against the territorial integrity of another state.

If the United Nations once admits that international disputes can be settled by using force, then we will have destroyed the very foundation of the organization and our best hope of establishing a world order. That would be a disaster for us all.

I would, I feel, be untrue to the standards of the high office to which you have chosen me if I were to lend the influence of the

United States to the proposition that a nation which invades another should be permitted to exact conditions for withdrawal.

Of course, we and all the members of the United Nations ought to support justice and conformity with international law. The first article of the Charter states the purpose of the United Nations to be "the suppression of acts of aggression or other breaches of the peace, and to bring about by peaceful means, and in conformity with . . . justice and international law, adjustment or settlement of international disputes." But it is to be observed that conformity with justice and international law are to be brought about "by peaceful means."

We cannot consider that the armed invasion and occupation of another country are "peaceful means" or proper means to achieve justice and conformity with international law.

We do, however, believe that upon the suppression of the present act of aggression and breach of the peace there should be a greater effort by the United Nations and its members to secure justice and conformity with international law. Peace and justice are two sides of the same coin.

Perhaps the world community has been at fault in not having paid enough attention to this basic truth. The United States, for its part, will vigorously seek solutions of the problems of the area in accordance with justice and international law. And we shall in this great effort seek the association of other like-minded nations which realize, as we do, that peace and justice are in the long run inseparable.

But the United Nations faces immediately the problem of what to do next. If it does nothing, if it accepts the ignoring of its repeated resolutions calling for the withdrawal of invading forces, then it will have admitted failure. That failure would be a blow to the authority and influence of the United Nations in the world and to the hopes which humanity placed in the United Nations as the means of achieving peace with justice.

I do not believe that Israel's default should be ignored because the United Nations has not been able effectively to carry out its resolutions condemning the Soviet Union for its armed suppression of the people of Hungary. Perhaps this is a case where the proverb applies that two wrongs do not make a right.

No one deplores more than I the fact that the Soviet Union ignores the resolutions of the United Nations. Also no nation is more vigorous than is the United States in seeking to exert moral pressure against the Soviet Union, which by reason of its size and power, and by reason of its veto in the Security Council, is relatively impervious to other types of sanction.

The United States and other free nations are making clear by every means at their command the evil of Soviet conduct in Hungary. It would indeed be a sad day if the United States ever felt that it had to subject Israel to the same type of moral pressure as is being applied to the Soviet Union.

There can, of course, be no equating of a nation like Israel with that of the Soviet Union. The people of Israel, like those of the United States, are imbued with a religious faith and a sense of moral values. We are entitled to expect, and do expect, from such peoples of the free world a contribution to world order which unhappily we cannot expect from a nation controlled by atheistic despots.

It has been suggested that United Nations actions against Israel should not be pressed because Egypt has in the past violated the Armistice Agreement and international law. It is true that both Egypt and Israel, prior to last October, engaged in reprisals in violation of the Armistice Agreements. Egypt ignored the United Nations in exercising belligerent rights in relation to Israeli shipping in the Suez Canal and in the Gulf of Aqaba. However, such violations constitute no justification for the armed invasion of Egypt by Israel which the United Nations is now seeking to undo.

Failure to withdraw would be harmful to the long-term good of Israel. It would, in addition to its injury to the United Nations, jeopardize the prospects of the peaceful solution of the problems of the Mid-East. This could bring incalculable ills to our friends and indeed to our nation itself. . . .

The United Nations must not fail. I believe that—in the interests of peace—the United Nations has no choice but to exert pressure upon Israel to comply with the withdrawal resolutions. Of course, we still hope that the Government of Israel will see that its best immediate and long-term interests lie in compliance with the United Nations and in placing its trust in the resolutions of the United Nations and in the declaration of the United States with reference to the future.

Egypt, by accepting the six principles adopted by the Security Council last October in relation to the Suez Canal, bound itself to free and open transit through the canal without discrimination and to the principle that the operation of the canal should be insulated from the politics of any country.

We should not assume that, if Israel withdraws, Egypt will prevent Israeli shipping from using the Suez Canal or the Gulf of Aqaba. If, unhappily, Egypt does hereafter violate the Armistice Agreement or other international obligations, then this should be dealt with firmly by the society of nations.

The present moment is a grave one, but we are hopeful that reason and right will prevail. Since the events of last October-November, solid progress has been made, in conformity with the Charter of the United Nations. . . .

What I have spoken about tonight is only one step in a long process calling for patience and diligence, but at this moment it is the critical issue on which future progress depends.

It is an issue which can be solved if only we will apply the principles of the United Nations.

That is why, my fellow Americans, I know that you want the United States to continue to use its maximum influence to sustain those principles as the world's best hope for peace.

2. THE SOVIET UNION AND THE UNITED NATIONS*

BY ALEXANDER DALLIN

A substantially constant ideological framework has permitted significant variations in Soviet strategy and tactics at the United Nations. The contrast between Moscow's policy in Stalin's days and in the Khrushchev era measures both the extent and the limits of variation.

But what has determined shifts in Moscow's policy? The primary determinant is to be found outside the U.N. system: This has been the Soviet view of changes in the "real world"—above all, changes

* From *The Soviet Union at the United Nations* by Alexander Dallin, pp. 196–213. Copyright © 1962 by Frederick A. Praeger, Inc.; reprinted by their permission.

of power and of opportunity. It was precisely the contrast between the glorious sense of growing Soviet world power and the lack of commensurate success or influence in the United Nations that permitted Moscow to argue for "realistic" adjustments in the organization's system of staffing and representation.

Another determinant is the system of ideological preconceptions. True, certain fundamental axioms—conflict, dichotomy, optimism—have shown remarkable tenacity, and certain generalities in the Soviet world view—the call for "realism," the approach to "sovereignty," the verdict that the United Nations is "useful" but not "important"—have remained virtually unchanged. Yet the doctrinal revisions of the Khrushchev era have been important in rationalizing the Soviet policy of nonviolent competition and widening the framework of permissible techniques.

This is not to suggest that the doctrinal reformulations preceded the new perception of a changing world. It should be clear, moreover, that the specifics of Soviet policy, in or out of the United Nations, are not explicable in ideological terms alone. Like the demand for parity, the *troika* proposition exemplifies a Soviet effort to gain as much as the other powers might concede—a demand fully consistent with, but not predictable solely in terms of, its world view. Political realism, as Moscow sees it, is thus superimposed on ideological commitments. Only the combination of the two can explain the nature and the timing of the Soviet reorganization proposals.

Soviet policy has been capable of crude and unprincipled practicality when the rewards have seemed to warrant it. The traditional commitment to the tenet of *pacta sunt servanda* is not allowed to stand in the way of demands for greater rights due to greater power. The most "principled" insistence on the reality of three power blocs easily yields to a plethora of Soviet formulae for four, five, six, or seven under-secretaries when Hammarskjold's successors are being discussed. Moscow refuses to finance or back U.N. action in the Congo, but simultaneously attempts to dictate U.N. policy there. Soviet opposition to the existing order in the United Nations, Moscow admits at times, is due not to the belief that a *single* group of powers controls the U.N., but that the *wrong* group—"reactionaries" and "monopolists"—does. Soviet insistence on unanimity as a *sine qua non* in the United Nations, which Moscow does not control, contrasts dramatically with its efforts to promote majority rule within the conclave of international Communism, where it does have most member-parties on its side, against Chinese Communist advocacy of unanimity. Even the sacred principle of sovereignty can be suspended when political utility demands it. "Principles," too, in other words, can be weapons in the struggle of systems, in and out of the U.N.

Among the strains of Soviet experience that contribute to the reassessment of strategy is the record of the United Nations itself. The U.N. action in the Congo is a case in point. While on the whole, events inside the U.N. have played a subordinate part in the crystallization of Soviet policies, the Soviet Union's own experience of being a "loser" for over a decade has no doubt reinforced Moscow's inclination to keep the United Nations' power down. The minority position of the Soviet bloc, during the early years, intensified its members' resentment and sense of isolation. Then their collective nonparticipation for a time set them apart even more. While a portion of this gap was bridged in the post-Stalin era, the suspicion that the United Nations was part of the hostile camp remained.

It was, of course, true that the majority of the United Nations—and of the Great Powers—was anti-Communist. With some exertion, the Western powers could usually command a majority of votes—something the U.S.S.R. could not do. At every step, from San Francisco to Korea and Suez, it must have seemed to Moscow that the United States had won out. Even as late as 1960–61, the U.N. was perhaps more indulgent toward the United States—over the U-2 flight and the attempted invasion of Cuba—than it might have been toward other nations. All this did not make the U.N. a "tool of the State Department," as Moscow alleged, but it provided an objective basis for the Soviet claims.

Finally, the Soviet world view contains a strong self-fulfilling element. George F. Kennan, among others, has suggested that Soviet expectation and behavior are bound to engender precisely the sort of response abroad and create just such a dichotomy as Moscow professes to see. In practice, too, many United Nations agencies became "Western" during the formative years, when the U.S.S.R. refused to take an active part in their work. The realization that this was the case was probably among the reasons for the later change in Soviet tactics—from absence to participation in many, though not all, activities of the U.N.

Nothing would be further from the truth than to suggest that the

Soviet Union has been the only culprit at the U.N. In fact, most powers have violated the spirit of the Charter, and many have ignored its letter time and again. Most members have failed to rely on the United Nations as a primary instrument of national policy—and with good reason. All nations have valued the U.N. for what they can get out of it. All states have loyalties transcending those to the U.N. All the Great Powers would refuse to surrender the veto. Others, too, have insisted on keeping the domestic-jurisdiction clause. Rather than entrusting their security to the United Nations, most states have bolstered their defenses or moved to regional-alliance systems. Other countries, too, have at times resisted U.N. regulation of their commerce and have preferred to put their own label on economic aid and exercise direct control over its distribution.

Moscow is right in arguing that if universality is an objective, the absence from the U.N. of Communist China and Germany is hard to defend. It is correct in stressing that "Great Power unanimity" *was* the original presupposition of the United Nations; if it implies the essentiality of agreement, it also spells the impotence of the U.N. when no such consensus exists. Many outside the Soviet bloc have also found the formula of "one state, one vote" in the Assembly highly unrealistic. Many new nations have felt their interests inadequately reflected on the United Nations staff and in the Security Council. Just as the Soviet Union came to look askance at a plain majority principle after its experience in the Assembly, so the United States and the United Kingdom appear to have lost some of their enthusiasm for that body since the accretion of Afro-Asian votes and the loosening of the Latin American bloc have made the Western powers a minority group, too. In its insistence on the imperative of change, the Soviet Union finds a considerable echo among other states, for there are many who—in H. G. Nicholas's words

have joined the U.N. less to preserve, by mechanisms of law and order, an existing state of affairs, than to effect, by the pressure of their votes and their voices, a change not only in their own circumstances but often in their relation with the rest of the world.

Even in its refusal to think and act in terms of a world community, the Soviet Union is by no means alone. Indeed, a series of studies on the U.N. prompted the conclusion that the idea of universal solidarity of man has not yet penetrated deeply. To use Maurice

Bourquin's expression, people the world over "don't *feel* the unity of humankind."

And yet, when all is said and done, the Soviet outlook on the United Nations remains unique in some essential ways. This unique feature is not so much Soviet defiance of the U.N., including its asserted willingness to use force to resist it, as illustrated by the Hungarian episode in 1956, when it ignored the body's verdict—at the same time that other violators of the Charter's spirit after all obeyed the U.N.'s call and stopped before Suez. Other states— notably France—have been known likewise to challenge and ignore the U.N.

The area of uniqueness lies above all in the Soviet view of the historical process and its translation into action. The profound conviction that, in the long run, neutrality and impartiality are impossible or nonexistent vitiates the fundamental assumption on which international organizations such as the United Nations are built. The Communist image of the United Nations as an arena of struggle is not a reluctant recognition of a tragic fact, but an exhilarating ride on the wave of the future.

The Soviet view, in sum, combines a revolutionary outlook with a conservative pursuit of its security and a pragmatic effort to make the most of the complex and shifting United Nations scene.

The hardheadedness of the Soviet approach contrasts strikingly with the fuzzy thinking about the U.N. that has often characterized others abroad. Yet—on this point the record should be convincing— Moscow has made its full share of errors and miscalculations. Soviet policy, Stalin told Anthony Eden in 1945, was "neither as simple as some thought nor as skillful as others believed." Indeed, we have too often mistaken absence of information for absence of conflict or absence of doubt on the Soviet side. We have been too much inclined to endow the masters of the Kremlin with infallible cleverness—and they to an even greater extent have seen a pattern, a design, a purpose, a conspiracy in every move and gesture of the outside world: "There are no accidents."

Soviet analyses and expectations have, in the Khrushchev era, tended to be fairly realistic about power relations, capabilities and vulnerabilities of states. They have permitted Moscow to ignore the United Nations as a decisive obstacle on its path. Indeed, what *could* the U.N. do in the face of overt Soviet hostility? But a substantial lack of realism intervenes when Soviet analysis concerns a pluralistic world. As bipolarity is the natural shape to which, Moscow imagines, the universe tends, the standard Soviet image of the United Nations, too, has been one of two opposites. So long as the facts can be made to fit such formulas, Soviet analysis is simple and often shrewd, even if its view of capitalism and democracy remains hopelessly out of date. But they don't always fit.

It is precisely with regard to neutralism and nonalignment that the Soviet view is apt to go awry. Which way the uncommitted will go when forced by the logic of international strife and Soviet (and American) prodding remains in doubt. But it is clear that the assumption that the ultimate interest of the neutral bloc is on the Soviet side is unwarranted and naïve. Moscow has ignored the fact that the United Nations occupies a far more important place in the thinking and expectations of the developing nations, with regard to their own security and progress, than in the thinking and security of the U.S.S.R.; their view of the U.N.'s welfare and economic activities is far more positive; and their perspective on U.N. financing differs drastically from the Soviet. While on issues such as anticolonialism the Soviet bloc has naturally identified itself with the new nations, Moscow may in fact have begun to realize that the "third" bloc is not necessarily—and surely not yet—to be counted on the Communist side. And it is no doubt at least a subsidiary purpose of the Soviet plan to deprive the United Nations of its ability to compete with the Communists for leadership of the "national-liberation" movement. In the last analysis, the Soviet assumption that the unaligned world—any more than the Western grouping—constitutes a cohesive, homogeneous, lasting bloc is plainly wrong. Whether or not the Communist orbit does, only the future will tell.

THE LIMITS OF LOGIC

The Soviet stand, enunciated in the fall of 1960, and reiterated since, is logical within the framework of Soviet assumptions and objectives. It is, to be sure, more extreme than the view Moscow had previously propounded about the United Nations. Allowing for some improvisations in the actual proposals, it has the virtue that the assumptions behind the *troika* plan remove an area of suppressed ambiguity that, during all these years, has inhered in the Soviet compromise between inward Communist hostility toward and outward identification with the U.N. The view that there exists no just arbiter or administrator above the two major camps revives, almost verbatim, positions voiced in days of greater Soviet candor.

The Soviet formula made little constitutional sense: it would have frozen the balance of three blocs by institutionalizing a haphazard and transient political alignment from which the sovereign member-states might choose to withdraw at some future time. Many borderline states could not easily be put into any of the three categories. The assumption that each of the blocs had unity and permanence was obviously open to serious challenge. Indeed, Soviet insistence on sovereign equality of states seemed to be violated by its plan to give equal weight to nine Communist states, some fifty neutrals, and the forty-odd Western powers and their allies.

Administratively, objections no less weighty were voiced by the United Nations staff itself. The *troika* would have stymied the Secretariat's work and made the use of the U.N. in another Korean or Congolese crisis impossible. But this was at least part of Moscow's purpose.

No elaborate evidence is required to show that Khrushchev has not been willing to tolerate an analogous *ménage à trois* either within the leadership in the Kremlin, or in Soviet industrial management, or in relations among Communist parties. Soviet insistence on tri-partite equality and veto in the executive organs conflicts directly with the time-honored Bolshevik administrative principle of *edinonachalie* —unity of authority—which has been reaffirmed on innumerable occasions as "the basic method of operating the Soviet economy and the Soviet state." Since the objective of *edinonachalie* is above all maximum efficiency, one may conclude that the Soviet purpose in opposing it in the United Nations is its reverse.

The political incongruity of the *troika* is well illustrated by Adlai Stevenson's remark that the application of the Soviet plan in the sixteenth century would have produced an organization "in which the administration of international affairs was entrusted to a trium-virate consisting of the Pope, the Sultan, and Martin Luther."

If adopted, the proposals would reduce the United Nations to the highest common denominator of its members' views. Moscow has gone so far as to insist that "the main goal of this organization consists in finding solutions acceptable to *all* its members." That this is no slip of the pen is shown by the recurrence of the theme on a number of occasions since Khrushchev's U.N. speech of September 19, 1959, in which he declared that "only such decisions should be taken in the United Nations that everyone would vote for." When asked, the following year, whether he would let a two-thirds majority of the member states decide whether or not Hammarskjold should stay, Khrushchev replied: "This is not a parliament. It is a forum in which questions should be resolved in such a way as not to endanger the interests of even a single state. . . ."

There is ground to question whether Moscow means quite what it says. While the extension of the unanimity rule to all members of the United Nations is consonant with one strain of Soviet thinking, the *liberum veto* would permit a single member—say, the Union of South Africa—to prevent the adoption of a decision favored by all other states. This clearly would not be welcome to the U.S.S.R. It would be impossible, under the circumstances, to "isolate" any state or bloc of states; yet this is precisely what Soviet spokesmen have time and again called for at the U.N.

What Moscow means, one may surmise, is that its own concurrence—as the leading power of the world, or so it likes to think—should be required at all times and in all organs of the United Nations. Tsarapkin reportedly told Arthur H. Dean in June, 1961, "Never again will any international organization take a vital decision without our consent." But this it cannot say openly, any more than it can afford to ask for a selective extension of the veto to a few favored nations at a time when it courts precisely those countries that would not benefit from such a move.

That the operation of a United Nations in which all of its hundred-odd members would possess a *liberum veto* would be destructive not only of the United Nations but of Soviet interests as well is nowhere better put than in a Soviet critique of the League of Nations. As Grigori Morozov writes in his volume on the U.N., a recent and authoritative Soviet account,

This impotence of the League flowed, in particular, from the fact that the Covenant required unanimity of all its members for the adoption of all political decisions taken by its Council and Assembly. This harmful pseudo democratism vitiated the role and responsibility of the several states in the cause of supporting international peace and practically rendered impossible the effective operation of an organization for the maintenance of peace and the prevention of aggression.

An extreme expression of the Soviet view is the contention that the "sovereign" member states need not be bound by what the United Nations says and does. This has been implicit in Khrushchev's references, since mid-1960, to the use of force. Speaking initially about the failure of the Security Council to support the Soviet demands stemming from the U-2 incident, he remarked (on June 3, 1960) that under such circumstances in the future "we have no other way out but to rely on our own strength." At the U.N. that fall, he went further: The Soviet Union would ignore United Nations decisions it deemed incompatible with its own interests. If it did not get its way, it would "uphold our interests outside this international body, outside the United Nations, by relying on our own strength." The final step in this progression came in Khrushchev's speech welcoming President Kwame Nkrumah of Ghana to Moscow in July, 1961:

Even if all the countries of the world adopted a decision which did not accord with the interests of the Soviet Union and threatened its security, the Soviet Union would not recognize such a decision and would uphold its rights, relying on force. And we have [plenty] to rely on.

What constituted a threat to its security was, of course, at all times up to Moscow to decide. Such strident formulations reveal the extent of Soviet determination to maintain its full freedom of action. Once again, Soviet insistence on "unanimity" and "sovereignty" turns the clock back. The unanimity rule, Nicolas Politis said in 1928, amounts to an admission that "among nations no real organization is possible, for the rule of unanimity may lead to paralysis and anarchy."

Moscow watched with unmitigated enmity the tragic—or pathetic—search for an international authority to deal effectively with forces greater than itself. The United Nations had not been expected to cope with disagreements among the Great Powers, and Moscow vigorously protested Western attempts to shape the U.N. into a serviceable tool in the conflicts between the "two camps." To its mind, what has taken place is an illegal "triple play" from Security Council to General Assembly to Secretariat, as the United States and its allies tried to use one organ after another for their ends. The Council, stymied by the veto, declined in importance and use, and was widely recognized to be unable to do its job. The General Assembly, even under the Uniting-for-Peace Resolution, could not compel compliance with its recommendations; and there were political and constitutional limits to what it could do. Disappointment was widespread—in the Soviet judgment as well as in that of the West. Both the inherent weakness of, and the increased membership in, the General Assembly finally encouraged an expansion of executive power in the U.N. Secretariat —a process likewise furthered by delegation of authority to the Secretary-General by the Security Council.

The United Nations Charter granted its Secretary-General explicitly far more authority than his inconspicuous and apolitical prototype in the League of Nations had possessed. If, in a recurrent pun, the problem of Trygve Lie and Dag Hammarskjold had been whether to be a Secretary or a General, one may claim that, by intent as well as by performance, the top executive of the U.N. has been a marshal rather than a clerk. His office has been not merely administrative but also political—legally, under Article 99; politically, "in response to developing needs." This was one reason why Hammarskjold's death initially left such a glaring void.

Experience shows that there are inherent flaws in the way the Secretariat was conceived. Stalin could choose to ignore the Secretary-General, who, like the Pope, "has no divisions." For the Secretary-General to exercise all the authority of his high office in a crisis often means antagonizing one or more of the Great Powers. The Secretary-General's effectiveness presupposes their continuous and unanimous trust. Both Lie and Hammarskjold antagonized the Soviet bloc. To have avoided doing so would have meant failing in the fulfillment of their duties.[1] To put it differently, the more effective the Secretary-General is in strengthening the U.N. itself, the more inevitable the opposition to him—especially on the part of the U.S.S.R.

The necessity to perform political tasks does not make "disinterested" or "objective" service impossible. Dag Hammarskjold put the problem sharply into focus in his Oxford speech, on May 30, 1961: If the demand for neutrality implies that an international public servant cannot take a stand on a political issue, even at the request of the General Assembly or the Security Council, the demand is in conflict with the Charter itself. If, on the other hand, neutrality

---

[1] H. G. Nicholas puts the dilemma effectively: "If the action of one or more of the members violates the Charter, the Secretary-General's duty is clear, but when the time comes, as it must, for healing the breach (unless there is to be world war *à outrance*), the Secretary-General's partiality, though it be the partiality of righteousness, is likely to be an offense in the nostrils of the returned prodigal."

means that he must remain wholly uninfluenced by national or group interests or ideologies, the obligation to observe such neutrality is just as basic to the Charter as it was in the Covenant of the League.

It has been a matter of honorable tradition and established policy, reiterated over generations, that an international staff, to be fair and effective, must not be imbued with the values and special interests of any one state.[2] Yet this is precisely what Moscow has challenged. As Walter Lippmann reported on the basis of his interview with Khrushchev,

the Soviet government has now come to the conclusion that there can be no such thing as an impartial civil servant in this deeply divided world, and that the kind of political celibacy which the British theory of the civil service calls for is in international affairs a fiction.

Beyond a doubt, the *troika* formula does radical violence to the entire U.N. approach, seeking to substitute for a distinguished civil service the crude arithmetic of political patronage.

It may well be that, from the Soviet viewpoint, the Secretary-General had gone beyond the original purview of his tasks. Once more, Moscow stuck to the minimal construction of the U.N.'s role, while the Secretary-General found support for his initiatives in the broad view (expressed, for instance, in the Report of the Preparatory Commission for the United Nations) that he, more than anyone else, "must embody the principles and ideals of the Charter."

Moscow objected not only to his arrogation of authority (at the behest of the "imperialists," it would maintain) but also to his philosophy under which the United Nations must be interposed between the major camps and fill the power vacuums wherever it can. In Moscow's reading, this is a pernicious doctrine incompatible with its view of the inevitable course of history. It is this attempt, more than anything else, that identified the Secretary-General, for

---

[2] Article 100 of the Charter stipulates that:

1. In the performance of their duties the Secretary-General and the staff shall not seek or receive instructions from any government or from any other authority external to the Organization. They shall refrain from any action which might reflect on their position as international officials responsible only to the Organization.

2. Each member of the United Nations undertakes to respect the exclusively international character of the responsibilities of the Secretary-General and the staff, and not to seek to influence in the discharge of their responsibilities.

the Communists, with reaction and that prompted the vigorous expression of Soviet determination not to tolerate efforts that would frustrate potential Communist gains in fluid areas around the globe.

WHERE DO WE GO FROM HERE?

The Soviet Union may at times silence the expression of its belief that ultimately "one or the other must prevail." It has never abandoned the "either-or" approach.

The choice of when to mute and when to trumpet the extreme formulation of incompatibility is up to Moscow. Even if the outside world can help fortify or provoke a given Soviet response, it can never expect to control it. The Soviet Union may alter at will its readiness to compromise on the organization of the United Nations or its resolve to cooperate on a given task. It cannot be compelled or effectively induced to do so. With some oversimplification, one may conclude that the United Nations is only as much as its least cooperative members want it to be.

The question was raised earlier whether a state committed to objectives at variance with those of the United Nations can—and should—operate in an international body such as the U.N. Sheer logic might well lead one to answer in the negative. In the long run, the contending forces as now defined and inspired may well be unable to coexist. Theoretically, or ultimately, one may indeed maintain that "international organization is hardly compatible with rampant imperialism by one state which seeks hegemony over the world." Yet in the short run—even on the brink of the thermonuclear precipice—restraint from recourse to extremes, retreat from the logical to the political, from incompatibility to coexistence, from the inexorable to the possible, refraining from the *ultima ratio,* remain the essence of power politics. So long as this is true, there is continuing and important room for the United Nations, and for the Soviet Union as part of it, in the duel of our age.

This would be true even if the Soviet long-range objective of controlling the U.N. had greater chances of success than now seems likely. Once its efforts succeeded, of course, the need for the U.N. would promptly disappear, for in the future commonwealth of Communist nations, the United Nations with its present complexion and philosophy can have no place.

The Soviet Union can be expected to pursue its own ends with all the vigor and determination that its "active, aggressive struggle" demands. Soviet policy-makers no doubt realize that their reorganization proposals are not likely to be adopted in their present form. On at least one occasion—the crisis induced by Dag Hammarskjold's death—Moscow has demonstrated that its demands need not always amount to ultimatums. In March, 1961, no one would have dared predict that within six months agreement on a successor to the Secretary-General was possible—even as an "interim" solution—without fundamentally modifying the structure and operation of the U.N. The deadlock likely to obtain when U Thant's term expires in April, 1963, may be expected to be fraught with even graver dangers, at a time when the Soviet position promises to be considerably less flexible—unless, once more, broader considerations of policy produce a propitious climate for Soviet moderation unforeseeable today. While various compromise formulas have been suggested in response to the *troika* plan, Moscow has actually allowed itself little room for negotiation or retreat without sacrificing the heart of its proposals—a veto over the activities of the Secretariat. It remains to be seen whether anything short of this will satisfy the U.S.S.R.; it is highly improbable that anything like it will be acceptable to the major non-Communist states.

To this extent, the future of the United Nations is in Soviet hands. Moscow can wreck it or build it up: In the U.N.'s present state, Moscow is unlikely to do either. It is, however, certain to keep the United Nations from taking that giant step that Dag Hammarskjold, in his final months, spoke of as the transition from "institutional systems of international coexistence" to "constitutional systems of international cooperation." That bridge between standing international conference and organized international community, which he saw embodied in the U.N. Charter, is certain to remain unfinished so long as Moscow has the right and the might to interpose its veto.

The Soviet bloc cannot be expected to adopt the philosophy of the U.N. and pursue the objectives of the U.N. As Adlai Stevenson put it to the Senate Foreign Relations Committee on January 18, 1961:

The United Nations—as an idea and as an institution—is an extension of Western ideas; of Western belief in the worth and dignity of the individual; of Western ideology. It is based on a Western parliamentary tradition. Its roots are in the Western idea of representative government. In short, it is thoroughly antitotalitarian.

Indeed, the United Nations is founded on the belief in a measure of perfectibility, gradualism, and consensus. In many respects, its outlook in international affairs is analogous to that of liberal democracy at home. We have been reminded that

international organization rests upon the belief that man is at liberty, not only to surrender to the operation of the iron laws of the system, or to attempt an apocalyptic leap from an era of determinism into an era of freedom, but to shape his collective destiny in the here and now.

The non-Western nations may, and perhaps will, overwhelmingly come to share these assumptions. The Communist states, as we know them, cannot.

But too much must not be expected, or asked, of the United Nations. It was never intended to clash with a Great Power or to resolve conflicts among them. Philip C. Jessup has realistically justified the veto as the safety valve "that prevents the United Nations from undertaking commitments in the political field which it lacks the power to fulfill." Senator James W. Fulbright has more recently argued that "the history of the United Nations has been in large measure a history of retreat from false hopes and of adjustment to the reality of a divided world. The veto is in fact an accurate reflection of that reality." The United Nations can alter neither the power relations among the states nor the motives of their rulers. This is not an argument against the United Nations: With all its inherent limitations, its uses and values, for all mankind, are many.

The West, and above all the United States, cannot of course expect the U.N. to "do its job" for it. The tendency occasionally implicit in American action (and inaction) to "let Dag do it" was a characteristic effort to escape responsibility. The Secretary-General himself was aware of it at one time. As he wrote, in a private letter, late in 1956:

It is one thing that, in the vacuum which suddenly developed in the Suez crisis, I had, for what it was worth, to throw in everything I had to try to tide us over. . . . But it is an entirely different thing, every time the big powers run into a deadlock, to place the problem in the Secretary-General's hands with the somewhat naïve expectation that he can continue to turn up with something. It is a matter of course that a continued use of the office of the Secretary-General in that way sooner or later leads to a point where he must break his neck. . . .

It may well be that Hammarskjold's own conception of the Secretary's office and authority contributed to such extravagant expectations on the part of some member states. His isolation and possible abuse of the Secretary-General's authority are problems that, sooner or later, deserve the most serious consideration. But the immediate task is to keep the U.N. and its Secretariat in effective trim.

If the United States—or any other power—cannot look on the U.N. as a substitute for a dynamic policy of its own, it must not turn its back on it either. No longer is it merely bigots, jingoists, and self-styled superpatriots who rant against the United Nations and American participation in it. Adlai Stevenson has aptly predicted that "the crisis of our loyalty to the United Nations is still ahead of us," as the passing of the majority to the new nations is bound to produce doubts and hesitation and, at times, bitterness as well. Henceforth, unlike in the days of the Korean conflict, the U.S. cannot expect to have the U.N. solidly on its side: The resulting proposals to forge a new and tighter concert of free nations or a cohesive international community endowed with force must be seen as complementary to the United Nations, not antagonistic to it, in conception or in future role.

The United Nations is not, and was never meant to be, an association of the like-minded. John Foster Dulles was once moved to write that the U.N. would be best served

if its Assembly is representative of what the world actually is, and not merely representative of the parts which we like. Therefore, we ought to be willing that all nations should be members without attempting to appraise closely those which are "good" and those which are "bad." Already this distinction is obliterated by the present membership of the United Nations.

It is essential then not to exaggerate the part the United Nations can perform in solving the awesome problems of our time. Moscow, on its part, does not expect any major impact on its world policy to come from or through the U.N. The roots of conflict lie outside the world organization and extend far beyond it. In this regard, "their" and "our" view is likely to coincide, for, in the words of George F. Kennan,

it is not fair to the Organization today to ask it to resolve the predica-
ments of the past as well as of the present. No international organization
can be stronger than the structure of relationships among the Great
Powers that underlies it; and to look to such an organization to resolve
deep-seated conflicts of interest among the Great Powers is to ignore its
limitations and to jeopardize its usefulness in other fields.

3. THE UNITED STATES IN THE UNITED NATIONS: AN INDEPENDENT AUDIT*

BY HENRY M. JACKSON

The place of the United Nations in American foreign policy
is now receiving a good deal of attention. Unfortunately, the debate
seems to be polarized around extreme positions. On the one hand,
there are those who say "The UN is the only source of hope"; "Let's
leave everything to the UN." On the other hand, there are those who
say "The UN is the source of catastrophe"; "Let's get out of the
UN." Each view is like the distorted reflection in a carnival mirror—
one too broad, the other too narrow. Neither view is really helpful.

No doubt the quiet, steadying majority of the American people
have a more balanced view of the United Nations, and see it for what
it is: an aspiration and a hope, the closest approximation we have to
a code of international good conduct, and a useful forum of diplomacy
for some purposes.

The United Nations is, and should continue to be, an important
avenue of American foreign policy. Yet practices have developed
which, I believe, lead to an undue influence of UN considerations in
our national decision-making. Indeed it is necessary to ask whether
the involvement of the UN in our policymaking has not at times
hampered the wise definition of our national interests and the development of sound policies for their advancement?

The test of the national security policy process is this: Does it
identify our vital interests and does it develop foreign and defense

---

* Address to the National Press Club, Washington, D. C., March 20, 1962.
Reprinted by permission of Senator Jackson.

policies which will defend and promote these interests? In our system, two men must bear the heaviest responsibility for giving our national security policy focus and structure. One is, of course, the President. The other is his first adviser, the Secretary of State.

The United Nations is not, and was never intended to be, a substitute for our own leaders as makers and movers of American policy. The shoulders of the Secretary General were never expected to carry the burdens of the President or the Secretary of State. But do we sometimes act as though we could somehow subcontract to the UN the responsibility for national decision-making?

At the founding of the United Nations there was the hope that all its members shared a common purpose—the search for a lasting peace. This hope was dashed.

The Soviet Union was not and is not a "peace-loving" nation. Khrushchev has announced his support for "wars of liberation." He has threatened to "bury" us. In their more agreeable moments the Russians promise to bury us nicely, but whatever their mood, the earth would still be six feet deep above us.

We must realize that the Soviet Union sees the UN not as a forum of cooperation, but as one more arena of struggle.

The maintenance of peace depends not on the United Nations as an organization but on the strength and will of its members to uphold the Charter.

The truth is, though we have not often spoken it in recent years, that the best hope for peace with justice does not lie in the United Nations. Indeed, the truth is almost exactly the reverse. The best hope for the United Nations lies in the maintenance of peace. In our deeply divided world, peace depends on the power and unity of the Atlantic Community and on the skill of our direct diplomacy.

In this light, some basic questions need to be asked:

FIRST: *Are we taking an exaggerated view of the UN's role?*

In one way and another the conduct of UN affairs absorbs a disproportionate amount of the energy of our highest officials. The President and the Secretary of State must ration their worry time— and the hours spent on the UN cannot be spent on other matters. All too often, furthermore, the energies devoted to the UN must be spent on defensive actions—trying to defeat this or that ill-advised resolution—rather than on more constructive programs.

The Secretary of State has called the United Nations "a forum in which almost every aspect of our foreign policy comes up." The fact is correctly stated, but does it reflect a desirable state of affairs? Should we take a more restricted view of the organization's capacity for helpfulness?

I think we should. The cold war may destroy the United Nations, if that organization becomes one of its main battlegrounds, but the United Nations cannot put an end to the cold war.

As a general rule, might it be more prudent, though less dramatic, not to push the UN into the fireman's suit unless we are sure the alternatives are worse and, above all, that we are not seeking to evade our own responsibilities.

I believe the United Nations can best gain stature and respect by undertaking tasks which are within its capabilities, and that its usefulness will be diminished if it is impelled into one cold war crisis after another and asked to shoulder responsibilities it cannot meet.

With these thoughts in mind, I read with some concern proposals to increase the "executive responsibilities" of the organization. Also, I have serious doubts about current suggestions to provide "more pervasive and efficient 'UN presences' " to help "halt infiltration of guerrillas across frontiers; and to help halt internal subversion instigated by a foreign power . . ."

Dag Hammarskjold, who was a brilliant and devoted servant of the United Nations, clearly saw the dangers in overrating the peacekeeping power of the organization. In a letter to a private citizen, he once decried the tendency to force the Secretary General into a key role in great power disputes "through sheer escapism from those who should carry the responsibility."

SECOND: *May not the most useful function of the United Nations lie in serving as a link between the West and the newly independent states?*

Most international business is best handled through normal bilateral contacts or through regional arrangements among the states concerned.

However, the United Nations provides a useful meeting ground for many new governments with other governments. These relationships may be of mutual benefit.

The UN affords good opportunities to explain Western policies, to correct misrepresentations of the Western position, and to expose the weaknesses in the Soviet line. In fact, the Soviet singing commercials themselves offend the most hardened ear. They inspire a healthy skepticism about Russian three-way cold war pills—guaranteed to end the arms race, relieve colonial oppression, and ease poverty, if taken regularly, as directed.

The UN and its specialized agencies may be of great usefulness in supplying technical assistance for economic development, in providing financial aid, and in preparing international development programs.

The organization may sometimes be helpful in reaching peaceful settlements of certain issues and disputes of concern to the newly independent states—especially if it is used to seek out areas of agreement rather than to dramatize conflicts of interest.

In this connection there has been too great a tendency to bring every issue to a vote. Indeed, there are too many votes on too many issues in the UN—and too much of the time and energy of every delegation is spent in lobbying for votes.

A vote requires a division of the house, a sharpening and even an exaggeration of points at issue, and it emphasizes the division of opinion rather than the area of agreement. Not every discussion needs to end in a vote. The purposes of the members might be better served if the UN forum becomes more often a place where diplomatic representatives quietly search for acceptable settlements of issues between their countries.

Voting has a way of raising the temperature of any body, and I think that we should be doing what we can to keep the temperature of the United Nations near normal.

THIRD: *In our approach to the UN, do we make too much of the talk and too little of the deed?*

New York City is the foremost communications center of the United States, if not of the world. Once the decision was made to locate the headquarters of the United Nations in New York, it was inevitable that what went on there would receive attention disproportionate to its significance. Newsmen and photographers have to produce news stories and pictures, and politicians from any land rival the celebrities of stage and screen in their hunger for free publicity.

The United States is of course host to the United Nations. Day in and day out we are conscious of the presence of the organization in our midst. And the role of host entails special obligations. Consequently, it is often difficult to keep one's sense of proportion. There is, for example, a tendency, to which the press itself is not immune, to believe the UN makes more history than it really does.

A Secretary of State—responsible for policy—must weigh his words carefully. For that reason he seldom makes good copy. One of the reasons for the extensive coverage of the United Nations is that the right to the floor of the General Assembly is not subject to the sobering influence of responsibility for action.

I have been struck, for example, by the serious disproportion in the press, radio, and television coverage of our UN delegation and the coverage of the Department of State. The space and time devoted to the former does not correctly reflect the relative importance of what is said in New York against what is said in Washington.

If the UN were used less for drumbeating on every nerve-tingling issue, and if its energies were quietly devoted to manageable problems, there might be fewer headlines from the UN but more contributions to the building of a peaceful world.

Everyone talks too much. It is a worldwide disease. Sometimes it seems that the appropriate legend to place above the portals of the UN might be: "Through these doors pass the most articulate men and women in the world."

FOURTH: *Should our delegation to the United Nations play a larger role in the policymaking process than our representatives to NATO or to major world capitals?*

I think the answer is no, and the burden of proof should lie with those who advocate a unique role for our embassy in New York.

Our delegation to the United Nations is, of course, frequently and necessarily involved in promoting or opposing particular actions by the United Nations which may have an important bearing on our national security policies. If it is not to commit the United States to positions inconsistent with our national security requirements, the delegation must be kept in closest touch with, and have a thorough understanding of, these requirements. Furthermore, the President and Secretary of State require information and advice from our UN delegation.

This is not to say, however, that the requirements of sound national policy can be more clearly seen in New York than elsewhere, or that our embassy in New York should play a different role in policymaking from that played by other important embassies.

The precedent set by President Eisenhower in this matter, and continued by this Administration, seems unfortunate. The Ambassador to the United Nations is not a second Secretary of State, but the present arrangement suggests a certain imbalance in the role assigned to the UN delegation in the policymaking process.

The problem is not to give the UN delegation a larger voice in policymaking but to give it the tools to help carry out the policy.

Rational, effective negotiation on complex and critical matters, like the reduction and control of armaments, requires unified guidance and instruction to those conducting the negotiations. This is a basic principle of sound administration and avoids the dangers of freewheeling. The unified source of information should be the Secretary of State, acting for the President, or the President himself—not others in the White House or the Executive Office, not lower levels in State, certainly not the UN delegation itself.

The UN delegation in New York should not operate as a second foreign office. Such confusion of responsibility reinforces a tendency to give undue weight in national policy formulation to considerations that seem more important in New York than they ought to seem in Washington, D.C. The effect of decisions on something called "our relations in the UN" may receive more weight than their effect on, say, the strength and unity of the Atlantic Community. The result may be a weakening or dilution of policy positions in deference to what is represented in New York as world opinion.

The concept of world opinion has been, I fear, much abused. Whatever it is and whatever the importance that should be attached to it, I doubt that it can be measured by taking the temperature of the General Assembly or successfully cultivated primarily by currying favor in New York. To hide behind something called "world opinion" is all too often the device of the timid, or the last resort of someone who has run out of arguments.

FIFTH: *Is our UN delegation properly manned for the diplomatic and technical tasks we require of it?*

We have established the tradition of choosing for top UN posts Americans of considerable prestige—prestige acquired, furthermore, not in the practice of diplomacy but in national politics, business, the arts and sciences and other fields of endeavor. For the most part, these people have served us well, in effective advocacy of America's concerns, and in persuasive championship of progress toward a world of good neighbors.

A start has been made in staffing the UN mission more as other embassies, with experienced diplomats and experts in technical fields in which the United Nations may be able to make quiet but useful contributions. Further progress in this direction should be encouraged.

The sum of the matter is this:

We need to take another look at our role in the United Nations, remembering that the UN is not a substitute for national policies wisely conceived to uphold our vital interests. We need to rethink the organization and staffing of our government for United Nations affairs.

For this purpose, we should have a top-level review conducted under the authority of the President and the Secretary of State. The review should, of course, be handled in a nonpartisan manner.

Debate over the United Nations is now centered on the UN bond issue. This debate reveals some of the symptoms of the basic disturbance. Congress has been requested to approve the purchase of UN bonds up to a total of 100 million dollars to help cover the cost of two controversial peace-keeping operations. The money in question has been spent and it would be a serious mistake to prolong the financial crisis. I trust the Congress can help find a wise way to help cover the deficit.

But the fundamental questions will still remain, and will plague us until they are answered:

Do our present relations with the United Nations assist the wise definition of our vital interests and the establishment of sound policies? Are we sometimes deferring to the United Nations in the hope that we may somehow escape the inescapable dilemmas of leadership? Are we failing to make the most of the United Nations by encouraging it to attempt too much?

Mr. Chairman, I close as I began: The United Nations is, and should continue to be, an important avenue of American foreign policy. But we need to revise our attitudes in the direction of a more realistic appreciation of its limitations, more modest hopes for its accomplishments, and a more mature sense of the burdens of responsible leadership.

Part Two

Struggle for Superiority

CHAPTER V

Politico-Economic Ideologies

Marxism-Leninism is our main weapon. We will conquer the capitalist world by using this mighty ideological weapon and not a hydrogen bomb.

— NIKITA S. KHRUSHCHEV

Mr. Khrushchev may have known his Marx—but his Marx did not know the United States of America.

— JOHN F. KENNEDY

Ideology, as a way of translating ideas into action, generates forceful passion. It may be said that the most important latent function of ideology is to tap emotion. Political ideology fuses those emotional energies and channels them into avenues of domestic and international politics. For Karl Marx, on whose doctrine the Soviet Union is supposedly based, the only real action was in politics. Revolutionary action, as Marx conceived it, was not mere social change but a consummate establishment of Communism on the ruins of capitalism. The followers of Marx are dedicated to the cause by the strength of their belief in the inevitability of Communist victory.

In the United States, many observers believe that the old nineteenth century ideologies and intellectual debates have been exhausted. They further believe that today there is a rough consensus on such political issues as: "the acceptance of a welfare state; the desirability of decentralized power; a system of mixed economy and of political pluralism." In that sense, they claim, the ideological age has ended in the United States and in the Western world as a whole.

This chapter is devoted to a comparative analysis of political ideologies of the United States and the Soviet Union.

The House Committee on Un-American Activities analyzes some of the fundamental, theoretical principles of the Communist ideology —class struggle and dialectic materialism.

127

Edwin G. Nourse, a member of the Joint Council on Economic Education, discusses four stages of capitalistic evolution through the eighteenth and the nineteenth centuries and analyzes the essence of "Laboristic Capitalism" and "People's Capitalism" of today.

Norman Cousins, Editor of the Saturday Review, *asserts that the Soviet leadership in recent years eschewed ideological rigidity by assuming the attitude: "Where ideology slows up production, ideology will be re-examined or revised." He further describes political and economic implications arising from such ideological flexibility.*

1. THE COMMUNIST IDEOLOGY*

BY THE HOUSE COMMITTEE ON UN-AMERICAN ACTIVITIES

Communist ideology was originally derived from a philosophy of history. And a view of history is still the very core of communism. What Marx took over from the philosopher G. W. F. Hegel and made the center of his own ideology is not a set of mere observations about historical events, but a complete theory about how history moves, why it moves, and the direction in which it moves. Since history is the entire field of human activities, such a theory of history supplies an explanation of the meaning of all human efforts (the direction of history), instruction on what people should be doing next (the "laws" of historical development), and a yardstick by which the value of men and things should be judged (forward—good; backward—bad). It can be readily seen that a comprehensive theory of history like that offers guidance similar to that provided by religion, and thus can be used as a substitute for religion by people who no longer believe in God.

The centerpiece of the Communist view of history is the doctrine which says that all societies above the primitive level are split into classes engaged in an unceasing and irreconcilable struggle: the doctrine of the class struggle. This is the concept that serves as a

---

* From *Facts on Communism,* House Document No. 336, Vol. 1 (December, 1959), pp. 15–31.

guiding criterion to all Communist thinking about society and politics. Communist ideology assumes that the basic reality of anything social is the class struggle. It thus explains in terms of the class struggle all salient events of history, the evils of human life, politics and the state, revolutions, ideas and religions, and many other phenomena. In presenting here the details of this doctrine, it will be pointed out that the doctrine consists of a characteristic mixture of scientific analysis, myth and prophesy, a mixture which enables it to impress men with the appeals of science along with those of religion.

If some men are able to wield oppressive power over others, Communists say, it is private property, and property alone, which enables them to do so. Property is what has brought about the division of society into classes. Property gives people exclusive control over things. Those who have exclusive control of the means of economic production can use their ownership as power over their fellow beings who do not own means of production. Thus we have classes, and power, both explained in terms of property.

Marx analyzed society by distinguishing in it several classes of people, according to the type of relationship which linked people with the process of production. As a mere observation, this is, of course, a valid method of scientific classification, just as scientists group plants and animals according to certain characteristics. But Marx went beyond mere observation. He claimed that the classes into which he had grouped people are real social and political forces which can and do act in history—nay, which are the chief actors in history. This is a bold thesis. Since classes have no external organization to act on their behalf, they can "act" as a unit only if the people grouped together in a class are themselves conscious of being parts of a "class." Classes can be actors in history only if people's minds are fully aware of their class interests and determined to promote them. This is indeed what communism claims. It asserts that people form different classes not only by virtue of the fact of their economic existence, but also because people living in similar circumstances also think alike. In a similar way, Hitler alleged that people with the same kind of physical build had the same kind of soul. Hitler believed men belonging to different races to *be essentially* different creatures. Marx taught that men belonging to different classes had no common values or ideas; that they had *essentially* differing consciousnesses. Let us note here that to classify phenomena—including people—for the purpose of observation, is one thing; to attribute to such classes will, purpose, and a common consciousness is quite another. To say that the classes into which one has divided people are authors of action, is an assertion which requires elaborate and hard-to-obtain proof.

Marx went beyond scientific methods in another respect. He described property as a source of power in society. But then he went beyond this analysis and claimed that property is, has been, and forever will be the sole root of oppressive power. In order to maintain this, he must, of course, discount such sources of power as bureaucracies, police machineries, military forces, taxation, or else he must claim that all these are merely derived from the power that flows from property. This indeed is the claim of Communists. It is another assertion that requires proof, a proof which no Communist thinker has ever attempted to offer. . . .

This concept of class struggle furnishes the Communists with an explanation of history. They say about recorded history (*a*) that everything that happened has ultimately been an aspect of class struggle; (*b*) that one can distinguish in these class struggles certain major phases; (*c*) that history moves along a certain line through these phases and cannot move otherwise; and (*d*) that this forward movement of history must culminate in communism. Let us take up each of these doctrines in turn.

History, a series of dramatic political changes, has happened, according to Communist ideology, because the division of society into classes makes the establishment of political power necessary, and political power rises, declines, and falls as its basis changes. The basis of political power, according to the Communist thesis, has been the ownership of the means of production. In the development of society the techniques of production have periodically changed, so that the means of production which were powerful yesterday gave way to new means of production today. The owners of these new means of production then were the up and coming class. But the owners of the old means of production still held sway by means of the machinery of political power they had established. It is political power which prevented a gradual change of peaceful progress from the rule of one class to that of another. So the up and coming class slowly gained influence and economic strength within the framework of political rule established by the old class, until one day this framework would be violently broken and the new class would take over political power. . . .

On the strength of this theory, the Communists believe that they are in possession of the key to history. They believe that the concept of classes, class struggle, forces of production, relations of production, and revolution, enable them not only to explain the past, but understand the present and recognize the direction events are taking into the future. In the realm of history, the process of change seems to them to have become as clear as that of mutation has as a result of Darwin's theories:

. . . Now Marx has proved that the whole of previous history is a history of class struggles, that in all the manifold and complicated political struggles the only thing at issue has been the social and political rule of social classes, the maintenance of domination by older classes and the conquest of domination by newly arising classes. To what, however, do these classes owe their origin and their continued existence? They owe it to the particular material, physically sensible conditions in which society at a given period produces and exchanges its means of subsistence.[1]

This view of history is called *historical materialism*. It is the special philosophy of Marx who developed it and applied it in his writings. Note that it attributes the ultimate moving power in human affairs to material factors, viz., the "forces of production," but insists that the actual movements are political, and, at the decisive points, violent. "Force is the midwife of history," said Marx.

Marx thought he had discovered the secret of social and political change and how it happens in history. His followers, particularly Lenin and Stalin (in most cases following Engels rather than Marx) went much further. They mapped out the entire course of human history, from the earliest beginnings, to what they believed must be the ultimate end. Engels, in a very superficial book called *The Origin of the Family, Private Property, and the State,* had distinguished certain phases of social development. Engels' already too simplified classification was reduced to even simpler terms, and now all Communists are taught that the history of mankind passes through *five* phases. These phases are distinguished in terms of the techniques of

[1] Engels, "Karl Marx" (1877), *Marx and Engels Selected Works* (Moscow: Foreign Languages Publishing House, 1955), vol. II, p. 163.

economic production and the relations of production with their corresponding social classes.

In the first and primitive phase, there was supposedly no private property, no class division and no state. With the introduction of private property, there came, according to the theory, the first division into classes. The first class society was a slaveholding society, with slaves owned as private property. When that society had run its course, and slavery was no longer profitable, a new class of feudal landowners supposedly emerged from the ruins and became the ruling class of the next type of society—feudal society.

In the framework of feudal society, in turn, the class of merchants grew into a revolutionary force which eventually overthrew feudal power and set up a new regime favorable to its own type of property —bourgeois or capitalistic society. And finally, capitalistic society is expected to nurture in its bosom its own gravediggers, the proletariat. The victorious revolution of the proletariat then would usher in the fifth phase—socialist society. Here the proletariat would be the ruling class, but, for reasons to be discussed later, there would be no more class struggles, no oppression, and no further revolutions.

What this amounts to is a complete outline of the course which human history, propelled by class struggles, must take. This theory is the most important piece in the entire structure of Communist ideology. For on it depends the Communist idea of the meaning of history (and, consequently, of politics), the Communist confidence in ultimate victory, the Communist attitude towards people, classes and nations, the Communist ethic (insofar as one can speak of an ethic here), and the Communist insistence on ideological conformity.

The five-phases theory goes far beyond Marx's analysis of revolutionary change through class struggle, because it pretends to give a complete and exhaustive list of the types of human society through which mankind must develop. It extends the theory of the class struggle to a comprehensive view of what past, present, and future of human society must be. Marx had left an analysis of capitalism, with positive assurance that capitalist society would engender the proletarian class which, in turn, would by its revolution abolish all classes and the class struggle. Now Communist ideology teaches that all roads of development in the world must eventually lead to capitalism and thus set up the proletarian revolution. That revolution is therefore seen as the destiny of all mankind. Not only is it bound to come about as the result of inevitable historical development, but it is also supposed to do away with the class struggle, the main source of evil, according to Communist thought. So the proletarian revolution is envisaged as something that is both necessary and good, both destiny and hope. To Communists, then, men are divided into those who ultimately help the revolution and those who oppose it. This is the basis of Communists' "ethics," and of the relation between the Communists and mankind. "Revolution" and "revolutionary" to the Communists are what Richard Weaver has called god-words. Those who oppose the proletarian revolution and its agents, the Communists, are not only oriented toward a past that is swept away by the powerful currents of history, but also opposed to the fulfillment of that destiny which holds the only hope for mankind. They stand condemned, in Communist eyes, on two counts: opposition to the march of history, and refusal to serve the good. Communists, on the other hand, draw from their view of history the double assurance that they are morally justified by their service to the redeeming cause of the proletarian revolution, and also are in accord with the movements of history toward a Communist future. Their struggle and the growth of their power is both good and necessary, because of the view which they have of history. One can therefore hardly exaggerate the importance of the Communist teaching of history, as the main foundation of Communist attitudes toward the world and toward people. . . .

If Communist ideology consisted of nothing but the teachings of Karl Marx, it would not have the view of history which has been here described. The main work of Marx, *Capital,* consisted of an analysis of modern society and its inner laws of development. It was based on the premise that the relations of men in the process of production contain the key to the structure of a society and the forces that make for change. This, as has already been mentioned, is a materialistic explanation of society, and the theory is called *Historical Materialism.* Historical materialism is as far as Marx himself went.

Modern Communist ideology, however, goes much further. It has developed a theory called *Dialectical Materialism.* This theory goes back largely to the writings of Engels, whose chief characteristic was that he generalized every concept that Marx developed. Marx applied the concept of the class struggle to one society: the industrial society of 19th century Western Europe. Engels wrote a brief book in which he claimed that the same concept applied to all societies ever known. Marx, in his earlier writings, reflected somewhat the influence of Hegel and Hegel's dialectic. Engels took these elements and, again in a short book, expanded them into a principle that explained everything in nature as well as in history. Lenin, following Engels more than Marx, developed a complete philosophy underpinning the Communist view of history, which is now taught under the name of Dialectical Materialism.

First, what is dialectic? In its modern use, the meaning of the term goes back to Hegel. It is a philosophy saying that all things are related with each other, that everything is in continuous flux, and that the flux occurs according to certain laws. In these laws, the concept of "opposites" plays a great role. Change occurs because there are opposites opposing each other. But in the course of the change it turns out that the opposites are not really opposed, but are really united. The "unity of opposites" is the name of this principle. It actually says that whenever we see struggle, there is hidden in it the meaning of unity on a higher level. Or, to turn it the other way around: struggle is the necessary form of progress, and all existing things carry in themselves the seed of something opposing them. Finally, this philosophy claims that all changes ultimately occur by way of a sudden leap, after the tension between opposites has been growing for a certain while; and in the leap something new is born, a new quality or essence.

. . . The principal features of the Marxist *dialectical method* are as follows:

(a) Contrary to metaphysics, dialectics does not regard nature . . . as a connected and integral whole, in which things, phenomena, are . . . determined by, each other.

(b) Contrary to metaphysics, dialectics holds that nature is . . . a state of continuous movement and change, of continuous renewal and development. . . .

(c) Contrary to metaphysics, dialectics does not regard the process of development as a simple process of growth . . . but as . . . a development in which the qualitative changes occur not gradually, but rapidly and abruptly, taking the form of a leap from one state to another. . . .

(d) Contrary to metaphysics, dialectics holds that internal contradictions are inherent in all things and phenomena of nature . . . and that the struggle between these opposites . . . constitutes the internal content of the process of development. . . .[2]

This goes far beyond anything Marx had taught and even far beyond an extension of the principle of class struggle to all of history. For this is a philosophy claiming knowledge about the way everything moves and exists—not merely societies and classes, but all of life. Engles expressly extended the philosophy of dialectic to the realm of nature. It is thus a philosophy of *being,* as comprehensive as any philosophy that has ever existed. Communists now represent not merely a political aspiration, or even the revolution of a social class, but an entire view of life which has become indissolubly linked with their political power. Communist power is used now, not only to bring about certain social changes or attain certain political goals, but also to impose authoritatively a world view with all its implications in art, science, literature, philosophy, and education.

The dialectic, i.e., a philosophy about the movement of all things in terms of opposites-in-unity, was combined with materialism, i.e., the explanation of all things in terms of matter. This combination does go back to Marx in the sense that Marx had been brought up in the dialectic of Hegel who said that the movement in terms of opposites-in-unity was a movement of ideas, and that history was nothing but the unfolding of ideas rooting in something he called Absolute Mind. Marx went on from there to say that Hegel's view of the world and history was upside down, in that ideas were but a reflection of material conditions. Marx undertook to put it "rightside up," that is, he asserted that the dialectic movement of history was ultimately a movement of matter rather than ideas. We have already seen how he carried out this proposition in his concept of the class struggle. As far as society is concerned, he said "matter" is the process of economic production. Thus matter moves, and its movement is dialectic—i.e., each condition already contains in itself the forces that oppose it, but from the opposition flows change and unity on a higher level. Capitalist society supposedly engenders within itself the tendency toward socialization and the proletarian class which opposes it and struggles with it. At one time, violent change will occur

[2] *History of the Communist Party of the Soviet Union* (Bolsheviks), *Short Course* (New York: International Publishers, 1939), pp. 106, 107, 109. Also Stalin, *Problems of Leninism* (Moscow: Foreign Languages Publishing House, 1953), pp. 714–717.

(the Revolution), and then the progressive elements of capitalist society (technology) and the proletarian forces will unite on a higher level (Communist society). As we have already seen, Marx himself dwelt almost exclusively on the materialistic explanation of history. It was Lenin who, following Engels, strongly emphasized the dialectic element and thus founded what is now known as *Diamat* (dialectical materialism). . . .

The materialistic component of the philosophy is, however, all-important in the following respect: Matter, being inanimate, can be observed and known by man, while ideas are creative and unpredictable. If history is a dialectic movement of material elements rather than of ideas, history can be known as much as material evolution can be known. One of the most important points in Communist ideology is the assertion that as history moves forward according to the laws of "matter," the laws of history can be known, and that Marxism-Leninism is the key to their knowledge. . . .

It is on this pretension of the knowability of history that the claim of the Communist Party to leadership is based, as we shall see. In Leninism, the "laws of history" and their knowledge become more and more the key to revolutionary and organizational policy. While Marx would say that the full development of capitalist society was the prerequisite for revolution, Lenin would claim that the existence of a group of people having the "consciousness" of the laws of history is the decisive factor.

The principle that history follows certain laws which, thanks to Marxism can now be known, is what Communists claim to be their mark of distinction from the so-called "utopian" socialists. Utopian socialists, in Communist definition, are those who dream of an ideal society, a regime of justice and equality, and in whose eyes "Future history resolves itself . . . into the propaganda and the practical carrying out of their social plans."[3] In other words, they are people who envisage a socialist society and believe that they can bring it into being by a direct action of their will.

Communists consider this a childish attitude, because it leaves out of consideration the "laws of history." Utopian socialists, they say, care for "the working class, as being the most suffering class. Only

[3] Marx and Engels, "The Manifesto of the Communist Party" (December 1847–January 1848), *Selected Works* (Moscow: Foreign Languages Publishing House, 1955), vol. I, p. 62.

from the point of view of being the most suffering class does the proletariat exist for them."[4] The correct attitude, according to Communists, would be to regard the proletariat not merely as the most suffering, but as the "most advanced," the "only really revolutionary" class, in other words, the class which is destined to bring about the fulfillment of history's scheme. What distinguishes communism from utopian socialism is that the latter is motivated by feelings of compassion and the will to realize justice, whereas the former is motivated by historical analysis and the will to help the movement of history. Since knowledge of history's laws is considered possible on the basis of the "science" of Marxism-Leninism, the history-motivated Communist calls himself a "scientific" socialist.

The term "scientific," as applied to Communist ideology, is in itself a jargon term connoting Communist insistence on the difference between their revolutionary cause, which is based on the alleged "laws of history," and other revolutionary causes based on ideas of justice, social order, etc. In terms of what is generally known as science, Communist ideology can of course not be called scientific. It is not scientific insofar as it indiscriminately mixes social analysis with prophesy, ignores facts that could refute its tenets, and prohibits critical examination of its basic propositions.

A "scientific" socialist refuses to fix his mind on the conditions of an ideal society. Instead, he keeps his eyes on the class struggle and its historical development. He firmly believes that the class struggle, if energetically pursued, will lead to the victory of a social force whose ascendancy will emancipate all mankind. Ultimate freedom is not a direct product of the human will but of historical development: the development of the political class struggle and of the forces of production. It is a mistake to say that communism is a blueprint for future society. It is rather the pretense of a foreknowledge of history, a trust in a beneficient outcome of a ruthless struggle for revolutionary power.

[4] *Ibid.*

2. THE PROMISE OF AMERICAN CAPITALISM*

BY EDWIN G. NOURSE

As used by Chairman Khrushchev, capitalism is a term of contempt and even hatred. To the typical American, the word bespeaks a proud tradition of national achievement and commands a personal allegiance. These Americans are spontaneously "agin" Communism and *for* "the American way" of economic life. But how many of the 67 millions who voted in November, 1960, could give a reasonably accurate description or make an effective defense of this system if confronted by their "opposite number" from the ranks of the skeptical and indoctrinated disciples of the Communist system? Exploration of the outer spaces of the capitalistic concept presents today as sharp a challenge to social scientists as orbital flight and excursions beyond the earth's orbit present to natural science.

Capitalism (as Gertrude Stein might have said) "is a word, is a word, is a word." In its first-word aspect it signifies property—saved from past labor to make future labor more productive. Capital formation dates back to the time when half-civilized men first began to save seeds for next year's planting, and to care for flocks and herds for their future product and fostered increase. Today, this physique of capitalism embraces a gigantic mechanical equipment and an ever-expanding research plant for discovering still mightier tools for the fructifying of human labor. In this basic sense, Mr. K., much as he reviles the word, is the greatest individual capitalist of all time. His overriding purpose is to see that the improvident masses do not fritter away in current consumption the productivity that he needs for building dams and factories and transport facilities with which to "bury" our form of capitalism.

In its second-word sense, capitalism is the price-profit-wage (and dividend) system by which we operate a market economy. It includes also a non-market apparatus of taxes, self-imposed in our democracy, and of legislatively directed spending and investment in "public

* From *The Virginia Quarterly Review,* Vol. 38 (Summer, 1962), pp. 369–379. Copyright © The *Virginia Quarterly Review,* the University of Virginia; reprinted by their permission.

works" that facilitates private production and provides quite an array of unpriced or underpriced services to the people.

In its third-word character, capitalism expresses the mystique through which our physical plant and commercial processes reflect our economic, and hence social, philosophy. It embodies the composite of theories and beliefs of our business, labor, and agricultural community as to how the modern capitalistic system *ought* to be run, or *needs* to be run. This popular philosophy of American capitalism holds tenaciously, in many quarters, to ancient folklores and parochial group demands. In other quarters, we see it aspiring to, and somewhat fitfully achieving, structures and practices more in keeping with standards progressively envisioned by modern social science. This outreach of capitalistic thinking should be readily apparent if we note four stages of capitalist evolution.

II

The first of these four stages was Owner-Capitalism or Proprietary Capitalism. It is a persistent and basic, but no longer exclusive, part of today's and tomorrow's capitalism. Only one thing needs to be said about it here. That is, it is monistic in form; the owner-capitalist is "the whole works."

Skipping over the primitive familial and feudal stages of our economic history, we note that, barely two centuries ago, the forward thrust of science and technology and the up-thrust of "the rights of man," the human individual, set the stage for the modern drama of private capitalism. This drama portrays the struggle between two mighty protagonists and has commonly been billed as "The Class Struggle." In the first act of this still-unfolding modern drama, the capitalist as such held the center of the stage. Steam (or water) power called for the building and equipping of costly mills, mines, factories, warehouses, and railways. Capital was the scarce factor in the new economy, whereas labor ran into surplus as machines took up their appointed task of "labor-saving"—socially beneficial but harsh in its impact on individuals. The capitalist easily vaulted into the driver's seat of this new economic machine.

Practical developments under early industrialism begot their relevant pattern of business relations. With crass complacency, the capitalist owner accepted a literal interpretation of supply-and-demand mechanics in the "free" labor market and exploited his strategic position by grasping the lion's share of the enlarged productivity. It was not he but "the iron law of wages," he said, that held workers down to a bare subsistence margin. By amassing capital and investing it, he was, in his own and the public esteem, the outstanding contributor to the expanding wealth of the nation.

The epoch dominated by Proprietary Capitalism presented a pretty sorry picture over-all. Great economic progress, yes, but at social costs that would be intolerable by modern standards. It was one of those things in human affairs that have to get worse before they can get better. Swiftly after the Civil War, the relatively feeble capitalistic device of individual proprietorship gave way to the fabulously powerful device of the limited liability corporation. The "soulless corporation," by its very fact of impersonality meant delegation of control to a special cadre of professional managers. Thus the centre of gravity of industrial and commercial capitalism passed from owner to trustee. We entered the age of Managerial Capitalism.

That the advent of the modern corporation was destined to make things worse before it could make them better accords with the classic dictum: "Power corrupts." The concentration of economic control made possible by the corporate form opened the door to an era of stock-jobbing, monopolistic pricing, and worker exploitation too well known to need review here. These youthful excesses of Big Business led rather promptly to the correctional measures of anti-trust legislation and other regulatory actions of government. And there was also a rising tide of resistance from the awakening giant, organized labor.

Before embarking on that story, however, justice demands a word about the tremendous service to human progress that was rendered by those hard-driving masters of early corporate capitalism—and is still rendered by their more refined successors of today. Theirs has been a vital and tremendous job of promoting that growth of the capital fund necessary to keep both physical plant and technology (science as well as engineering) abreast of or one step in advance of consumers' needs and dreams. They worked—while the feckless consumer slept—to make the electric, automotive, synthetic chemistry, and electronics age come to full flower.

The best of these corporation leaders early raised the torch of dependability of product and equity of treatment of employees in pay, working conditions, and economic security. They co-operated in governmental regulatory measures and discouraged or disciplined "chiselers" within their own ranks.

It may be guessed that, on balance, for the whole area of corporate capitalism, more managers have fought rear-guard actions against such reforms than have kept pace with them or been themselves pace-makers. But Managerial Capitalism did, in time, come to stand for a professional code which, though still greatly honored in the breach, is something very far removed from the callous or predatory outlook of the "tycoons," "robber barons," and "malefactors of great wealth" of the late nineteenth century. In the words of one prominent business executive leader of twenty-five years ago:

Management no longer represents, as it once did, merely the single interest of ownership. Increasingly, it functions on the basis of trusteeship . . . accountable not only to stockholders but to the members of the working organization, to our customers, and to the public. . . . Decisions must now be evaluated in terms of consequences not merely to one individual company but to an entire industry.

This statement of management's responsibility might seem to offer an ideal formulation for a healthy economy under the aegis of Managerial Capitalism. But even at its best there was one large fly in that ointment. The "responsibility" formula retains a strongly feudal flavor of unilateral decision-making. Organized labor long ago repudiated such a monistic philosophy of economic life. And so we turn to their version of an acceptable capitalistic society.

III

Labor's challenge to the right of the capitalist-manager to run the whole business show by unilateral decision began in the first half of the nineteenth century, even under small proprietary capitalism. It gained momentum rapidly after the coming of corporate big business. But in fact, from the very advent of collective bargaining and indeed from the first successful strike for higher wages or better working conditions, labor was asserting a right to some voice in the business process. Through unremitting attacks, at first by small partisan bands of stubborn and ambitious workers and, eventually, through the formidable battalions of the A.F.L. and the C.I.O., this insurgent power gained a footing in the domain of traditional capitalism. This did not mean usurpation of the capitalist manager's operational control. But it did mean effective intervention in management's authoritarian administration of the private distributive process—affecting wages and salaries directly, but also dividends, retained earnings, and prices of the product to buyers indirectly.

Until 1936, the legal status of the labor union was ambiguous. Workers did organize and they did bargain collectively with employers. On the other hand, they were harassed by anti-trust prosecutions, by court injunctions, and by the "yellow-dog contract," which made union membership a bar to employment. Partial liberation took place under the Railway Labor Act (1926) and the Norris-LaGuardia Act (1932-anti-injunction). But it was not until the National Labor Relations Act of 1935 that permanent Federal legislation made a general declaration of the rights of labor to organize and bargain collectively. This Wagner Act is often called the Magna Carta of the labor union; but it was much more than a grant of power to labor. It defined union responsibilities as well as rights, and also the rights as well as the responsibilities of management. Thus, it drew up a written constitution for the government of a new bilateral type of capitalism. This may well be called Laboristic Capitalism.

Though Laboristic Capitalism is a third major phase of capitalism in America, it does not supersede the earlier forms, proprietary capitalism and managerial capitalism. It complements them in a natural process of evolution in a free-enterprise economy. The legal constitution of Laboristic Capitalism, like our Federal Constitution, soon revealed need of perfecting amendments, and the first batch of such amendments was adopted in the well-known Taft-Hartley law of 1947. Proceeding from the premise that the Wagner Act had overcorrected the situation in favor of labor, Taft-Hartley undertook to strike a balance more equitable to both parties and more salutary for the economy.

The unions with great unanimity denounced the Taft-Hartley law as a "slave labor act" and made its repeal a major issue in their political program for a decade. Similarly, management, quite widely, had fought the Wagner Act as a betrayal of free enterprise to socialistic bureaucracy. But time and experience have softened the lines of this controversy. In August, 1961, with contract negotiations with the United Automobile Workers pending, the General Motors Corporation addressed both its workers and the public with a 36-page brochure under the title, "Free Collective Bargaining Works!" Citing five GM-UAW National Agreements covering the years 1948–1960, each of two to five years duration, the company avers:

Throughout the years, General Motors and the UAW have demonstrated time and again that they can work out agreements by direct negotiation between the parties concerned. Both understood early that labor and management both have the same goal—continued successful operation of the business as the key to progress for all. Both have publicly recognized that they must co-operate in order to obtain that goal . . . sincere and patient effort on both sides has made it possible for GM and UAW to work out agreements on the basis of mutual respect and confidence and without the intervention of third parties.

As a postscript, the General Motors pamphlet quotes Walter Reuther, in testimony before a Senate committee:

If you want to talk about the pattern of our collective bargaining relationships, just take a look at the General Motors Corporation. We will lay that parallel to any comparable group in the free world in terms of responsible labor-management relations.

This may be taken as endorsement from the very summit of American industrialism of the fact and the acceptability of Laboristic Capitalism. From here on, there will, of course, be the continuing tussle of conflicting minds and wills to find workable solutions to ever-recurring spot dilemmas. The hardcore issue for Big Business, for Big Labor, and for you and me as citizens is to arrive at a conceptual basis and a legal structure that will realize "equality of bargaining power" between the two protagonists. There is an uneasy suspicion in many quarters today that organized labor, now rescued from its nineteenth- and twentieth-century limbo as "under-dog" in the economic world or "second-class citizens" in our society, has conceived an ambition to become top-dog or to become special-class citizens.

Those fears and suspicions are based not only on the words and actions of the more arrogant labor leaders, (notably the three James boys—"Jimmy" Hoffa, James Cesare Petrillo, and "Jim" Carey) but on the widespread if not universal claim of unions to basic exemption from the antitrust laws. It is hard to reconcile such a claim with labor's own principle of "equality of bargaining power." If labor's long struggle for equal status in a system of Laboristic Capitalism is to be crowned with success, it would seem incumbent on the unions to renounce any claims to special powers or immunities for themselves.

IV

Even if organized labor and professional management find ways of peaceful and productive co-existence among themselves, it is patent that they do not operate within a "closed" business system but within a larger social system that embraces public as well as private enterprise. An all-embracing and co-ordinated structure of modern capitalism is beginning to emerge in American thought and action. This fourth stage of capitalistic evolution has been well named People's Capitalism.

The term People's Capitalism was formerly proposed several years ago by a national public-relations organization, after a rather extended survey of public opinion. The phrase seemed richer in meaning than "democratic capitalism," less likely than "socialized capitalism" to be confused with socialism, and not, as is "welfare capitalism," vulnerable to the accumulated resentments of those political fundamentalists who equate the liberal creed with "being liberal with other people's money." There are those who are dubious about the term People's Capitalism because of the debauchment of meaning conveyed in Communist tags like "people's army," "people's communes," or the "People's Republic of China." But all doubts about its rightness would seem to me to be resolved by the positive fact that the phrase People's Capitalism recalls and exemplifies our original and enduring intention that the American way of life shall be "of the people, by the people, for the people." The economy we seek to achieve, and are somewhat fitfully achieving, is truly capitalism of the people, by the people, for the people.

It is *of the people* because the ever-expanding flow of savings into the enlarging and modernizing of plant (including its research facilities) comes in large measure from the myriad trickles of dollars and even dimes of many millions of people who earn something, and in some millions of cases a good bit, above mere current subsistence needs. There are many large streams of capital formation too, but the system is not dependent mainly on the surpluses of the rich. It is the mass of the population that maintains the high level of capital inflow through insurance premiums, savings accounts, building and loan investments, stock and bond purchases, and pension fund contributions. These masses are able to save for the rainy day of misfortune and for the sunny day of comfortable retirement; for the education of their children and grandchildren; and for such "culture" endowments as churches and private recreational and artistic facilities —part of our social capital. This provident saving by the modestly prosperous is both a more dependable and a more healthy source of the economy's capital fund than the manipulative impounding and investment behavior of a monied class. Finally, through self-taxation, we the people accumulate, renew, and enlarge a gigantic public capital of educational, health, communication, and recreational "public works."

People's Capitalism is *by the people* because it rests on the voluntary decisions of individual proprietors, organization executives, and elected public officials, both local and central. These government taxing and spending officers are under constant scrutiny, frequent check, and periodic mandate by the citizen body which they represent. In the private sector, to be sure, corporation stockholders are to a considerable extent disfranchised by self-seeking and self-perpetuating boards of directors and union members disfranchised by their own lethargy or the machinations of union bosses. Likewise, many citizens are careless or venal in the exercise of their franchise. But trusteeship is the principle on which our system is organized in all three of these departments. And "reformers" indomitably return to the crusade to raise or restore general practice to the high level of that principle.

Modern American Capitalism is *for the people* in a sense and to a degree undreamed of by, and indeed unwelcome to, those who made norms of opinion and action from the Civil War to the first World War—and their hold-over brothers in the current scene. But today's sophisticated capitalist manager justifies his unilateral administration in the private sector of the economy on the ground that it serves the ends of national prosperity and growth most fully and surely. Organized labor similarly justifies its intervention in this private sector on the ground that it has peculiar competence to see that the basic claims of the laboring masses are not subordinated to the special interests of capital control and that consumers as such shall have priority rights over the machine as such.

V

But an adequate philosophy of modern capitalism must go beyond Laboristic Capitalism as sophisticated collective bargaining (i.e., negotiated coexistence) between Big Business and Big Labor. The goals of economic policy for America as torch bearer and chief underwriter of the free world cannot be limited to whatever achievement or frustration of economic service to the whole people may be forthcoming from the astute compromises and the dubious deals that will emerge from bipartisan private administration of the nation's capital and labor resources.

Modern capitalism of the people, by the people, for the people complements the traditional and well-proven institutions of the free private market with an increased amount of activation and financial implementation of national resources use through governmental policy-making, fiscal and monetary administration, and institutional regulation. This maturing public philosophy, presaged by Theodore Roosevelt and Woodrow Wilson, became widely accepted during the twenty years of the New Deal-Fair Deal. Neither Thomas E. Dewey nor, more recently, Richard Nixon dared (or, I believe, cared) to challenge it. Its future hopes of still richer fulfillment and its peril of arrest or retrogression now ride with the guidon of John Fitzgerald Kennedy.

In the words and actions of the President may be seen touches of prophetic insight as to what American capitalism may become. But the mind and heart of the people must be lifted up if he is to march at the head of a victorious army of free capitalistic enterprise. The minds of the people must be sharpened to comprehend the novel issues raised by new technology and accompanying concentrations of economic power and to show the "Yankee ingenuity" by which to preserve the dynamism of the individual and still achieve the full efficiency of large organization. The hearts of the people must be fortified to renounce the ways of economic war among special-interest groups and to seek honestly such rewards as match their several contributions to the joint economic enterprise, these contributions to be evaluated by the tools of scientific method.

3. CHANGE—POSSIBLY FOR THE BETTER*

BY NORMAN COUSINS

At the heart of the dispute between the Chinese Communist leaders is a conflicting interpretation of Karl Marx. Mao Tse-tung is aghast at the economic incentives being introduced in the Soviet Union. To his mind, increases in private property, bonuses tied to extra production, and the accumulation of private capital—just to mention a few developments—prove that the Soviet Union has veered sharply away from Marx. In fact, Mao has accused the Russians of putting bourgeois satisfactions ahead of socialist sacrifices.

What Mao may be missing is that high productivity in the minds of the Soviet leaders is a matter of national survival. Where ideology serves the purposes of production, ideology will be followed. Where ideology slows up production, ideology will be re-examined or re-vised. It was no accident that anxiety over inadequate production figured so largely in the recurrent debates inside the Soviet hierarchy. And out of those debates has come apparent agreement that the system of enlarged incentives associated with Khrushchev must be expanded.

The question, therefore, is whether Soviet leaders have ignored Marx. A careful reading of *Das Kapital* may indicate that Marx has figured largely in recent decisions, even though the course of action flowing out of these decisions may be somewhat different from the trend of Marx's own hopes. Specifically, it is possible that Soviet leaders have been profoundly impressed by Marx's examination of what he considered to be the fundamental characteristics of capital-ism. Chief among these characteristics, said Marx, was a natural and prodigious facility for production. As he saw it, this resulted in chronic overproduction, maldistribution, and an inevitable struggle for foreign markets.

It is possible, however, that what Marx saw as a dead end may be seen by Soviet leaders today as a way out. For if their main problem

* From *Saturday Review* (February 6, 1965), p. 22 ff. Reprinted by per-mission.

is underproduction, and it is true that high production flows almost automatically out of the elements of a free economy, then this is too significant to ignore. With high production in today's world, all things are possible. Without it, nothing is possible. People can't eat theories. They can't wear ideology. They can't find shelter inside statues to national heroes.

Whatever philosophical or ideological goals may animate a national leader on coming into office in today's world, he isn't in power very long before he finds himself preoccupied with pressures inside his own country—too many people without adequate housing; not enough wheat or corn or meat to take care of hungry people whose grumbles become ominous thunder if ignored; not enough brainpower or skilled labor to translate technological prospects into productive reality. What happens in the outside world is vital—but the top priorities go to internal needs. When Nikita Khrushchev was in office, he looked around and he saw ineptness, inertia, and incompetence resulting from the massive bureaucracy that had been built up in the name of Marxism and Leninism. When we met with him in December 1962, he referred to the inability of the Soviet economy to meet expectations, especially in agriculture. We asked whether he didn't feel that such failures were inherent in the Soviet system of economic organization. He replied that there was nothing rigid about that system. "We are not too proud to learn from others," he added. "We can even learn from you."

In scrutinizing the United States and the West in general, therefore, Nikita Khrushchev—and his present successors—have undoubtedly caught the significance of Marx's remark; namely, that free economic societies like the U.S. and Great Britain have no difficulty in making things and in growing things. It would appear that a word from Marx to the wise is sufficient. As for the specter of maldistribution and a fearsome world struggle for markets that Marx also associated with the highly productive society, there is reason to believe that the Russian leaders would prefer to take their chances with too much rather than too little.

With the upgrading of the Russian economy has come some degree of political unfreezing and opening up of intercourse with the West. The positive possibilities of these developments, however, have not always been apparent to Western policy-makers. Indeed, some of these political strategists are still acting and reacting as they did back in the Twenties and Thirties. For a long time they held to the view that improvement in the living conditions of the Russian people were inimical to the West and to the cause of freedom in general. They favored an arms race not on military grounds alone but as a means of putting pressure on the Soviet economy, diverting resources and manpower away from Russian consumer needs. Fortunately, this no longer is the predominant view in U.S. government thinking and planning. It is now recognized that a condition of maximum economic stress inside the Soviet Union doesn't decrease the ideological and military danger from Russia but may actually strengthen it. Conversely, upgrading of living conditions—especially in view of the modifications that are required to achieve it—add to the chances for durable peace. The American search for effective disarmament agreements, therefore, is a genuine one.

Meanwhile, a parallel fallacy about the American economy has existed for many years among Soviet planners. For if the United States thought it could crack the Soviet economy by stepping up the arms race, the Soviet Union thought it could crack the American economy by ending it. More recently, however, Soviet leaders appear to be unburdening themselves of that particular fallacy. No longer are they committed to the view that disarmament in the United States would touch off a massive depression. Their economists have undertaken detailed studies of the American economy and now believe that the conversion possibilities are substantial and would offset the downward effects of cutback and dislocation. They realize that the continuation and extension of the nuclear arms race would lead to a holocaust that would be just as real to them as it is to us. And they are less inclined today to see the question of disarmament in terms of ideological or economic gain or loss than they are in terms of their own national survival. In this respect, the changed thinking in both countries provides a broader base for constructive and useful dialogue than has previously existed.

The great hope for the future, as in the past, lies in the fact of change. The question is not whether history is moving in the direction of sparing modern man from nuclear incineration but whether modern man can recognize auspicious change when he sees it.

Chapter VI

Economic Power and Goals

We must meet the world challenge and at the same time permit no stagnation in America. Unless we progress, we regress.
—Dwight D. Eisenhower

The Soviet Government has maintained and continues to maintain that capitalist and socialist systems can peacefully coexist and compete economically with each other.
—Georgi M. Malenkov

In February, 1959, Premier Khrushchev in a radio broadcast told his countrymen: "The capitalist ringleaders are, for the time being, succeeding in keeping around them certain strata of society and even part of the working people. Our Seven-Year Plan is the sun at its highest point which will disperse with its rays the fog of doubt of a certain part of the working people in the capitalist countries about the superiority of the socialist system. We hope that the time will come when the absolute majority of the peoples of the world will recognize that there is but one path for mankind, which desires peace on earth and wants to enjoy the goods of its labor—the path showed by Marx, Engels, and Lenin, the path of building the Communist society."

Nearly five years later, Khrushchev's contention of "the superiority of the socialist system" was most eloquently challenged by President Kennedy in his undelivered Dallas speech, November 22, 1963: "It is clear, therefore, that we are strengthening our security as well as our economy by our recent record increases in national income and output—by surging ahead of most of Western Europe in the rate of business expansion and the margin of corporate profits, by maintaining a more stable level of prices than almost any of our overseas competitors. . . . This nation's total output—which three years ago was at the $500 billion mark—will soon pass $600 billion, for a record rise of over $100 billion in three years. For the first time in history, average factory earnings have exceeded $100 a week. For *the first time in history, corporation profits after taxes—which have risen 43 percent in less than three years—have reached an annual level of $27.4 billion." Let the fact speak for itself: which system— capitalism or socialism—is superior.*

This chapter focuses on economic factors as instruments of competition between the United States and the Soviet Union.

Premier Khrushchev, in his speech delivered to the Ukraine Republic Supreme Soviet in late 1957, prided himself on the phenomenal growth of Soviet economic productivity, urged the Ukrainians to "overtake" and "surpass" the United States in farm production, and reemphasized the great advantage of the socialist system over the capitalist system.

Willard L. Thorp, Professor of Economics at Amherst College, offers a critical examination of the wisdom, purpose, and effectiveness of United States trade restrictions on the Communist bloc, clarifies the nature and extent of Soviet aid programs to underdeveloped countries, which have come to constitute the arena of US-Soviet rivalry, and urges the United States to take a positive approach toward these emerging nations.

Leon M. Herman, Adjunct Professor in the School of International Studies at the American University, points out the aspirations of the Soviet leaders for rapid economic development, examines various criticisms of Soviet economists on their regimented production system, and asserts that, in economic competition with the West, the Soviet leaders "will have to undertake an agonizing reappraisal" of their institutions of forced economic growth.

1. THE TASK OF SURPASSING THE USA*

BY NIKITA S. KHRUSHCHEV

The memorable anniversary of the establishment of Soviet power in the Ukraine is being observed by Soviet men and women

* From *The Current Digest of the Soviet Press*, Vol. 9 (February 5, 1958), pp. 12–17, published weekly at Columbia University by the Joint Committee on Slavic Studies, appointed by the American Council of Learned Societies and the Social Science Research Council. Copyright 1958; reprinted by their permission.

amid a great patriotic upsurge among the peoples of the USSR and further growth in the might of our homeland.

The year 1957, which ends in a few days, has been an anniversary year, the 40th year in the life of the Soviet socialist state. It has been rich in events both in the domestic life of our country and in the international arena. This year has been marked by the successful fulfillment of the historic decisions of the 20th Party Congress, which outlined a magnificent program of communist construction.

The celebration of the 40th anniversary of Great October was a great festive occasion not only for the peoples of the Soviet Union but for all progressive mankind, since the October Socialist Revolution, because it initiated the building of a new world on socialist principles, was an event of world significance.

The 40 years of work by the working class, the peasantry and the intelligentsia and by the peoples of the Soviet Union under the leadership of the Communist Party, which was founded by the great Lenin, have been marked by historic victories. The building of socialism and the successful construction of communism is the principal result of our people's labor effort. All our country's successes are a result of the consistent application of the Leninist policy of the Communist Party of the Soviet Union. The unbreakable unity between the Communist Party and the Soviet people is the inexhaustible wellspring of the creative forces of our Soviet motherland, which is advancing to new communist triumphs. (*Prolonged applause.*)

The enemies of socialism deny the creative abilities of the working class, of the working people, who, having taken power into their own hands, began building life on socialist principles. They advertised in every way the advantages of capitalism over socialism and lauded the merits of "private enterprise," the prime mover of which is profit and gain. But life has refuted their assertions.

The socialist system has proved its great vital force. It has opened up immense possibilities for an economic and cultural upsurge, for development of all the creative forces of the people. As a result of socialist transformations, our country, which before the revolution was backward in comparison with other countries, has been turned into a mighty industrial state in an historically short period of time.

Now even the most diehard enemies of socialism have been obliged to admit that the Soviet Union has scored exceptional successes in the development of industry, agriculture, science and technology, in the technical equipping of the various branches of the national economy and in the training of highly qualified specialists and workers.

The decisions of the 20th Party Congress evoked a fresh surge of energy and creative activity on the part of the working people. All Soviet people are working with tremendous patriotic enthusiasm to realize the Party Congress decisions and to carry out the measures charted by the Communist Party and the Soviet government for the further development of socialist industry, agriculture, science and culture and for increasing the output of consumer goods.

We note with great satisfaction that the period since the 20th Party Congress has been marked by major new successes in the development of our country. (*Applause.*) . . .

All industry in the Soviet Union is on a sharp rise. The reorganization of the management of industry and construction by economic regions, the transfer of the administration of industry and construction to the Union republics, the setting up of economic councils and bringing management into direct, close contact with the enterprises have had a favorable effect on the work of our industry. This is attested to by the work results at enterprises and construction projects throughout the country, and is eloquently attested to by the achievements of the Soviet Ukraine as well. (*Applause.*)

The 1957 plan called for a 7.1% increase in our country's industrial output. The actual growth in industrial output this year will be 10%. (*Applause.*)

It is important to note that in the second half of 1957 industry fulfilled its quotas on a higher level than in the corresponding period of 1956. While last year the third-quarter plan for gross production was fulfilled by 101%, the third-quarter plan for this year was fulfilled by 104%. In October and November of 1956 the plan for industrial output was fulfilled by an average of 103%; the plan for the corresponding period of 1957 was fulfilled by 105%. . . .

Of course, there are still many shortcomings in the work of industry and construction, both in the country as a whole and in the Ukraine. But, contrary to the assertions of the "skeptics," things have gone not worse but much better since the reorganization of the management of industry and construction. (*Applause.*)

The task now is to improve the work of the economic councils, to have them probe more deeply into the work of each enterprise, manage the enterprises effectively, know their needs, and give enterprises and construction projects the necessary assistance in fulfilling national economic tasks. The economic councils have a great deal of work to do in further improving the specialization, integrated mechanization and automation of production, and in improving cooperation among enterprises in order to bring about a substantial rise in labor productivity, expand production and cut unit costs.

A major task of the economic councils is to fill orders from other economic areas promptly and with high-quality goods. It is necessary that our industry fill all orders on time. But the filling of orders for other economic areas must be unflaggingly supervised by the economic councils. We must remember, comrades, that failure to fill these orders on time impedes integration and specialization of industry and harms the planned functioning of the economy. Our industry's fulfillment of all foreign orders promptly and with high-quality goods must be put under the same unflagging supervision.

We are convinced that the heroic working class of the Soviet Union and the workers in the industry of the Ukraine will achieve new and great successes in the continued mighty advance of heavy industry and in the development of all light and food industries. (*Stormy applause.*)

Comrades! Allow me to tell you about certain agricultural problems. It is common knowledge that 1956 was a record year as regards the total grain harvest and grain procurements. This year has been unfavorable because of the drought in a number of areas, particularly in the Volga region, the Urals and some provinces of Kazakhstan. But thanks to the development of the virgin and idle lands, the country has procured approximately as much grain in 1957 as in 1955, while in comparison with 1953 grain procurements have increased 18%, including a 41% increase for wheat. (*Applause.*) . . .

On Dec. 1, 1957, there were 4,200,000 more cattle (including 600,000 more cows), 6,400,000 more pigs and 8,900,000 more sheep on the Soviet Union's collective and state farms than on Dec. 1, 1956.

Along with the growth in the number of livestock, the productivity of animal husbandry has increased markedly; the output of milk, meat, wool and other products has increased.

The Soviet people are gladdened by the agricultural workers' achievements in increasing milk output. . . .

The growth in the output of milk and the considerable rise in the collective and state farms' share of the country's livestock have made it possible to increase milk procurements. The plenary session's decisions called for an increase in milk procurements of no less than 80% in 1960 as compared with 1954. This task has been achieved in three years rather than in six. (*Prolonged applause.*) . . .

All the Union republics have joined in the struggle for a further increase in the output of animal husbandry products. Many collective farms, state farms and entire districts report that they are successfully fulfilling their pledges to obtain 100 or more centners of meat and 400 to 500 centners of milk per 100 hectares of farm land. This attests to the feasibility of our goal and to our agriculture's great potentialities and latent reserves. . . .

The achievements of leading collective farms attest to the fact that the Ukraine has immense latent potentialities for further increasing the production of grain, meat, milk and other farm products. But you also have collective and state farms that are still producing low yields per 100 hectares of land. You pledged to produce not less than 100 centners of meat and 400 centners of milk per 100 hectares of land for the republic as a whole, and not less than 64 centners of meat and 247 centners of milk per 100 hectares for collective farms.

If such results are to be achieved, a great deal of work must still be done, and all collective and state farms must rise to the level of the leading farms. In order to do this it is necessary first of all to improve organizing work in rural areas and to train collective farmers, team and brigade leaders and collective farm chairmen carefully. This must be mentioned since there are still grave shortcomings in your work with people and particularly with the managerial cadres of collective farms. Persistent application of advanced experience and of the discoveries of agricultural science is also necessary.

I wish to say a few words about how the call to overtake the United States in per capita output of animal husbandry products in the next few years should be properly understood. When the Party Central Committee gave its support to the appeal by our leading collective and state farms to overtake the United States in per capita output of animal husbandry products, and in this connection set the task of increasing meat production, for example, by 250%, it had in mind the country as a whole.

But such an average yardstick cannot be applied to the individual republics. Take the Ukraine as an example; collective and state farms and all rural workers must strive to surpass the United States' indices by a considerable margin.

The amount by which the Ukraine must surpass the United States must be calculated. You Ukrainian comrades must not only overtake the United States in the output of animal husbandry products, you must considerably surpass it—perhaps by 100%, or even more. Unquestionably you have every requisite for obtaining much more farm produce per 100 hectares of land than is obtained in the United States. (*Applause.*) . . .

The Party and government express their firm conviction that the glorious collective farm peasantry and all workers in socialist agriculture will continue to struggle selflessly to increase the output of farm products and will make their worthy contribution to the achievement of an abundance of food for the public and raw materials for light industry. (*Stormy applause.*)

There can be no doubt that the collective farmers and Machine and Tractor Stations and state farm employees of the Ukraine, who have often initiated all-Union competition and introduced new work methods in agriculture, will continue to show creative initiative and to march in the front ranks of the struggle for a further advance in agriculture and for full sufficiency of products in the country. (*Stormy applause.*)

Comrades! The Communist Party and the Soviet government have always devoted a great deal of attention to raising the people's living standard. A number of important measures have been taken in recent years to improve the life of the Soviet people and raise the real incomes of workers, employees and collective farmers.

Our country's national income more than doubled between 1950 and 1957. During the same period the number of workers and employees increased by nearly 14,000,000. Real wages of workers and employees and the income of the peasants have grown considerably during this period.

It must be said that an increase in the working people's real earnings can be achieved in essentially two ways: by reducing the retail prices of consumer goods or by increasing monetary wages, pensions, benefits and other cash income.

As is known, between 1947 and 1954 we mainly followed the path of reducing retail prices. Today state retail prices are 2.3 times lower than in 1947 [i.e., they are 43.48% of 1947 prices], while the price of bread, meat, butter and certain other necessities has been cut even more. This year the prices of a number of articles of mass consumption have also been reduced. We will continue to carry out such measures. (*Applause.*)

It is necessary to bear in mind, however, that a reduction of retail prices is of greatest benefit to those who buy the most, i.e., the higher-paid groups of workers and employees, while the lower-paid groups benefit to a lesser extent.

We proceed from the socialist principle of payment according to the quantity and quality of work and, naturally, cannot allow levelling in wages. But the gap in wages between the higher- and lower-paid groups must be reduced; and as time goes on this gap will be progressively narrowed by raising the wages of the lower-paid categories of working people and by increasing pensions. (*Applause.*). . .

The Communist Party and the Soviet government will continue to strive to raise the people's living standards, will apply the policy of reducing the gap between the maximum and minimum wage levels. We must bear in mind that a rise in the living standard of the working people, an increase in wages and further reduction of prices all depend on the increase in labor productivity. There is direct dependence here, and this must be made clear to workers, employees, collective farmers and all the working people of our country.

In conformity with the resolutions of the 20th Party Congress, enterprises began a conversion to a shorter workday starting with the second half of 1956. Donets Basin coal miners were put on a shorter workday in the fourth quarter of 1956. Workers and employees in the mining, metallurgical and coke and chemical enterprises of ferrous metallurgy are presently being shifted to a shorter workday.

During the Sixth Five-Year Plan all workers and employees will switch over to a seven-hour day, and workers in a number of jobs to a six-hour day. Reducing the workday at a time when we have a growing need for manpower is yet another proof of the unflagging concern of the Party and government for the well-being of our country's working people. . . .

In recent years the collective and state farms have achieved a significant rise in output. As a result, procurements of farm products from collective and state farms have increased, permitting the state to lower the quotas for obligatory deliveries from the households of collective farmers, workers and employees.

You know that the Party Central Committee and the Council of Ministers adopted a resolution freeing all the households of collective farmers, workers and employees from all obligatory deliveries of farm products to the state beginning with 1958. This means that between 17,000,000 and 18,000,000 households of collective farmers, workers and employees will be able to sell their farm products at more advantageous prices through the state and collective farm-cooperative trade networks instead of turning them over to the state in the form of obligatory deliveries; as a result, they will increase their earnings by more than 3,000,000,000 rubles. This measure will also make possible a reduction in the number of employees in the procurement apparatus. . . .

Comrades! The 20th Party Congress set the task of working out a long-range plan for development of the national economy to cover several five-year plan periods. Preliminary estimates by officials of the planning agencies show that within the next 15 years the Soviet Union not only can overtake, but can surpass the present gross output of the most important types of industrial goods in the United States of America. Of course the U.S.A. can also move ahead somewhat, but thanks to the higher rate of growth of our industry, we can still overtake and surpass it.

All the necessary conditions have now been created in the Soviet Union for economic development to proceed at an ever more rapid pace. . . . Our present level of investment in the national economy is 14 times what it was in the years of the First Five-Year Plan, and investment in industry is more than 15 times what it was. . . .

We are moving ahead considerably faster than the capitalist countries. In the 40 years from 1918 to 1957 the average annual rate of increase in industrial output in the U.S.S.R. was 10% while in the United States it was 3.2%, in Britain 1.9% and in France 3.2%. . . .

In the prewar year of 1940 we produced 18,300,000 tons of steel and the United States produced 60,800,000 tons, i.e., somewhat more than three times as much. As a result of the losses we suffered in the war, our steel output in 1954 dropped to 12,300,000 tons, while in the United States it stood at 72,300,000 tons, six times as much.

In 1957 the U.S.S.R. will produce 51,000,000 tons of steel and the United States about 106,000,000 tons, i.e., twice as much.

There is every reason to assume that in steel output, just as in the output of other industrial goods, we can overtake and surpass the United States in a very brief historical period.   (*Prolonged applause.*)

Thus the successful accomplishment of the basic economic task of the U.S.S.R.—to overtake and surpass the principal capitalist countries in per capita industrial output—is becoming a real actuality. (*Applause.*) . . .

The economy, science and technology have reached a level of development in the Soviet Union that now enables us to develop light industry at a faster pace without impairing the country's defenses and the further expansion of heavy industry, and, in particular, to produce footwear and fabrics for the people in quantities that will make possible the full satisfaction, within the next five to seven years, of the people's growing demand for these goods.

All the Union republics will have to do a great deal of work to accomplish the tasks set forth in the estimates of the long-range plan. We must make considerably better use of available reserves in all branches of the national economy, persistently raise labor productivity, practice the strictest economy, show true thrift in all matters and fight against extravagance and waste.

I wish to stress once again that a steady rise in labor productivity is the main source of the accumulations we need for the further development of industry, agriculture, science and culture; for consolidating the country's defenses and raising the people's living standard. A rise in labor productivity is the fundamental question of the development of a socialist economy and the attention of all our workers must be constantly directed toward it.

In evaluating the work of industrial enterprises, construction projects, M.T.S. and collective and state farms, account must always be taken of how labor productivity is being raised, how the expenditure of labor per unit of output is being reduced, how the unit cost of production is being lowered and how quality is being improved.

Comrades! One of the greatest achievements of our people in the years of Soviet rule is that we showed the entire world that only socialism opens up the widest possibilities for tempestuous and comprehensive development of the spiritual life of society, opens boundless expanses for the development of science, technology, literature and art and for the development of the people's talents and gifts.

As a result of the cultural revolution accomplished in our country, millions of people, formerly deprived of education, enlightenment and knowledge, have in Soviet times been exposed to the great treasure of culture and have become active creators of culture.

The outstanding successes of the Soviet Union in the sphere of culture are most strikingly manifested in the large-scale training of highly qualified specialists.

While Soviet higher educational institutions are graduating 250,000 to 260,000 persons annually, including 70,000 to 75,000 engineers, the United States of America, with about the same size graduating class, graduates only 25,000 to 26,000 engineers, and other countries even fewer.

The pride of our people is the remarkable cadres of Soviet intelligentsia—reared by socialist society and trained by the Communist Party in the spirit of loyalty to Marxism-Leninism and to their socialist motherland and the people.

Our people are rightly proud of the outstanding achievements of Soviet science and technology. Soviet scientists and industrial personnel have created high-speed computing machines, have elaborated new principles of accelerating elementary particles and have developed powerful accelerators; they have surpassed the scientists of other countries in this important work.

It was in the Soviet Union that the world's first atomic power station was built, the world's first atomic ice-breaker, the "Lenin," was launched, and substantial advances were made in the peaceful uses of atomic energy, and first-rate passenger planes powered by jet and turboprop engines were produced. The development of an intercontinental ballistic rocket is an outstanding achievement.

The successes of Soviet industry, science and technology are another conclusive demonstration of the great advantage of the socialist system over the capitalism system; they have demonstrated how socialist society brings out the inexhaustible forces and potentialities of the people.

Soviet scientists, designers and workers have performed the greatest of feats, launching the artificial earth satellites. The launching of the satellites is the work of the Soviet people, who, under socialism, are making fairy tales into reality. By their heroic labors the people have created a mighty industry, trained remarkable cadres in all spheres of economic and cultural construction, and raised science and technology to unprecedented heights.

Not long ago at all we were considered backward. How much ink and paper was wasted by bourgeois scribblers! Many representatives of the capitalist world spouted streams of lies and slander to the effect that there is no freedom of creativity in the Soviet land. Who today will believe these fables when Soviet satellites are circling our planet, proclaiming to all the world what the creative genius of our people, freed from the shackles of capitalism, can do? (*Stormy applause.*)

Not long ago at all the inordinately boastful American reactionaries, loudly advertising their preparations to launch an earth satellite, were prepared to gloat over our backwardness.

But, as the popular saying goes, "Don't cry 'hup' until you've made your jump." (*Animation in the hall, applause.*) But they often cry "hup" and brag ahead of time. This time again they embarrassed themselves before the whole world.

The Soviet people give due recognition to the scientists, designers and workers who have gladdened our country with outstanding achievement. . . .

Comrades!

The talented Ukrainian people are making their own notable contribution to our common treasurehouse of socialist science, technology and culture. More than 1,250,000 specialists with a higher or secondary specialized education are presently employed in the Ukraine's national economy.

The culture of the Ukrainian people, national in form and socialist in content, is flourishing. Ukraine writers, artists, sculptors, composers, film makers and men of other creative professions have produced many vivid works that have enriched Soviet and world literature and art.

The Ukraine's unions of writers, artists and composers have demonstrated that they are ideologically stable, close-knit collectives that are fighting consistently to carry out Party policy in literature and the arts. Their principled stand in the struggle against unsound sentiments and tendencies has exerted a great positive influence on raising the level of the ideological and creative life of our writers, artists and composers.

Allow me to express confidence in the fact that Ukraine scientists, cultural figures, writers, artists and composers will gladden our country with remarkable new discoveries and works, and will continue actively to assist our party in its ideological struggle and in the communist education of the Soviet people.   (*Prolonged applause.*)

Comrades! The building of communism is now not only our great ideal but a direct, practical task of Soviet society, a task in which are engaged millions and millions of toilers of city and countryside—all the Soviet people, under the leadership of our Leninist Communist Party.

Marching with us are the peoples of the Chinese People's Republic and all the countries of the mighty socialist camp; with us are millions of our friends in all countries and on all the continents.

The working people abroad note with tremendous admiration the historic triumphs that the Soviet Union has achieved in the years of Soviet rule.

Under the leadership of the Communist Party the Soviet people are accomplishing tremendous tasks in building communist society. In the name of achieving this great goal our party is mobilizing the creative efforts of the working class, the collective farm peasantry and the intelligentsia. Our party's general line, expressing the fundamental interests of the people, is embodied in the 20th Party Congress decisions and the subsequent Party and government decrees. Every Soviet man turns with boundless love and warm gratitude to the Communist Party, the experienced leader, inspirer and organizer of communist construction. . . .

In the struggle for the great cause of building communism the Soviet people are rallying even closer around the Communist Party of the Soviet Union and its Central Committee, which carries high the triumphant banner of Marxism-Leninism.   (*Stormy applause.*)

In the fifth decade of its existence the Land of the Soviets has entered into the full flower of its mighty forces. The Soviet Union now has every requirement for further rapid development of productive forces, for bettering the people's life and raising their cultural level.

Our successes in economic and cultural construction, in science and technology and in foreign policy are genuinely great, and this causes joy and legitimate pride among Soviet people. But the strength of our party lies in the fact that it constantly looks ahead and mobilizes the people to meet ever new tasks. That is why in our work conceit, complacency and an uncritical evaluation of our activities cannot be tolerated. . . .

The national economic plan for 1958, approved by the recently concluded session of the U.S.S.R. Supreme Soviet, envisages a new advance of industry and agriculture and a further increase in the people's well-being and culture. Successful accomplishment of this plan will be an important landmark along the path of communist construction. . . .

Allow me, comrades, on the eve of the new year of 1958 to wish the working people of the Ukraine Soviet Socialist Republic further success in all spheres of economic, political and cultural life. (*Stormy applause.*)

2. AMERICAN POLICY AND THE SOVIET ECONOMIC OFFENSIVE*

BY WILLARD L. THORP

In the early years after the war, the Russians expanded their ideological exports while pursuing a policy of economic isolationism whenever more tangible goods were involved. Wherever they could make themselves heard, they challenged United States concepts of trade and aid as exploitation and imperialism, but they did not compete in substance. Within its own self-imposed limitations, American foreign economic policy was relatively free to engage in trade and aid with the countries not in the Soviet bloc.

The partial oxidation of the Iron Curtain by Bulganin and Khrushchev has not only made possible some degree of controlled artistic, athletic and scientific interchange, but it appears also to have important economic implications. Soviet bloc economic negotiators are busy in both the industrial and the underdeveloped countries. Arrangements are being made for the expanded bartering of commod-

* From *The Soviet Union, 1922–1962,* Philip E. Mosely, ed. (New York: Praeger, 1963), pp. 324–335. Copyright © 1963 by Council on Foreign Relations, Inc.; reprinted by their permission.

ities, the extension of credit and the provision of technical assistance. At the same time, American policy in this area has become even more hesitant and vacillating, awaiting the results of half a dozen new Administrative reappraisals and Congressional investigations.

The background of the Soviet economic offensive is relatively simple. In 1937, the Soviet Union carried on 96 percent of its limited foreign trade with countries now in the free world. Taking all the Eastern European countries as a group, their prewar trade with the present free world was more than 85 percent of their total trade.

The postwar period witnessed not only a political convergence of the Soviet Union and her new satellites but also an economic integration. By the end of the postwar decade, the trade pattern was completely altered. After eliminating the effect of changes in price level, the volume of their trade with each other has expanded more than 2.5 times while their trade with the rest of the world was less than half its prewar level. Thus in 1954 only 20 to 30 percent of the trade of most Eastern European countries (21 percent for the U.S.S.R.) was with the rest of the world. Within the Eastern European group, the Soviet Union had emerged as the most important trading partner. Even by 1948, its exports to the other countries in the bloc had multiplied by 25 times and imports by 10 times, compared to the very low prewar levels.

The basis of this new trade pattern was primarily the effort to develop the Soviet bloc as a self-contained economic unit. There were four reasons for this. First was the concentration on military strength and development, an objective which obviously involves reducing economic dependence upon unreliable (foreign) sources of strategic raw materials and finished goods. Second was the Iron Curtain policy, with its effort to reduce contacts with the Western world to a minimum in order to insure discipline and acceptance of the régime. Third was the reliance upon economic planning and the consequent effort to eliminate those uncertainties which are introduced by dependence upon transactions with buyers and sellers beyond the control of the planners. Finally, many of the arguments were applied to the bloc as a whole which are now being advanced for a "common market" in Europe. At first the plans were essentially nationalist, but more recently special emphasis has been given to the desirability of organizing to permit large-scale production and specialization, thereby increasing productivity for the group as a whole.

Even had there not been internal reasons for developing this Soviet-bloc autarky, other forces would have contributed to reducing their trade with the free world. Their industrial expansion and lagging agriculture ran counter to the reconstruction of the prewar trade pattern when they exported food and feedstuffs in return for manufactured goods, largely consumer items. Furthermore, the imposition of strategic trade restrictions by Western countries put obstacles in the way of trade in those very items for which presumably these countries had the greatest demand.

For all these reasons, in spite of economic expansion within the Soviet bloc and rapid recovery and growth in the free world, the trade between the two declined from a not very high postwar peak in 1948 to a low point in the first half of 1953. Since then, trade between the bloc and the rest of the world has more than doubled and is still expanding rapidly, although it is not large in volume. Trade with the bloc countries, which was 7.4 percent of the free world's trade in 1938, was only 2.3 percent in 1954 and 2.6 percent in 1955. And it is still true that the countries within the bloc do about 75 percent of their trade with each other.

The increases in trade with the free world since 1953 are not merely random economic variables. They represent a definite shift in policy and emphasis. There has been an even greater increase in the volume of talk by Soviet leaders, broadcasting their desire for increased trade with the free world. This recent development is clearly a part of the new post-Stalin picture. It is consistent with the so-called peace offensive and the call for reduced international tensions. But it seems to be more than an adaptation to the new mood. It looks as though the past occasional and insignificant use of economic means to achieve foreign objectives (*i.e.,* a shipload of wheat to Italy at a critical time) is being replaced by a positive utilization of foreign economic policy as a major instrument in the struggle to win friends and influence people.

On the more strictly economic side, the new structure of trade is suggestive. There is a definite tendency to expand exports of manufacturers in exchange for imports of food and raw materials, and this would seem to correspond to the productivity record in the Communist countries. There may therefore be some economic logic behind the expansion of trade as well as its use to further the continuing political objectives of Soviet Communism.

So far as Western Europe and the United States are concerned, the main expression of trade policy toward the bloc in recent years has been the operation of the so-called strategic controls. While American economic foreign policy in general has sought to lower trade barriers and encourage trade expansion, trade with the bloc countries has been restricted with respect to items which might contribute to Communist military strength. Furthermore, so far as the United States is concerned, the reductions in tariffs negotiated under the Trade Agreements Act, usually generalized to other countries in accordance with most-favored-nation commitments, have not been extended to countries in the Soviet bloc. Nevertheless, there is a considerable area for trade in so-called "peaceful trade" items not covered in the restrictive trade program. However, although a wide network of trade agreements has been negotiated, the volume of trade actually achieved has been relatively small.

Strategic controls originated at the time when it became apparent that we were engaged in an arms race with a dangerous adversary. We had demobilized while the Russians had not, and our immediate defense lay in the atomic bomb, obviously a temporary advantage. Military strength is relative, and it was important to gain time by delaying Russian progress. Thus the policy was adopted of restricting trade in goods which might contribute to Soviet military strength. In general, the other industrial countries joined in the program, although its specific application was a constant source of friction. That it was incorporated as a condition for the receipt of United States assistance made it an even greater irritant. Nevertheless, it undoubtedly created some delays in the Russian military program and helped hold the line until the NATO defenses could be developed.

Assuming that there will continue to be an embargo on actual military items, additional restrictions no longer can be said to have much importance for our security. Whatever bottlenecks were created by the original policy have undoubtedly been broken by this time. In fact, it was clear at the beginning that one of the results of the restrictive policy would be to force the Soviet bloc to develop its own production of the prohibited items. With such a primary position in planning given to the military, it is hard to conceive that the Soviet bloc has left itself in any way dependent upon foreign trade to meet its military requirements.

If the significance of the strategic controls in terms of military requirements is reduced to a minimum, there still remains the possibility of using controls to hamper the general economic progress of the countries in the bloc. However, this cuts both ways. From the economic point of view, it is impossible to conclude that trade in one direction is more valuable than trade in the other. How can one say that fuel and raw materials flowing out of Eastern Europe are more or less valuable than wheat and tobacco flowing in, or than small ships, or even than electric motors?

The changing pattern of trade is clearly relevant to this argument for continuing controls. In 1954, the increase in bloc imports was largely in consumer goods—food, tobacco, textiles and paper. In 1955, imports of consumer goods held level and the chief increases were in ships, iron and steel, and nonferrous metals. The imports of machinery, which had been declining in earlier years, did not increase in 1955 even though there was some relaxation of the strategic controls by the Western countries in August 1954.

The largest export items from the bloc were coal (although in 1955 United States shipments of coal to Western Europe were larger than those from Eastern Europe by two and a half times), petroleum and petroleum products, and timber, but iron and steel products and machinery exports are increasing rapidly. In 1955, for the first time, Eastern European exports of manufactured products to Western Europe exceeded food exports. However, the two categories together were less than fuel and raw material exports. The new pattern which is developing, particularly in relation to overseas trade, is the export by the bloc of manufactured goods and the import of foodstuffs and raw materials.

In the light of the present situation, it seems more appropriate that efforts should be made by Western Europe and the United States to increase their trade with the bloc, particularly with the satellite countries. This can have much more than economic importance. When Yugoslavia pulled out from under Soviet domination, its most difficult problem was created by the trade embargo immediately placed upon it by the Soviet bloc. In 1948, 50.7 percent of its exports and 45.6 percent of its imports came from Eastern Europe. From then until 1954, its trade with the bloc was zero. The success of its effort to throw off the Moscow yoke depended in large part upon how quickly its trade could be reoriented toward the free world. This was no easy matter, and it was only because the United States, the United Kingdom and France gave special assistance that "Titoism" was possible. Similar assistance may be used again to encourage satellite independence, but this can be only a temporary substitute for the development of trade channels.

The Soviet Union clearly recognizes the importance of binding the satellites to itself and to each other by strong economic ties. Drew Middleton reported in *The New York Times,* shortly after the political developments in Poland, that the Soviet Union had offered to buy the Polish coal now going to the West. Clearly, this is an effort to strengthen the economic interdependence of Poland and the U.S.S.R. Furthermore, in the Soviet Union's policy statement of October 30, 1956, on relations with other Communist nations, the subject is raised but not resolved, by the statement that "the Soviet Government is ready to discuss, together with the governments of other Socialist states, measures insuring the further development of economic ties between Socialist countries."

It will not be an easy matter to make any substantial break in the volume of intra-bloc trade. The more recent East-West trade agreements, negotiated, to be sure, before the unrest broke out in the satellites, all provide for increases in trade, and the early months of 1956 show both imports and exports up by about 15 percent above early 1955. While there have been talks of very large increases (the Russian tourist-team talked in London of a fivefold increase in five years), it is difficult to envisage what the bloc might supply in such a case. Since this trade is such a small proportion of free Europe's trade, it probably could easily be supplied on the Western side, but the necessary reverse flow is more difficult to envisage. Foodstuffs are out of the picture, but increases in petroleum and coal may be possible, as well as the kind of diversified trade with which countries such as Czechoslovakia are familiar. In short, there seems to be little possibility for any spectacular developments in trade between Western and Eastern Europe, but such increases as are possible should now be encouraged as at least one step in the process of liberation.

Two fears which have often been expressed are that the Soviet bloc might use any significant trade position to disturb and disrupt markets, and that expanded trade might create dependence upon it by countries that are now free. So far as market disturbance is concerned, such leverage is largely on the selling side of the market and is a matter of magnitudes and alternatives. When Soviet manganese was withdrawn from the world market, it did create a shortage and there was a delay before other sources such as India were able to fill the gap. On the other hand, the Western purchasers of Polish coal have always known that American coal was readily available if the bargaining became too difficult. Russian and Rumanian petroleum are also easily replaceable, assuming normal channels are open. To be sure, sudden dumping on a market can cause short-run confusion, but this might raise a serious problem only if it took the form of dumping large quantities of precious metals. A large gold flow, not a likely development, might conceivably lead to inflation in countries with weak monetary controls.

There are a few countries for whose products the Soviet bloc provides an important market, notably Iceland and Finland. These are both special cases and the free world has perhaps been somewhat negligent in permitting them to slip so far into the Soviet economic orbit. In 1953, after desperate efforts to find other markets, Iceland began to sell its fish products in quantity to the Soviet bloc, and the volume and percentage of its exports to the bloc have increased each year since then. Finland's trade was directed to the Soviet bloc in large part by its reparations commitments. Although its exports to the bloc were larger in 1955 than ever before, the proportion of its trade which this volume represented has declined somewhat since the peak in 1953.

There are two other countries in the free world where one can expect that trade with Eastern Europe may soon reach the 20 percent mark, Austria and Yugoslavia. The signing of the Austrian State Treaty in May 1955 was followed by a payments agreement relating to former German assets and by a series of trade agreements. As a matter of fact, it may well be that most of any apparent statistical increase in Austrian exports to the bloc will be merely the explicit recognition of unrecorded exports during the Soviet occupation. However, of all the Western European countries, Austria had the greatest Eastern European trade before the war and is still far below those earlier percentages.

In the case of Yugoslavia, after a period of orientation toward the Soviet bloc, trade relations were completely severed in late 1948. Trade was resumed in 1954 and increased rapidly in 1955. Larger quotas plus substantial Soviet credits augur a further substantial increase in 1956. Some of Yugoslavia's traditional exports, such as fruit, vegetables and tobacco, were never easily marketed in Western

European markets and her trade with the West has had to be supported by grants and credits.

For Western Europe as a whole, trade with Eastern Europe (excluding trade between West and East Germany) is still exceedingly small—3.4 percent of its imports and 3.2 percent of its exports, less than half the prewar figures.

In the special cases described above, the problem for the free world is one of providing alternatives—not necessarily alternatives which need to be used but options which are there as a protection against increasing dependence and the threat of coercion. And the same considerations, directed at the satellites, would argue for the effort to increase their trade with the free world.

II

The new economic policy has been much more spectacular in relation to the underdeveloped countries. Although the expansion of trade with countries supplying food and raw material is explained by some analysts in terms of economic advantage, the fact that this new interest in trade is not solely an economic matter was made clear by Mr. Khrushchev in speaking to a group of visiting United States Senators: "We value trade least for economic reasons and most for political purposes as a means of promoting better relations between our countries." Although he was talking about United States-Soviet relations, this pronouncement takes on even greater significance when related to the underdeveloped countries, where the Communists have their greatest hope for further accessions to their ranks. With this in mind, a whole series of new policies has been put into practice by the Soviet bloc.

One technique has been to provide a market for goods which are proving difficult to sell in the free world. The purchase of fish from Iceland, rice from Burma and cotton from Egypt are all illustrations of this approach. In 1955, the Sino-Soviet bloc purchased more than 10 percent of the exports of nine countries: Iceland (27.8 percent), Egypt (26.7), Finland (25.8), Turkey (21.8), Iran (15.2), Yugoslavia (13.8), Burma (12.0), Austria (10.2) and Afghanistan (estimated at 50 percent). Only five countries purchased as much as 10 percent from the bloc: Finland (27.0), Hong Kong (24.2), Iceland (22.2), Turkey (18.3) and Afghanistan (exact percent not known). These are important percentages, many of which are still rising, but they still do not indicate that dominance over any considerable area is being achieved through trade.

The Soviet effort to expand economic relations with the underdeveloped countries has involved not only trade but also credits, technical assistance, trade fairs, technical exchange, trade missions and propaganda. The most common trade pattern is the exchange of primary products for manufactured goods on an intergovernmental basis. In addition, credits have been extended on an expanding scale. Credit agreements concluded during 1955 amounted to nearly $600 millions, most of which went to Yugoslavia, Egypt, Afghanistan and India. These credits involved low interest rates, long periods of repayment and sometimes arrangements for compensation in kind, as in the case of Egyptian cotton. In addition to credit, substantial technical assistance has been made available, ranging from aid in oil exploration (India) to the setting up of a technical institute in Rangoon and a 100-bed hospital in Kabul.

These new programs are not to be regarded lightly. To be sure, the members of the Soviet bloc would probably be embarrassed if all their offers were accepted but they do have the capacity to carry out substantial programs. In fact, they could probably equal our present levels of non-defense-support aid to the underdeveloped countries if they should determine to do so. Of course, the extension of substantial credits in any one year cannot be compared with an actual flow of trade, since the credit usually relates to shipments to be made over a period of several years. The Soviet bloc is starting from a very low level of trade with most underdeveloped countries. However, its emphasis is on support of economic development and this is undoubtedly the area of greatest political impact.

The political values are clearly uppermost. The economic effects are decidedly marginal. By expanding trade, they may even improve the position of their own consumers by obtaining rice for a product such as cement. By exporting capital, they may slow down their own rate of expansion a little or even delay the rate at which their growth is reflected in the standard of living, but neither of these will clearly appear to their citizens as a calculated and explicit burden. For various reasons, they can easily send more technicians abroad than can we under our present procedures. Furthermore, their programs often have more appeal than ours, even if they may be less sensible in terms of the allocation of resources. They may do the more conspicuous or symbolic project, such as paving the streets in Kabul, or the more impressive, such as building a steel mill in India. And always there is the steady beat of propaganda asserting that Soviet programs are disinterested, without strings, while Western programs are militaristic, imperialistic and set about with conditions.

What is the basis for this new Soviet activity? One can of course find many self-serving declarations by the Russian leaders. Marx originally predicted the revolution as the result of the explosion of misery and clearly the present-day Communists are not acting on that basis, for assistance interferes with Marx's economic determinism. Nor can they be operating upon the American thesis that improvement will deter the embrace of Communism. There is very little evidence that the Slavic temperament or the Soviet rulers have ever relied on gratitude as an important source of motivation. But they always have placed great weight on economic factors. Perhaps this new policy is simply a combination of a desire to demonstrate the economic strength of the Communist bloc and an effort to establish closer economic ties as a basis for political rapprochement. From our point of view, it would appear to imply a recognition that the American programs, which took their shape in the first five years after the War, were sufficiently effective and successful to require some counteraction.

The problems already mentioned with respect to Iceland and Finland appear also among the underdeveloped countries. In several instances, the Soviet bloc has been able to inject itself by purchasing commodities not easily marketed in the free world. In the cases of cotton, rubber and rice, American developments contributed to the marketing difficulties of the underdeveloped countries, and Egypt, Ceylon and Burma found outlets in the Soviet bloc. All these arrangements were more or less barter deals and they obtained manufactured goods which they wanted in exchange for their own surpluses. In strictly economic terms, such arrangements cannot be automatically censured. The bartering of commodities for which there is no market in the free world can be a definite economic gain provided useful commodities are obtained in exchange. Furthermore, assistance presently available to the underdeveloped countries is not at the limit of their absorptive capacity. Such aid and assistance as can come from the Soviet bloc (and it is likely to prove disappointing over time) will add to the resources available for economic development.

This having been said, there appears to be no justification for adopting a nonchalant view of the new Soviet offensive. The great danger, of course, is that some countries may get into the position where economic pressure can be applied as a method of obtaining political concessions. As in the case of countries in Western Europe, the amount of leverage which can be obtained from economic ties is related in large part to the degree to which alternatives are readily available. If economic opportunities and assistance are readily available from the West, then the danger is less one of coercion and is reduced to the level of contact and persuasion.

This new situation has a real bearing upon our own policy of economic assistance. We may well find ourselves in the difficult position of competing against a fairly secretive competitor, and be dependent upon the beneficiary for our information or misinformation about the score (as in the case of Egypt and the Aswan Dam). We can of course withdraw from the scene or make it an all-or-none issue, but neither course is likely to improve our international relations. In the last analysis, the consequence of the new Soviet offensive should be to improve the performance of the competitors. So long as we were the main source of economic aid, we could function with a kind of positive and magisterial assurance. But now, even more than before, we must review our methods and procedures to see whether or not we can do a better job of it.

We still have substantial assets in our hands. We can outbid the Soviet bloc with economic goods and services whenever we wish to do so. In one area, that of foodstuffs, we have surpluses where they are hard pressed. In fact, our recent programs for agricultural disposal have indicated one promising way of contributing to economic development. Unfortunately, the fact that our internal political discussion of this problem has been in terms of getting rid of surpluses rather than contributing to economic development has created the notion in the beneficiary countries that they are performing a service for us rather than receiving assistance. And the fact that the citizens in the recipient country pay for the products in their local currency conceals the fact that our action is creating a fund for economic development which would otherwise not be available to the government. Perhaps this is merely a matter of public education, both at home and abroad. Since our own reports are in terms of how much surplus we have managed to dispose of, how can we expect the program to be put in its proper perspective? The agricultural disposal program suggests that the weakness in our assistance programs is less in what they are than in how they are done and what they are believed to be.

The centralized character of Soviet operation gives it certain advantages in developing the assistance aspect of foreign policy. There is no public debate involving the antecedents, present performance and future prospects of the prospective beneficiary. There is no framework fixed by legislation within which each operating act must fit. There is no limitation with respect to the period of time to be covered by a commitment. And people and goods can be coöpted without due process of law. To be sure, we are convinced that the development of individualism, the review of public policy by the people and their representatives, and the operation of government within a process of checks and balances are all essential to democracy. That this may lead to delays, unfortunate publicity and inflexibility is a price we have always been willing to pay in dealing with domestic problems. But it does raise difficulties for the detailed operation of foreign policy, and we should be ingenious enough to find ways and means of reducing the obstacles which we continually place in our own way.

It does not now appear that the new programs will place the Soviet Union in a position within the next few years to take over political control through economic domination, except possibly in the case of Afghanistan. Yet it is still quite likely that the new policies may strengthen its political position and possibly weaken that of the Western countries. However, this is clearly the objective of the new total policy and not merely of the new "aid through trade" programs.

In the ideological competition, Soviet policy now looks toward a great expansion in contacts. Trade and technical assistance will contribute added opportunities for Communist enthusiasts to spread their ideas. That more Communist propaganda will be loose in the world adds to the danger. However, the important impact of the new economic programs may be less in terms of the personnel which goes along with them than in the encouragement that these programs will give to those already in the country with a tendency to lean toward the left.

If our basic concern is to make it possible for the underdeveloped countries to maintain their independence, giving them freedom to design their own future in so far as any nation is ever able to do so, we must be concerned not only about political ties but also about economic independence. This involves two considerations—enough economic progress so that internal pressures do not force them to turn to a dictatorship of the extreme right or left, and sufficient economic alternatives so that they do not become exposed to economic coercion. These are not negative goals, but essential bases for the development of free nations. Perhaps the most important objective for American policy must be to convince the underdeveloped countries that our interest is not in using them as pawns in the cold war, but rather in supporting their freedom and assisting in their own development.

3. THE LIMITS OF THE FORCED ECONOMIC GROWTH IN THE USSR*

BY LEON M. HERMAN

I

Official economic doctrine in the Soviet Union continues to hold fast to the view that growth conquers everything. A rapid rise in the level of economic output remains the magic key to the solution of all problems facing the Soviet Union, large and small alike. First of all, of course, economic growth at the highest possible rate remains an indispensable goal, in the official viewpoint, if the USSR is to be assured a firm position in the forefront of major world powers. There was surely no doubt in Stalin's mind that only a forced pace of growth in the economic capabilities of the Soviet state could prevent a dangerous backward drift in the international power position of Soviet Russia. This theme, as we know, was utilized by the former dictator to the hilt in his fierce drive to mobilize the physical and human resources of his country, and to motivate the political elite, for an all-out campaign against the strategic threat to the survival of the state that he considered to be inherent in economic backwardness.

Nor is this, from the viewpoint of the Soviet leaders, the only pot

* From *World Politics*, Vol. 16 (April, 1964), pp. 407–417. Reprinted by permission of the Princeton University Press.

of gold at the end of the rainbow of economic growth. By displaying to the world a unique record of performance in this respect, the Russian leadership also hopes to persuade world public opinion to equate communism with economic progress. In a world in which the swamp of poverty continues to be the natural habitat of the mass of people, such a reputation would indeed be extremely helpful toward winning a large following for the ideology of communism. In the less-developed countries, above all, this particular feature of the Soviet social order—namely, rapid economic growth—has always been expected by the Soviet leadership to have its most telling historic effect.

There is still another type of objective that the Soviet Union has consciously pursued through its policy of forcing the expansion of its basic industrial capacities at the highest possible tempo. The Communist hierarchy has long anticipated that continued spectacular performance on the part of the Soviet Union in the sphere of economic growth would exercise a demoralizing effect upon the advanced industrial nations of the West. Thus, for example, one "inevitable" outcome of continued Soviet success on the "production front" has always been expected to be an increase in the discontent of the industrial proletariat in the capitalist world. Like Stalin before him, Khrushchev continues to draw inspiration from this enduring Soviet hope. A typical passage from an inspirational address that he delivered to a meeting of Soviet writers and artists articulates it as follows: "Many bourgeois politicians are frankly saying that they are frightened by the rate of growth of Soviet industry, frightened by the influence of the Soviet example on the workers of the whole world. And you and I know very well how convincing our example is to the minds of the workers of all countries."[1]

Internally, too, Soviet politicians have counted heavily upon rapid economic growth as a potential corrective force that would, among other things, ultimately relieve the all too visible strains and stresses in the economic structure. Since all serious tensions in the economy, in the official view, are generated in one way or another by the distortive pressure of physical shortages, it follows that a rapidly expanding scale of production will in time provide the appropriate cure. With the aid of so powerful a panacea, Soviet planners have believed, the Soviet economy will inevitably "outgrow" all the familiar disorders of its own "infantile" stage of development.

[1] *Kommunist,* No. 12 (1957), II.

This central objective of forced economic growth has been vigorously pursued in the USSR for some three and a half decades—since the late 1920's, to be exact. An objective of this kind has, of necessity, its own conditions of fulfillment. In freely choosing a maximum annual rate of growth as their main goal in the economic sphere, the Soviet rulers thereby committed themselves to a number of inescapable conditions of economic organization. They were bound to (a) a highly centralist policy of decision-making in regard to the proportion of saving and direction of investment; (b) the restriction of consumption in the city and village to a low but tolerable level; (c) the deliberate channeling of the lion's share of labor, material, and capital to the primary, growth-inducing branches of industrial production; and (d) the administrative manipulation from the center of large numbers of production managers at the local level.

In turn, this commitment to a method of administrative allocation of resources, firmly controlled from the center, has over the years given rise to a distinctive set of economic institutions that have become the hallmark of the Soviet production system. The Soviet leaders eventually settled upon these institutions, by means of trial and error, as being most responsive, dependable, and generally suitable for their chosen purposes. They are now in fact so firmly implanted in the economic soil of the USSR, as we know from the recent attempts at administrative reform, that the leaders themselves are finding it difficult to carry out any material changes in the basic institutional landscape.

To name just a few, these institutions include a centralized mechanism both for planning production levels in great detail, and for allocating the major physical inputs of the economic process; an arbitrary price system that frustrates most attempts at normal communication between the planners and the enterprise managers; a massive, open-ended bonus system that makes it possible for managers to get their premium pay while, in fact, they evade the true intent of the center; a lack of lateral lines of communication in the economy; and an absence of meaningful economic sanctions for the wasteful use of resources or the violation of established supply schedules.

Readers of the Western literature on the Soviet economy have long been familiar with the curious, but persisting, modes of behavior that this overcentralized system has tended to thrust upon the individual production manager. Although he is the pivotal agent in the process of production, the plant manager finds himself entangled in a bewildering cobweb of administrative fiats. He has been described as resorting to such tried and true weapons as trading favors illegally (*blat*) and as applying improper influence in the course of seeking to achieve his maddeningly detailed assignments. He has been reported as falling back on the tested device of understatement of his production capacities; on the use of the slush fund and the "pusher" (*tolkach*) in the unauthorized procurement of supplies; the padding of production reports; the bribing of inspectors; the falsification of account books.

II

What is both interesting and remarkable at the present time, however, are signs of a kind of convergence of the main lines of criticism of the Soviet economy as they have evolved in the West with a cautiously emerging flow of economic criticism in the USSR. To be sure, criticism in the Soviet Union is still anything but a universal right: one needs an explicit license, besides a great deal of civic courage, to exercise it. However, the more permissive atmosphere of the past few years has made a difference. It has made it somewhat less hazardous for prominent individuals in the USSR to express their personal misgivings in public, even where the explosion of some long-cherished official myth may be involved. In this recent mild rumbling of criticism, the misgivings voiced and the remedies proposed have often been remarkably explicit and substantive. Moreover, a discernible note of urgency has been sounded by the several prominent men in the USSR who have recently expressed in print the need for a new approach to the organization of economic planning and managerial practices.

One theme that runs through many of these discussions is the urgent need for more rational ways of making use of the vast economic assets of the country, including its mammoth labor force. Most of the participants in this novel kind of discussion in the Soviet press appear to agree with the admonition of the respected mathematician A. Berg, who has warned that "We cannot permit ourselves the luxury of wasting time, if we soberly consider the tasks that face us and also the difficulties which we must overcome as quickly as possible."[2]

[2] *Pravda*, October 24, 1962.

What seems to lend urgency to the present appeals for economic realism in the Soviet press is the clear implication on the part of the participants that the heavy burden of irrationality now weighing down the Soviet economy is inherent in, and swelling along with, the basic administrative apparatus by which forced economic growth has been sustained in the USSR over the past several decades. This is indeed a prominent thesis in the present internal discussion. And, if true, it would certainly tend to impose a heavy handicap upon the Soviet Union in its all-out race against the capitalist method of production, in the face of the counting-house tradition of economic discipline among the market-oriented economies.

One outspoken critic of the present regimen of decision-making in the Soviet economy, the plane-designer O. Antonov, deals most unceremoniously with some of the sacred cows of the economic planning system. He is unmistakably a person who is licensed to give advice in public by dint of his own record as a successful production man. He can also show that he is genuinely interested not only in pointing out the symptoms, but also in tracing the causes of the chronic disorders in the industrial sector of the economy. Antonov holds one major cause of the haphazard, unresponsive mode of production in Soviet industry to be the fact that "the output of the individual plant is oriented toward the warehouse rather than toward the sales counter." This is certainly a familiar theme in Western comment. Because of this tendency, Antonov argues, the production flow lacks the benefit of what he and his engineers call the "feedback factor"—namely, the signal for needed improvements that is normally provided by the plant-consumer. The successful manager in Russian industry, he complains, is one who can prove that he has pumped his full quota of production into the pipeline. This done, he does not need to pay any heed to the reaction of the consumer of his product. His immunity, moreover, is the same, whether the consumer happens to be another important state enterprise or the lowly private customer of the state store.[3]

Antonov is especially critical of the official overall "success indicator" used by the planners to judge, and to reward, the performance of the plant manager. He believes that most of the known irrational decisions made at the plant level stem directly from "this one-sided, ill-conceived indicator"—namely, the "gross value of output" of the

[3] *Izvestia,* May 25, 1962.

individual industrial plant. Among the examples of erratic behavior of local managers under the pressure of the center for ever more "gross output," he cites the following practice: A plant manager keeps regularly at his warehouse an inordinate stock of spare parts and components. Why? First, because the manager does not have faith in the precision of the supply apparatus; and secondly, because when the plant is hard-pressed, when performance is running dangerously behind the plan, these parts and components can be withdrawn from storage and included in the monthly total of new "gross output." This sort of management, in Antonov's opinion, yields the national economy nothing more than "padded figures and confusion, to put it mildly."

Such preoccupation with growth at any cost, Antonov suggests, inevitably impels the Soviet plant managers in the direction of "short-changing the future." He is persuaded that the pressure for volume growth, which continues to be the order of the day in the Soviet economy, can result only in bequeathing serious deficits to the next generation. He warns, for example, that the substandard machine which is turned out in haste today, and forced upon the helpless plant-producer, will serve to produce poor quality goods in the years to come.

Being a practical, production-minded man, Antonov rounds out his argument by offering this rather broad judgment on the choices confronting the Soviet economy: "Such is the dialectic of relations between quantity and quality that by changing our approach in favor of the production of goods of a higher quality, though somewhat reduced in volume, we will assuredly attain a growth in the quality as well as the quantity of goods for the national economy as a whole." To many Russians, such an argument has an appealing ring. It clearly echoes Lenin's well-remembered motto: "Better less, but better!"

This close link between the rush for record quantity output and the neglect of quality of product constitutes a major theme in the current flow of internal criticism. One high official of the cabinet-level State Committee on Automation cites a typical experience in his own field —namely, the production of electric motors: "The overwhelming majority of production equipment in the country is powered by electric prime movers, of which there are at present several million units at work. However, the life span of these engines is short. . . . The predominant majority of engines break down as a result of the unsatisfactory execution of the armature and insulation work. Every year we are compelled to spend vast sums on the repair of electric engines and to maintain large staffs of repair men."[4]

Similarly, two Soviet scientists recently reported in the press one of the findings of a new Committee for Quality Control—namely, that "40 per cent of all failures of machinery in the course of operation are the result of low quality of manufacture." There is no real force at work in the economy, they asserted, to assure high-quality output. "The official agencies for technical quality control actually do nothing more than place the tag 'reject' on the finished product and try to influence the production process chiefly through slogans and chants!"[5]

With much the same concern in mind, a group of Soviet scientists not long ago took the unusual step of addressing a letter to the Central Committee of the CPSU about what they considered the crucial problem in regard to the supply of fertilizer in the economy. It would do no good, they argued, to try to solve the present shortage by the standard approach: by ordering another increase in output. What must be done first, in their view, was "to take resolute measures . . . to put the utilization of fertilizer in proper order." What really was necessary, they stated, was to provide adequate transport, packing materials, storage facilities, and machines for the application of fertilizers. Because of the lack of these ingredients of an adequate distribution system, the scientists concluded, "the country does not get from the use of fertilizers half of what could be obtained with good organization."[6]

III

It is quite natural, of course, that the most systematic criticism of the growth-oriented economic practices followed by the Soviet government comes from the ranks of the academic economists. They, too, are today recommending strong, if unpleasant, remedies that entail abandoning the present philosophy of maximum growth of output in response to ill-considered production commands. From their writings it emerges that it is now quite clear to them, as it long has been to Western economists, that Communist economic theory has

[4] *Pravda*, December 17, 1962.
[5] *Izvestia*, October 8, 1963.
[6] *Pravda*, November 17, 1963.

very little to say outside the area of broad macro-economic decisions. It is wholly concerned with the issues of overall national economic policy, such as rates of growth, fiscal policy, volume and distribution of investment, etc. Even prices are treated by Soviet planners as a macro-economic problem, a matter of financial security for the state. Conversely, there is in Soviet economic theory no rational guide or practical yardstick for resource allocation at the enterprise level.

Yet, the lack of such a yardstick has emerged as one of the crucial deficiencies at the present juncture in Soviet economic development. The distinguished Soviet economist Novozhilov, among others, has been recommending for the past several years, in sober and unvarnished language, that the government turn its back on the present system of detailed quantitative guidance of the economy from the center. The entire system of performance and record-keeping at the plant level in response to commands from the center, he contends, is founded on an illusion—namely, that what is profitable for the enterprise is also beneficial for the economy as a whole. From the standpoint of the plant manager, Novozhilov reasons, most of the assignments he receives fall into either a "profitable" or an "unprofitable" category. Most unsurprisingly, his self-interest impels him to take care of his own balance-sheet first. When that happens, says Novozhilov, the articles that are produced in abundance show a good record for the plant, while the goods of high national economic interest often are neglected in the process.[7]

The main source of distortion, as Novozhilov sees it, stems from the fact that Soviet economic practice has lost sight of the distinction between the receipts and the expenditures of an enterprise—i.e., between input and output in production. "It would be hard to imagine a more gross error in economic calculation," in his opinion. As accounts are kept now, the "gross output" of an enterprise embodies a lot more than the actual work of the given enterprise; it also includes the value of the inputs employed in the process of production. Hence, a plant can generally increase its own "gross output" simply by increasing its expenditures on purchased materials. Thus, he points out, by including materials received from outside in the indicator of output, the present planning system is rewarding extravagance rather than economy in the use of materials, labor, and capital.

[7] V. V. Novozhilov, *Proceedings of the Leningrad Engineering-Economic Institute* (in Russian), No. 24 (Leningrad 1958), 150–56.

There is only one way, Novozhilov suggests, to bring the wishes of the state into harmony with the interests of the plant managers. This is to devise a uniform basis for price-setting throughout the economy, and thereby "make the accounting system into a reliable tool of the plan." Once the plant manager was given a reliable, generalized yardstick of value, in the form of meaningful prices, he would, in Novozhilov's opinion, have the necessary incentive to behave rationally. He would then be motivated to fulfill his plan not only for total output but for the given product-mix as well. By working with a set of prices that reflect his own real costs, the plant manager would be impelled to effect savings in costs for his own account-keeping in a way that would reflect a saving of inputs in real terms. He would, moreover, be motivated to make more efficient use of his fixed capital and, above all, would see his genuine economic interest in the installation of more advanced industrial technology in his plant.

IV

Highly significant evidence to the effect that the Soviet method of forced economic growth has begun to reveal its limitations in rather compelling terms has been provided by the recent pronouncements, as well as the actions, of Premier Khrushchev. In his widely ranging, often angry address to the meeting of the Central Committee of the Communist Party in November 1962, he expressed so many biting criticisms of established economic practice as to suggest a gnawing discontent with the uncertain course of Soviet economic progress.

In this address, Khrushchev showed an acute awareness that the atmosphere of forced, mechanical growth in effect in Soviet plants is all too apt to foster bad production habits. There appears to be, in his view, too little interest on the part of plant managers in the critical elements in a modern economy—namely, in more advanced productive equipment, in inputs of the least cost, in new materials, in products of higher quality and greater durability. Whenever he learned of some remarkable new type of production equipment employed in the West, Khrushchev complained, he was told that "our own engineers are also working on the idea." He was beginning to wonder, he said, whether this "proves our inability to utilize technical progress."

Khrushchev seemed to be displeased, in particular, with the state of affairs in regard to innovation in Soviet industry. The designers, who are found in large numbers in a wide network of Soviet research institutes, appear to be working in isolation from one another, unaware of whether they are repeating each other's inventions or mistakes. There is no clearing house, he complained, no center for the coordination of new ideas. "Everybody, you might say, is inventing the bicycle all over again." What Khrushchev found most disturbing was that the country's plants, at the same time, were not pressing eagerly for the most advanced production machinery they could get.

It is not difficult to recognize the main source of Khrushchev's discontent. It must have become quite apparent to him by this time that the economic race against capitalism has turned out to be a more complex and taxing undertaking than he had anticipated. It is not necessary to marshal a great array of statistics to indicate that in terms of employment in industry the Soviet Union has for some time "caught up" with the United States. The smaller size of Russia's industrial manpower has long been one of the main "reserves" for the achievement of parity in output. At present, Soviet industry, upon which the lion's share of the nation's investment capital is lavished, already employs 57 per cent more workers than does the same basic sector of the economy in the United States.[8] Furthermore, the number of engineers employed in Soviet industry is more than double that of ours. The annual supply of new machine tools going into Soviet industry also exceeds ours by a sizable margin. Thousands of machine tools, valued at about $100 million, are imported annually from Eastern Europe, and the total number of machine tools in use in Soviet industry (2.3 million units) is at present roughly equal to that of the United States.

V

The chief problem confronting the Soviet policy-makers in industry, however, appears to be the lack of a real, appreciable rise in the productivity of its vast resources, human and physical. At present, the Soviet Union's enormous industrial plant is yielding an annual product that is equal to just about 56 per cent of its United States counterpart. This statement is based on the Soviet planners' own calculations of an average labor productivity in Soviet industry equal to 36 per cent of the average output per worker in the United States.[9]

[8] *Vestnik Statistiki,* No. 11 (1963), 35.
[9] *Voprosy Ekonomiki,* No. 5 (May 1961), 21.

The institutionalized bias in favor of quantity has also tended, in Soviet practice, to discourage the necessary steady search for new materials, or for new mixtures in the use of old materials, in the production process. It is a matter of record that the most notable innovations in this regard recently carried out in the USSR have been inspired by the example of the West. In one major specific case, the recent shift in the fuel balance from the predominance of coal to gas and oil, was undertaken in the light of the better results obtained in the West. This is equally true with respect to the recent shift toward large-scale production of such new products as man-made fibers, new types of synthetic rubber, plastics, and other chemical materials. The same tendency toward emulation, with consciously varied delays, has been displayed by Soviet industrial planners in such fields, among many others, as railway traction, farm implements, fishing trawlers, automobiles, and metal-cutting and metal-forming machinery.

Is there anything inherently wrong, it may be asked, with this observed Soviet practice of allowing the West to develop and thoroughly test a given innovation before putting it into operation in the USSR? After all, the Soviet Union is strong in the advancement of its military technology, well-supplied in volume and variety of weapons. One answer that suggests itself is that the practice of systematic borrowing from the West is manifestly an involuntary rather than a deliberate form of behavior; and that, as such, it places the Soviet Union at a disadvantage in the long-run economic race against the market-oriented economies at work in the democratic societies. For one thing, systematic reliance on foreign innovation surely tends to dry up the springs of creativity among domestic producers. Another and more tangible result is that it builds obsolescence into the Soviet production system: by the time a machine or process is copied and fully mastered by the Soviet plants, in the West that particular piece of equipment or practice has often reached a later stage of design and improved productivity.

The critical elements in the Soviet race for economic parity are certain, in the long run, to be the qualitative indicators in production. For it is abundantly clear that the competition with the West will be determined not by the volume but by the productivity of available economic resources in the USSR. A steadily improving climate of productivity, for instance, has made it possible for the Western nations to raise the standard of national economic performance in recent years. Step by step, in this process, they have in fact expanded the terms of the economic competition with the Soviet Union and its allies. Today, the minimum national economic goals among the advanced Western nations encompass a great deal more than heavy industry and military security. They include such objectives as industrial innovation on the basis of new scientific findings; an economy oriented toward consumer welfare; an abundant supply and variety of housing; steady economic growth; an active exchange of goods with the developing nations; grants, credits, and industrial machinery for development; and the maintenance and support of a durable system of alliances.

There is no doubt, of course, that the Soviet Union is determined to increase its own capability in all these spheres of economic endeavor. In the light of their commitment to defend the prestige of their economic system, the Soviet leaders cannot do otherwise. Before the USSR can make an adequate showing in this regard, however, the leadership will have to undertake an agonizing reappraisal of its devotion to the institutions of forced economic growth. It will most likely find it imperative to clean its economic house of the cobwebs of bad practices that have accumulated during the decades of hypnotic preoccupation with the physical aggrandizement of its industrial establishment and the mobilization of a maximum of manpower for the achievement of record levels in the quantity of industrial production.

To paraphrase Gibbon's famous dictum about the security of modern Europe against invasion from Asia, one might say, in this context, that before the Soviet leaders can "conquer" the Western nations economically, "they must cease to be barbarous in their habits." They must abandon the magic horse of hypertrophic growth and settle down to learn the homely art of economic calculus. For it is by means of this art that the nations of the West have learned to husband their human and physical resources in a way best calculated to achieve an acceptable balance between the need for an effective national community and the need for the self-realization of the individual citizen in the modern industrial society.

CHAPTER VII

Science and Technology

*One of the most critical problems facing the Nation is the inade-
quacy of the supply of scientific and technical manpower.*

—JOHN F. KENNEDY

*We are proud that the Russian words "Sputnik" and "Lunik" are
understood all over the world without translation.*

—NIKITA S. KHRUSHCHEV

    *The twentieth century is characterized as the "Age of
Revolutions"—political revolution, ideological revolution, demographic revolution, and scientific revolution. In recent years the
spectacular developments of science and technology, ranging from
atomic energy to zoology, have given mankind, for the first time in
history, the ability and opportunity not only to advance toward universal prosperity and freedom from disease, but also, ironically, to
bring about the universal destruction of human civilization.*

    *The contributions of the scientific revolution, and the US-Soviet
competition in the technological breakthrough, should be hinged on
the promotion of full benefits for all mankind. "For science is the
most powerful means we have for the unification of knowledge, and
a main obligation of its future must be to deal with problems which
cut across boundaries, whether boundaries between the sciences,
boundaries between nations or boundaries between man's scientific
and his humane concerns." In this sense, the argument on the superiority of capitalist science over socialist science, or vice versa, really
matters little. But, in view of the fact that the advancement of science
and technology is unavoidably related to the state of military preparedness, quality of national education, degree of economic growth,
and many other vital areas of national power, such an argument seems
inevitable and understandable.*

    This chapter is intended to examine some implications of the

187

scientific and technological developments both in the United States and in the Soviet Union.

John von Neumann, mathematician and former member of the Atomic Energy Commission, discusses the prospects and problems of a constantly expanding science and technology, and attempts to answer the question: Within this expanding framework, will it be possible, as it was in the past, to accommodate the major tensions created by technological progress?

The Soviet Communist Party Program of 1961 sets forth two important tasks in Soviet science: development of theoretical investigations and ties between science and production.

Kenneth R. Whiting, Professor of European History at the Research Studies Institute of the Air University, asserts that in 1960 the United States was lagging far behind the Soviet Union in the training of technicians and engineers.

1. CAN WE SURVIVE TECHNOLOGY?*

BY JOHN VON NEUMANN

"The great globe itself" is in a rapidly maturing crisis—a crisis attributable to the fact that the environment in which technological progress must occur has become both undersized and underorganized. To define the crisis with any accuracy, and to explore possibilities of dealing with it, we must not only look at relevant facts, but also engage in some speculation. The process will illuminate some potential technological developments of the next quarter-century.

In the first half of this century the accelerating industrial revolution encountered an absolute limitation—not on technological progress as such but on an essential safety factor. This safety factor, which had permitted the industrial revolution to roll on from the mid-eighteenth to the early twentieth century, was essentially a matter of geographical and political *Lebensraum*: an ever broader geographical scope for technological activities, combined with an ever broader

* From *Fortune* magazine (June, 1955), p. 106 ff. Copyright © 1955 by Time Inc.; reprinted by their permission.

political integration of the world. Within this expanding framework it was possible to accommodate the major tensions created by technological progress.

Now this safety mechanism is being sharply inhibited; literally and figuratively, we are running out of room. At long last, we begin to feel the effects of the finite, actual size of the earth in a critical way.

Thus the crisis does not arise from accidental events or human errors. It is inherent in technology's relation to geography on the one hand and to political organization on the other. The crisis was developing visibly in the 1940's, and some phases can be traced back to 1914. In the years between now and 1980 the crisis will probably develop far beyond all earlier patterns. When or how it will end—or to what state of affairs it will yield—nobody can say.

In all its stages the industrial revolution consisted of making available more and cheaper energy, more and easier controls of human actions and reactions, and more and faster communications. Each development increased the effectiveness of the other two. All three factors increased the speed of performing large-scale operations— industrial, mercantile, political, and migratory. But throughout the development, increased speed did not so much shorten time requirements of processes as extend the areas of the earth affected by them. The reason is clear. Since most *time* scales are fixed by human reaction times, habits, and other physiological and psychological factors, the effect of the increased speed of technological processes was to enlarge the *size* of units—political, organizational, economic, and cultural—affected by technological operations. That is, instead of performing the same operations as before in less time, now larger-scale operations were performed in the same time. This important evolution has a natural limit, that of the earth's actual size. The limit is now being reached, or at least closely approached.

Indications of this appeared early and with dramatic force in the military sphere. By 1940 even the larger countries of continental Western Europe were inadequate as military units. Only Russia could sustain a major military reverse without collapsing. Since 1945, improved aeronautics and communications alone might have sufficed to make any geographical unit, including Russia, inadequate in a future war. The advent of nuclear weapons merely climaxes the development. Now the effectiveness of offensive weapons is such as to stultify all plausible defensive time scales. As early as World War

I, it was observed that the admiral commanding the battle field could "lose the British Empire in one afternoon." Yet navies of that epoch were relatively stable entities, tolerably safe against technological surprises. Today there is every reason to fear that even minor inventions and feints in the field of nuclear weapons can be decisive in less time than would be required to devise specific countermeasures. Soon existing nations will be as unstable in war as a nation the size of Manhattan Island would have been in a contest fought with the weapons of 1900.

Such military instability has already found its political expression. Two superpowers, the U.S. and U.S.S.R., represent such enormous destructive potentials as to afford little chance of a purely passive equilibrium. Other countries, including possible "neutrals," are militarily defenseless in the ordinary sense. At best they will acquire destructive capabilities of their own. . . . Consequently, the "concert of powers"—or its equivalent international organization—rests on a basis much more fragile than ever before. The situation is further embroiled by the newly achieved political effectiveness of non-European nationalisms.

These factors would "normally"—that is, in any recent century—have led to war. Will they lead to war before 1980? Or soon thereafter? It would be presumptuous to try to answer such a question firmly. In any case, the present and the near future are both dangerous. While the immediate problem is to cope with the actual danger, it is also essential to envisage how the problem is going to evolve in the 1955–80 period, even assuming that all will go reasonably well for the moment. This does not mean belittling immediate problems of weaponry, of U.S.-U.S.S.R. tensions, of the evolution and revolutions of Asia. These first things must come first. But we must be ready for the follow-up, lest possible immediate successes prove futile. We must think beyond the present forms of problems to those of later decades.

Technological evolution is still accelerating. Technologies are always constructive and beneficial, directly or indirectly. Yet their consequences tend to increase instability—a point that will get closer attention after we have had a look at certain aspects of continuing technological evolution.

First of all, there is a rapidly expanding supply of energy. It is generally agreed that even conventional, chemical fuel—coal or oil—

will be available in increased quantity in the next two decades. Increasing demand tends to keep fuel prices high, yet improvements in methods of generation seem to bring the price of power down. There is little doubt that the most significant event affecting energy is the advent of nuclear power. Its only available controlled source today is the nuclear-fission reactor. Reactor techniques appear to be approaching a condition in which they will be competitive with conventional (chemical) power sources within the U.S.; however, because of generally higher fuel prices abroad, they could already be more than competitive in many important foreign areas. Yet reactor technology is but a decade and a half old, during most of which period effort has been directed primarily not toward power but toward plutonium production. Given a decade of really large-scale industrial effort, the economic characteristics of reactors will undoubtedly surpass those of the present by far.

Moreover, it is not a law of nature that all controlled release of nuclear energy should be tied to fission reactions as it has been thus far. It is true that nuclear energy appears to be the primary source of practically all energy now visible in nature. Furthermore, it is not surprising that the first break into the intranuclear domain occurred at the unstable "high end" of the system of nuclei (that is, by fission). Yet fission is not nature's normal way of releasing nuclear energy. In the long run, systematic industrial exploitation of nuclear energy may shift reliance onto other and still more abundant modes. Again, reactors have been bound thus far to the traditional heat-steam-generator-electricity cycle, just as automobiles were at first constructed to look like buggies. It is likely that we shall gradually develop procedures more naturally and effectively adjusted to the new source of energy, abandoning the conventional kinks and detours inherited from chemical-fuel processes. Consequently, a few decades hence energy may be free—just like the unmetered air—with coal and oil used mainly as raw materials for organic chemical synthesis, to which, as experience has shown, their properties are best suited.

It is worth emphasizing that the main trend will be systematic exploration of nuclear reactions—that is, the transmutation of elements, or alchemy rather than chemistry. The main point in developing the industrial use of nuclear processes is to make them suitable for large-scale exploitation on the relatively small site that is the earth or, rather, any plausible terrestrial industrial establishment.

Nature has, of course, been operating nuclear processes all along, well and massively, but her "natural" sites for this industry are entire stars. There is reason to believe that the minimum space requirements for her way of operating are the minimum sizes of stars. Forced by the limitations of our real estate, we must in this respect do much better than nature. That this may not be impossible has been demonstrated in the somewhat extreme and unnatural instance of fission, that remarkable breakthrough of the past decade.

What massive transmutation of elements will do to technology in general is hard to imagine, but the effects will be radical indeed. This can already be sensed in related fields. The general revolution clearly under way in the military sphere, and its already realized special aspect, the terrible possibilities of mass destruction, should not be viewed as typical of what the nuclear revolution stands for. Yet they may well be typical of how deeply that revolution will transform whatever it touches. And the revolution will probably touch most things technological.

Also likely to evolve fast—and quite apart from nuclear evolution —is automation. Interesting analyses of recent developments in this field, and of near future potentialities, have appeared in the last few years. Automatic control, of course, is as old as the industrial revolution, for the decisive new feature of Watt's steam engine was its automatic valve control, including speed control by a "governor." In our century, however, small electric amplifying and switching devices put automation on an entirely new footing. This development began with the electromechanical (telephone) relay, continued and unfolded with the vacuum tube, and appears to accelerate with various solid-state devices (semi-conductor crystals, ferromagnetic cores, etc.). The last decade or two has also witnessed an increasing ability to control and "discipline" large numbers of such devices within one machine. Even in an airplane the number of vacuum tubes now approaches or exceeds a thousand. Other machines, containing up to 10,000 vacuum tubes, up to five times more crystals, and possibly more than 100,000 cores, now operate faultlessly over long periods, performing many millions of regulated, preplanned actions per second, with an expectation of only a few errors per day or week.

Many such machines have been built to perform complicated scientific and engineering calculations and large-scale accounting and logistical surveys. There is no doubt that they will be used for elaborate industrial process control, logistical, economic, and other planning, and many other purposes heretofore lying entirely outside the compass of quantitative and automatic control and preplanning. Thanks to simplified forms of automatic or semi-automatic control, the efficiency of important branches of industry has increased considerably during recent decades. It is therefore to be expected that the considerably elaborated newer forms, now becoming increasingly available, will effect much more along these lines.

Fundamentally, improvements in control are really improvements in communicating information within an organization or mechanism. The sum total of progress in this sphere is explosive. Improvements in communication in its direct, physical sense—transportation—while less dramatic, have been considerable and steady. If nuclear developments make energy unrestrictedly available, transportation developments are likely to accelerate even more. But even "normal" progress in sea, land, and air media is extremely important. Just such "normal" progress molded the world's economic development, producing the present global ideas in politics and economics.

Let us now consider a thoroughly "abnormal" industry and its potentialities—that is, an industry as yet without a place in any list of major activities: the control of weather or, to use a more ambitious but justified term, climate. One phase of this activity that has received a good deal of public attention is "rain making." . . .

But weather control and climate control are really much broader than rain making. All major weather phenomena, as well as climate as such, are ultimately controlled by the solar energy that falls on the earth. To modify the amount of solar energy is, of course, beyond human power. But what really matters is not the amount that hits the earth, but the fraction retained by the earth, since that reflected back into space is no more useful than if it had never arrived. Now, the amount absorbed by the solid earth, the sea, or the atmosphere seems to be subject to delicate influences. True, none of these has so far been substantially controlled by human will, but there are strong indications of control possibilities.

The carbon dioxide released into the atmosphere by industry's burning of coal and oil—more than half of it during the last generation—may have changed the atmosphere's composition sufficiently to account for a general warming of the world by about one degree Fahrenheit. The volcano Krakatao erupted in 1883 and released an amount of energy by no means exorbitant. Had the dust of the eruption stayed in the stratosphere for fifteen years, reflecting sunlight away from the earth, it might have sufficed to lower the world's temperature by six degrees (in fact, it stayed for about three years, and five such eruptions would probably have achieved the result mentioned). This would have been a substantial cooling; the last Ice Age, when half of North America and all of northern and western Europe were under an ice cap like that of Greenland or Antarctica, was only fifteen degrees colder than the present age. On the other hand, another fifteen degrees of warming would probably melt the ice of Greenland and Antarctica and produce worldwide tropical to semi-tropical climate.

Furthermore, it is known that the persistence of large ice fields is due to the fact that ice both reflects sunlight energy and radiates away terrestrial energy at an even higher rate than ordinary soil. Microscopic layers of colored matter spread on an icy surface, or in the atmosphere above one, could inhibit the reflection-radiation process, melt the ice, and change the local climate. Measures that would effect such changes are technically possible, and the amount of investment required would be only of the order of magnitude that sufficed to develop rail systems and other major industries. The main difficulty lies in predicting in detail the effects of any such drastic intervention. But our knowledge of the dynamics and the controlling processes in the atmosphere is rapidly approaching a level that would permit such prediction. Probably intervention in atmospheric and climatic matters will come in a few decades, and will unfold on a scale difficult to imagine at present.

What could be done, of course, is no index to what should be done; to make a new ice age in order to annoy others, or a new tropical, "interglacial" age in order to please everybody, is not necessarily a rational program. In fact, to evaluate the ultimate consequences of either a general cooling or a general heating would be a complex matter. Changes would affect the level of the seas, and hence the habitability of the continental coastal shelves; the evaporation of the seas, and hence general precipitation and glaciation levels; and so on. What would be harmful and what beneficial—and to which regions of the earth—is not immediately obvious. But there is little doubt that one *could* carry out analyses needed to predict results, intervene on any desired scale, and ultimately achieve rather fantastic effects. The climate of specific regions and levels of precipitation might be altered. For example, temporary disturbances—including invasions of cold (polar) air that constitute the typical winter of the middle latitudes, and tropical storms (hurricanes)—might be corrected or at least depressed.

There is no need to detail what such things would mean to agriculture or, indeed, to all phases of human, animal, and plant ecology. What power over our environment, over all nature, is implied!

Such actions would be more directly and truly worldwide than recent or, presumably, future wars, or than the economy at any time. Extensive human intervention would deeply affect the atmosphere's general circulation, which depends on the earth's rotation and intensive solar heating of the tropics. Measures in the arctic may control the weather in temperate regions, or measures in one temperate region critically affect one another, one-quarter around the globe. All this will merge each nation's affairs with those of every other, more thoroughly than the threat of a nuclear or any other war may already have done.

Such developments as free energy, greater automation, improved communications, partial or total climate control have common traits deserving special mention. First, though all are intrinsically useful, they can lend themselves to destruction. Even the most formidable tools of nuclear destruction are only extreme members of a genus that includes useful methods of energy release or element transmutation. The most constructive schemes for climate control would have to be based on insights and techniques that would also lend themselves to forms of climatic warfare as yet unimagined. Technology—like science—is neutral all through, providing only means of control applicable to any purpose, indifferent to all.

Second, there is in most of these developments a trend toward affecting the earth as a whole, or to be more exact, toward producing effects that can be projected from any one to any other point on the earth. There is an intrinsic conflict with geography—and institutions based thereon—as understood today. Of course, any technology interacts with geography, and each imposes its own geographical rules and modalities. The technology that is now developing and that will dominate the next decades seems to be in total conflict with traditional and, in the main, momentarily still valid, geographical and political units and concepts. This is the maturing crisis of technology.

What kind of action does this situation call for? *Whatever* one feels inclined to do, one decisive trait must be considered: the very techniques that create the dangers and the instabilities are in themselves useful, or closely related to the useful. In fact, the more useful they could be, the more unstabilizing their effects can also be. It is not a particular perverse destructiveness of one particular invention that creates danger. Technological power, technological efficiency as such, is an ambivalent achievement. Its danger is intrinsic.

In looking for a solution, it is well to exclude one pseudosolution at the start. The crisis will not be resolved by inhibiting this or that apparently particularly obnoxious form of technology. For one thing, the parts of technology, as well as of the underlying sciences, are so intertwined that in the long run nothing less than a total elimination of all technological progress would suffice for inhibition. Also, on a more pedestrian and immediate basis, useful and harmful techniques lie everywhere so close together that it is never possible to separate the lions from the lambs. This is known to all who have so laboriously tried to separate secret, "classified" science or technology (military) from the "open" kind; success is never more—nor intended to be more—than transient, lasting perhaps half a decade. Similarly, a separation into useful and harmful subjects in any technological sphere would probably diffuse into nothing in a decade.

Moreover, in this case successful separation would have to be enduring (unlike the case of military "classification," in which even a few years' gain may be important). Also, the proximity of useful techniques to harmful ones, and the possibility of putting the harmful ones to military use, puts a competitive premium on infringement. Hence the banning of particular technologies would have to be enforced on a worldwide basis. But the only authority that could do this effectively would have to be of such scope and perfection as to signal the *resolution* of international problems rather than the discovery of a *means* to resolve them. . . .

What safeguard remains? Apparently only day-to-day—or perhaps year-to-year—opportunistic measures, a long sequence of small, correct decisions. And this is not surprising. After all, the crisis is due to the rapidity of progress, to the probable further acceleration thereof, and to the reaching of certain critical relationships. Specifically, the effects that we are now beginning to produce are of the same order of magnitude as that of "the great globe itself." Indeed, they affect the earth as an entity. Hence further acceleration can no longer be absorbed as in the past by an extension of the area of operations. Under present conditions it is unreasonable to expect a novel cure-all.

For progress there is no cure. Any attempt to find automatically safe channels for the present explosive variety of progress must lead to frustration. The only safety possible is relative, and it lies in an intelligent exercise of day-to-day judgment.

The problems created by the combination of the presently possible forms of nuclear warfare and the rather unusually unstable international situation are formidable and not to be solved easily. Those of the next decades are likely to be similarly vexing, "only more so." The U.S.-U.S.S.R. tension is bad, but when other nations begin to make felt their full offensive potential weight, things will not become simpler.

Present awful possibilities of nuclear warfare may give way to others even more awful. After global climate control becomes possible, perhaps all our present involvements will seem simple. We should not deceive ourselves: once such possibilities become actual, they will be exploited. It will, therefore, be necessary to develop suitable new political forms and procedures. All experience shows that even smaller technological changes than those now in the cards profoundly transform political and social relationships. Experience also shows that these transformations are not *a priori* predictable and that most contemporary "first guesses" concerning them are wrong. For all these reasons, one should take neither present difficulties nor presently proposed reforms too seriously.

The one solid fact is that the difficulties are due to an evolution that, while useful and constructive, is also dangerous. Can we produce the required adjustments with the necessary speed? The most hopeful answer is that the human species has been subjected to similar tests before and seems to have a congenital ability to come through, after varying amounts of trouble. To ask in advance for a complete recipe would be unreasonable. We can specify only the human qualities required: patience, flexibility, intelligence.

2. SOVIET COMMUNIST PARTY PROGRAM IN SCIENCE*

Under the socialist system of economy, scientific and technical progress enables man to employ the riches and forces of nature most effectively in the interests of the people, to discover new forms of energy and to create new materials, to develop means of weather control, and to master outer space. Application of science in production becomes a decisive factor of rapid growth of the productive forces of society. Scientific progress and the introduction of scientific achievements into the economy will remain an object of special concern to the Party.

Most important are the following tasks:

(*a*) *Development of Theoretical Investigations*. The further perspectives of scientific and technical progress depend in the present period primarily on the achievements of *the key branches of natural science*. A high level of development in *mathematics, physics, chemistry, and biology* is a necessary condition for the advancement and the effectiveness of the technical, medical, agricultural, and other sciences.

Theoretical research will be promoted to the utmost, primarily in such decisive fields of technical progress as electrification of the whole country, comprehensive mechanisation and automation of production, transport and communications, the application of chemistry to the leading branches of the national economy, industrial uses of atomic energy. This applies to:

studying the power and fuel balance of the country, finding the best ways and means of utilising the natural sources of power, working out the scientific fundamentals of a single power grid, discovering new power sources and developing methods of direct conversion of thermal, nuclear, solar, and chemical energy into electric power, and solving problems related to control of thermonuclear reactions;

working out the theory and principles of designing new machines,

* From *The U.S.S.R. and the Future,* Leonard Schapiro, ed. (New York: Praeger, 1963), pp. 306–307. Copyright © 1962 by Forschungsinstitut, Munich, Germany; reprinted by their permission.

automatic and telemechanical systems, intensively developing radio-electronics, elaborating the theoretical foundations of computing, control and information machines, and technically improving them;

investigating chemical processes, working out new, more efficient technologies and creating inexpensive high-quality artificial and synthetic materials for all branches of the national economy: mechanical engineering, building, the manufacture of household goods and mineral fertilisers, and creating new preparations for use in medicine and agriculture;

improving existing methods and devising new, more effective methods of prospecting minerals and making comprehensive use of natural wealth.

Big advances are to be made in the development of all the biological sciences in order successfully to solve medical problems and achieve further progress in agriculture. The main tasks to be solved by these sciences in the interests of mankind are: ascertainment of the essence of the phenomena of life, the biological laws governing the development of the organic world, study of the physics and chemistry of living matter, elaboration of various methods of controlling vital processes, in particular, metabolism, heredity and directed changes in organism. It is essential to develop more broadly and deeply the Michurin line in biology, which is based on the proposition that conditions of life are primary in the development of the organic world. Medicine must concentrate on discovering means of preventing and conquering cancer, virulent, cardiovascular, and other dangerous diseases. It is important to study and extensively use microorganisms in the economy and the health services, among other things for the production of foods and foodstuffs, vitamins, antibiotics and enzymes, and for the development of new agricultural techniques.

Artificial earth satellites and spaceships have, by enabling man to penetrate into outer space, provided great opportunities for discovering new natural phenomena and laws and of investigating the planets and the sun.

In the age of rapid scientific progress, the elaboration of the philosophical problems of modern natural science on the basis of dialectical materialism, the only scientific method of cognition, becomes still more urgent.

There must be intensive development of research work in the *social sciences,* which constitute the scientific basis for the guidance of the development of society. Most important in this field is the study and theoretical generalisation of the experience gained in communist construction; investigation of the key objective laws governing the economic, political and cultural progress of socialism and its development into communism, and elaboration of the problems of communist education.

The task of economic science is to generalise new phenomena in the economic life of society, and to work out the national economic problems whose solution promotes successful communist construction. Economists must concentrate on finding the most effective ways of utilising material and labour resources in the economy, the best methods of planning and organising industrial and agricultural production, and elaborating the principles of a rational distribution of the productive forces and of the technical and economic problems of communist construction.

The investigation of the problems of world history and contemporary world development must disclose the law-governed process of mankind's advance towards communism, the change in the balance of forces in favour of socialism, the aggravation of the general crisis of capitalism, the break-up of the colonial system of imperialism and its consequences, and the upsurge of the national-liberation movement of peoples.

It is important to study the historical experience of the Communist Party and the Soviet people, tried and proved successful in practice, the objective laws of development of the world socialist system and the world communist and working-class movement.

It is essential, in the future as well, to firmly defend and develop dialectical and historical materialism as the science of the most general laws of development of nature, society and human thinking.

The social sciences must continue to struggle with determination against bourgeois ideology, against Right-Socialist theory and practice, and against revisionism and dogmatism; they must uphold the purity of the principles of Marxism-Leninism.

(b) *Ties Between Science and Production.* Close ties with the creative labour of the people and practical communist construction are an earnest of a fruitful development of science.

In conformity with the requirements of economic and cultural development, it is essential to extend and improve the network of research institutions, including those attached to the central bodies directing economic development and those attached to the economic councils, and the network of research laboratories and institutes at the major industrial plants and in farming areas; to develop research at higher educational establishments; to improve the geographical distribution of research institutions and higher educational establishments, and to ensure the further development of science in all the Union republics and major economic areas.

The research institutions must plan and co-ordinate their work in the most important fields of research in accordance with the plans of economic and cultural development. The role of the collective opinion of scientists in directing scientific work will increase. Free comradely discussions promoting the creative solution of pressing problems are an essential condition for scientific development.

The Party will adopt measures to extend and improve the material facilities of science and to enlist the most capable creative forces in scientific pursuits.

It is a point of honour for Soviet scientists to consolidate the advanced positions which Soviet science has won in major branches of knowledge and to take a *leading place in world science* in all the key fields.

3. THE TECHNOLOGICAL RACE*

BY K. R. WHITING

In the present Cold War contest between the free world and the Communist bloc, the technological and economic-production race seems destined to become a decisive factor. Since the death of Stalin, the Soviet leadership has apparently taken a long-range view of the conflict and is making every effort not only to catch up with Western Europe and the United States, but to surpass them.

The Soviet leadership has recognized that education is a mighty factor in this contest, and a very large part of the Soviet budget is devoted to education and research. In recent years, the Soviet press

* From *The Soviet Union Today* by Kenneth R. Whiting, pp. 260–264. Copyright © 1962 by Frederick A. Praeger, Inc.; reprinted by their permission.

has proclaimed the "furious" growth in the number of schools, students, and teachers. The official report on the Plan fulfillment for 1960 stated that more than 52 million Soviet citizens were in some kind of an educational program. More than 1.3 million students completed their secondary education and received Maturity Certificates; more than 4.4 million students were enrolled in higher and specialized secondary educational institutions, and 820,000 graduated from these schools, with 340,000 of them in technical specialties; and 117,000 engineers were graduated.

Sheer numbers, however, are only a part of the contest. More to the point is the problem of obtaining trained manpower for the critical fields. Here the Soviets have an advantage. They can use a degree of compulsion to get the results they want. Budget allotments, compulsory job assignments, and curricula determination are all used to steer the bright students into the scientific and technical fields.

But compulsion has its limitations, and more subtle incentives must be employed as well. Here, too, the Soviets have an advantage. The materialistic basis of Communist ideology gives things scientific an aura of the religious, and Soviet youth has almost been persuaded that science can provide the answer to all problems. Everything from the explanation of human history to the building of an ideal future is credited to science; Soviet youth can aspire to nothing higher than to become scientists or technicians.

Another motivation toward technical training is provided by the vast and well-organized paramilitary society for Soviet youth, the DOSAAF (All-Union Voluntary Society for Assistance to the Army, Air Force, and Navy). This is the new name, since 1951, for the former Osoaviakhim (Voluntary Society for Assistance in Defense, Aviation, and Chemistry), which was formed in the late 1920's. This society, numbering more than 15 million members, sponsors all kinds of military training and the development of skills that will be useful to the armed forces.

A further impetus to scientific careers derives from the new surge of patriotism in the Soviet Union. This is partly the result of the constant barrage by all the Soviet organs of propaganda and partly the result of the victory over the Germans in World War II. One manifestation of the extreme nationalism has been the series of "firsts" claimed as Russian inventions and technical discoveries. But beneath this lies a pride in Russian achievement.

The United States still leads the U.S.S.R. in education so far as total number of students. But in the training of engineers, the story is different. In 1953, the United States had a total of 530,000 engineers; the Soviet Union, 500,000, but the rate of increase since then has been in favor of the Soviets. In 1954, the Soviet Union graduated 53,000 engineers; the United States, only 20,000. In 1960, the Soviets had raised their production of engineers to 117,000, and the United States was lagging far behind.

The output of scientists and engineers in the next decade will depend largely on the interests and training of the students now in elementary and secondary schools—and on an adequate number of well-trained teachers in the precollege schools. It is precisely here that the United States is lagging. Of the Soviet teachers trained in pedagogical institutes, around 50 per cent now take as their major science and mathematics and teach these subjects in the Soviet educational system. In the United States, not only is there a smaller percentage of teachers trained to specialize in mathematics and science, but a staggering number of these never become science teachers, or do so for only a short period of time. Many are attracted to the better-paying jobs in industry.

Although the exact percentage of time given to science and mathematics by pupils in the secondary schools of the United States cannot be determined, there is little doubt that it is below the 40 per cent of the Soviet secondary school. And since there is no nationwide standard for U. S. secondary schools, the training in mathematics and science varies from excellent to very poor. Recent surveys have shown that the secondary-school pupils in the United States try to avoid what are considered "tough" courses—mathematics and sciences— and resent the poor teaching that often accompanies these courses. The U.S.S.R. has several advantages in this area. First, the Soviet pupil is given no choice in mathematics and science courses in the lower grades and secondary school. Second, the extremely centralized structure of the Soviet educational system enables the authorities to set up uniform standards throughout the country. Furthermore, the Soviet teacher employs "old-fashioned" methods of drill and repetition, highly effective in teaching the basic materials in mathematics and the sciences—which the Soviet pupil must have mastered by the end of the tenth grade.

A major weakness of the Soviet educational system is the extreme concentration of higher educational institutions in the two areas of Moscow and Leningrad. Moscow has ninety such institutions, with almost 300,000 students; Leningrad has fifty, with 150,000 students. As a result, much potential talent may remain untapped. The Soviet press has carried many articles recently on the need for expanding rural school facilities, for raising the standards of the outlying universities and higher-educational institutions, and, in general, for decentralizing education.

On August 5, 1956, *Pravda* reported that the Council of Ministers had ordered the organization of a research department in nuclear physics at the Tashkent Institute, in Uzbekistan, under the Academy of Sciences of the Uzbekistan S.S.R. The institute was authorized to obtain an atomic reactor and the necessary equipment for first-class research in nuclear physics. It was to become a center for Central Asian scholars in this field. However, the great emphasis upon practical experience in the Soviet technical schools demands a proximity of school and industrial plant. Since no plant exists at Tashkent, the institute has not yet turned out its first nuclear physicist. Several all union-republic universities and institutes have no industrial facilities in their immediate neighborhood—a factor that is a hindrance to the wide dispersal of technical schools. But as the industrial base of the Soviet Union is decentralized, the schools should follow.

In analyzing the race for the production of technically trained manpower, it is likely that Soviet statistics exclude one important group from the totals—the number of graduates turned out by military-engineering schools. There are a large number of Soviet military schools, both secondary and on the higher levels, but the number of graduates is not reported. When Stalin presented the figures for higher education to the Communist Party Congress of 1939, he pointed out that he was not including the military figure. The *Narodnoe Khozyaystvo SSSR* omits military schools in its otherwise comprehensive compilation of statistics. Many educational institutions under the various ministries have military engineering sections under "special faculties," and their figures are likewise not given. Engineers involved in the production of special weapons are not counted in any breakdown, nor is there any tabulation of the graduate students working in such establishments. Gorokhoff suggests that some idea of the magnitude of this group can be obtained from a study of the atomic-energy system of the United States and the number of engineers engaged in it. One must assume that a rather sizable group of engineers is being trained and recognize that figures on this group are never included in published Soviet statistics.

In the field of Soviet education, statistical evaluations are less likely to be widely erroneous than in other areas of the Soviet world. What is most important is an estimate of the current direction and velocity of Soviet education. The only estimate consistent with available information is that the Soviet Union is indeed attaining its goal of first matching and then surpassing the United States, both quantitatively and qualitatively, in the production of technically trained manpower.

CHAPTER VIII

The Race into Space

> The launching of artificial satellites is a kind of culmination of the competition between socialist and capitalist countries. And socialism has won it.
>
> —NIKITA S. KHRUSHCHEV

> I believe that this Nation should commit itself to achieving the goal before this decade is out of landing a man on the moon and returning him safely to the earth. No single space project in this period would be more impressive to mankind or more important for long-range exploration of space, and none would be so difficult or expensive to accomplish.
>
> —JOHN F. KENNEDY

The US-Soviet competition in science and technology is most conspicuously reflected in the race into space. The successful launching of the first Sputnik in 1957 gave the Soviet Union an immeasurable degree of pride and prestige in its technological skill and impressed the peoples of the world with what it claimed to be "unmistakable proofs" of Soviet superiority in space science. Successive achievements such as sending a rocket to circumnavigate the moon to relay pictures of its dark side and the first manned orbital flight (Yuri Gagarin in 1961) further convinced the world that the Soviet Union was leading the United States in space technology.

The following table is a record of manned orbital flights in the US-Soviet space race.

Country	Astronaut or Cosmonaut	Spacecraft	Date	Number of orbits
USSR	Yuri Gagarin	Vostok I	April 12, 1961	1
USSR	Gherman Titov	Vostok II	August 6, 1961	17½
USA	John Glenn	Friendship 7	February 20, 1962	3
USA	Scott Carpenter	Aurora 7	May 24, 1962	3

Country	Astronaut or Cosmonaut	Spacecraft	Date	Number of orbits
USSR	Andriyan Nikolayev	Vostok III	August 11, 1962	64
USSR	Pavel Popovich	Vostok IV	August 12, 1962	48
USA	Walter Schirra	Sigma 7	October 3, 1963	6
USA	Gordon Cooper	Faith 7	May 15, 1963	22
USSR	Valery Bykovsky	Vostok V	June 14, 1963	81
USSR	Valentina Tereshkova (Woman)	Vostok VI	June 16, 1963	48
USSR	Vladmir Komarov Boris Yegorov Konstantin Feoktistov (3-man flight)	Voskhod I	October 12, 1964	16
USSR	Alexei Leonov Pavel Belyayev (2-man flight)	Voskhod II	March 18, 1965	17
USA	Virgil Grissom John Young (2-man flight)	Molly Brown	March 23, 1965	3
USA	James A. McDivitt Edward H. White (2-man flight)	Gemini IV	June 3, 1965	62
USA	Gordon Cooper Charles Conrad (2-man flight)	Gemini V	August 21, 1965	120
USA	Frank Borman James A. Lovell, Jr. (2-man flight)	Gemini VII	December 4, 1965	206
USA	Walter Schirra Thomas T. Stafford (2-man flight)	Gemini VI	December 15, 1965	16

The United States, in its efforts to gather scientific data for space exploration and to narrow the gap in the space race with the Soviet Union, launched a series of highly sophisticated space vehicles such as the Explorer, the Pioneer, the Tiros (weather satellites), the Midas (early warning satellites), the Samos ("spy in space"), the Echo (radio wave reflector), the Telstar and the Syncom (communication satellites), the Ranger, and the Mariner. (Mariner IV, launched November 28, 1964, sent the first closeup "pictures" of Mars millions of miles through space in July, 1965.) Meanwhile the United States has successfully completed the Mercury Project and is concentrating on the Gemini Project. At present the immediate goal of the US-Soviet space race is to achieve a "soft landing" of an instrument package on the moon, followed by a "manned flight around the moon" and eventual landing on its surface.

For the first time in history, mankind has learned how to escape the earth's gravitational field into interplanetary space. The three-dimensional "New Frontiers"—President Kennedy's political ideals—summon not only Americans to a supreme national effort, but also all mankind to noble common endeavors—to cultivate unbounded human intelligence, to build undying peace on earth, and to explore unlimited outer space.

This chapter deals with the nature and scope of the space probe of the United States and the Soviet Union.

James W. Fulbright, Senator from Arkansas, urges that the space program, important and desirable as it is for national security and prestige, should be treated in the light of other more urgent questions, such as education and unemployment, which call for immediate and effective national action.

Robert A. Kilmarx, an expert on Soviet military affairs in the United States Department of Defense, carefully analyzes the relationships of Soviet space technology to its military goals, and points to the Soviet intent of selecting space as their "battlefield" to defeat the West in the cold war.

Walter Sullivan, a member of the New York Times staff on scientific affairs, briefly examines the recent history of the space race between the United States and the Soviet Union, discusses scientific and technical aspects of landing a man on the moon, and speculates on the ultimate goal of the Soviet space program.

1. SPACE AND NATIONAL PRIORITIES*

BY JAMES W. FULBRIGHT

Mr. President, the question which Congress must answer in determining this year's appropriation for the National Aeronautics and Space Administration is not whether we should or should not explore outer space, or even whether we should or should not try to land American astronauts on the moon. Space exploration is a great

* Address delivered in the United States Senate, October 17, 1963. Reprinted by permission of Senator Fulbright.

challenge to the human mind and spirit which may bring great benefits to humanity. The United States is uniquely endowed with the human and material resources to meet this challenge. It is within our means and in our interests to sustain a continuing effort in the exploration of outer space.

The real question before Congress is one of priorities, of how we are to allocate our great but not unlimited resources among many important national programs, of which space is only one. We must consider the NASA appropriation in the context of overall national needs, distinguishing between urgent and marginal goals, between programs which are essential and those which are merely desirable.

For reasons which I shall attempt to set forth, I believe that we are placing excessive emphasis on space in relation to other national programs, notably in the areas of education and employment. The benefits of space exploration may indeed be considerable, but they are remote and incalculable. The need for schools and jobs is immediate and pressing. The space program, we are told, is important for our security and especially our prestige. This is perhaps true, but the education of our people and the growth of our economy are far more important because these are the foundations of national power. To allow them to deteriorate is to undermine our national security as surely as would the dismantling of our military power.

There is, I believe, a dangerous imbalance between our efforts in armaments and space on the one hand and employment and education on the other. The proposed appropriation for NASA, in my opinion, reflects this imbalance. I believe that it should be substantially reduced. I further believe that any funds which are withheld from the space program should be reallocated to programs of education and employment which are before Congress this year.

The question before us, as I have said, is not whether we should or should not send a manned rocket ship to the moon but whether the project is so vital and so urgent as to warrant the indefinite postponement of other national efforts. This question has been debated at length in recent months, both in the Congress and in various publications. I have heard nothing to persuade me that it would be a national calamity if the landing on the moon were delayed until 1980 or 1990. I have heard and seen a great deal which persuades me that our continuing neglect of deteriorating schools and rising unemployment would be a national calamity.

The argument most frequently heard in support of Project Apollo is that if we do not pursue a crash program in space the Russians will get to the moon ahead of us. This argument can be challenged on two grounds: first, it is not at all clear that the Russians are trying to beat us to the moon; second—and more important—it is even less clear that it would be an irretrievable disaster if they did.

Sir Bernard Lovell, director of the Jodrell Bank Observatory in Britain, reported after a visit in July to Soviet space observatories that he saw no evidence of a high priority manned moon program. Sir Bernard was told by Russian scientists that they saw insuperable economic and technical problems to landing a man on the moon and that in any case they believed they could get nearly all the information they wanted by a soft landing of instruments on the moon. "I think, at the moment," said Sir Bernard, "the Americans are racing themselves concerning moon research."

What if Sir Bernard is wrong and the Russians really are committed to a race to the moon? What if they do get there first? Would that be an unmitigated disaster and disgrace for America? Would it make us a second-rate people, shamed in the eyes of the world, and in our own eyes, as well? I do not think so. I think it would be a temporary embarrassment and annoyance, but not a calamity. It would hurt our pride, but not our lives as free men in a free society. Most emphatically, it would not change the course of history.

The issue, as I have said, is one of priorities. It would be a fine thing indeed to have an American landing party on the moon before 1970. The question which we must ask ourselves is whether it is really worth 20 or 30 billion dollars for the glory and prestige of being first. Sir Bernard Lovell, himself an advocate of a manned moon flight, admitted recently that "people everywhere now are getting so inured to the amazing success in space that by 1967 or 1970 the landing of a man on the moon might not cause more stir than the launching of another cosmonaut or astronaut does now." But even if the world were to react with enormous enthusiasm to a landing on the moon, is it really worth 20 billion dollars or more solely for the pleasure and satisfaction of dazzling the world with our prowess and our skill? Again, I do not think so.

The conflict between freedom and dictatorship is a great deal more than a competition in technological stunts. The real issue is between two conflicting concepts of man and of his life in organized societies.

It is on this level that the contest between freedom and communism will ultimately be resolved. Does it not follow that our success in this struggle has a great deal to do with our capacity to employ and educate our people, to create the conditions for human happiness and individual fulfillment in a free society?

If, at the end of this decade, the Russians should have reached the moon, and we should not, but if we, instead, have succeeded in building the best system of public education in the world, in the renovation of our cities and transport, in the virtual elimination of slums and crime, in the alleviation of poverty and disease, whose prestige would be higher, who would then be ahead in the worldwide struggle for the minds and the allegiance of men?

The mind does not readily grasp the significance of a sum of $20 or $30 billion. Warren Weaver, vice president of the Alfred P. Sloan Foundation, has provided some dramatic comparisons between the cost of the moon race and that of some urgently needed projects here on earth. With $30 billion, he points out, we could give a 10-percent raise in salary, over a 10-year period, to every teacher in the United States, from kindergarten through universities—about $9.8 billion; could give $10 million each to 200 colleges—$2 billion; could finance 7-year fellowships at $4,000 per person per year for 50,000 new scientists and engineers—$1.4 billion; could contribute $200 million each toward the creation of 10 new medical schools—$2 billion; could build and largely endow complete universities with liberal arts, medical, engineering, and agricultural faculties for all 53 of the nations which have been added to the United Nations since its founding—$13.2 billion; could create three more permanent Rockefeller Foundations—$1.5 billion; and we would still have left $100 million for a program of informing the public about science.

It is frequently said that we did not provide adequate funds for education and other vital domestic needs before we had a space program, and that there is no assurance that we would increase our efforts in these areas if the space program were abandoned or reduced. This, I am bound to concede, may well be true, although the Congress has come close, several times, and very close, last year, to adopting a meaningful program of Federal aid to education, and it is possible that the reduction of our space expenditures would provide the impetus for the enactment of a really good education bill. In any case, I see little merit in the view that since we will not spend money, anyway, on things we urgently need, we might as well spend it on things we do not need. If it comes to that, I, for one, would rather not spend the money at all.

Another rather specious argument that is put forward for a crash program to reach the moon is that of inaccurate and oversimplified historical analogy. We are told, for example, that, like Spain in the time of Columbus, we are living in an age of discovery, and that, like Columbus, we must not fail to seize our moment of greatness. The analogy is a stirring and dramatic one, but it is hardly a sound basis for the shaping of public policy. If Columbus is to be brought into our discussion of outer space, it is worth noting that he raised a substantial part of the costs of his voyages from private sources, and that in any case he was not at all interested in discovering new lands, but only in discovering a shorter and less costly route to the Indies. It is also worth noting that the conquest of the New World brought Spain only a brief period of glory, which was followed by four centuries of political and economic decay. Finally, I am not at all sure that it would have been one of the great tragedies of history if America had been discovered in 1500, or even 1600, instead of 1492.

Another questionable argument that is made for Project Apollo is that instruments cannot be substituted for men in our exploration of the moon. There is, in fact, a very impressive body of scientific testimony to the contrary. Philip Abelson, for example, the editor of *Science Magazine,* and he himself a noted physical chemist, pointed out recently that "The cost of unmanned lunar vehicles is on the order of 1 percent of the cost of the manned variety," and that "most of the interesting questions concerning the moon can be studied by electronic devices." And Dr. Vannevar Bush, who is well known in this city for his great work during the war, stated recently:

"There is nothing a man can do in space that cannot be done better and more cheaply by instruments. There is very little scientific knowledge to be gained by rushing to hurtle men into space. To me such exploits are little more than stunts that appeal to the gladiator instincts."

British physicist R. L. F. Boyd maintains that:

"For scientific purposes, man is a nuisance in space. The plain fact of the matter is that for one-tenth of the cost one could get 90 percent of the valuable information—without having to overcome the enormous difficulties of putting a man on the moon and getting him back alive."

Warren Weaver of the National Academy of Sciences, wrote recently:

"I do not think that scientific considerations justify the proposed magnitude of the program, and even more emphatically I do not believe that scientific considerations justify its frantic, costly and disastrous pace."

If, in fact, as these eminent scientists believe, we can gain most of the information we want about the moon at one-tenth of the projected cost of Project Apollo, by using instruments instead of men, Congress could make a very substantial reduction in the space appropriation without impairing our national space effort in any important way. It becomes increasingly clear that the principal object of our moon program is the glory and distinction of being "first in space." I for one do not believe we can afford a program which, if we assume its minimum cost of $20 billion, will add up to $2 billion for science and $18 billion for prestige.

Perhaps more important than the costs of space research is the fact that it is drawing urgently needed scientific talent away from the civilian economy. In 1961, for example, of 400,000 scientists and engineers engaged in research and development work in the United States, 250,000 were doing it for space and defense. Since 1954, the number of research and development scientists and engineers in industry has increased by 160,000, but all but 30,000 of these have been drawn into Government-sponsored projects. As one research director of a private company commented recently: "We need good people, but my company can't compete with projects paid for by the U. S. Treasury."

Technically qualified manpower has become a critically scarce resource. The increase in the supply of research scientists and engineers this year is expected to be about 27,000, but some 25,000 of these—virtually the entire supply—will be drawn into space research and development. Prof. Barry Commoner of Washington University in St. Louis has said that the space agency will require the services of one in every four U. S. scientists by 1970.

There is thus a real danger that our national programs in defense and space will become a drain on the civilian economy and will jeopardize our position in world trade. At present only 25 percent of our total national research and development spending is going into industrial research for civilian purposes. Western European countries are spending twice as large a proportion of their gross national products as the United States for civilian research and development. The Japanese, largely as a result of progress through civilian research, have introduced the first transistorized television sets into the United States, are getting twice our rate of production from textile machinery, and are turning out automated ships that can carry more cargo than our ships with smaller crews.

Equally alarming is the prospective diversion of scientists and engineers from careers in university teaching. In the next decade there will be a great increase in our college population. If the present teacher-student ratio is to be maintained, the universities in the next several years will have to retain two-thirds of their current output of new Ph.D.'s instead of the present one-third. Thus, the current flow of graduate research scholars to Government and industry would have to be cut in half. It is just at this critical point that the demand for scientific talent for the space program is rapidly rising. It is increasingly clear that the supply of scientists and engineers in the present decade will not be sufficient to meet the demands of a mushrooming space program, a rapidly expanding college population, and all the other needs of the civilian economy.

These, I believe, are some of the compelling reasons for bringing our space program into a more realistic relationship to pressing national needs. In the face of all the unsolved problems of our country—problems of inadequate education and rising unemployment, of urban blight and rising crime and many others—I cannot bring myself to believe that landing an American on the moon represents the most urgent need, the most compelling challenge, or the most promising opportunity before the American people in this decade. The incongruousness and distortion of priorities that is involved in a crash program in space is admirably expressed in a story that is told of a Russian pupil in a physics class, who, when told of the plans to land a Russian on the moon, agreed that this was a fine thing and asked: "But when may we go to Vienna?"

I believe, Mr. President, for the reasons I have set forth, that in its appropriation for NASA for fiscal year 1964 the Congress should substantially reduce the amount of the authorization. It should be made quite clear that such a reduction in funds for the space program in no way implies a lack of confidence in the space agency itself or in the competent and dedicated people who have made our space program so great a success over the last several years. The meaning and purpose of a reduction in funds, as I see it, is to register a judgment by the Congress on national priorities, a judgment that space exploration, though valuable and desirable, is only one of many valuable and desirable national programs, some of which under existing circumstances, have a prior and more pressing claim on our limited national resources.

The highest priority need of America in the 1960's is the expansion and improvement of public education. While a vast proportion of the wealth and talent of America are expended on defense and space, our public schools, the ultimate source of our national strength and welfare, are deteriorating under the pressures of inadequate funds, inadequate numbers of teachers with inadequate training, and a rapidly mounting school-age population.

Horace Mann wrote: An undereducated nation is like an obscene giant who has waxed strong in his youth and grown wanton in his strength; whose brain has been developed only in the region of the appetites and passions. Such a republic, with all its noble capacities for beneficence, will rush with the speed of a whirlwind to an ignominious end.

Is America an undereducated nation? The answer lies all around us, in the growing number of our "unemployables," in mounting rates of crime and juvenile delinquency, in lingering vestiges of poverty within our affluent society. Consider, for example, a recent report by the Army Surgeon General's Office showing that one out of every four young Americans who were called before the draft boards in 1962 was rejected for failing the Army's intelligence test. In North Dakota, with the best record, only 7 percent of the draftees failed the mental examination; in South Carolina, with the worst record, 5 out of every 10 draftees failed the mental test. In the District of Columbia, one out of every three draftees failed the mental test, and even in New York, with one of the best financed systems of education in the Nation, one of every three draftees could not pass the Army's mental examination.

A recent report by the National Committee for the Support of the Public Schools shows that fewer than one-third of the people of my own State of Arkansas have completed 4 years of high school and that only a half have completed the eighth grade. According to the report, only 4.8 percent of the people of my State have completed 4 years of college and 15.4 percent of the population are considered functionally illiterate, having completed less than 5 years of schooling. The correction of this situation, in my opinion, and of similar situations in many other States, is far more urgent and important than the landing of an American on the moon in 1970 or at any time in this century.

There is no problem more pressing in our national life than the need for improving and expanding our public education. Although expenditures on public education have risen rapidly in the last decade, they have not nearly kept pace with the increase in our school age population, which since 1950 has been growing twice as fast as the total population. We have been economizing on education and for this false economy we cannot avoid paying a heavy price in the prosperity and happiness of our people and, ultimately, in the security and defense of freedom.

The correlation between lack of education and unemployment is high and continually rising. In March 1961 the unemployment rate among professional and technical workers was 1.6 percent; among clerical workers 4.9 percent; skilled workers, 9.1 percent; semiskilled workers, 12.1 percent; and unskilled workers, 19.1 percent. In the complex and increasingly automated American economy of the 1960's the unskilled and untrained worker is increasingly relegated to a life of intermittent or chronic unemployment, to a hopeless shuffling from one menial job to another, to a life of diminishing hopes and mounting disillusion. While the demand for highly skilled workers continues to rise, the unskilled worker is increasingly destined to be not only unemployed but unemployable.

The slow but continuing increase in unemployment among the work force as a whole, and the very rapid increase of unemployment among young people, is largely the result of grave shortcomings in our public education, especially for the 80 percent of American youth who do not go to college. The vocational education bill passed by the House and by the Senate will, if enacted, make a powerful contribution toward remedying this situation, but it will be only a valuable first step toward meeting an overriding national problem. It should be followed by further measures in the field of education, including the adoption of the President's program for basic education for the 8 million adult Americans who, lacking the ability to read, write, and do simple arithmetic, are "functional illiterates." At present, these people would be unable to benefit from vocational training programs even if they were available to them because they lack the basic educational tools for training and employment. Surely, a major national effort to remedy these problems, with their enormously destructive social, economic, and political implications, warrants a high priority in our public policy.

We live in a society which, though affluent beyond all others, has not yet succeeded in eliminating widespread poverty and deprivation. As President Kennedy pointed out in his last State of the Union message, some 32 million Americans "still live on the outskirts of poverty." Some authorities cite much higher figures. The Conference on Economic Progress has said that 38 million Americans live in poverty and another 39 million live in substantial deprivation.

Throughout the country there is a high correlation between poverty and dependency and lack of education. In my own State of Arkansas 89.4 percent of all the people on public welfare rolls have less than a fourth-grade education. The $4.5 billion which is spent on welfare payments each year by Federal, State, and local authorities is of course only a small part of the cost of inadequate education. Crime and delinquency, losses of economic productivity, and the destructive social and political consequences of inadequate education are also part of the equation, and their costs to the Nation are beyond calculation.

Until we have gone much farther toward the solution of these critical problems of our national life, I do not see how we can regard a voyage to the moon as one of the high priority objectives of our public policy. The conquest of outer space is a worthy and inspiring aspiration, but the education and employment of our people is a basic and immediate necessity. With will and dedication, it is entirely within our means to overcome the problems of poverty and unemployment and inadequate education. When we have done so, it will be time enough to direct our aspirations toward the moon and whatever lies beyond.

2. THE SOVIET SPACE PROGRAM*

BY ROBERT A. KILMARX

The Soviet space program is entering a period of more accelerated advance as a result of careful planning, high priority investment of resources and a step-by-step approach to problem-solving. There is good reason to believe that this new period will include the development of operational space systems within the next few years to augment the military as well as the political strength of the U.S.S.R. Evidence of this intent can be found in the recent record of Soviet astronautical activity, in statements by Soviet political and military leaders concerning program objectives, in organizational changes, in revisions in Soviet positions in the field of space jurisprudence and even in reorientations in Soviet space technology. The flames of the cold war may be dampened on earth but the spark has already risen in space and may soon ignite this new dimension.

The importance the Russians attach to their space program is attested to by the fact that it has received increased allocations of scarce resources at a time when the Soviet economy has been facing severe economic problems: the rate of industrial growth is down, the pace of new investment has faltered, agriculture is in the doldrums and the consumer's needs are still not being met.

It is also a time when pressures from the military sector have been more intense to build up strategic, nuclear forces while retaining modern mass armies and conventional weapons systems. Despite Premier Khrushchev's ambitious plans to equal and surpass the West in economic strength, the annual rate of the increase in the Soviet gross national product (GNP) has probably fallen below that of the United States, at least for a while, largely because of military and space requirements.

The increased pace of the Soviet space program in 1962 and 1963 can be statistically or qualitatively demonstrated in many ways. For example, of the 35-plus space launchings from 1957 through 1962

* From *Current History,* Vol. 45 (October, 1963), pp. 200–4 +. Reprinted by permission of the author and *Current History.*

which were at least partially successful, 20 occurred in 1962 and the rate remains high in 1963. In 1962 and early 1963, the Soviets stepped up the pace of their failure-plagued interplanetary program with a number of attempts to probe Mars and Venus, resumed their lunar launchings, began an active new *Cosmos* series of earth satellite launchings, and took a giant step in their primary area of concentration, manned space flight near the earth.

On August 11–12, 1962, there were the twin orbital flights of Andriyan Nikolayev and Pavel Popovich, who approached within 6.5 km of each other in space. In June, 1963, similar dual flights followed of 48 and 81 orbits, respectively, by Valentina Tereshkova and Lieutenant Colonel Valery Bykovsky.

All these flights demonstrated advanced capabilities and prospects for successful orbital systems which seemed highly uncertain only a few years ago. Space rendezvous, docking and inter-satellite transfer may soon follow, as well as some soft landings on the moon.

Prior to 1962, the Soviets repeatedly claimed that their space program was directed only towards peaceful, scientific purposes. Later this hackneyed theme began to change. Following Premier Khrushchev's implication in December, 1961, that the "space ships" of Gagarin and Titov could be used to carry nuclear weapons "to any point on the globe," a number of Soviet military leaders and strategists developed this new theme. The list includes Soviet Minister of Defense Marshal Malinovsky, who characterized space as one of the areas of future warfare in Soviet military doctrine. This followed articles in *Red Star* in March, 1962, which stated that "The Soviet Union is forced to accept the necessity of studying military operations utilizing outer-space means."[1]

A few months later, statements appeared in Marshal Sokolovsky's book, *Military Strategy,* to the effect that the use of outer space and of space vehicles to strengthen Soviet defenses "is considered essential in Soviet military strategy." According to this text, "an important problem now is warfare with artificial earth satellites which can be launched for the most diverse reasons, even as carriers of nuclear weapons."

On February 21, 1963, the developing crescendo of suggestions concerning a Soviet military space program went into a higher gear

---

[1] Propaganda aspects of such pronouncements, however, obscure any assessment of the feasibility of the concepts discussed by the Soviets.

when the former Commander-in-Chief of the Strategic Rocket Forces, Marshal Biryuzov, claimed over Moscow Radio that rockets can be launched from satellites "at any desirable time and at any point of the satellites' trajectory, on command from earth." Marshal Biryuzov was formerly Commander-in-Chief of the Strategic Rocket Forces; he was placed at the head of the General Staff after the failure to establish an offensive missile base in Cuba led to a reassertion by Premier Khrushchev of his radical military doctrine of January, 1960, with its primary emphasis on advanced means of waging war, particularly on strategic rocket nuclear weapons.

In view of these pronouncements, the possibility certainly exists that the Soviets have already decided to develop a number of military space systems. Thus it is prudent to recall the history of other weapons programs, as did *The Economist* over two years ago. "The Russians . . .," stated *The Economist,* "persistently maintained that their nuclear research programme was devoted to peaceful purposes right up to the moment when it produced weapons." According to a United States authority on the Soviet space program, F. J. Krieger, the current *Cosmos* series of Soviet heavy satellites is to be a program of directly military-oriented space development.

Looking to the future, one may visualize the possible development of a Soviet hypersonic-glide, sub-orbital weapons system or an orbital, maneuverable space plane. Recently Soviet aircraft designer Mikoyan predicted hypersonic flight with variable-wing aircraft, traveling six or seven times the speed of sound. He said that such aircraft might have ranges of several thousand miles and might be capable of making several circuits of the earth. Judging from the configuration of re-entry systems for Soviet space boosters appearing on Soviet monuments and postage stamps, greater emphasis will be given by the Soviets in the years ahead to aerodynamic vehicles that fly at hypersonic speeds, i.e., vehicles that literally ride the head of a ballistic missile.

Since the establishment of space stations may be considered one of the most important intermediate goals of Soviet astronautics, the not-too-distant future offers the prospect of giant, Soviet space stations in near-earth and then in more distant orbits; these space stations will be capable of performing a wide variety of missions. At a later date the Soviets may seek to extend such capabilities to moon-bases and even to interplanetary space.

The offensive and defensive weapons available to such vehicles may be nuclear or perhaps of the radiation type, capable of destroying select targets instantaneously and from great distances. The demonstrable conformity between the early dreams of science fiction and the probable realities of astronautics offers a major challenge to those who postulate stability in strategic forces in the decades to come.

To the Soviets, calculations of cost effectiveness for space systems seem to be broadly construed, to include political values and not just comparative tests of true military worth. The Soviets are primarily interested in providing a "back-drop" of military power to support a forward political policy and in improving the world's image concerning the alleged benefits of the Communist formula for progressive development.

The Soviet Union has already learned that missile and space spectaculars can impress the uncommitted as well as the free world, can enhance the image of deterrent strength and can substitute temporarily for real fighting capability. The utility of scientific space spectaculars as hallmarks of power, however, has depreciated with time. As *The Economist* noted in April, 1961, ". . . the successive marvels of the space age are already tending to yield diminishing moral returns." To reinvigorate the political value of space achievements, the Soviets may now establish a closer, perhaps demonstrable, relationship between space experiments and real strategic military strength.

Another clue that a major change has occurred in scope, pace and direction of the Soviet space program is revealed by an examination of organizational realignment in the U.S.S.R.

Initially, when scientific orientation was the paramount requirement, the program was managed primarily by a scientific committee under the Astronomical Council of the Academy of Science. This committee, called the Interagency Committee for Interplanetary Communication, included representatives of the military establishment; the initial steps towards the conquest of space were viewed as a joint military-civilian effort. Furthermore, the Ministry of Defense and several State Committees concerned with defense production provided the facilities, the launching vehicles and other supports used to carry scientific instruments and pioneer astronauts into the cosmos.

The program in this early phase was governed in large measure by actual and anticipated requirements of national power, i.e., by prospects for obtaining short-term political benefits as a result of space spectaculars and probably for developing future military space systems. The likelihood that military systems objectives were a governing priority for the Soviet space program from its earliest days is indicated by Soviet concentration on manned satellite operations in a limited envelope of near-earth space.

By 1962, important organizational changes are believed to have been made in the Soviet space program. The requirements of systems development and production were probably broadening the scope of scientific and industrial activity. Furthermore, the need was becoming greater for more concentrated basic research on the operational environment in which Soviet space systems would function. As a result, the Soviet space program today probably has at its apex a committee of the Council of Ministers, with the military program controlled by Minister of Defense Malinovsky. His requirements for production resources are under the over-all purview of Dimitry Ustinov, head of the newly formed Supreme Council of the National Economy.

Research needs are coordinated through the State Committee for the Coordination of Scientific Research, established in April, 1961, and now headed by K. N. Rudnev. Both officials are experienced leaders in the field of defense technology. Basic research is conducted under the Academy of Science, which probably also controls the "peaceful uses" of space programs. This aspect of the Soviet space program includes cooperation with the West in such fields as meteorological and communications satellites.

The gradual evolution of a separate organizational and institutional relationship for the military and non-military aspects of the Soviet space program is in keeping with the historical pattern noted in the Soviet nuclear program. In time, we may expect to see the emergence of a Main Administration on the Uses of Space to handle the non-military aspects of the Soviet space program, although developments in this area could also contribute to the support of Soviet military capabilities. The organization of the military space program will probably remain obscured by concealed directorships, complex institutional relationships and even misleading organizational names. This path was followed in the Soviet nuclear weapons program, which cloaked its extensive weapons development and production operations under the innocent label of the Ministry of Medium Machine Building.

Extensive investment of resources over a long period of time has already provided the Soviet Union with a technological base. The technological base is sufficiently broad to permit the development of military space capabilities without long lead-times after basic policy decisions have been made and without protracted research and development. This aspect of space may also be compared with a "peaceful" nuclear program which can be translated into at least limited, war-making capabilities without much delay. The unique and disturbing features of broadly-based, modern technology add to the risks of technological surprise and weapons proliferation and complicate problems of disarmament.

United States awareness of this vulnerability in regard to space weapons has been called to the attention of Congress.

It is worth noting that the Air Force Research and Development Chief reportedly told the House Space Committee that it is conceivable that some object put into orbit around the earth by the Soviet Union might carry a nuclear warhead without the United States knowing it.

Concurrently the United States is seeking to explore all prospects for military roles in this dimension. In the words of Eugene Fubini, Assistant Secretary of Defense (Deputy Director, Defense Research and Engineering),

> We are proceeding with the *Dyna-Soar* and *Gemini* programs as insurance against what lies behind the curtain that veils requirements for manned military space efforts; the curtain we shall try to lift.

The United States already has many projects under way to meet recognized military requirements in space with unmanned vehicles.

The technology of the Soviet space program has been entering a period of change. Established practice has revealed emphasis on proven design and a certain conservatism in production processes, where possible, to reduce risks and avoid costly efforts to find sophisticated, new solutions to old problems. Soviet space vehicles, for example, have combined advanced designs and engineering techniques with off-the-shelf items and standard practices; Soviet design has utilized proven components and sub-systems and the gradual accumulation of test experience.

However, new demands are being made because of the greater sophistication required of new components, the increases needed in performance parameters and the rise in the complexity of experimental goals. The Soviet space program must now give more attention to original, perfectionist and novel designs, to new materials and engineering methods and to higher quality production techniques. State-of-the-art advances have become more important. Soviet space scientists and engineers must depart even more from the past focus on ease-of-production, reliability, simplicity and short developmental lead-times. They probably can benefit even less from Western advances than in the past.

This transformation is made possible by the gradual reduction or removal of the constraints of past industrial backwardness; of shortages of skilled personnel, quality materials and equipment; and of institutional and managerial blockages. There are many indices of this change in capabilities and prospects. The Soviet investment in basic research has grown at a very high rate; the number of research and test centers and facilities is mounting; the available pool of scientists and engineers with advanced degrees who are seeking to make their mark in research is reaching new levels in numbers and in qualifications.

Supporting industries are also gaining in experience and thus are lightening the burden on the research and development sector. Furthermore, the outlook for better planning, organization and managerial methods through cybernetics will promote more effective use of and control over scientific and production resources, in spite of Premier Khrushchev's recent complaints about the efficiency of the armament industry and his new efforts to improve economic management. In short, from the technological standpoint, the Soviet space program is entering a period of innovation and quality advance on expanding economic foundations. Long term risk-taking has always been attractive to the Soviet Union when the costs were low and opportunities great; now more consideration must be given to shorter-term risks and to their reduction through scientific investigation and experimentation.

Other indications of a new phase in the Soviet space program have been provided by developments concerning Soviet jurisprudence in space. According to Robert Crane, who has ably analyzed developments in this field in the *American Journal of International Law,* "during 1962 the first indications appeared that Soviet space law was developing into an instrument to support the shift of [the Soviet space] offensive from the political into the military realm." One of the most significant indications reported is "the refinement and even the rejection of the previous Soviet position that military uses of space are illegal. . . ."

As recently stated by Soviet legal space experts in the spring of 1962, there is no "organic contradiction" between the use of space for scientific purposes and its use to protect national security. In August, 1962, the Executive Secretary of the Space Law Commission of the Soviet Academy of Sciences stated: ". . . it by no means follows that it is forbidden to use this space for striking through it or with its aid a retaliatory blow at the aggressor in the course of legitimate self-defense."

The significance of this trend can be evaluated only with caution at this point in history because of the uncertainties of politics, the pressures of economics, the many remaining mysteries of space, and the wide scope and nature of the cold war power assets of both East and West. It is evident, however, that space warfare capabilities will assume an ever-increasing role in strategic calculations during this decade. It would appear that the conquest of space has become a primary route that the U.S.S.R. will follow in an effort to reinvigorate both the image and reality of its power in the cold war.

Space already may have been selected as the key medium in which the Soviets hope to attain military superiority over the West. A pronounced affirmation of the goal of military superiority by top Soviet military leaders occurred in 1962 and was concurrent with the new emphasis on the military uses of space.

Perhaps with the space program in mind, Marshal Malinovsky said that "New scientific ideas and technical inventions, as a role, are evaluated not only from the standpoint of their general importance, but also from the standpoint of the prospects for military use." Close analysis of this document reveals that the stated goal does not represent special pleading by the military sector but has been politically determined by top Soviet leadership. Subsequent articles by Marshal Greshko in *Izvestia* and by a Colonel Ratnikov in *Red Star* reiterated the theme of military superiority. Marshal Greshko openly stated that the Communist party and the Soviet government "are basing their military policy" on the superiority of the armed forces of "the soundest commonwealth" over those of the West.

Mention of "the soundest commonwealth" may be the harbinger

of an effort to reaffirm the paramountcy of the Soviet Union within the Communist bloc, based on superior military technology. To the Russians, the polycentrism of the Communist world movement, unlike the polycentrism of the universe, is not governed by immutable, natural laws. The Sino-Soviet controversy, especially, could provide an additional stimulus to Soviet planners to attain clear superiority in new weapons fields.

The prospect that the Soviets already may have decided to seek military superiority over the West in space warfare places a special responsibility for vigilance on the United States. As recently stated by General William F. McKee, Vice Chief of Staff of the United States Air Force: ". . . we must watch our own and the Soviets' space programs carefully. This is probably the area of greatest demand on our vision as a nation. For it is here that one of us, probably, will find the key to the strategic superiority of the 1970's."

3. A RUSSIAN STEPS INTO SPACE*

BY WALTER SULLIVAN

In Moscow last week [March 18, 1965] a Soviet space official said, "The target now before us is the moon, and we hope to reach it in the not distant future."

In the U.S., a spaceman said glumly, "The Russians upstage us every time."

The remarks reflected contrasting moods in the two countries in the aftermath of a new Soviet "space spectacular" at a moment when the United States was preparing for a more modest one of its own. The Soviet feat was the first venture by a spaceman out of his spacecraft into the void of space. It lasted only ten minutes, but it had a dramatic impact that was heightened by the fact that millions in Russia and elsewhere watched it on live TV.

American officials suspected the Soviet achievement was timed for psychological effect. It came only five days before a scheduled

* From *The New York Times,* March 21, 1965, p. E3. Reprinted by permission.

resumption of manned flight by the United States after a pause of nearly two years. This week the next stage of the American space program is to get under way with the first launching of a two-man Gemini spacecraft into orbit.

Attainment of the major goal now sought—a landing on the moon —is still years away for both nations. But the Russians clearly hold the lead now—as they have ever since the space age dawned with the flight of the first earth satellite seven and a half years ago.

Last week's feat was the latest of many Soviet "firsts" in the space race, starting with the launching of Sputnik 1, the pioneer earth satellite, on Oct. 4, 1957.

The Russians took an early lead in the race, and concentrated on spectacular achievements with high propaganda potential. Their initial advantage derived from the big rockets they developed after World War II. Lacking adequate bombers, the Russians needed the rockets as propellants for nuclear missiles which, at the time, were heavy and bulky. These large rockets enabled the Russians to launch bigger manned capsules capable of supporting their passengers on flights far longer than those attempted by the U.S.

After Sputnik 1 there came a series of unmanned "firsts," including a satellite with an animal aboard, a sun satellite, photographs of the hidden side of the moon, and a Venus probe launched from orbit.

Yuri Gagarin became the first spaceman on April 12, 1961, with one circuit of the earth. He was followed by the first double launching with humans in August, 1962; the first woman in space in June, 1963, and the first triple-manned launching last October.

The U.S. started much more slowly. After the war the U.S. relied on planes to carry its A-bombs; it began rocket work on a major scale only after developing light-weight nuclear weapons in 1954.

Though American payloads as a result have been smaller than Russia's, the U.S. space program has had a broader scope. American space science has developed highly sophisticated satellites to probe space secrets, to aid navigation, to provide data on weather on earth, to link continents in telecommunications. A notable "first" was achieved last August when Ranger 7, an unmanned vehicle, hit the moon and sent back close-up pictures.

Still manned space flight accounts for much of the U.S. effort in space. The U.S. currently is in the second phase of its moon program. The first phase was the Mercury series that began with Alan Shepard's suborbital flight in 1961 and ended with Gordon Cooper's flight of 22 orbits in May, 1963.

The second phase—Project Gemini—calls for the launching of a larger space capsule, carrying two astronauts who will test the complicated devices and techniques to help us in Project Apollo, the culminating phase that will carry a three-man expedition to the moon. The first of at least 10 manned Gemini flights is scheduled for this week.

The biggest "first" sought by both Russia and the U.S., of course, is landing a man on the moon. This will require a much more powerful rocket than either country has at present. Thus, it is possible that the Americans may be the first to develop such a rocket and thereby take the lead.

But the Russians lead now—as they showed dramatically last week.

The Soviet space shot came as a surprise to many people throughout the world. There had been no advance hints that anything special was pending. After hearing the first announcement of the flight, some Americans speculated that the Russians were only trying to take some of the gloss off the U.S.'s scheduled Gemini flight.

But then on television screens throughout the Soviet Union and other nations in Europe came the blurred but startling pictures of the cosmonaut in the black void of space. A television camera fixed to the side of the spaceship Voshkod II allowed the world to see him push himself away, attached only by an "umbilical" line, to roll, float and tumble for 10 minutes before pulling himself back into the vehicle—a science fiction story become reality.

The spaceship, apparently essentially the same as the Voskhod I which last October carried a three-man crew into space, had been launched only hours before from the Soviet cosmodrome near Baikonur, in the Central Asian deserts of Kazakhstan. It was under the command of a colonel in the Soviet Air Force, Pavel I. Belyayev. His co-pilot was Lieut. Col. Aleksei A. Leonov, the man who floated in space.

The ship flew the customary route of Soviet space vehicles—northeasterly across Siberia, then southeast along the central axis of the Pacific Ocean, crossing the Atlantic at an angle of 65 degrees. Its orbit had an apogee, or high point, of 399 miles, which is higher than any other manned spaceship has flown. The previous high point of

254 miles was reached by Voskhod I. The perigee, or low point, of this week's orbit was given as 108 miles.

It is assumed that as the Voshkod II completed its first orbit, Colonel Leonov entered a special compartment, or air lock, sealed off from the main cabin in which Colonel Belyayev continued to pilot the craft. Both men would have been breathing pure oxygen at just under half the normal atmospheric pressure to clear all nitrogen from their bodies.

With the nitrogen expelled, they could endure far lower air pressure than normal without danger of "the bends," or decompression sickness. This ailment, which afflicts divers who surface too quickly, is caused when, under condition of quick changes in air pressure, nitrogen forms bubbles in the blood. These can cause acute pain in the limbs and abdomen, paralysis and even death.

The oxygen was then slowly drained from the air lock simply by allowing it to escape into the void of space. At the same time, the internal pressure of Colonel Leonov's space suit—from all indications a relatively unsophisticated costume without the self-supporting oxygen or propulsion systems essential for a moon landing—was correspondingly reduced so it would not blow up into an unmanageable balloon as the outside pressure dropped.

With the air lock drained—had this not been done first the cosmonaut would have been blown out like a pea from a peashooter—the hatch was opened. Colonel Leonov then stuck his head and shoulders out. He grasped a handrail, lifted his feet out of the airlock and extended them sideways, like a gymnast working out on parallel bars. With a gentle shove, he then sailed off about 15 feet from the spacecraft, linked to it only by his tether line. This line carried his communication link with his fellow astronaut and the oxygen that he breathed. He also appeared to be wearing oxygen tanks on his back, probably an emergency supply in case the tether line broke or became kinked.

After 10 minutes of gentle acrobatics, he pulled himself back through the hatch by the tether cord. The door was then sealed and oxygen readmitted to the air lock until the pressure in the chamber equalled that in the rest of the craft. He was then free to rejoin his fellow spaceman.

Why did he drift along with the space ship instead of falling behind it or dropping toward the earth? The explanation involves Newton's first law of motion: that a body in motion will remain in a state of uniform motion unless acted upon by some outside force. Since Colonel Leonov had gone through the same acceleration as his ship, he was in orbit just as it was. Since both were speeding through a virtual vacuum, there was no air drag. Thus when he stepped outside the vehicle he continued to sail along at the same speed. Even if his tether cord had broken, he would not have strayed far from the vehicle unless something pushed him.

Twenty-six hours and two minutes after launch, at the end of their 17th orbit of earth, the two cosmonauts landed the Voskhod II near Perm, a town west of the Ural Mountains and 700 miles northeast of Moscow. Both were reported to "feel well."

There is no record of any other Soviet cosmonauts landing in the Perm area and heavy forests there would appear to make it an unsuitable site for space operations. This, plus the fact that Moscow gave no progress reports for nearly seven hours toward the end of the flight, prompted speculation that something had gone wrong and the landing had not been as planned.

The Russian people rejoiced as the world applauded the feat. A British expert hailed it as "the most incredible achievement yet" and a top French specialist called it "a very, very great step forward." President Johnson sent Soviet leaders, cosmonauts and scientists his congratulations saying: "all of us have been deeply impressed."

From the scientific standpoint, the importance of the feat lies in the fact that it proves the feasibility of some of the space planners ideas. It has been assumed that astronauts eventually would be able to float in space, on a tether, to make repairs on and inspect vehicles and perform other tasks, including even the assembly of platforms and other craft in space.

Politically, the space success gives the Russians a much-needed shot in the arm at a time when they are under fire because of their split with the Chinese, their policy in Vietnam and their failure to achieve predicted economic advances.

At Cape Kennedy all last week, reporters, photographers and TV crews gathered for what was to be a big American week in the space race: a new Ranger shot to the moon scheduled for today; the two-man Gemini flight scheduled for this week. There was anticipation and excitement in the air.

It quickly turned to gloom and frustration with the news of the Soviet feat. Nevertheless, the plans went forward with attention focused mainly on the Gemini flight as an important milestone in the American reach for the moon.

The Gemini spacecraft is a two-man vehicle designed for evolution of the techniques that are vital for a landing on the moon. Paramount in this respect is rendezvous between spacecraft in orbit and docking —the joining together of vehicles in space.

In Project Apollo, the American scheme for landing men on the moon, a composite vehicle will be maneuvered into orbit around the moon. Two of the astronauts will then climb into one unit of the vehicle—the "bug"—which will separate and descend to the moon, leaving the main vehicle in orbit with the third man aboard.

For the return trip the bug will lift the explorers from the moon to rendezvous with the main vehicle. Upon this difficult maneuver will depend the lives of the two men. Once aboard their home spaceship they and their third companion will return to earth. Thus, at least in the American program, rendezvous and docking are the key to the success of the moon project.

America's first operational steps toward rendezvous and docking will be taken in this week's Gemini flight, if all goes well. Astronauts Virgil I. Grissom, a major in the Air Force, and John W. Young, a Navy lieutenant commander, will carry out a series of preliminary maneuvers.

They are to be launched into a comparatively lopsided orbit, reaching out 150 miles from the earth and with a perigee or low point of about 100 miles. As they complete their first orbit (flying over Texas) they will fire a rocket tending to drive the ship backwards. At this point they will be near low point of the orbit and the effect will be to deprive them of the inertia needed to sail out to their original high point, or apogee, on the far side of the world. Instead, their maximum height on the second orbit will be only about 107 miles. The orbital path will thus be almost a perfect circle. Shortly past the midpoint of this orbit they will fire another complex of small rockets that will push the vehicle sideways, changing the plane of its orbit. In most, if not all, manned space flights to date the plane of the orbit has remained fixed in space. It has been like a rabbit running in loops on a slope. The shape of the loops might change, but not the tilt of the slope.

To change the orbital plane requires considerable thrust. In the first manned Gemini flight the change will only be slight.

Thus first priority, in Gemini, has been given to maneuvers. On the second manned flight, perhaps in June, an astronaut may open the hatch and poke his head and shoulders out to test the airtight integrity of the space suit, but it may be a year before anyone pushes from a Gemini space ship into the void.

There has been much perplexity as to the prime goal of the Soviet space program. The Russians are obviously going somewhere in a very determined manner. Is it to beat American astronauts to the moon? Is it, instead, to construct a large space station in orbit around the earth—one capable of performing a variety of scientific and military tasks? The question persists despite the Soviet official's remark last week about the moon as "the target before us." The next day a dispatch by Tass, the official Soviet press agency, spoke of the advantages of free-floating astronauts in assembling "heavy inter-mediate stations" in orbit around the earth. These stations would be composed of units launched by separate rockets. Later, the dispatch said, vehicles would be launched from such platforms towards the moon and planets.

But if the Russians have, in fact, set the moon as their next major goal in space, some find it strange that they have launched no effort for studying the lunar surface comparable to the American Ranger project. The Ranger vehicles carry a nest of six cameras that televise images of the surface to earth as they plunge into the moon. They are to be followed by the so-called Surveyor vehicles that will be landed intact, by means of breaking rockets, and will then transmit to earth information on the composition of the surface and its bearing strength.

It is possible that the Russians have decided to embark directly upon such a project. Or, some have suggested, they may be counting on the United States to provide data on the surface.

It was proposed last week that the next logical step for the Russians would be some long-duration orbital flights, followed by the launching of cosmonauts to orbit the moon and return. This would not tell much about what the moon is made of, but it would be another Soviet "spectacular."

To send one of the known Soviet cosmonaut vehicles into a lunar orbit would require a rocket with about five times as much thrust as that of the rocket that launched Voskhod II last Thursday. The latter is thought to have developed a thrust of some 900,000 pounds.

If the Russians are shooting for the moon, they must have a far larger rocket under development. Some believe it might be available for a shot into a manned lunar orbit within a year. At the moment the United States seems to hold the edge in demonstrated thrust, since the Saturn I rocket develops 1.5 million pounds, but it is far short of what will be needed for the manned moon shots. The United States will ultimately have the Saturn-V, producing 7.5 million pounds thrust, and it is probable that the Russians will also come forward with such a giant.

Lieutenant Colonel Leonov's step into space, last Thursday, was a step towards the moon, but the road ahead is a long one. It has many steps—the perfection of rendezvous, the development of a new generation of giant rockets, and scouting of the moon itself by such vehicles as the Ranger and Surveyor spacecraft. It is still far from certain whose will be the first footprints on the moon—a Soviet cosmonaut or an American astronaut.

Part Three
Trade, Aid, and the Aided

Chapter IX

Emerging Nations

> *The United States, once itself a colony, shares and sympathizes with the aspirations of peoples for political independence. . . . We can and should play an important part in finding the policies to cope with the political and social ferment of much of the human race.*
>
> —John Foster Dulles

> *The revolutionary energy of the popular masses of the countries of Asia, Africa, and Latin America, having awakened to political life, acts as an accelerator of the historical process and progress of all mankind.*
>
> —Kommunist

The ambiguity of the term "underdeveloped countries" prevents a precise definition. In 1951 a group of experts appointed by the Secretary-General of the United Nations wrote:

We have had some difficulty in interpreting the term "underdeveloped countries." We use it to mean countries in which per capita real income is low when compared with the per capita real incomes of the United States of America, Canada, Australia and Western Europe. In this sense, an adequate synonym would be "poor countries."

Another synonym of "underdeveloped countries" in popular usage is "emerging nations." They are "emerging" as modern, independent, sovereign nations; they are "emerging" from the ignoble state of affairs—politically unstable, economically backward, socially disturbed, and technologically inexperienced. And they are swept by anticolonial, anti-imperialistic, nationalistic sentiments, mingled with burning aspirations for industrialization, modernization, and westernization of their societies and institutions. This epochal phenomenon then is their "Revolution of Rising Expectations." This Revolution— the combination of increasing awareness of their intolerable plight and accentuating aspiration for a better life—is politically explosive,

237

and creates not only a fertile field for jealousy, unrest, and suspicion, which threaten international peace, but also an arena for big-power competition, which jeopardizes international security.

This chapter is devoted to an analysis of emerging nations in terms of their characteristics, aspirations, and transformations.

B. K. Nehru, India's Ambassador to the United States, points to the fact that the problems of underdeveloped countries become problems of advanced countries in this shrunken world community, and calls for a much more substantial, rational, and planned assistance to the developing countries. He cites India as an example to show how an underdeveloped nation can approach the problem of economic progress.

United Nations Courier *discusses the main aspects of the economic development process, the different characteristics of "underdevelopment," and the problems arising from traditional attitudes in the modernization process.*

Janez Stanovnik traces the changing political context of aid to underdeveloped countries in the last decade and a half, and proposes that the energy and force of "competitive coexistence" between capitalist and socialist systems should be directed toward progress in these less developed countries.

1. UNDERDEVELOPED WORLD TODAY*

BY B. K. NEHRU

I am greatly honoured at being given this opportunity to address the members of the Commonwealth Club of San Francisco. The problems of the under-developed world are already beginning to assume an importance in world affairs and are likely to over-shadow, in the long run, all the other international problems which occupy the centre of the stage today; they are also likely to continue with us for a very considerable time to come. It is, therefore, appropriate that I should take some of your time this afternoon to present

* From *Vital Speeches*, Vol. 27 (March 1, 1961), pp. 315–318. Reprinted by permission.

to you some of my thoughts on what these problems are, why they are important to the rest of humanity, and what can be done to solve them, both by the people of the under-developed world themselves and by those more fortunately placed.

If you look at a map of the earth's surface, you will find that only a small portion of it has been economically developed. With the exception of Australasia and Japan, this developed part consists of a narrow Northern belt encompassing Western Europe and the continent of North America. The riches of the rest of this planet have been inadequately exploited. The result has been that the inhabitants of the developed parts of the world enjoy wealth and prosperity and standards of living which have never before been attained in human history, whereas most of the inhabitants of the rest of the world continue to live materially in almost the same state as their forefathers did a thousand years ago or more. The industrial revolution which, in the last couple of hundred years, transformed and transfigured Western society has passed these countries by. The population of the developed parts of the world is about a thousand million; that of the under-developed parts about two thousand million. The contrast between these two sets of countries can perhaps best be exemplified by citing their figures of per capita income. The average per capita income of the richer parts of the world is $1200 per annum; the average in the under-developed world is $125 per annum. But averages, as always, conceal the true contrasts for, at one end of the scale, is the United States with a per capita income about to reach somewhere around $2700 and at the other end are countries, such as my own which has a per capita income of no more than $70 per annum.

These inequalities of income are great but one of the problems of the world is that instead of decreasing, they are increasing at a very rapid rate. The rich are getting richer and the poor, though they are not getting poorer in absolute terms, are certainly getting poorer, relatively speaking. That this should be so is easily explicable in terms of economics for the growth of income is a function of the investment of capital. Rich societies, by the very fact of their being rich, not only consume more but save more than the poorer societies. Consequently, the annual growth of a rich country, even though percentagewise it may be small, is very much greater than that of a poor country. In the last ten years, by dint of great self-sacrifice, we in India have managed to invest in the Indian economy a sum of $22 billion. We have thereby raised the Indian per capita income at the rate of one dollar per year. A similar amount is invested in the economy of the United States practically every three months; and as a consequence the United States increases its national income every three months by about as much as we have done in the last ten years.

This international mal-distribution of wealth or the growing inequality of international incomes raises certain problems in international society today which are the exact counterparts of the problems which the nation-state in Western Europe had to face in the nineteenth century. This is not surprising in the least for we are today, whether we like it or not, an international society, communicating with each other much more freely and dependent on each other in much greater measure than national societies a hundred years ago. Differences in wealth and opportunity, the existence of privilege divorced from function, the absolute physical misery in which the vast majority of the people of Western Europe lived in the era in which the industrial revolution was working in their midst, caused stresses and strains leading to riots and revolution and ultimately resulted in substantial changes in the structure of society in those countries before social and political stability was achieved. I would suggest to you that the stresses and strains apparent in the international world today, confused and compounded as they are by the existence of East-West differences, are nevertheless traceable basically to the same roots as the discontents of Western European society in the nineteenth century. And if my analysis is correct, it follows that the remedies that were applied within those national societies in response to these discontents are the same as are applicable on the international scale today for the restoration of international stability.

The interest of the rest of humanity in the problems of the underdeveloped world is basically threefold. First, it appears morally wrong that, in an age in which human technology has developed to the point at which it can remove poverty from the whole surface of the globe, the use of that technology should be limited to small areas and for the benefit of a minority of the human race. When human beings did not have the wherewithal or the knowledge to produce material goods in adequate quantities, their consciences when faced with poverty and misery, could have been satisfied in the knowledge that when there was an overall insufficiency, some would undoubtedly have to suffer. But in an age of overall abundance, the human conscience cannot escape its responsibility by pleading the inevitability of poverty. If we have to make human life more bearable and to give to it the dignity that it deserves, it seems to me that it is incumbent upon us to use the productive powers of science and technology to achieve these ends.

Secondly, the existence of vast areas of the world whose wealth is not exploited is of great harm to the developed world itself. International trade which has been a source of wealth from time immemorial consists of the exchange of goods. The under-developed world, though greatly in need of the goods produced in the developed societies, has an insufficiency of goods to exchange for the goods it needs. The consequence is that international trade does not grow, and therefore does not add to human wealth, to the extent it could if the productive capacity and consequently the purchasing power of people in the under-developed world were increased. To cite one example, the entire trade of the United States with South East Asia which contains more than 600 million people, amounts to exactly two per cent of the total trade of this country. If the purchasing power of the countries comprising this area could be even fractionally increased, they would present markets for American products vastly in excess of the market today.

Thirdly, the existence and the increase of these vast disparities of income and, in particular, the absolutely low material level at which human life has to be lived over large areas of the earth's surface constitute a continuing and growing threat to the political stability of the world. We have moved very far from the days of the first great war when it appeared that the world was in stable equilibrium with Western Europe dominating most parts of it and the United States content in its own isolation. The equilibrium the world had then was manifestly unjust; and like all unjust systems it had within it the seeds of its own destruction. The colonial system is now on its way out and a majority of the countries of Asia and Africa are now free to manage their own political affairs or will be so free in the near future. These countries vary greatly from each other in their histories and traditions, in their geography and their economy, in their social systems and their attitudes of mind. But all of them have three things in common. They are all determined to maintain their political independence; they are all very poor; and they are all determined to get rid of this poverty. Having attained the first of their objectives, they are not faced with the task of so organising themselves as to be able to develop themselves in the shortest possible time. One of the major problems before them, even though they may not all clearly recognise this themselves, is the choice of the form of society that is best suited to achieve the categorical imperative of economic development which can no longer be denied.

Turning again to the lessons of history, there is the striking fact that, apart from those vast empty spaces which are now the United States of America, Canada and Australasia, no country has had that kind of upsurge in economic growth which is required in the under-developed societies except under a non-democratic institution. The United Kingdom at the time of the industrial revolution and for a long time thereafter was no democracy as we understand the term today. Most of the states of Western Europe when they went through a similar transformation of their societies could hardly be described as democracies. Japan achieved its basic economic growth long before the democratic system took root in that country and the Soviet Union and China have deliberately chosen a totalitarian form of society. Once again, in economic terms this phenomenon is easily explicable. Capital is the difference between current production and current consumption. In poor societies, current production is so low that there is very little margin between consumption and production. This gap has to be increased as rapidly as possible if economic growth is to be achieved. The societies of Western Europe increased this surplus by not permitting the labourer to consume the fruits of his labour. The communist countries, though they have a different social system, have adopted the same techniques and do not permit the farmer or the working man to increase his consumption beyond the point necessary to enable him to go on producing. This process of increased production but restrained consumption can and does lead to very rapid economic development.

Is the European method of development open to the countries which have recently regained their freedom? It is not possible today, even in those societies which are under-developed in ways other than economic, to reproduce the conditions of unfettered capitalism which were characteristic of the nineteenth century. In most societies, such as my own, which have undergone a political revolution before the industrial revolution, the difficulties of recreating these conditions are absolute. The farmers who have the vote and the labourers who have trades unions are hardly likely to permit themselves to be exploited for what appears to them to be the benefit of the individual capitalist. If, in the national interest, exploitation there has to be, then it has to be communal and not individual exploitation.

Nor are the people of the under-developed world anxious to give up their hard-won individual freedoms if this can be possibly avoided. The desire for liberty, not only from foreign domination which we have already achieved, but the desire for individual liberty, for freedom of speech and freedom of religion and freedom of association is as deeply rooted among the poor as among the rich. But the poor have another desire which grows in direct proportion to their poverty, namely the desire for bread. Historically as well as theoretically, there would seem to be a conflict, at least in the early stages of development, between the maintenance of individual liberty and the production of material goods. Are the under-developed countries, therefore, doomed to pass through a period of totalitarianism if they wish to develop materially or can a way be found to reconcile bread with liberty?

My answer is that it can: But only on condition that the outside world helps the developing countries in a much more substantial, rational and planned way than it has hitherto done. And as an example, though I admit by no means a typical example, of the alternative that is open to the under-developed world, I should like to explain to you how we have approached the problem in India, with what success and with what hopes and to explain to you the difficulties with which we are beset. I have said that India is not a typical example, basically because it is not under-developed in any but an economic sense. In other words, it possesses all the requisites of economic growth except one, namely capital. It has a stable government, an administrative apparatus second to none in the world, managerial and technical ability to no mean order and sophistication in financial and economic affairs which enables it to make the best use of such resources as it may have or is able to get. I make no apology for choosing India as an illustration not only because I come from that country but because India is by itself one-third of the non-communist under-developed world. It is also important because the Indian example, partly because of its size, partly because of the fact that it was the first country to break the bonds of colonial domination, partly because it has chosen the path of free and unadulterated democracy, tends to be followed by a large number of underdeveloped countries who have the same ends in view but who are groping to find the best means to achieve them.

India regained her independence in 1947 and chose for herself a political constitution guaranteeing to her citizens all the individual freedoms that are generally associated with the democratic framework of society. I am proud to say that for the last 13 years we have not only been the largest democracy in the world on paper but we have observed in the spirit and to the letter the practices of a free and democratic society. Having thus satisfied the need for liberty, we had to devote our attention to the possibly more overriding need for bread. When we achieved control of our own affairs, the Indian per capita income was no more than $50 per annum or less than a dollar a week. These dry figures cannot give you any idea at all of the extent of Indian poverty and the misery that it entails. It is beyond the imagination of a rich society to visualize the manner of life, if life it can be called, which people have to live on the kind of income that we have. The Indian was, and unfortunately is, under-nourished, under-clothed, under-housed, under-educated and under-nursed. Agricultural production was not enough to give many Indians two square meals a day. The consumption of cotton cloth was no more than 10 yards per head per annum. Outside the towns housing, such as there was, consisted of mud huts. In the urban area the overcrowding was unimaginable; and even so, large numbers of people had no housing of any kind and actually lived on the streets. There were 59,000 doctors in the entire country and as they were largely concentrated in the cities, the majority of the Indian population had no medical facilities and would not have been able to pay for medical services even if the facilities had been available. The absence of roads made communication between village and village extremely difficult and diseases such as malaria, cholera and the like, continued to take their toll of human beings whose powers of resistance were low owing to under-nourishment.

This was the inheritance that we received and it is clear that, apart from the immorality of allowing this state of affairs to continue, neither the Government of India nor the Republic of the Union of India itself would have a chance to survive if efforts were not made rapidly and on a large enough scale to change these conditions. Given our resolve to continue to live as a democracy, to strengthen and to preserve the democratic framework of society, to eschew wholly the totalitarian methods of organisation, we certainly did handicap ourselves in getting the best and earliest possible economic results. We established in 1950 a Planning Commission, the function of which was to take stock of our needs and of our resources and to draw up blueprints for economic progress, it being clear all the time that no element of totalitarianism was to creep into these plans. The Planning Commission has produced two five-year plans of economic development and the country has progressed under them to a certain extent. Agricultural production has in the last ten years been increased by 42 per cent; we are still however unable to feed our people on an adequate level; but the hardship that would have been caused by this fact has been substantially alleviated by the generous allocations which the U. S. Government has made to us from its stocks of surplus wheat. Cloth consumption has increased from 10 yards per head to 15 yards per head per annum. The number of doctors is now 84,000. The number of hospitals and dispensaries has gone up from 8600 to 12,600. Malaria and cholera have both been virtually eliminated. The total number of schools in the country has increased from 230,000 to 400,000. 50,000 miles of new surfaced roads have been built. Industrial production has increased at an average rate of 5 to 6 per cent per annum and industry has been diversified. The installed capacity of electrical power has gone up from 2.3 million kw to 5.8 million kw and the installed capacity of steel from 1.2 million tons to 6 million tons per annum.

This progress seems good. It is also remarkable that, in spite of the poverty of the society and in spite of the fact that no compulsion has been used, by far the greater proportion of the investment that has made this progress possible has come from the sacrifices of the Indian people themselves. Out of the total of $22 billion invested in the Indian economy in this period, no more than one-sixth has come from outside, mainly in the form of foreign aid; the remaining 84 per cent has come out of that meagre $50 per head income that I have spoken to you about. The rate of saving in India has increased from 5 per cent of national income to a little over 8 per cent in the last ten years. The fact that the people of India have borne with patience and with fortitude the substantial increases in taxation and some increases in prices that have been loaded upon them speaks volumes not only for their desire to develop on a basis of self-reliance but for the self-sacrificing discipline which they are prepared to undergo.

The progress that we have made is, as I have said, impressive in absolute terms. It must be remembered, however, that India is a large country with over 400 million people and the increases in production have to be divided over this vast number in order to assess their effect on the life of the individual. The rate of growth of the economy has been on the average 3½ per cent per annum. The rate of growth of the population has been somewhere under 2 per cent per annum. The net increase in per capita incomes has, therefore, been no more than 1.5 per cent per annum. In other words, we have not been able to increase the per capita income of the Indian people in real terms by more than about a dollar a year or less than 2 cents per week.

We feel, and those of our friends abroad who have devoted time and attention to the problem agree with us, that in order to maintain the social and political stability of Indian society, this rate of development is too slow. We cannot compete and we do not wish to compete with the phenomenal rates of growth that are prevalent in certain communistic countries. We are prepared to sacrifice, poor as we are, rapid material advancement in favour of the maintenance of our individual liberties. But there are limits beyond which this sacrifice cannot go. It is generally agreed that if we are to continue as an orderly and a free society, our rate of growth should be increased to a minimum of 5 per cent per annum. This requires a substantial increase of the rate of investment in the economy. We calculate that if an investment of an additional $50 billion were made in the Indian economy, we could achieve this rate of growth and if this investment were made wisely we could so strengthen the Indian economy that its further growth at this acceptable rate could be financed from within its own resources. We believe that, given the limitations of organisation, administration and man-power, it will take us ten years to make this investment in physical terms on the assumption, of course, that the financial resources will be made available as required. We calculate also that out of this $50 billion, the Indian people can themselves raise $40 billion without altering our present democratic structure of society. But beyond this our poor economy will not bear the burden of development; and if the remainder of the money has also to be extracted from the people, methods of regimentation and compulsion will have to be introduced and the liberties of the individual curtailed beyond the point at which the system can still be called democratic. We are, therefore, hopeful that, understanding our situation, appreciating our sacrifices, and having regard to the stakes involved for the whole human race, it will be made possible for us to obtain from abroad the $1 billion a year we need for the next ten years to make democratic India a going concern. We should like to get as much of this money as we possibly can through private foreign investment or from the capital market. But our experience, which has corresponded with that of the other under-developed countries, is that private capital is extremely hesitant to face the difficulties and uncertainties of an under-developed country. We are, therefore, forced to rely on financial assistance from international financial institutions and the governments of friendly countries.

I have taken you briefly through the Indian developmental story and shown to you clearly where and in what form the outside world can help in Indian development. As I said, India is not a typical case. It is atypical because in the Indian economy there is only one factor of growth missing and that is capital. It is atypical also in that in the case of India one can clearly foresee a time, which is not very far off, at which economic aid from the outside will no longer be necessary. And it is perhaps also slightly atypical in that the Indian people have shown themselves capable of self-sacrifice to an extent that has not yet been matched by any other country similarly placed. If one were to analyse the problems of each country in the under-developed world, one would discover that there are many in which a number of other factors of growth are missing and these can with advantage be supplied from abroad. There are countries whose need at this stage is for basic education; there are others whose lack is that of technically qualified personnel; others need administrators, doctors, lawyers, scientists. Others yet need industrial know-how or knowledge of agricultural techniques. The outside world can help by the provision of whatever factors of growth may be missing in any particular under-developed society. The costs have really never been adequately estimated because no individual survey of the needs of various countries has ever taken place. But from such rough estimates as have been made, it would appear that the total bill for the developed world, both for capital assistance and for technical assistance, is not likely to be more than $6 to 7 billion a year. Considering that the gross national product of the richer societies of the Western world is some-where around $900 billion a year and that it is increasing at about $30 billion annually, it would appear to me that a sacrifice of the order involved would be well worth making having regard not only to the direct advantages that would follow from the development of the under-developed economies but to the direct dangers to the peace and stability of the world if these newly emerging countries are left to fend for themselves.

2. ANATOMY OF UNDERDEVELOPMENT*

BY UNESCO

What do economists mean when they call a country under-developed? The expression "underdeveloped" is difficult to define in precise terms.

All countries are in some respects underdeveloped, for all are still in the developing process. There is none which has reached the stage where no further progress is possible or where no useful changes could be introduced. It is nevertheless clear that we can distinguish between those countries which have reached an advanced stage of economic development and those who are still in a more primitive phase.

Probably the broadest distinction is to be found in the distribution of the national income through various levels of the population. Those countries which are economically advanced have a much higher general level of prosperity and superior standards of living among the mass of their people.

Industrialization, or the opportunity for all to partake of its benefits, is essential to economic progress. It is not, however, an end in itself. Schools, hospitals, museums, art galleries, theatres are built not for their own sake, but to serve specific purposes, and factories are no exception. They are indispensable tools in the struggle to raise living standards among the less fortunate of the world's people. This

* From *UNESCO Courier,* Vol. 15 (July, September, November, 1962, and March, 1963). Reprinted by permission.

is a fundamental objective of the United Nations and the sole purpose of the technical assistance programmes.

Factories, mines, power stations, transport undertakings and so on are symbols of the economic development by which this raising of living standards can be achieved. Economic development must go hand in hand with the production of more food, the improvement of health, the spread of education and the promotion of social welfare and human rights. It will help to put more money into the pockets of the people who need it. Without that increase in spending power, the people in the "underdeveloped" countries cannot know freedom from misery and want.

The most striking difference between the developed and the underdeveloped countries lies, as we have seen, in the standard of living attained by the majority of their people—in other words, in the extent to which the national income is distributed through wide strata of the population. It is, however, possible to attempt some more exact definition of the term underdeveloped.

An underdeveloped country might be described as one in which the natural and human resources are used for economic purposes to only a very limited degree. The trained personnel, the capital and the administrative machinery necessary to make proper use of them are partly, or wholly lacking. Such a definition is no more than rough and ready. The word "resource" itself needs clarification. We might say that, in the economic sense a resource only becomes a resource when it can be put to an appropriate use. Until that time, the richest resources are valueless in themselves.

If we look back over the long history of mankind, we see a period, perhaps lasting up to a half a million years or more, during which the food gatherers and hunters of the Palaeolithic, or Old Stone Age, wandered countless times across what was later to be recognized as rich arable land without being able to make the slightest use of it. It was probably not more than ten thousand years ago that the first Neolithic farmers, by sowing and harvesting grain, discovered the possibilities inherent in such land. Thanks to this innovation, they took to living in settled communities and so changed the course of human history.

We can find plenty of examples nearer our own time. In fact, the more complex civilization has become, the more intense has been the search for new resources or new uses for old resources. Coal was occasionally used in the Middle Ages, but its real value as a natural resource was discovered only when the factories of the industrial revolution created a demand for fuel which could not be met by the diminishing woodlands of late eighteenth and early nineteenth-century England.

At a further stage in the industrial revolution, oil began to take the place of coal as a fuel and the vast deposits lying under the Middle East, Central America, Texas, the Caspian Sea area and elsewhere acquired immense economic importance for the industrialized civilization of the twentieth century.

This type of society remains more or less self-contained, but it includes the elements of an exchange of commercial economy, the promise of bigger things to come. It is typical of much of contemporary Africa and also of parts of Latin America and Southeast Asia.

By organizing a system of trade, such societies take the first step leading from the subsistence agriculture stage to that of industry. There is, however, no elaborate transformation of materials, no use of complex machines and no employment of specialized wage earners in a common place of work. Nevertheless, the emergence of better transportation and the increasing sale of goods open the way to further specialization.

commercial stage with its simple industries grows out of the subsistence agriculture phase. Later, and generally much later, comes the stage of more complex manufacturing industry, with the use of machines on an ever-increasing scale, an increasing specialization of many workers and the creation of more and more elaborate administrative and financial techniques to keep pace with heavier economic demands.

Industry first appears with the processing of primary products. Grain is milled, leather is tanned, wool or vegetable fibres are spun, ores are smelted. These processes obviously call for the next level of industrial development, when materials are transformed and not merely processed. The grain so milled is turned into bread, the leather into footwear, the cloth into wearing apparel, the smelted ores into ploughshares, horseshoes and other metal goods.

At this stage, goods are still produced for immediate use by the person who buys them. The major difference between this phase and the next, more complex, stage of large-scale industry is that capital equipment now begins to be produced not to satisfy immediate consumer demand, but to help in the future production of such goods over a long period of time and with far more elaborate marketing facilities in mind.

Civilizations do not pass through these phases in clearly defined historical periods. Human history is an untidy phenomenon. It allows for much disorder and for the existence side by side of processes of varying age and efficiency. The so-called industrial civilization of our time is distinguished by a tremendous emphasis on the third, or machine-dominated stage.

The railroad, the steamship, the internal-combustion engine, flight, atomic power, electronics, all of them Western discoveries or inventions, have vastly broadened the horizon of man's possibilities. Their advantages are now becoming available by degree to countries which have never experienced the preliminary stages of industrial progress.

As a result, our contemporary world presents the picture of an economically advanced minority of peoples on the one hand and, on the other, a highly diversified group of peoples who make up the majority of mankind and who, at varying stages of economic under-development, are seeking to narrow the broad gap which separates them from the economic leaders. It may be possible perhaps to distinguish various categories among these underdeveloped countries and the distinction will help to make clearer both their economic problems and their potentialities.

(a) First there are societies in which there has as yet been practically no autonomous economic growth. Most of the people wrest a meagre livelihood from the soil as subsistence farmers. A very elementary marketing system exists, but the exchange of products is on too small a scale to allow any real division of labour into different skills and crafts, and thus the incentive to progress is lacking.

Great areas of Africa would be typical of this phase of economic development, as would a territory like New Guinea, hardly affected as yet by outside civilization. In such regions, the people themselves lack all the essential means to promote their economic growth. They must be helped to modify the pattern of subsistence agriculture. A more complex exchange system must be introduced to promote buying and selling and the manufacture or preparation of products.

In these simply constituted economic societies (personal and tribal relationships, like the indigenous languages, are often far more complex than any in the "civilized" world) this will always require both technical assistance and capital from outside to get the static economy moving.

(b) The second category is more common in the contemporary world. Here, we are dealing with underdeveloped countries where foreign enterprise, capital and management, have introduced themselves into a relatively simple economic society and have caused a rapid evolution in certain sectors. This situation is to be seen in a number of ex-colonial countries such as Indonesia and Malaya.

Here, valuable raw materials like rubber and tin have been exploited through foreign technical skill and capital. As a result, a few highly developed industries have been set up to obtain and export such raw materials. The coming of these industries has introduced, in part at least, a commercial economy into the country concerned. This has brought with it an elaborate exchange mechanism and has provided commercial employment for some of the local population.

Meanwhile, the primitive agricultural economy goes on as before over the country as a whole. The scale and complexity of local industries which may arise to process raw materials on the spot will vary according to the nature of the product removed and exported with foreign help. If this is a mineral, the local processing plant is likely to be more complicated than in the case of a vegetable product like sisal, for example, which is grown and processed in Tanganyika. Much more complex are the copper refineries in Katanga and Northern Rhodesia and the oil refineries of the Middle East.

(c) A third category of countries differs from the rest mainly as a result of internal, rather than external, economic factors. How far will domestic demand encourage industrial enterprise? We have seen above how the partial economic development of an underdeveloped country may be stimulated by demand from abroad for a particular raw material or product. Where this foreign demand is absent, economic growth will occur only when a local demand for goods exists.

This demand, in turn, will depend upon the way in which income is distributed among the people and the tastes of potential customers. If only small numbers of the population can afford to buy consumer goods, they may prefer imported articles. Local manufacturers will then receive little encouragement to enter the field and there will be as little impulse to extend the industrialization process. A number of Latin American countries are in this situation.

At this point a word must be said about the important factor of government intervention. Government intervention has tended to increase markedly in our time. It is particularly noticeable in countries which have recently gained their political independence and which find themselves faced with the great task of raising the living standards of their people with a minimum of delay.

This task requires some degree of central direction. Essential data about natural resources, both natural and human, have to be centrally collected and assessed. Plans must be centrally drawn up for the development of these resources, as part of an overall national programme of economic and social development. Priorities must be centrally established, official encouragement must be given to projects and industries which are likely to promote the welfare of the people as a whole, and technical assistance and foreign loans must be applied for through recognized government channels.

This government intervention ranges from encouragement and advice, as seen, for example, in community development projects sponsored by the authorities in India and elsewhere, to actual direction by the state in the U.S.S.R., the countries associated with her and in the mainland of China. The methods applied to achieve economic development will reflect the prevailing ideology. But it should be borne in mind that the conditions favouring spontaneous economic growth are present only in a small measure in the underdeveloped

At first individuals, then organized groups, devote themselves entirely to secondary occupations away from the land, such as the transformation, preparation or carrying of raw materials. This early countries and, without some degree of government action, no substantial progress could be expected in the foreseeable future.

There are, of course, many underdeveloped countries in which these views are not held, or are restricted to certain spiritual teachers and their disciples. Few Indians would today see an irreconcilable conflict between the Hindu religion and an effort to improve standards of living. The existence in nonindustrial societies of such widespread reluctance to submit for long to the monotony of industrial labour should however be noted.

Critics of the West have pointed out what they believe to be a certain selfishness and superficiality in the attitudes which have made Western industrial civilization possible. They see in Western man a desire to "have" rather than to "be," and they compare this unfavourably with the more communal, less individualistic and acquisitive state of mind that prevails in much of Asia and Africa. There, at least in many rural communities, personal aggrandizement tends to be condemned as a motive for human conduct. Sharing with one's fellows is taken more readily for granted and time is something to be enjoyed, rather than used, like a song by firelight that enriches companionship, even if it leaves the coffers as empty as ever. Such attitudes could perhaps restore to the "acquisitive society" a dimension of human warmth which it has, to some extent, lost. In any event, they cannot be overlooked if we seek to compare the mentality of today's underdeveloped countries with that of industrial England or America.

In the attempt to move from an earlier, rural culture into the mobile, machine-conscious, urbanized, technological society, the "less developed" countries may risk losing precious social values consecrated by tradition and also art forms which satisfy æsthetically as manufactured goods can never do. Only economic development and industrialization can reduce the material sufferings and insecurity of the less privileged peoples, but respect for these social and artistic values may still be a guiding principle both of those who are seeking to diversify their economies and of the experts from industrialized countries who go among them, sometimes without fully realizing what treasures an "underdeveloped" culture may conceal. . . .

Today's underdeveloped countries face formidable obstacles in the struggle to increase the earning power of their people. Often there is no mercantile class ready to become the entrepreneurs of a new historical phase, and in many lands the educated classes show active distaste for the industrial or commercial life. Inadequate knowledge of the prospects before a new industry is an added deterrent to those who have capital. The mass of the people is far too poor to have money for investment or for the purchase of manufactured goods.

Land reform and other social changes may be an essential preliminary to any substantial increase in the earnings of the people. New attitudes of mind which machinery and industrialization require on the part of masses of men are also a conspicuous need. At the same time, care must be taken to preserve, as far as possible, those social and other values of the non-industrialized culture which might otherwise be needlessly sacrificed in the helter-skelter of change.

In these circumstances, governments have come to play an important role in economic development, for in all the countries concerned, development involves tasks—economic, educational and social—of a magnitude which calls for some degree of central planning and coordination. But, while the role of national governments may be vital, governments themselves require international help in carrying out these huge tasks.

3. THE CHANGING POLITICAL CONTEXT*

BY JANEZ STANOVNIK

The Sino-Soviet rift and the first improvements in Soviet-American relations affect not only relations between East and West but also between North and South. The problems of the Southern Hemisphere are predominantly economic. Policies of trade and aid pursued thus far toward the developing countries, evolving as they did within the terms of the cold war, have not yielded encouraging results. The developing countries can no longer be an object in world policy; they must become a subject of policy on an equal footing with others. In order to attain that status, however, they must be able to exploit fully their own resources, both material and human. International action can serve as a catalyst. But for it to do so successfully, there must be a thorough reconsideration not only of present aid policy but also of international trade and financial policy. China's challenge introduces new elements in this field. The new international economic policy should not rest on political alliances, pacts and blocs but must try to assist the transformation of the developing countries internally so as to promote their consolidation and stabilization. . . .

Early in the fifties—at the time, that is, of the Korean conflict—the main emphasis in aid to underdeveloped countries was military. It was only after Stalin's death that economic aid began to develop increasingly. The policy of aid to the developing countries went through three stages in the fifties: "trade not aid"—"trade or aid"—"trade and aid." Yet throughout this period the policy of assistance

* From *Foreign Affairs*, Vol. 42 (January, 1964), pp. 242–254. Reprinted by permission of the Council on Foreign Relations, Inc.

evolved within the general framework of "competitive coexistence."

Beginning in 1954, the Soviet Union also started granting aid, mainly in the form of long-term, low-interest loans to individual developing countries. From mid-1955 to the end of 1960, the socialist countries granted assistance to the developing countries amounting to $3.6 billion while the United States gave them, in corresponding categories of aid, about $7.3 billion. . . .

Toward the close of the fifties, various attempts at reform somehow stabilized policy on the basis of "trade and aid." That concept aimed to maintain trade relations on traditional patterns, but admitted implicitly that this could succeed only if supplemented with a deliberate policy of governmental aid. Thus international economic relations with the developing countries evolved according to a dualistic pattern: in the field of trade, the attempt was made to maintain existing economic and commercial principles and motivations, while in the field of aid the principles and motivations applied were preponderantly political. This made the international economic relations of the developing countries highly dependent upon the general course of international political relations.

The concepts of "competitive coexistence" and of the "economic competition of two systems" proceeded in fact from the same basic assumptions. Both sides became increasingly aware that they could not resolve their differences by thermonuclear war. This does not mean, however, that in this period there had as yet matured the awareness, which President Tito forcefully expressed before the U.N. General Assembly last October, that "the time is past when economic and material benefits might have been achieved by war, by the conquests of foreign territories or the like." Quite the contrary, it was largely an attempt to attain the same goals by new means; and aid was an important one of them. Although in many instances aid led to a more rapid economic evolution in the developing countries, its basic aim, nevertheless, was not economic development as such but as a component of the political aim being pursued. This policy evolved in general from the belief that the destiny of our civilization rested on some solution of the rivalry between East and West. Each side endeavored to expand its influence in the Southern Hemisphere, feeling that this might help it achieve its ultimate goals.

But this kind of aid policy made the situation of the developing countries more and more critical. Often it did not yield economic results—which is not surprising, as the motives and criteria for it were not primarily economic—while its long-term political effects proved dubious.

The fact that the experience of the fifties was unfavorable does not necessarily mean that international aid as such is an unsuccessful instrument for promoting economic growth. However, that experience does show unmistakably that international aid is a dubious instrument of international policy. . . .

The world situation in the sixties is a new one and it requires a reconsideration of certain basic assumptions as to policy approaches. First of all, in a time of "competitive coexistence" and "economic competition between two systems," it will be necessary to reëxamine the notion of "system."

The capitalistic "system" was the term used to designate the private-enterprise economies in North America, Western Europe, Oceania and Japan. The socialist "system" incorporated the centrally planned economies in the U.S.S.R., Eastern Europe and Asia. Stalin carried this concept to its ultimate consistency with the theory of "socialist" and "capitalist" world markets, which served as a basis for the concept of the international division of labor on "socialist" and "capitalist" lines.

Although both the East and the West could aspire to giving practical application to the monolithic aspect of their territorial "systems," this concept met with serious difficulties when applied to the developing countries. The idea of the troika represented an attempt to reach a compromise in the concrete situation existing in the United Nations; but it only proved that a sharp territorial division of the world according to socio-economic systems was not feasible. The majority of the developing countries adopted a mixed economy as an institutional framework. However, as "competitive coexistence" and "economic competition between two systems" continued to grow, an increasing tendency set in toward non-alignment and toward African, Arab, Indian, Cuban and other paths to socialism. The Belgrade and Cairo Conferences were clear reflections of this development.

If it was true that inconsistencies in the old concept of a "system" had been demonstrated in the past, it is even more true today when the general principles of coexistence are being applied. The basic premise of coexistence and the prerequisite for its further progress are the establishment of mutual confidence. But as long as the "systems" continue to have a territorial connotation, practical policies will encounter a wide range of difficulties.

If the countries of the Western alliance consider themselves identified with the capitalist system, while those of the Eastern alliance are identified with the socialist system, then either coexistence or confidence may come into question. Marxists cannot renounce the class struggle between the socialist and capitalist systems. Both the adherents of capitalism and of socialism logically aspire to extend their influence and their ideas. If this extension is identified with the territorial expansion of "systems" or the spread of spheres of interest, then coexistence must sooner or later damage the confidence which is the precondition of progress and the fulfillment of the policy of coexistence. In short, coexistence is possible only under the condition that neither territorial grouping should be committed to "bury" its opponent and inherit its territory.

Coexistence is possible on the basis of strict respect for territorial integrity, noninterference in internal affairs, the renunciation of force as an instrument in settling disputes, respect for sovereignty and the realization of a minimal system of collective security. That is why coexistence can and should be the principle underlying the relations among states, regardless of whether such states are associated in some territorial alliances or not; among various countries, regardless of whether they are large or small; among national economies, regardless of whether they are organized into capitalist, socialist, feudal or traditional institutional patterns. Progress and fulfillment of the policy of coexistence is therefore possible if both sides give up their claim that their territorial alliances of states are the sole embodiment of one system or another. Thus, systems should again be conceived as they properly are: the institutional organization of economy, a social organization of life, production and distribution, and not an international political or military alliance. "Systems" relate to internal and not international relations. Coexistence therefore need not involve the renunciation of the class struggle or further social evolution or the sanctioning of the status quo. Coexistence as thus conceived is essential not only for the East and the West but for the developing countries as well.

Such a clarification of general conceptions, which seems to be a logical consequence of the further evolution of the policy of coexistence, will have far-reaching implications for international economic policy regarding the developing countries within the framework of a re-formulated policy of "competitive coexistence" or the "economic competition of two systems."

It thus becomes possible for there to be an independent institutional evolution of the socio-economic systems in the developing countries which is acceptable to both the developed parts of the world and which does not change the basic balance of power. Relations with the developing countries in the new situation need no longer evolve in the shadow of attempts to enlarge spheres of interest. The new situation thus creates new conditions in which relations with the developing countries can be based primarily on economic and no longer on political or military motivations.

The need for a new international policy vis-à-vis the developing countries is obvious. It must take into account the new world reality; it must be founded on the experiences and lessons of the fifties; it must also be adapted to the internal experiences and needs of economic and social growth.

Aid for development purposes during the fifties was primarily motivated by political considerations, with humanitarian and economic motives of secondary importance. Trade policy toward the developing countries, however, remained subject to the rules of the game, inherited from the past. And since there was no inner connection between trade and aid policy, it is no wonder that the aid policy did not succeed in mitigating or neutralizing the negative effects of the trade policy.

The new world developments diminish the likelihood that aid will be extended for the purpose of attracting political sympathizers and allies. This does not mean, however, that it weakens the motivation for constructive and effective economic policies toward the developing countries in general. Reduced tension decreases the political motivation but at the same time increases the economic motivation.

The problem confronting the world community does not arise from the alternatives of "development" or "stagnation" in the developing countries. The demand for economic growth is a *sine qua non* in our day and as such it is only a sequel to the play of those same forces which during the past decade led to the liberation from colonial rule. President Kennedy was right when he told the United Nations that "political independence is but a mockery without economic advancement." The problem facing the world community is whether the developing countries will be compelled to develop primarily with their own resources or whether they will enjoy the advantages of international coöperation. The implications of one or the other path are today clear (as the developments in China may serve to illustrate).

Out of approximately 80 independent developing countries, about 50 are so small that the annual gross national product of each amounts to less than one billion dollars. If these countries are compelled to develop by relying solely on their own resources, they will be forced to undertake a much more intensive substitution for imports than is economically reasonable, they will have to introduce a much more rigid internal discipline than they wish, they will have to "tighten their belts" much more than their populations would freely be ready to do. The internal and external consequences of such a policy can easily be foreseen. If, on the other hand, they are to enjoy the advantages of full international coöperation—trade and aid— then the transition will be much smoother and the international implications much more favorable.

It is not a question of neutralizing Chinese demagoguery. Chinese propaganda cannot secure mass support in the developing countries either with its theories on the inevitability of war, or by such actions as its territorial expansion toward India, or with such policies as breaking up the family. The case is different when it comes to economic and social achievements in China. China cannot become a sympathetic symbol with its foreign policy, but only with its internal policy and with its opposition to those whom the masses in the developing countries blame for their plight—supposing, that is, that the international community does not provide a better alternative through change and economic and social advancement.

Despite a certain measure of progress in the last decade, economic progress in the developing countries is still largely restricted to a thin upper layer. Dr. Raul Prebisch recently noted that 5 percent of the upper strata of society enjoy 30 percent of the entire consumption in Latin America. The dualistic character of economy and society, inherited from colonialism, stubbornly continues to prevail. The dependence of a tiny commercialized sector of the economy upon foreign trade—in circumstances where there is an unfavorable trend in commodity exports—is the Achilles' heel in the economies of these countries.

Under the changed conditions, the political alignment of the developing countries is of lesser significance than their economic and social advancement. This advancement, however, is being impeded by inherited international trade relations. The terms of trade are still determined largely by the concentrations of economic power which put the peoples of those countries in the status of "hewers of wood and drawers of water." Just as economic and political stability is inconceivable in a national economy in which the workers and farmers are exposed to the pressures of a concentrated economic force under the pretext of the "law of supply and demand," so world stability is inconceivable under conditions in which the world's workers and farmers—the primary commodity producers, that is, the developing countries—are exposed to the pressure of the concentrated economic force of those who have already attained a degree of economic maturity.

The new world trade policy should make it possible for the developing countries to put their natural and human resources to productive use, and thus to earn their own way. But though it should provide new opportunities for the developing countries, it will not automatically increase production. Trade policy should therefore be coördinated and supplemented by an aid policy.

Such a trade and aid policy does not necessarily mean a new "sacrifice" on the part of the industrial countries. The launching of development activities on the territory of one-half of the globe will give to the whole world economy an impulse similar to that produced in the American economy with the opening up of the American West. The effects will be felt in greater employment, the transfer of economic activities to sectors of high productivity, and in many other ways. A new trade and aid policy toward the developing countries will thereby become not a liability but an asset for world progress.

CHAPTER X

United States Foreign Aid

I believe that in carrying out this program the American people will get full value for their money. Indeed, we cannot afford to do less. Russia and Red China have tripled their promises of aid in the past year [1964]. They are doing more than they have ever done before; the competition between them has led to increased efforts by each to influence the course of events in the developing nations.
—LYNDON B. JOHNSON

The colonizers give a dollar in "aid" in order to receive ten dollars later in return by exploiting the peoples who have accepted such "aid." After this, they enslave the peoples politically. Such are the "new" forms of economic domination.
—NIKITA S. KHRUSHCHEV

Realistically speaking, the United States foreign aid program transcends humanitarian and economic motives—important as they are. The real stake is the political interest which arises from the conviction that the best chance of peace and security can be maintained by strengthening, militarily and economically, the free world as well as the underdeveloped and uncommitted countries of Asia, Africa, and Latin America, which are especially susceptible to Communism.

The United States makes no secret of its intention and design to promote in these countries a democratic political system by economic advancement induced by American foreign aid. The United States has recognized since the end of World War II that these nations' national independence, economic progress, and democratic evolution deserved America's grave concern.

Within the framework of this general objective, the United States foreign aid program aims more specifically at encouraging the recipient countries to meet and resolve their internal problems without

262

resorting to totalitarian measures. The strengthening of democratic forces in these countries, a fulfillment of their nationalistic aspirations, and strict maintenance of their political independence are considered to provide an impregnable bulwark against the spread of Communism, thus contributing to the interests of the United States.

An accurate assessment of the foreign aid program in the context of overall American foreign policy is intricate and complex. Such evaluation, however, must include the impact of the program, scrutiny of the program's achievement, and areas for improvement. The crucial question is no longer whether the program advances the foreign policy of the United States but rather how effective it is in view of the money, material and manpower put into it.

This chapter is designed to present the philosophy, purpose, and performance of United States foreign aid in a proper perspective.

President Kennedy, in his message to Congress in 1963, reviews the historical accomplishments of foreign aid in promoting the cause of freedom the world over and stresses the overriding importance of its continuation to meet the challenge of our time. He further specifies six key recommendations for the future and evaluates the Alliance for Progress.

Barbara Ward, the British economist and author, maintains that the United States foreign aid has succeeded, by and large, in checking Communist expansion and that its greater significance lies in the possibilities of building up the institutions and the solidarity of a fraternal world order.

Isaiah Frank, Clayton Professor of International Economics at Johns Hopkins University, presents a detailed examination of four major criticisms of American foreign aid: 1) the enormity of the program, 2) the character of recipients, 3) the inefficiency in aid administration, and 4) the disproportionate share of the United States' burden. He suggests means to rectify some of the administrative defects.

1. FOREIGN AID, 1963*

BY JOHN F. KENNEDY

To the Congress of the United States:

"Peace hath her victories no less renowned than war," wrote Milton. And no peace-time victory in history has been as far-reaching in its impact, nor served the cause of freedom so well, as the victories scored in the last 17 years by this nation's mutual defense and assistance programs. These victories have been, in the main, quiet instead of dramatic. Their aim has been, not to gain territories for the United States or support in the United Nations, but to preserve freedom and hope, and to prevent tyranny and subversion, in dozens of key nations all over the world.

The United States today is spending over 10 per cent of its gross national product on programs primarily aimed at improving our national security. Somewhat less than 1/20th of this amount, and less than 0.7 per cent of our gross national product, goes into the mutual assistance program: Roughly half for economic development, and half for military and other short-term assistance. The contribution of this program to our national interest clearly outweighs its cost. The richest nation in the world would surely be justified in spending less than 1 per cent of its national income on assistance to its less fortunate sister nations solely as a matter of international responsibility; but inasmuch as these programs are not merely the right thing to do, but clearly in our national self-interest, all criticisms should be placed in that perspective. That our aid programs can be improved is not a matter of debate. But that our aid programs serve both our national traditions and our national interests is beyond all reasonable doubt.

History records that our aid programs to Turkey and Greece were the crucial element that enabled Turkey to stand up against heavy-handed Soviet pressures, Greece to put down Communist aggression, and both to re-create stable societies and to move forward in the direction of economic and social growth.

* From "Message of the President to the Congress," *The New York Times* (April 3, 1963), p. 34. Reprinted by permission.

History records that the Marshall Plan made it possible for the nations of Western Europe, including the United Kingdom, to recover from the devastation of the world's most destructive war, to rebuild military strength, to withstand the expansionist thrust of Stalinist Russia, and to embark on an economic renaissance which has made Western Europe the second greatest and richest industrial complex in the world today—a vital center of free world strength, itself now contributing to the growth and strength of less developed countries.

History records that our military and economic assistance to nations on the frontiers of the Communist world—such as Iran, Pakistan, India, Vietnam and Free China—has enabled threatened peoples to stay free and independent, when they otherwise would have either been overrun by aggressive Communist power or fallen victim of utter chaos, poverty and despair.

History records that our contributions to international aid have been the critical factor in the growth of a whole family of international financial institutions and agencies, playing an ever more important role in the ceaseless war against want and the struggle for growth and freedom.

And finally, history will record that today our technical assistance and development loans are giving hope where hope was lacking, sparking action where life was static, and stimulating progress around the earth—simultaneously supporting the military security of the free world, helping to erect barriers against the growth of Communism where those barriers count the most, helping to build the kind of world community of independent, self-supporting nations in which we want to live, and helping to serve the deep American urge to extend a generous hand to those working toward a better life for themselves and their children.

Despite noisy opposition from the very first days—despite dire predictions that foreign aid would "bankrupt" the republic—despite warnings that the Marshall Plan and successor programs were "throwing our money down a rat-hole"—despite great practical difficulties and some mistakes and disappointments—the fact is that our aid programs generally and consistently have done what they were expected to do.

Freedom is not on the run anywhere in the world—not in Europe, Asia, Africa, or Latin America—as it might well have been without United States aid. And we now know that freedom—all freedom, including our own—is diminished when other countries fall under Communist domination, as in China in 1949, North Vietnam and the northern provinces of Laos in 1954, and Cuba in 1959. Freedom, all freedom, is threatened by the subtle, varied and unceasing Communist efforts at subversion in Latin America, Africa, the Middle East, and Asia. And the prospect for freedom is also endangered or eroded in countries which see no hope—no hope for a better life based on economic progress, education, social justice and the development of stable institutions. These are the frontiers of freedom which our military and economic aid programs seek to advance; and in so doing, they serve our deepest national interest.

This view has been held by three successive Presidents—Democratic and Republican alike. It has been endorsed by a bipartisan majority of nine successive Congresses. It has been supported for 17 years by a bipartisan majority of the American people.

And it has only recently been reconfirmed by a distinguished committee of private citizens, headed by General Lucius Clay. . . . Their report stated: "We believe these programs, properly conceived and implemented, to be essential to the security of our nation and necessary to the exercise of its world-wide responsibilities."

There is, in short, a national consensus of many years standing on the vital importance of these programs. The principle and purpose of United States assistance to less secure and less fortunate nations are not and cannot be seriously in doubt.

The question now is: What about the future? In the perspective of these past gains, what is the dimension of present needs, what are our opportunities, and what changes do we face at this juncture in world history?

I believe it is a crucial juncture. Our world is near the climax of an historic convulsion. A tidal wave of national independence has nearly finished its sweep through lands which contain one out of every three people in the world. The industrial and scientific revolution is spreading to the far corners of the earth. And two irreconcilable views of the value, the rights and the role of the individual human being confront the peoples of the world.

In some 80 developing nations, countless large and small decisions will be made in the days and months and years ahead—decisions which, taken together, will establish the economic and social system, determine the political leadership, shape the political practices, and mold the structure of the institutions which will promote either consent or coercion for one-third of humanity. And these decisions will drastically affect the shape of the world in which our children grow to maturity.

Africa is stirring restlessly to consolidate its independence and to make that independence meaningful for its people through economic and social development. The people of America have affirmed and reaffirmed their sympathy with these objectives.

Free Asia is responding resolutely to the political, economic and military challenge of Communist China's relentless efforts to dominate the continent.

Latin America is striving to take decisive steps toward effective democracy—amid the turbulence of rapid social change and the menace of Communist subversion.

The United States—the richest and most powerful of all peoples, a nation committed to the independence of nations and to a better life for all peoples—can no more stand aside in this climactic age of decision than we can withdraw from the community of free nations. Our effort is not merely symbolic. It is addressed to our vital security interests.

It is in this context that I hope the American people through their representatives in Congress will consider our request for foreign aid funds designed carefully and explicitly to meet these specific challenges. This is not a wearisome burden. It is a new chapter in our involvement in a continuously vital struggle—the most challenging and constructive effort ever undertaken by man on behalf of freedom and his fellow man.

OBJECTIVES

In a changing world, our programs of mutual defense and assistance must be kept under constant review. My recommendations herein reflect the work of the Clay committee, the scrutiny undertaken by the new administrator of the Agency for International Development, and the experience gained in our first full year of administering the new and improved program enacted by the Congress in 1961. There is fundamental agreement throughout these reviews: That these assistance programs are of great value to our deepest national interest—

that their basic concepts and organization, as embodied in the existing legislation, are properly conceived—that progress has been made and is being made in translating these concepts into action—but that much still remains to be done to improve our performance and make the best possible use of these programs.

In addition, there is fundamental agreement in all these reviews regarding six key recommendations for the future.

Objective No. 1: To apply stricter standards of selectivity and self-help in aiding developing countries. . . .

Considerable progress has already been made along these lines. While the number of former colonies achieving independence has lengthened the total list of countries receiving assistance, 80 per cent of all economic assistance now goes to only 30 countries; and military assistance is even more narrowly concentrated. The proportion of development loans, as contrasted with outright grants, has increased from 10 per cent to 60 per cent. We have placed all our development lending on a dollar repayable basis; and this year we are increasing our efforts, as the Clay committee recommended, to tailor our loan terms so that interest rates and maturities will reflect to a greater extent the differences in the ability of different countries to service debt.

In the Alliance for Progress in particular, and increasingly in other aid programs, emphasis is placed upon self-help and self-reform by the recipients themselves, using our aid as a catalyst for progress and not as a handout. Finally, in addition to emphasizing primarily economic rather than military assistance, wherever conditions permit, we are taking a sharp new look at both the size and purpose of those local military forces which receive our assistance. Our increased stress on internal security and civic action in military assistance is in keeping with our experience that in developing countries, military forces can have an important economic as well as protective role to play. . . .

Objective No. 2: To achieve a reduction and ultimate elimination of United States assistance by enabling nations to stand on their own as rapidly as possible. Both this nation and the countries we help have a stake in their reaching the point of self-sustaining growth—the point where they no longer require external aid to maintain their independence. Our goal is not an arbitrary cutoff date but the earliest possible "takeoff" date—the date when their economies will have been launched with sufficient momentum to enable them to become self-supporting, requiring only the same normal sources of external financing to meet expanding capital needs that this country required for many decades. . . .

The record clearly shows that foreign aid is not an endless or unchanging process. Fifteen years ago our assistance went almost entirely to the advanced countries of Europe and Japan—today it is directed almost entirely to the developing world. Ten years ago most of our assistance was given to shoring up military forces and unstable economies—today this kind of aid has been cut in half, and our assistance goes increasingly toward economic development. There are still, however, important cases where there has been no diminution in the Communist military threat, and both military and economic aid are still required. Such cases range from relatively stabilized frontiers, as in Korea and Turkey, to areas of active aggression, such as Vietnam.

Objective No. 3: To secure the increased participation of other industrialized nations in sharing the cost of international development assistance. . . .

Objective No. 4: To lighten any adverse impact of the aid program on our own balance of payments and economy. . . .

Objective No. 5: To continue to assist in the defense of countries under threat of external and internal Communist attack. Our military assistance program has been an essential element in keeping the boundary of Soviet and Chinese military power relatively stable for over a decade. Without its protection the substantial economic progress made by underdeveloped countries along the Sino-Soviet periphery would hardly have been possible. As these countries build economic strength, they will be able to assume more of the burden of their defense. But we must not assume that military assistance to these countries—or to others primarily exposed to subversive internal attack—can be ended in the foreseeable future. On the contrary, while it will be possible to reduce and terminate some programs, we should anticipate the need for new and expanded programs.

India is a case in point. The wisdom of earlier United States aid in helping the Indian subcontinent's considerable and fruitful efforts toward progress and stability can hardly now be in question. The threat made plain by the Chinese attack on India last fall may require additional efforts on our part to help bolster the security of this crucial area, assuming these efforts can be matched in an appropriate way by the efforts of India and Pakistan.

But overall, the magnitude of military assistance is small in relation to our national security expenditures; in this fiscal year it amounts to about 3 per cent of our defense budget. "Dollar for dollar," said the Clay committee with particular reference to the border areas, "these programs contribute more to the security of the free world than corresponding expenditures in our defense appropriations. . . . These countries are providing more than 2 million armed men ready, for the most part, for an emergency." Clearly, if this program did not exist, our defense budget would undoubtedly have to be increased substantially to provide an equivalent contribution to the free world's defense.

Objective No. 6: To increase the role of private investment and other non-Federal resources in assisting developing nations. . . .

ALLIANCE FOR PROGRESS

In a special sense, the achievements of the Alliance for Progress in the coming years will be the measure of our determination, our ideals, and our wisdom. Here in this hemisphere, in this last year, our resourcefulness as a people was challenged in the clearest terms. We moved at once to resist the threat of aggressive nuclear weapons in Cuba, and we found the nations of Latin America at our side. They, like ourselves, were brought to a new awareness of the danger of permitting the poverty and despair of a whole people to continue long anywhere in this continent.

Had the needs of the people of Cuba been met in the pre-Castro period—their need for food, for housing, for education, for jobs, above all, for a democratic responsibility in the fulfillment of their own hopes—there would have been no Castro, no missiles in Cuba, and no need for Cuba's neighbors to incur the immense risks of resistance to threatened aggression from that island.

There is but one way to avoid being faced with similar dilemmas in the future. It is to bring about in all the countries of Latin America the conditions of hope, in which the peoples of this continent will know that they can shape a better future for themselves, not through obeying the inhumane commands of an alien and cynical ideology, but through personal self-expression, individual judgment, and the acts of responsible citizenship.

As Americans, we have long recognized the legitimacy of these aspirations; in recent months we have been able to see, as never before, their urgency and, I believe, the concrete means for their realization.

In less than two years the 10-year program of the Alliance for Progress has become more than an idea and more than a commitment of governments. The necessary initial effort to develop plans to organize institutions, to test and experiment has itself required and achieved a new dedication—a new dedication to intelligent compromise between old and new ways of life. In the long run, it is this effort—and not the threat of Communism—that will determine the fate of freedom in the Western Hemisphere.

These years have not been easy ones for any group in Latin America. A similar change in the fundamental orientation of our own society would have been no easier. The difficulty of the changes to be brought about makes all the more heartening the success of many nations of Latin America in achieving reforms which will make their fundamental economic and social structures both more efficient and more equitable. . . .

Since 1961, eleven Latin-American countries—Argentina, Bolivia, Brazil, Colombia, Chile, Costa Rica, the Dominican Republic, El Salvador, Mexico, Panama, and Venezuela—have made structural reforms in their tax systems. Twelve countries have improved their income tax laws and administration.

New large-scale programs for improved land use and land reform have been undertaken in Venezuela, the Dominican Republic and two states in Brazil. More limited plans are being carried out in Chile, Colombia, Panama, Uruguay and Central America.

Six Latin-American countries—Colombia, Chile, Bolivia, Honduras, Mexico, and Venezuela—have submitted development programs to the panel of experts of the Organization of American States. The panel has evaluated and reported on the first three and will soon offer its views on the balance.

Viewed against the background of decades of neglect—or, at most, intermittent bursts of attention to basic problems—the start that has been made is encouraging. Perhaps most significant of all is a change in the hearts and minds of the people—a growing will to develop their countries. We can only help Latin Americans to save themselves. It is for this reason that the increasing determination of the peoples of the region to build modern societies is heartening. And it is for this reason that responsible leadership in Latin America must respond to this popular will with a greater sense of urgency and purpose, lest aspirations turn into frustrations and hope turn into despair. Pending reform legislation must be enacted, statutes already on the books must be enforced, and mechanisms for carrying out programs must be organized and invigorated. These steps are not easy, as we know from our own experience, but they must be taken.

Our own intention is to concentrate our support in Latin America on those countries adhering to the principles established in the Charter of Punta del Este, and to work with our neighbors to indicate more precisely the particular policy changes, reforms and other self-help measures which are necessary to make our assistance effective and the Alliance a success. . . .

A beginning has been made in the first two years of the Alliance; but the job that is still ahead must be tackled with continuing urgency. Many of the ingredients for a successful decade are at hand, and the fundamental course for the future is clear. It remains for all parties to the Alliance to provide the continuous will and effort needed to move steadily along that course. . . .

CONCLUSION

In closing, let me again emphasize the overriding importance of the efforts in which we are engaged.

At this point in history we can look back to many successes in the struggle to preserve freedom. Our nation is still daily winning unseen victories in the fight against Communist subversion in the slums and hamlets, in the hospitals and schools, and in the offices of governments across a world bent on lifting itself. Two centuries of pioneering and growth must be telescoped into decades and even years. This is a field of action for which our history has prepared us, to which our aspirations have drawn us, and into which our national interest moves us.

Around the world cracks in the monolithic apparatus of our adversary are there for all to see. This, for the American people, is a time for vision, for patience, for work and for wisdom. For better or worse, we are the pacesetters. Freedom's leader cannot flag or falter, or another runner will set the pace.

We have dared to label the sixties the decade of development. But it is not the eloquence of our slogans, but the quality of our endurance, which will determine whether this generation of Americans deserves the leadership which history has thrust upon us.

2. FOREIGN AID HAS SUCCEEDED*

by Barbara Ward

Against all the Cassandra warnings of hatchet work to come, the Foreign Aid Bill has gone through the House in a uniquely untruncated state. Yet one can still say no more than that the tendency to reduce aid, which has been gathering momentum in Congress for several years, has been halted, at least for the time being. A trend has been checked, time gained for reappraisal. But not even the most potent political magic can be expected, year in, year out, to force through programs from which public opinion is thoroughly alienated.

Is this the case with foreign aid? Have the American people, after a 17-year experiment, decided against it? Has Congress in recent years accurately reflected a growing popular disillusion? If so, is it one that can no longer be reversed? There is time, this year, to ask these questions. And on the answers depends any possibility of renewing and sustaining economic assistance for the longer run.

The first difficulty lies in establishing the facts. Whenever public opinion polls test the popular reaction to foreign aid in general terms, the answer is invariably that a sizable majority believe that aid should continue. It cannot be said that the American people have gone on record against economic assistance. Yet every Congressman who opposes aid tends to include among his reasons the argument that it is highly unpopular in his own constituency.

A lot, of course, depends upon the way in which the question is put. "Would you use some of America's abundant wealth to fight

* From *The New York Times Magazine* (July 12, 1964), p. 9 ff. Reprinted by permission of the author and *The New York Times*.

hunger, misery and ignorance abroad?" invites the generous answer: "Yes." The question: "Would you continue to shore up corrupt and lascivious generals with your aid money?" invites an equally emphatic negative.

Foreign aid can cover either or both propositions, and since many Congressmen display a built-in tendency to distrust Federal spending and an equal tendency to confine it, if possible, to expenditures which have immediate impact on American voters—especially their own— it is quite conceivable that the supposed unpopular reactions from the grass roots are in response to heavily loaded questions: "Would you rather see this fertilizer plant set up in Adel County or Bombay?" "Would you rather have flood control on the Upper Missouri or the Lower Nile?" The sampling is very far from clinically pure and the evidence must therefore be held to be somewhat inconclusive.

These loaded questions point to an even greater difficulty in the way of judging either the effectiveness of foreign aid or the real nature of popular reactions to it. Any judgment implies some standard of comparison. A teacher in a slum area contriving to pass on some instruction and a little sense of purpose to a class of potential juvenile delinquents may, in fact, be doing a far more testing and brilliant job than a university instructor successfully coaching a group of straight-A students. Most judgments, therefore, imply expectations— of what it is reasonable to achieve in given circumstances and hence of what the circumstances actually are.

At this point, one encounters the most formidable of all obstacles to the forming of any clear and convincing judgments about the success of foreign aid. Such judgments depend directly upon people's expectations—and there are some good reasons for supposing that, over the past 17 years, the link between American expectations and world facts has not always been very close.

Can one, without caricature, give some sort of profile of America's worldwide hopes and interests in the postwar years? Certainly a central strand is the concern for freedom—freedom from colonial rule by Western powers, freedom from post-colonial domination by Communists. But this is an aspiration at a very high level of generality. When Americans have thought in concrete terms about the policies needed to create or preserve freedom, it is arguable that their minds have been strongly colored by two great historical experiences —one old, one new, but both felt to be relevant.

The old experience is America's own anticolonial revolution. The archetype for the world is a band of vigorous men acting together to throw off colonial rule, setting up the institutions of free government, keeping foreign tyranny at bay and setting to work, by their own free efforts and enterprise, to develop a whole underdeveloped continent. When a Sukarno comes to Washington and speaks of the leadership Jefferson and Lincoln have offered an aspiring world, the American subconscious stirs with sympathetic images of freedom won and tyrants overthrown.

The new experience is the triumphant success of the Marshall Plan. After 1947, a group of free nations, shattered by war, endangered by Communist pressure, prostrate in the wake of an appalling winter, were enabled, by American aid, to rebuild the foundations of their shaken continent. In four years, they achieved new standards of wealth and unity and decisively defeated the risk of Communist expansion. American assistance, though vast—some $13 billion in free grants—was only the spark to ignite a whole conflagration of local investment which, in its turn, launched the European community into a new orbit of growth in which it has happily circled ever since. With this triumph behind them, Americans have understandably been inclined to believe that capital assistance, judiciously injected at strategic points in stagnant economies, can provide the extra element of élan needed to insure take-off into sustained growth.

Out of these two experiences it has been all too easy to construct an ideal pattern of aspiration for the world at large—that of responsible local leaders throwing off colonialism in the name of free government and then, supported by appropriate American aid, building up independent economies, closed to Communism and open to productive private investment. Aid, in such a context, is largely what the distinguished Clay Committee thought it should be—an instrument of American foreign policy designed to frustrate the spread of Communism and to foster not only the public but also the private development and management of free economies—certainly not an ignoble aim but, in the event, wildly out of line with the realities of the post-colonial world.

For what in fact is the record in recent years? There have been one or two resounding examples of success within the framework of America's expectations. Greece, Israel, Taiwan—all have been massively aided. All have used the aid to strengthen and diversify their mixed economies. All are now more or less in orbit, economically. None has succumbed to left-wing extremism.

But one cannot call the achievement typical. Whether the arena is Asia or Africa or the less developed parts of Latin America, the normal pattern is a shaky economy still far from "self-sustaining growth"; a government of dubious stability and authoritarian leanings, announcing a wide variety of "Socialistic patterns" for its economy; an international stance which, far from upholding anti-Communism, refuses to take sides, proffering an equal variety of variants on the theme of nonalignment—and all this in spite of a continuing under-cover threat of Communist subversion.

There are exceptions to this discouraging picture. India has main-tained the rule of law and a functioning democracy among a popula-tion that makes up nearly half the "third world." Egypt and Guinea have accepted Communist aid and locked up local Communists. Venezuela has survived a violent Castroite onslaught with democratic procedures and rates of growth intact. But these can be dismissed as exceptions. The norm remains. And if Americans are gloomy about the apparent results of a decade of assistance to the developing nations, it would be less than candid to maintain that they have not a good deal to be gloomy about.

But how much of the disillusion is due to fact, to reality, how much to disappointed expectations? The world seen from Westchester County (or Sunningdale or Passy, for that matter) may look a little less than reassuring. But this is not the only view. How, for instance, may it have looked from Peking in the early nineteen-fifties? The view from there would certainly not have raised the same expecta-tions. Indeed, it would not have overlapped at all in any but the crudest geographical sense. Yet it would have seemed real enough to the Chinese and remarkably close to *their* historical experience.

All around the world they would have seen poor, colored nations on the point of getting rid of Western tutelage, or, in more flamboyant language, "throwing off the imperialist yoke." The economies of these countries in some ways repeated China's own early obstacles to growth—stagnant, often bankrupt agriculture; modernization chiefly confined to the import-export sectors and concentrated in large, foreign-dominated coastal cities; industry in an embryonic state and largely in foreign hands. In politics a small, wealthy local group would be likely to be in close and even compromising touch with foreign interests; foreign businessmen, administrators, technicians and visitors would hold aloof on the other side of a color bar. Local education, though it would be large enough to spark hope, would be neither technical nor widespread enough to underpin a vigorous, modernizing economy (one thinks of the Congo, with only 12 college graduates at the time of its independence). In short, the typical post-colonial pattern could be held to be one of societies aware of new opportunities, open to the "revolution of rising expectations," but frustrated by internal unbalance and caught between an old world that would not die and a new order still unborn.

Only violence, it was easy to feel, would break the impasse. Like Russia in 1917—a comparable case of deadlock—China in 1949 embarked on the Leninist short cut to modernization—Lenin himself had thought that the conquest of the world might lie through Peking and Delhi. In China, in the early fifties, the world-wide triumph of Communism, as the "contradictions" of the ex-colonial world turned into revolution, must have seemed a foregone conclusion. Aid in the shape of loans and guerrilla instruction would simply hasten a historic inevitability.

Two views, two sets of expectations, one world, presumably one reality—but who has proved to be nearer the facts? So far, at least, one has surely to admit the curious paradox that while the Communists' picture of the developing world is on the whole more accurate their expectations have proved far wider of the mark.

The developing world of the sixties *is* infinitely more like China of the late forties than Europe at the same time or America in the days of the Founding Fathers. Economies *are* unbalanced as a result of the old Western dominance which stimulated exports and little else. Trade patterns *do* induce one-crop dependence and unsatisfactory primary prices. Western investment plans and tariff structures *do* tend to favor growth where it is already profitable—in the developed world—while poor countries grow poorer still. All this experience of disequilibrium and dependences *does* create its resentments—racial resentment, economic resentment, growing realization of the gap between rich nations and poor.

Meanwhile, new governments, composed all too often of no more than a fringe of fully literate and experienced men, could hardly be more unlike the Madisons and Jeffersons of America's own revolution. Nor can one compare the reactions of the sturdy yeoman electorate of the United States in the late 18th century with the inchoate ambitions and measureless miseries of the poor majority in today's new states. A double revolution of equality sweeps the world—against the élite at the national level, against the wealthy West at the world level.

It is a crisis apparently tailormade for Communism. Yet, by and large, Communist pressure is no more effective today than it was 10 years ago. In fact, it can be argued that in some areas it is receding, as Africa develops strange new varieties of home-grown Socialism, as Latin America learns the lean look of the Castro experiment, as Eastern Europe wriggles out of Soviet tutelage and as the Communist bloc tears itself apart in a new ideological struggle in which one element is, precisely, China's denunciation of Russia as a "bourgeois" state.

Why have Communist expectations for the developing world been even more brutally disappointed than Western hopes? Certainly, no one will assign all the credit to foreign aid. Communist policies have often contributed to their own discrediting. Their aid—as in Africa— has often been expensive and unfit for tropical conditions. On occasion, their technicians have been shown to be without the needed skills or languages. They have been caught out in subversion. They have been found guilty of such "capitalist tricks" as unloading unwanted goods, or reselling tropical produce at less than world market prices.

Again, many new governments have proved fully as anxious as any American could wish to avoid substituting Eastern ideological control for Western colonialism. President Nyerere's present maneuvers to regain control over Zanzibar have precisely this aim in view. Nasser, Touré, Nkrumah—to name some of America's possibly less favorite leaders—do not wear "positive neutrality" as a cloak. It means what it implies—independence from either great world bloc. For, as President Nkrumah once put it: "When the bull elephants fight, the grass is trampled down."

Such detachment may rile Western enthusiasts, but at least they can console themselves with a reminder that they are supposed to believe in variety. It is infinitely more galling for the Communists, for whom world uniformity is the aim.

Yet while allowing for Communist mistakes and for the developing nations' own sturdy sense of independence, one must also give Western policies—above all, the policies of economic assistance—some credit for the continuance of a largely open world. Western aid to the development plans of India and Pakistan in the shape of crucial foreign exchange and surplus food supplies has permitted the huge subcontinent to secure industrial growth of the order of 8 per cent a year and to keep just ahead in the task of producing more food for its bursting population. America's assistance to Latin America has offset the decades-long fall in primary prices and at least permitted trade to continue at the old levels. Western aid of all kinds to Africa has brought about an educational revolution in a continent in which a shortage of skills of all kinds is the greatest obstacle to growth. A dozen universities, primary schools for half the population, places for perhaps 4 per cent of the children in secondary education—these are targets either achieved or within reach as a result of Western activity.

It can therefore be argued that foreign aid has succeeded in the profoundest sense—at the level of human imagination and understanding. It has begun to change the whole context within which the developing nations, the vast majority of mankind, look at the West and assess Western policies and intentions. This does not mean that aid cannot be better administered and better used. A very valuable tightening up of the administrative machinery is now taking place in America's agency for aid. The international agencies have also acquired a great deal of valuable experience about the best methods, the best channels, and the right kind of supervision to be applied in aid programs.

Nor, in the longer run, is even the check to potential Communist expansion the most important feature of the aid effort. Its *positive* possibilities in building up the institutions and solidarity of a brotherly world order are ultimately of far greater significance and, for Western nations—wealthy beyond the dreams of avarice—of much greater moral validity as well.

But, given the present questioning mood of America, the first point to be made, when the effectiveness or continuance of aid is discussed, is that even within the single context of checking Communism the program cannot be said to have failed. On the contrary, the failure—the setback, the surprised disappointment—is largely on the Communist side. For this reason, if for no other, any decision to support foreign aid is profoundly in America's interest.

3. FOREIGN AID AND THE LIBERAL DISSENT*

BY ISAIAH FRANK

Ever since the United States began to provide economic assistance to less developed countries, the program has been under sharp attack. Traditional opponents continue to denounce the give-away of taxpayers' money, the bleeding of the American economy and the encouragement of socialism abroad. But this familiar refrain has in recent years been joined by expressions of doubt and frustration by others, by men who ought to be for foreign aid but who have lost heart. The *New Republic* is scarcely the place to have to defend foreign aid against its traditional detractors, but readers of the magazine ought to be deeply concerned with what it is that troubles men of goodwill about the present state of the program.

In seeking to gauge the extent of the recent disquiet, one discovers a curious fact. The complaints have not come widely from liberal individuals or groups across the country who feel that something has now gone wrong with foreign aid. Their enthusiasm may have declined but by and large doubts have not been expressed openly. The opposition has rather been concentrated among members of Congress who have supported the program in the past but who each year find it more and more difficult to defend its complex workings and to assess its results. A private individual, well-disposed toward the general idea of helping the poor of other lands, can shrug off the technicalities as not really his business. But a conscientious Congressman, who must vote on billions of dollars in appropriations and who must speak to the doubts and questions of both his constituents and opposing legislators, cannot rest his case on repeated assertions that the national interest is being served.

Because the annual battle for foreign aid appropriations has been going on practically since the end of the Second World War, a widespread case of combat fatigue has set in on Capitol Hill. As in any

* From the *New Republic,* Vol. 152 (January 23, 1965), pp. 17–22. Reprinted by permission of the *New Republic,* © 1965, Harrison-Blaine of New Jersey, Inc.

long-drawn-out struggle, the fighters have grown weary and bored. Even toward the end of the Eisenhower Administration, when Senator Fulbright rose to introduce the foreign aid bill, he declared: "I do not, it will be noticed, leap to my feet ablaze with excitement and enthusiasm. . . ." And last month the Senator threw in the towel as manager of the foreign aid bill in the Senate. Although objecting specifically to the continued inclusion of both military and economic aid in a single bill, it was clear that he was tired of going through the whole dreary chore year after year. "I have served my time on this kind of bill," he declared. "If they want to pursue that same kind, they ought to turn it over to someone else, someone who is fresher and more enthusiastic than I am."

Most Congressmen accept the official statement of the objectives of our foreign aid—to further US security by helping other countries maintain their independence and develop into self-supporting nations. They also realize that our security interest in the developing countries is far broader than simply fighting Communism and that economic aid, in serving this interest, also satisfies strong humanitarian impulses of the American people.

But where are the results, ask the Congressmen. Why, despite huge amounts of aid, have major countries continued to be wracked by turbulence, subversion and economic stagnation? In reply, they are offered the cold comfort that the program's results can in most cases be realized only over the long run and that in many areas the situation may get worse before it gets better. And when will it all end? As of today, the Administration can only promise that, as AID Administrator David E. Bell said last month, "the concept of temporary assistance . . . is a feasible idea." But how temporary no one can say. The truth is that the need for foreign aid will be with us for a long time. Although individual developing countries may soon be off the list because self-sustained growth will have been achieved, the total need for economic assistance over the next decade will be greater than ever before. With no end of the road in sight, the tedious and protracted annual congressional debate generates an atmosphere of impatience and frustration within which a rational assessment of the economic assistance program can scarcely take place.

This situation is compounded by the fact that roughly half the $3,250 million in the 1964 Foreign Assistance Act is not intended primarily for economic development assistance but rather for direct security purposes. (Military assistance, supporting assistance, and the contingency fund are included in the security category.) The aid bill as a whole, therefore, becomes a focus of attack for those who, like Senators Wayne Morse and Frank Church, question the conduct of our foreign policy in such places as Vietnam, Laos, Korea or Taiwan, where a large share of the military assistance goes. Moreover, the economic development component of the foreign aid bill bears the brunt of the attack on foreign economic aid as a whole, even though it constitutes only about $1,700 million out of a total US economic aid program of $4,000 million. Most of the rest consists of programs that are closely tied to domestic interests in the United States—shipments of surplus agricultural products which are now an integral element of our domestic farm support program, and Export-Import Bank loans designed to further export of American machinery and other capital goods.

In short, any dissatisfaction with the scale of our economic aid effort as a whole tends to concentrate on the most politically vulnerable part of it—namely, the development assistance funds appropriated for the Agency for International Development (AID).

With this general background, let us examine four major criticisms of the economic aid program as synthesized out of the welter of objections and charges most commonly put forward by liberals in Congress.

Charge number one is that the aid program is too big. Too big not in terms of the US ability to afford a program amounting to less than two-thirds of one percent of its gross national product, but rather in terms of the ability of the receiving countries to use the funds effectively. Today, it is charged, we provide aid indiscriminately to almost 100 countries, regardless of whether promises of social reform and self-help measures are fulfilled. Much of the aid never reaches the ordinary people but ends up in the pockets (or the Swiss bank accounts) of the oligarchies.

In line with this concern, Senator Ernest Gruening has put forward a list of 10 criteria which should be "rigidly adhered to" in determining which countries are worthy of receiving US foreign economic assistance. Among them are an efficient government and trained administrators; an austere budget and a readiness to sacrifice for future economic growth; assurance of an equitable share of the benefits of development to workers and peasants; absence of capital flight; a workable long-range development plan; and tax and land reform measures. If only these criteria were followed, we could discontinue aid to many recipients and substantially cut down the size of the total program.

The trouble with this approach is that it rests on a basic misconception of the very nature of the problem our government faces in the underdeveloped parts of the world. If a country fully satisfied the Gruening pre-conditions for assistance, the chances are that it would not need any outside aid at all. It would probably be well on its way to self-sustained growth simply with the help of whatever external capital would be forthcoming on normal commercial terms.

Our concern is with promoting growth and stability in those countries which, precisely because they have in varying degrees lacked the attributes enumerated by Senator Gruening, have become victims of stagnation and frustration and are promising breeding grounds for subversion, violence and chaos. It is true that in situations of this kind, aid, viewed purely as a net addition to a country's resources, would be equivalent to pouring money down a rathole. But there *are* underdeveloped countries where governments are determined to battle against the obstacles to development, and where an aid program can be a means of getting involved in their struggle. Through an assistance program we can supply not only capital and skills but also the moral support needed to withstand and overcome resistance to change on the part of entrenched domestic interest groups. In many cases, it is only with such support that progress can be made toward the social and political transformation implied by the Gruening preconditions. And we must reconcile ourselves to the fact that this process of change is bound to be accompanied by inefficiencies in the use of resources.

Nevertheless, it is legitimate to ask whether the program as a whole would not benefit from a greater degree of country selectivity. Currently, 76 developing countries are receiving AID economic assistance and a larger number when other forms of aid are included. Surely there must be a significant number of countries in this group where the prospects for development and the realistic possibilities of exerting effective influence are so limited as to call into question the rationale for US assistance. There may also be a certain institutional sluggishness in phasing out a program even where the case for withdrawal is recognized.

The fact is, however, that the general desirability of concentrating the aid effort has been fully accepted by AID, and the wholesale congressional charges of "scatteration" have been met in extensive testimony by the Administration. The bulk of AID funds goes to only a small fraction of the 76 recipient countries. Specifically, 50 percent of all AID economic assistance is received by seven countries—Chile, Colombia, Nigeria, Tunisia, Turkey, Pakistan and India—where the prospects for growth are promising. At the other extreme there are some 37 countries, accounting for only 10 percent of total AID economic assistance, where the US has quite limited programs.

Conditions in some of the latter countries may well warrant US withdrawal as soon as existing programs can be phased out. In others, although we may not be able to work effectively with present governments, we can accomplish useful results in selected sectors, while maintaining at small cost a US presence in the country. In still others, favorable conditions for growth may exist but the US aid program is merely supplementary to more substantial assistance by other donors.

Apart from the question of the distribution of US aid, how large should the program be in total? In last year's hearings Senator Morse complained that although the number of countries receiving help had fallen by 10, no commensurate cut was made in the Administration's request for new funds. The Senator's assumption that needs elsewhere did not increase is, however, quite at variance with recent official and unofficial estimates of aid requirements.

Although the estimates vary a good deal, they tend to suggest that, if the poorer countries of the world are to achieve a per capita annual increase in real income of about 2.5 percent, they will require by 1975 external capital from all sources equal to at least twice the present inflow of about $8 billion. Part of the reason for the rapidly growing need is the expectation that, even with satisfactory internal performance, the essential import needs of the developing countries will outstrip their capacity to finance those needs through the growth of their exports. And part of the reason for the anticipated lag in their exports is the restrictive commercial policies of the advanced countries—as exemplified by US import quotas on sugar, lead, zinc and cotton textiles.

Charge number two is that the US continues to give aid to countries which threaten war against neighbors, oppose us in the United Nations, or otherwise adopt foreign policy measures counter to our interests. In some instances, it is claimed, our economic aid has freed domestic resources for use in military adventures disruptive to international peace and security. Among the countries cited in connection with these charges are Syria, Brazil under Goulart, and most consistently Indonesia and the United Arab Republic.

In the forthcoming aid hearings the spotlight will undoubtedly be on the UAR. In the last few weeks of 1964 an American library was burned in Cairo, an American oil company plane was shot down over UAR territory and UAR officials announced arms shipments to the Congolese rebels while telling the United States to jump in the lake with its aid program. What was the US response? No suggestion of cutting down existing aid, consisting primarily of $143 million in surplus food. Instead, the US postponed until 1965 a decision as to whether to give the UAR $35 million more in surplus food over and above the existing level.

According to *The New York Times* of December 29, the Administration strategy was as follows: "Washington is holding back on a decision until it sees what course President Nasser intends to pursue in his relations with the US. By delaying, but not slamming the door on the request, the Administration obviously hopes to steer President Nasser away from the apparent anti-American course he has taken. However, the Administration is deliberately not emphasizing the diplomatic bargaining aspects of the delay. President Nasser is extremely sensitive to the suggestion that American aid is conditioned on Cairo's behavior and the State Department does not want to complicate already frayed relations by openly treating the surplus food request as a bargaining lever."

The Administration's sensitivity to President Nasser's feelings will have to be weighed against the likely effect of this type of strategy on the fate of the aid bill as a whole. It is a safe guess that more than a few Senators may turn out to be lacking in the sophistication required to appreciate why an additional $35 million of aid is likely to alter President Nasser's course when $143 million has so signally failed to do so. In any case, a lot of questions are going to be asked about the probable results of cutting off aid to the UAR and precisely how the consequent situation is likely to be worse than the present one.

We are told that the benefits of the US assistance program must be viewed in long-term perspective—in the gradual strengthening of the political independence and economic performance of the recipient countries and the consequent contribution of aid to peace and stability in the world. So long as countries show a determination to preserve their independence and promote their economic growth, the US should assist them without expecting short-run compliance with its wishes in foreign affairs. Without necessarily disputing this doctrine, a number of Senators are going to want to know why the US is precluded from using this particular instrument of foreign policy more boldly to press for conformity to certain elementary standards of responsible international conduct.

Charge number three is that the aid program is poorly administered, primarily in the sense that much of the money is advanced in the form of "program loans." As stated by Senator Morse, *"project* loans finance the importing of commodities for specific projects whose soundness can be verified by AID officials; but *program* loans go to balance accounts and finance imports in general. In many countries these include imports that contribute nothing to local development."

It is true that a large portion of the development loan funds advanced by AID are not tied to specific projects like dams or cement plants, and that the so-called program approach is the predominant form of assistance for countries, like India, Pakistan, Nigeria and Brazil which are among the largest aid recipients. But it is an optical illusion to believe that because project aid provides visible or tangible results, it necessarily makes a greater contribution to growth than does program support.

From the development point of view, the crucial question is not how specific aid funds are used, but rather what effect provision of these funds has on total disposition of resources in the receiving country. If a country has a well-articulated development plan consisting of a series of capital projects to be undertaken in a particular time sequence, the financing of one of these projects through foreign aid may not affect the country's investment program at all. If the project falls within the country's scale of priorities for the use of its own resources, the consequence of providing foreign assistance for the project is simply to free an equivalent volume of domestic resources for some other purpose. Although it may appear, therefore, that the donor is financing the equipment for an electric power plant, he may in fact be permitting the country to step up its volume of imports of consumer goods.

In general, where a country is in the early stages of growth and does not possess an operable development plan, the case is strong for following a project approach. Such a country is likely to have inadequate control over the use of its resources and program support is quite apt to be dissipated. Project assistance, however, will at least provide close control over a small portion of available investment resources and foreign exchange. At the other extreme, for a country like India with an internationally accepted development plan and a good record of performance, the program approach is an effective way of providing aid. It substitutes for the narrower project control an over-all understanding with the country as to its use of resources under government control, including the foreign exchange needed to carry out the development program.

In practice, AID recognizes that the wisest course for many countries is a blend of the two types of assistance. Each has certain disadvantages that can be minimized when combined with the other. Project aid tends to overemphasize public sector activities and large schemes. Exclusive reliance on program aid, on the other hand, may tend to establish a politically frozen level of aid, and would sacrifice the public relations advantages of separately identifiable, successful aid-financed projects. But regardless of the blend of aid used, it is clear that many Congressmen will continue to be suspicious of program assistance unless a much greater effort is made to explain its rationale.

Charge number four is that other affluent nations take a back seat when it comes to helping poorer countries. As a result, the US is forced to assume a disproportionate share of the aid burden. In the words of Senator Morse, "our so-called allies are permitted to shirk their responsibilities because of our often feckless generosity."

Discussions of burden-sharing inevitably get complicated because of the need to specify precisely what burden one is talking about, and because of the difficulty of commensurating assistance that is conveyed in a variety of different forms. If, for example, one includes military assistance to the developing countries on the periphery of the Communist world, the US share of free-world assistance increases substantially. Other countries have not accepted responsibility for the defense of these areas and we are the only large-scale provider of military aid to them. If, on the other hand, only economic development assistance is included, the US share would appear to amount to about 60 percent of the total, a proportion just about equal to the US share of the total gross national product of the aid-contributing countries of the free world. Among other countries, France contributes a substantially larger share of its national income than the US; most other countries contribute a smaller share.

These figures, however, can only be viewed as the roughest approximations. Again with the exception of France, US aid is conveyed on more liberal terms than that of other countries. Most of our aid is in the form of grants and low-interest, long-term loans, whereas a substantial proportion of aid from other countries is in the form of loans of shorter maturity and higher interest rates. Over the period 1961-63, however, Western European countries have increased their commitments and generally softened their terms, whereas US commitments have not risen and our lending terms have progressively hardened. In any event, over a third of all US economic aid is in the form of shipments of surplus farm products, a form of assistance that can hardly be viewed as a burden or sacrifice since it is largely a by-product of farm support programs.

In short, so far as economic aid is concerned, the facts do not lend support to the charge that the US is carrying an undue share of the load.

Most signs indicate that the US foreign economic aid program is in trouble. In an undertaking of such complexity and scope there are bound to be mistakes and false starts. But the program is in trouble not because it suffers from basic defects of conception, policy or administration. Nor is it in trouble because of a lack of success in achieving its basic purposes. Economic growth in the less developed world as a whole since 1950 has been at an unprecedented rate of 4.2 percent per year. Even on a per capita basis the rate of growth of about two percent per year has been an impressive achievement in the perspective of history. And in most countries, growth has been accompanied by some improvement in the lot of the ordinary man and by the strengthening of national independence.

The aid program is in trouble because both sides—the Administration and Congress—are tired of the annual cycle of preparation, presentation and hearings on authorizations and appropriations extending over the entire congressional session. It is unlikely, moreover, that the prospects for appropriations would be improved by merely following Senator William Fulbright's suggestion of separating economic and military aid requests into different pieces of legislation. Representative Thomas Morgan may be right in believing that this strategy by itself would be apt to expose economic aid to even bigger cuts than in the past. In order to rescue the aid program, its most vulnerable part must somehow be removed from the annual battle for survival on Capitol Hill.

I suggest that serious consideration be given to turning over, to the World Bank's International Development Association (IDA), development loan funds now administered by AID. In the current fiscal year, these amount to $774 million. This sum is not intended to be used as a slush fund for short-term political objectives but as a development fund for long-term, low-interest loans similar in purpose to those made by IDA.

The United States is already contributing $100 million a year to IDA against a three-year commitment, a sum equal to approximately 40 percent of total annual contributions to IDA by all individual country donors. The extent of the proposed additional contribution would be conditioned on matching grants by other countries. Equally important would be at least the retention of the present practice of three-year commitments to IDA but, preferably, the lengthening of the commitment period in the future.

I see advantages in a move along the following lines:

1. The development loan funds are the most vulnerable component of the aid program. To the extent that they can be shifted to IDA, on a multi-year commitment basis of at least three years, the program as a whole will be better protected from the congressional chopping-block. In general, the World Bank group has achieved an excellent public image and has been relatively free from the carping criticism to which AID has been subjected.

2. Even in the unlikely event that all development loan funds could, under the specified conditions, be shifted to IDA, the US would still be left with the bulk of its development aid program administered on a bilateral basis. As a minimum, the bilateral program would then include virtually all agricultural-commodity assistance, Export-Import Bank loans, funds for the Alliance for Progress and a substantial amount of technical assistance. By and large, these programs have been less controversial than development lending. There would also remain supporting assistance and the contingency fund, but these funds are so closely linked to military programs or

short-range political objectives that they can scarcely be regarded as development aid.

3. IDA's current policy is to lend at extremely liberal terms: 50 years, three-quarters of one percent interest, and 10-year grace periods for repayment of principal. To the extent that a US offer to shift its development loan funds to the IDA induces other countries to do likewise, it will accelerate the present tendency of our allies to soften the average term of their total development contribution.

4. In sensitive political situations, the IDA may be able to press more effectively for necessary changes in internal economic policies than the US government. Recipient countries tend to react with less resentment to tough conditions on the use of aid when imposed by international institutions than when insisted upon by bilateral donors.

Despite advantages, one cannot be sanguine that this proposal would find ready acceptability. While Congress has been sharply critical of the administration of our assistance on a bilateral basis, it has not shown an equivalent eagerness to relinquish US control over large portions of the development lending program. Approval of the US contribution to last year's replenishment of IDA funds was obtained only with great difficulty. But attitudes can be changed and a major effort to convince Congress to move along the lines proposed here may well pay off.

However, no change of this sort, or any other organizational rearrangement, is likely to be effective in bringing forth the necessary funds unless the full weight of the President's prestige is placed squarely behind the development assistance program. We need more of the spirit generated by President Johnson when he spoke on April 21, 1964, to a group of editors and broadcasters in the Rose Garden of the White House. Referring to foreign aid, he said:

"Because of what we call it, and because of how it has been administered, and because it is far away, we don't realize that this investment is not only one of the most Christian acts that this great, powerful rich country could do, but it is an act of necessity if we are to preserve our image in the world and our leadership in the world and, most of all, our society. . . . No President who looks beyond the immediate problems which crowd his desk can fail to extend the hand and heart of the country to those who are struggling elsewhere."

CHAPTER XI

Soviet Aid and Trade

Socialist aid is called upon to promote the economic liberation of the Asian, African, and Latin American countries from the bonds of foreign monopolist capital.

—PRAVDA

The USSR takes opportunity to side with these new countries against the West to foster the community-of-interest attitude.

—THE COUNCIL FOR ECONOMIC AND
INDUSTRIAL RESEARCH, INC.

Viewed from the standpoint of myopic Marxists, the United States foreign aid program was a new venture in economic imperialism—the last hope of the capitalists to prolong their search for "surplus value" and to extend the life of their self-contradicting economic system which is doomed to a self-destruction. The Soviets, however, came to recognize the success and impact of the program which, in spite of their vituperative accusations against it, "must look like one of the smartest moves the non-Soviet world has made, and one to be discouraged in every possible fashion."

The Soviets, therefore, in 1953 set out to use their own economic and technical aid to gain greater influence in the underdeveloped countries, which were struggling for their national identification and economic improvement. Through accelerated trade with, and aid to, these countries the Soviets are determined to promote their political objectives, to minimize the influence of the United States and its Allies, to disrupt the free world's defense alliances, and to increase their own prestige and power. They feel that the political advantage to be gained is greater than any financial or economic loss they may incur. It would be naïve to assume that the Soviet Union will use its capacity to provide economic and technical assistance in such a way as to help consolidate genuinely democratic, non-Communist regimes in the newly emerging nations.

291

This chapter is intended to show the motive, character, and result of the Soviet economic offensive in the emerging countries.

The editor of this book examines the characteristics of the under-developed countries, attempts to determine the reasons for their susceptibility to Soviet aid, and cites the United Arab Republic (Egypt) as an example to illustrate the impact of the Soviet aid affecting the United States program.

V. Rymalov, a Soviet economist, contends that the Soviet economic aid enables the emerging nations to strengthen their position in the struggle for the national liberation movement and that "in the course of economic competition of the two systems the logic of events will lead them to the conclusion that the socialist road to progress is unquestionably superior."

C. P. FitzGerald, Professor of Far Eastern History at the Australian National University in Canberra, discusses the conflicting views between the Soviet Union and Communist China in their approaches to the problems of underdeveloped countries, and analyzes Chinese Communist tactics to win Southeast Asia and Africa through their revolutionary spirit and method.

1. SUSCEPTIBILITY AND IMPACT

BY YOUNG HUM KIM

"Underdeveloped countries," when defined in a loose and general term as "poor countries," cover most nations in Latin America, nearly all of Africa, and most of the Middle and Far East, as well as vast tropical areas of the earth. These countries include more than two-thirds of the world's population.

The most striking feature of the underdeveloped countries is the low standard of living as compared with that enjoyed by advanced countries. Disease and a high mortality rate, illiteracy and ignorance, insufficient food supplies with accompanying malnutrition, social disorganization and political unrest—all these are still the rule rather than the exception.

Most of these countries have only recently achieved their national political independence after decades or centuries of struggle against colonial domination. The consequent outburst of nationalism and anti-imperialism makes them hesitant to accept large amounts of foreign capital and economic assistance.

The most apparent aspirations and ambitions of the newly independent states are largely a reflection of the reasoning and activity of a small minority of leaders, drawn from, and supported by, a relatively limited number of intelligentsia. These intellectuals, or elites, chiefly of western education but often not unsympathetic with Communist cause and doctrine, usually determine decisively the politics of their countries. Such a situation is in itself indicative of disharmonies in the total social process.

While they view the past with distaste, deeply cognizant of their economic and social backwardness, fully aware that both the Soviet Union and the Western nations are far beyond them in power, prestige, and standards of living, they are at the same time conscious of their elitism, their intellectual achievements, and their ability to emulate the success of more advanced countries. Believing that their power and capacity to achieve political and economic development at an accelerated pace toward the desired goals will be enhanced only if they bring their nations out of poverty, these leaders tend to select one particular factor—the industrialization of the national economy—as a panacea for existing ills and the state of inequality. They are, therefore, intent on including heavy industry in their economic development plans. These programs for economic progress are, however, frequently handicapped by the more apparent political instability resulting from the struggle for power within the elites.

The use of potentially abundant resources for economic development is only partially and inefficiently explored. Crucial factors are the lack of capital, technology, and qualified technicians. The economic progress has been further handicapped by political chaos which frequently resulted from the dislocation and devastation of World War II, as well as the turbulent transition from war to peace, and subsequent civil strife following the change from dependent to independent status. Also, serious economic maladjustment has resulted from the increased disorganization of the production and transportation of foodstuffs and raw materials.

Though predominantly agrarian and potentially wealthy in mineral resources, the standard of living and the per capita income of these countries are extremely low. In the early 1960's the average per capita income was over $2,500 for the United States, about $1,000 for some of the Western European countries. In contrast, for the underdeveloped countries as a whole it was in the neighborhood of $100 with an average of only $70-$80 over vast areas of Asia, Africa, and Latin America. The average real income is barely sufficient to maintain a minimum level of subsistence, and industrial output constitutes only a small proportion of the total production. The lack of modern forms of industrial production is accompanied by an insufficiency of modern transportation, distribution, and consumption. Low productivity and the low living standard reinforce each other to form the familiar "vicious circle" in these countries.

While the peoples in underdeveloped countries have access to sufficient resources, they are deficient in actual technological skills for advancement. Moreover, they have traditions, customs, and taboos which are frequently detrimental to economic development and social reform. Their attitudes are primarily fatalistic and defeatist, which, probably enhanced by their religious beliefs, brew a natural reluctance to advance and change by ordinary means. These attitudes are further intensified by the bitter experiences of the past, a past filled with memories of all forms of inequality, humiliation, and submission to alien subjugation and relentless exploitation.

The history of colonial Asia and Africa is replete with examples of assistance programs undertaken not for the benefit of colonial people but with ulterior motives for financial, political, cultural, and religious interests of the colonizers. In addition, the great masses were exploited by local, conservative, and landed "aristocrats"—sheiks, warlords, maharajahs, sultans, etc.

Those responsible for misery in the Middle East are not, on the whole, the Western powers, but its own feudal aristocracy. This class, which is naturally conservative, has found in the plethora of organizations trying to help the area, the perfect field for its ancient pastime of playing one foreigner off against another. Their very numbers enable this class to pay lip service to reform, while postponing the day of action because there are inexhaustible ranges of authorities that need to be consulted.[1]

It is not surprising, then, that among the masses of these countries there is an incorrigible conviction that any alteration by this class is

[1] *The Economist,* CLXI (November 24, 1951), 1253.

not necessarily for their benefit. Such a conviction, in turn, generates sentiments of revolt against the aliens and suspicion of their helping hand.

The birth and death rates of the underdeveloped countries are characteristically high. Estimates of birth rates for Asia were in the range of forty to forty-five per 1,000 population between 1930 and 1937. Data for later years which are available for some countries in the Far East and Southeast Asia show that the birth rate remained relatively constant at this high level. In the 1950's, according to available information, birth rates in most of Asia, Africa, and Latin America were generally somewhat higher than those of Western Europe around the beginning of the nineteenth century.

Social and economic conditions in these areas are less favorable to the nature of the small-family idea. Hence, Asian, African, and Latin American birth rates may fall less quickly—if they fall at all—in response to economic development.[2]

Viewed from the standpoint of contemporary power politics, the underdeveloped countries are mostly uncommitted to either side of the vast confrontation of power between the United States and the Soviet Union; each attempting to draw a large number of countries toward its own political, economic, cultural, ideological, and psychological orbit.

The underdeveloped countries are compelled to seek foreign financing for their development programs from three possible sources: (1) from private investors, (2) from international institutions, and (3) from foreign countries, either of the Communist bloc or of the free world.

There is little hope, under existing economic and political conditions, of a revival of the flow of private capital and investment, the volume of which has been considerably reduced. The guarantees offered by the recipient countries are insufficient; in many cases the investors believe the political and military risks outbalance the possible gains. In addition, most underdeveloped countries are reluctant to take loans from moneylenders or from foreign governments. Such loans are often thought to be fraught with exploitation, imperialistic tendencies, and political pressures of every kind.

These countries, therefore, turn to the second source—international

[2] *United Nations Documents,* E/CN.9/55/Add. 2 (May 2, 1950), p. 8.

institutions—for financial help. The two agencies designed to provide such assistance are the International Monetary Fund, though it is not directly concerned with economic development, and the International Bank for Reconstruction and Development (World Bank), which thus far has been unable to meet the requirements of the needy countries. The financial needs have been so vast, and the prospect of return so remote and difficult to estimate in terms of money, that it is impractical for the Bank to provide the necessary capital and at the same time adhere to the principles laid down in its Articles of Agreement. The inauguration of the Expanded Program of Technical Assistance and the establishment of the United Nations Special Fund were designed to provide the answer to this problem.

In seeking assistance from other nations, the underdeveloped countries have two choices: the Communist bloc led by the Soviet Union (although the Soviet leadership in some regions is challenged by Communist China) or the Western bloc led by the United States. The Soviet Union is not unmindful of the opportunity to gain considerable political credit by associating its technical, financial, economic, and military aid with the profound urge for a better life and economic advancement that has been sweeping the backward countries.

The Communist leaders use trade and aid as political weapons. Even though their assistance may be unaccompanied by formal political conditions, the spread of their capital, technology and manpower throughout the underdeveloped countries is calculated in advance to have a beneficial political effect for Communism.[3]

Against this background, these countries are susceptible to the blandishments and promises of the Soviet Union. These nations, now undergoing the process of disintegration of traditions, are receptive to new things; new institutions and attitudes must replace those in process of dissolution. In this ferment, the Soviet bloc is active with its propaganda. Western powers have the disadvantage of their discredited colonial past, and the Soviet Union makes every effort to identify the United States with the colonial powers. The Soviets frequently chide the leaders of formerly colonial countries for insufficient bitterness toward the colonialists, insisting that "if aid is to be rendered, we will render it ourselves." The underdeveloped

[3] U.S., *Congressional Record,* 86th Cong., 1st Sess., 1959, CV, Part 6, 7257.

countries, being poor, have inadequate internal sources to achieve expansion by themselves and, therefore, they are willing to go along with the Soviet "trade and aid" offensive.

In the undertaking of economic assistance programs, the Soviet Union has some definite advantages over the United States. First, the Soviet Union itself is only a short step ahead of these new countries in its economic development. Indeed, vast areas of the Soviet Union are still "underdeveloped" or only slowly emerging from such a condition. Consequently, the Soviet Union is likely to understand them better. Second, having diverse ethnic origins, the Soviet Union is in a position to send technicians of the same or similar race and cultural background to its adjacent underdeveloped countries. This tends to lend substance to their propaganda theme that they are of ethnic affinity.

Soviet Russia has no equivalent of the Monroe Doctrine for Southeast Asia. But Moscow has made plain that it feels a special kinship with the peoples of Southeast Asia and it has spared no effort to combat and undermine Western influence there. The Russians clearly regard the underdeveloped nations of the area, with their history of colonialism, as inviting territory for Communist penetration.[4]

Many underdeveloped countries, on the other hand, have set goals which exceed their resources and technical knowledge. They face particular difficulties in trying to materialize the rapid industrialization on which they place such a high premium as a symbol of economic independence, and they frequently find the process of their economic growth in Western style is slow and arduous. Then they tend to discredit and blame democratic methods for the inadequate and insufficient result in attaining the pre-set goals.

While many people in these countries are opposed to Communist political institutions and methods, they are frequently impressed by Soviet industrial growth and technical achievements, although in general these have yet to attain Western European and North American levels.[5]

Soviet leaders capitalize on this sentiment among the peoples of underdeveloped countries and reportedly insist that Soviet scientific and economic achievements demonstrate superiority over the "deca-

[4] *The New York Times,* February 28, 1960, Sec. 4, p. 1.
[5] U. S. Department of State, *The Communist Economic Threat,* 1959, pp. 2–3.

dent bourgeois" system in the West. Premier Khrushchev said: "Our competition in the economic field with the United States can be compared to a marathon race. We are still trailing the United States, but this does not mean anything because they started first. Now the speed of the United States is slower. They are exhausted."

The underdeveloped countries are, in various degrees, susceptible to the Soviet economic offensive. How the United States is to meet this problem is one of the major questions of policy to be decided in Washington. The answer may determine whether the United States or the Soviet Union will exert the greater influence on the direction that the underdeveloped countries take. With the Communist bloc attempting to displace the Western powers in every corner of the earth, the United States faces the choice of either withdrawing from the race or challenging it with added vigor.

The impropriety of withdrawal is obvious; it would signal a birth of neo-isolationism. The realities of thermonuclear war are probably as apparent to the Soviet Union as they are to the United States and its allies. The conflict between the free world and the Communist bloc, patterned as "competitive coexistence," has not only altered the traditional balance of power in world politics, but has also created an entirely new prospect in international affairs—the prospect that no nation, however powerful and prosperous, can long enjoy its power and prosperity in isolation.

The choice for the United States, then, must be at least to stay in the race. In 1959, President Eisenhower stated: "In recent years the rising social and economic aspirations of the free world's less fortunate peoples have been seized upon by the Communists as fertile ground in which to accomplish what they have successfully been deterred from achieving by military aggression. Accordingly, the mutual security program, now more than ever, offers the most economically effective means of blunting and turning back this latest Communist challenge." President Kennedy, in his second State of the Union Message, declared: "These programs help people; and, by helping people, they help freedom. The views of their governments may sometimes be very different from ours, but events in Africa, the Middle East and Eastern Europe teach us never to write off any nation as lost to the Communists. That is the lesson of our time." In the same vein President Johnson defined, in his legislative message to Congress in January, 1965, the fundamental aims of the foreign aid program: "Here is our difference with the Communists—and our strength. They would use their skills to forge new chains of tyranny. We would use ours to free man from the bonds of the past."

The impact of Soviet aid activities cannot be treated separately from the overall Soviet diplomatic efforts in larger international power politics. Soviet diplomacy during the last decade has been directed toward improving its relations with major sectors of the free world. It has sought to create an impression that the Soviet Union is a peace-loving, progressive nation harboring no aggressive design. This pattern of diplomacy has been tailored differently for different parts of the world for different purposes, depending on the prevailing circumstances; for example, taking the rebel side in the Congo dispute, and the Arab side in the Middle East issue. The purpose and intent of this diplomatic offensive has been to allay possible fears of Soviet aggressive design among the nations of Asia, Africa, and Latin America; at the same time it has been designed to weaken popular and official support for the defensive alliances of the United States, i.e., the North Atlantic Treaty Organization, the Central Treaty Organization (formerly the Baghdad Pact), the Southeast Asia Treaty Organization, and the Organization of American States.

As part of this general offensive the Soviet Union sought to establish closer trade relations with Western Europe, offered economic and technical assistance to underdeveloped countries, and played up its friendly and helpful intentions among former colonial territories. The theme it reverted to repeatedly was that the nations of the underdeveloped areas should look to the Soviet Union rather than to the United States for economic and technical assistance. Premier Khrushchev, during his second visit to Southeast Asia in February, 1960, laid special emphasis on this point in India—clearly his principal target in the foreign aid competition with the United States. In a speech in Calcutta, Khrushchev called Western assistance to under-developed countries a "weapon of a new colonial policy."

Within the confines of this general pattern of Soviet international politics, one example may be cited to show the impact of Soviet assistance in negating the United States program.

This example is found in the Middle East, especially in Egypt. The long-festering Arab-Israel controversy, the Anglo-Egyptian issue over Suez, and the anti-colonial sentiment in the Arab world presented a series of crises seeking some solution or exploitation. The Soviet

Union exploited them politically by arms aid to Egypt and Syria (the United Arab Republic).

The outcome was apparent in the degree of Soviet penetration into parts of this region. Prior to the summer of 1955, the Soviet Union attempted to achieve its objectives in the Near and Middle East by means other than economic assistance. Since the autumn of 1955, however, the entire Communist bloc appeared to have concentrated upon winning the Middle East. The offensive, which extended into North Africa, included military and economic aid, technical assistance, increased trade, and cultural exchange. One observer described this offensive in the following fashion:

Ever since the Communist-Egyptian arms deal in the autumn of 1955, there has been an accustomed, busy traffic of delegations to and from the Soviet bloc and the Arab countries, pledging undying friendship and (from the Soviet side) all kinds of economic aid. The Soviet Union has agreed to install Egypt's first nuclear laboratory; Hungary is going to build new bridges across the Nile; Bulgaria will carry out construction work in Alexandria harbor. The East Germans will be drilling for water in the Sudan, the Czechs are going to construct oil refineries in Syria, the Poles are building new railroads in Saudi Arabia. Soviet engineers are already busy in Yemen and Lebanon, and the Poles have received a bid to build steel plants in Egypt. In the last few months, China has become the single most important buyer of Egyptian cotton. This list could be prolonged indefinitely.[6]

Following the conclusion of an arms agreement between Egypt and Czechoslovakia, in September 1955, the Soviet Union offered technical assistance to Egypt for the construction of the Aswan Dam. Up to that time Gamel Abdul Nasser, the President of Egypt, had stated on several occasions that Egypt would accept technical assistance, economic aid, and trade from Communist countries if it were in the national interest. The terms of the Soviet offer for the cost of building the Aswan Dam contained a loan of $200 million, which could be payable in Egyptian cotton and rice supplies over a period of thirty years at 2 percent interest. It was estimated that the loan would represent about one-third of the estimated cost of the dam.

On the other hand, the United States, from 1951 to the fall of 1955, was not very helpful in assisting Egypt to meet its great prob-

[6] Walter Z. Laqueur, "The Moscow-Cairo Axis," *Commentary* (May, 1956), pp. 409–416.

lems. A total of $59 million had been allocated for Egypt, but only $7 million of this was spent. In a report to the Congress in January, 1956, Senator Theodore F. Green stated:

> Even when allowance is made for the fact that more than two-thirds of the obligations were made within the last fiscal year, this is a disappointing showing for which both ICA/Washington and ICA/Cairo must share responsibility. Further, the funds which have been spent appear to have been too widely dispersed without benefit of clear planning or precise objective.[7]

On December 7, 1955, as a countermeasure to the Soviet move, the United States offered to grant $45 million and Great Britain $14 million to Egypt. It was implicit in these offers that the Soviet Union be excluded from the Aswan project. The United States at the same time urged Egypt to accept military assistance, but negotiations broke down when Nasser refused to conclude such an agreement. The refusal was followed by the revocation of an American promise to make Export-Import Bank funds available to help build the Aswan Dam, as Egypt commenced her large-scale arms purchases from Communist Czechoslovakia. Thus, a chain of reaction was set in motion: the need of funds for the Aswan project was, at least in part, a reason for Egypt to nationalize the Suez Canal Company; the nationalization of the company was, in turn, a cause for the Anglo-Franco-Israeli invasion into Egypt.

Although, in 1956, the Soviet Union had officially disclaimed interest in assisting Egypt with the building of the Aswan High Dam, the Soviet Union and the United Arab Republic subsequently signed, on December 26, 1958, an agreement on Soviet aid in the first four-year phase of the dam project. The agreement provided that the Soviet Union would supply the necessary materials and equipment, together with the services of Soviet technicians and experts, and that the Soviet 400-million ruble loan for this purpose would be repaid in twelve annual installments starting in 1964, calculated in Egyptian pounds and bearing 2.5 percent interest per annum. The Aswan Dam project had been a focus of East-West political struggle in the Middle East for more than two years, and the sudden signing of the agreement after numerous postponements appeared to take the West by surprise.

[7] U. S. Senate, Committee on Foreign Relations, *Technical Assistance,* 1957, p. 545.

A general contract for Soviet technical assistance and equipment in the first stage of the dam project was signed in Moscow on September 9, 1959, and the work was officially started as of January 9, 1960. At the opening ceremony President Nasser expressed gratitude to the Soviet Government for its technical and economic assistance, which, he said, had been prompted solely by a feeling of friendship.

In the same month another agreement on the second stage construction of the dam by the Soviet Union was reached in letters exchanged between President Nasser and Premier Khrushchev. It was reported that only a few days before the announcement, President Eisenhower had stated at a press conference that the United States would support the financing of the second stage by the World Bank.

As regards the United States assistance program to Egypt, a new agreement was signed on June 27, 1959, as part of a series of measures taken by the United States with a view to resuming economic relations with, and economic assistance to, the United Arab Republic, which had been suspended after the 1956 Suez crisis. The overall cost of the program included in the new agreement was not made public.

The first stage of the dam—the construction of the diversionary canal—was completed on May 14, 1964. Premier Khrushchev, who journeyed to Egypt to participate in the ceremony, declared: "It should be called the eighth wonder of the world; it is a triumph over foreign exploitation." President Nasser echoed that the Soviet aid to the Aswan project was a symbol of Soviet friendship which helped strengthen his people's will to break the bonds of imperialism. Premier Khrushchev further committed himself to lavish aid promises, which many observers believe contributed to his downfall in October, 1964. Indications were that the new Soviet leaders would review their vast aid program everywhere in the world, and within the scope of this reappraisal they would continue to aid Nasser. As an evidence of this policy, Soviet Deputy Premier Alexander N. Shelepin visited Egypt in December, 1964, and pledged his government's continued assistance. During his stay in Egypt, Nasser scorned publicly that the United States could "go jump in the lake" with its aid program.

Although there had been persistent strains and stresses in American-Egyptian relations, the first public indication of Egyptian antagonism toward the United States came with the burning of the

John F. Kennedy Memorial Library in Cairo in November, 1964. Less than a month later a private United States oil company plane was shot down by Egyptian fighters. Then the real clash of policy erupted over the Stanleyville rescue operation by the United States. Egyptian leaders regarded this operation and Western support of Premier Tshombe as the return of neo-colonialism, and joined Algeria, with the Soviet material support in airlifting arms to the Congo rebels. These developments undoubtedly served to heighten American apprehension about the future direction of Nasser's policy and may cause a change in Washington's basic policy toward Cairo, but the two countries were not at swords' points.

So far, the economic aid of the United States to Egypt, totaling nearly one billion dollars, has outstripped that of the Soviet Union, totaling over $800 million of industrial credit, more than half of which is still unused. The Soviet Union, however, has provided Nasser with approximately $750 million worth of military aid such as MIG fighters, TU bombers, air defense missiles, and tanks. Nasser's policy of "nonalignment" or of playing off the Soviet Union against the United States to induce both to help build his country's future has proved fruitful.

In short, the impact of the Soviet economic offensive in the United Arab Republic may be stated in the following terms. The Soviet aid provided Nasser with an alternative to Western aid. Operating from the base of Arab nationalism and Arab socialism, and refusing to ally permanently with either side, Nasser welcomed Soviet aid; he stated that his country needed loans which "can be taken from the East at low interest or from the West at high interest. Of course, the one who offers me loans at better conditions, I take. It is not a matter of preference between East and West." In reality, however, by virtue of receiving more economic as well as military aid from the East than from the West, Nasser has been steadily gravitating toward the former. An important outcome of this development was the realization, to a great extent, of the short-term objective of the Soviet economic offensive—to push the West out of the Arab world. Before Nasser's rise to power and prestige, the West in general, and the United States in particular, was on friendly terms, or allied, with most Arab nations; after his rise, many governments having close ties with the West have been either ousted or overthrown by Nasserite pressure and coup. Whenever a political vacuum or instability was created in this fashion, there always have been possibilities for the Soviet Union to move in to fill the gap by using Nasserites who consciously or unconsciously paved the way for Communist inroads.

In general summary, the Soviet aid activities—in steel mills, new dams, stadium construction, highways, laboratories, irrigation works —bring into the underdeveloped countries not only manufactured goods and machinery from the Soviet Union but also Communist technicians who will act in a dual capacity as skilled industrial specialists and as expert propagandists for the Communist cause and its way of life. At the same time, local Communist parties in recipient countries may, as a result of Soviet performance in technical and economic assistance, acquire a new opportunity for respectability, responsibility, and added political appeal. To date, Soviet technicians sent abroad appear to have been regarded as able and competent, and their behavior has given rise to few complaints. As the implementation of Soviet programs progresses, the number of Soviet technicians working in recipient countries will increase, although some of the underdeveloped countries have so far been wary of accepting any large number of Communist personnel since they recognize the potential for subversive activities. But how well can the underdeveloped countries resist the temptation to accept Soviet offers of "trade and aid" which seem, at the moment, very attractive and useful? To a great extent these countries are susceptible to the overt blandishment and the occasional covert threat of the Soviet Union.

2. ECONOMIC COMPETITION AND AID
TO UNDERDEVELOPED COUNTRIES*

BY V. RYMALOV

The economic competition of the two systems has entered a decisive stage. While socialism aims at equaling and surpassing in the shortest historical period the leading capitalist countries, it is at the same time fulfilling another task of paramount importance: that

* From *Problems of Economics,* Vol. 3 (December, 1960), pp. 43–52. Reprinted by permission of International Arts and Sciences Press.

of fully liquidating in the near future the discrepancies in the development of the countries forming the new world system by raising the level of the lagging countries up to the level of the more advanced ones.

In his report to the 21st Congress of the CPSU N. S. Khrushchev set forth and substantiated the extremely important proposition that within the framework of the socialist system, due to fraternal mutual assistance and close cooperation, all socialist countries are afforded the opportunity of attaining such a degree of development of their material and spiritual forces that they will be able more or less simultaneously to achieve the transition to the higher stage of communist society. The resolution of the Party Congress on N. S. Khrushchev's report stated: "As the world socialist system continues to grow and become stronger, all the socialist countries will develop successfully. The countries which in the past lagged economically are now rapidly developing their economy and culture, availing themselves of the experience of the other socialist countries on the basis of cooperation and mutual assistance with them. Thus, the general standards of economic and cultural development of all the socialist countries are reaching a common level, and the necessary conditions for transition from the first stage of communist society to its second stage will be created at an increasingly rapid rate." [1]

This is one of the basic laws governing the development of the world socialist economy. It is exercising a growing influence on the course of the economic competition of socialism and capitalism, which is the dominant factor in world history at this stage. The disinterested fraternal aid extended by some countries to others speeds up the process of eliminating the economic and cultural backwardness inherited by many socialist countries from the capitalist era, and greatly accelerates the rate of progress of the new world economic system as a whole.

Under these conditions it is vitally important to analyze the trends of future development of the underdeveloped countries which are outside the socialist system. The significance of this question is emphasized by the fact that in the postwar period the overwhelming majority of these countries have become independent states.

Marxism-Leninism has comprehensively explained the inner eco-

[1] *Extraordinary 21st Congress of the CPSU, January 27–February 5, 1959,* Stenographic Report, Vol. II, Moscow, 1959, p. 447.

nomic laws governing the capitalist social system. It has demonstrated, and life has fully supported this conclusion, that the development of capitalism brings about a polarization of wealth and poverty, both within individual countries and on a world scale.

The fantastic disproportions between the social and economic standards of a handful of wealthy imperialist countries, on the one hand, and the vast mass of the destitute, underdeveloped, exploited countries, on the other, is the logical consequence of the prolonged development of the world capitalist economy which reached full maturity when it attained the stage of imperialism. . . .

The emergence of the socialist system struck an irreparable blow at imperialism, and this could not fail to have its effect on the development of the world capitalist economy as a system of enslavement and exploitation of weak nations by strong ones. The mere existence of a new world system, its readiness to extend the utmost aid to the underdeveloped countries in their efforts to achieve genuine national independence is exercising an increasingly far reaching effect on the position these countries occupy within the capitalist framework. The birth and vigorous development of the socialist countries has damaged the exclusive position of the imperialist powers in the world economy and brought about the collapse of their monopoly in the field of production of machinery and equipment, weapons and military supplies, technological know-how, as well as in respect to their absorption of the basic exports of the countries producing raw materials and farm products. This has created unprecedentedly favorable external conditions for accelerating the rate of growth of productive forces in the underdeveloped countries which have achieved national independence.

In turn, the emergence of new sovereign states in the East is having an increasing effect on the economic processes at work in the world capitalist economy. Achievement of political independence by the underdeveloped nations which account for the great majority of the population in the capitalist world is not an end in itself; it is in fact the only way out of the disastrous economic consequences of colonialist and imperialist exploitation.

The anti-imperialist struggles waged by the colonial peoples in order to achieve national independence and promote economic progress under the conditions of coexistence and peaceful competition of socialism and capitalism has brought to the fore of social life a number of new and important international problems which have to be thoroughly and scientifically analyzed and understood. One of them, which is acquiring added urgency and significance with each passing year, is the problem of aid to the developing economies of the underdeveloped countries.

This problem stems directly from the growing national-liberation movement and the socialist countries' support to the anti-imperialist struggle waged by the peoples of Asia, Africa and Latin America.

The socialist states' aid to the underdeveloped countries is a new form of international economic cooperation which is gradually restricting the imperialist powers' possibilities of exploiting these countries. The feverish efforts of monopoly capital to obstruct the extension of this aid miscarry time after time. Evidence of this is supplied by the growing number of agreements on economic and technical aid, as well as by the rapid expansion of trade turnover between the underdeveloped countries and the world socialist system. For example, the underdeveloped countries' trade turnover with the Soviet Union during the period covering 1953 to 1958 increased more than sixfold. In the past five years the total of Soviet long-term credits and other forms of aid for promoting the economic development of non-socialist countries in Asia, Africa and Latin America have increased several hundred times and now amount to several billion rubles. (See Table 1 below.)

Thanks to the aid of the Soviet Union and the other socialist states, some underdeveloped countries are already at work on many projects that are vitally important for advancing their industry and economy as a whole. These countries can sell to the socialist states, on stable and mutually profitable terms, raw materials and other export commodities. In exchange, they can purchase industrial equipment and any other commodity they need on very favorable terms to promote their independent national development.

As this system of equitable cooperation and aid is being strengthened, and as the process of bringing up the lagging socialist countries to the level of the more advanced ones proceeds, the ruling circles in the leading capitalist countries are realizing to an increasing extent the necessity of taking into account the measures adopted by the socialist states for the purpose of extending genuine economic aid to the underdeveloped countries. The leaders of the capitalist states cannot afford to ignore the fact that the underdeveloped nations are not assuming control of their own destiny merely to vegetate in destitution for many years to come and to watch with equanimity how their wealth is being channeled into the safes of overseas monopolies. . . .

Table 1. Development of Soviet Economic Relations
with Some Eastern Countries

Country	Trade turnover (in million rubles)				Soviet long-term credits (in million rubles)
	1955	1956	1957	1958	
Afghanistan	98.1	133.5	154.2	142.9	480
India	46.9	234.8	506.4	723.7	2,600
UAR	107.0	465.0	811.2	933.9	1,100*
Indonesia	15.3	52.3	101.5	155.0	400

* Credits to Egyptian Area of the UAR.

As matters stand, since socialism is no longer confined within the boundaries of one country but has grown into a rapidly developing world system, since the task of completely doing away with colonialism and its consequences has been placed on the order of the day in the most pressing manner, aid for promoting the economic advancement of underdeveloped countries constitutes a complex set of closely related international problems which includes the following factors: (1) aid extended by the leading socialist states to the underdeveloped countries of the world capitalist system in their anti-imperialist struggle to achieve independent economic development; (2) economic aid extended by the leading capitalist powers to the colonial and other underdeveloped countries as a means of offsetting the aid of the socialist states, of safeguarding their own positions, and of enhancing the waning prestige of capitalism in those countries.

This, of course, does not mean that one should altogether discount the danger of a possible imperialist venture in some area of the colonial world. This danger will be removed only when imperialism itself disappears, for the existence of imperialism hinges on the exploitation and oppression of the backward countries.

Although the economic competition of the two systems compels the imperialist powers to aid underdeveloped countries, this has not modified their nature—they are merely seeking to adapt themselves to a new situation. If one wishes to obtain a clear picture of the actual relations between those countries, one need only compare the amount of aid granted by the capitalist states to the underdeveloped countries with the size of the tribute the latter have to pay to the former as ransom for their backwardness. . . .

We know from history that the outcome of the struggle between different social and economic systems is determined in the final analysis by the system which at the given stage of development offers more favorable conditions for the growth of the productive forces of society. This was indeed the reason why capitalism defeated feudalism. It is, moreover, a fact that when social groups of exploiters were struggling for supremacy, the problem of the well-being of the popular masses was not and could not be raised. On the contrary, the development of these social structures was based on intensified exploitation and plundering of the actual producers of material values.

All capitalism needed in order to triumph on a world scale was to ensure a rapid rate of growth of the productive forces in just a few countries. As for the overwhelming majority of the countries, as Lenin aptly remarked, they were converted into civilization's fertilizer, becoming the colonial slaves of a handful of imperialist powers. These powers' rapid economic advance was to a large extent achieved by means of indiscriminate exploitation and obstruction of the development of the countries which were by-passed by capitalist civilization. Only a relatively small number of countries succeeded in achieving a high rate of development of their productive forces on the basis of the capitalist mode of production. For instance, the leading capitalist states which have less than one-third of the capitalist world's population account for close to nine-tenths of total capitalist industrial production. The United States alone produces about five times as much industrial output as all the underdeveloped countries which account for two-thirds of the capitalist world's population.

While in the world socialist system the process of eliminating the disparity in the economic development of different countries is continuously at work, the opposite is the case within the capitalist system. This situation is a cause of serious alarm to the defenders of modern capitalism. Prof. Gunnar Myrdal, the Swedish economist, remarks that the underdeveloped countries are not going to consent "to a course of world development which will leave them poor, or as was recently the case in certain parts of the world, a course which will make them even poorer while the wealthy countries are becoming still wealthier." The more realistically minded partisans of the dying social order are compelled to consider these developments from the point of view of the competition of the two systems. Walter Lippmann wrote in the *New York Herald Tribune*: "I would like to define the reason why, in the present state of affairs, the West is losing and the communists are winning the competition in the underdeveloped countries. The main reason is that the advanced, industrialized western countries in North America, Western Europe and Australia are enriching themselves, while the poorly developed countries which are not within the communist orbit are continuing to experience extreme want and are making very slow progress."

This alarm for the fate of capitalism in the underdeveloped countries is entirely justified. The data of the UN *World Economic Survey 1958* supply the evidence that in the past few years in the world capitalist economy the gap in the levels of economic development between a relatively small group of industrially advanced countries and the bulk of countries producing raw materials and agricultural commodities, far from narrowing, on the contrary is continuing to widen to a certain extent. . . .

It stands to reason that the expansion of mutually profitable economic relations between socialist and non-socialist states helps to reduce international tensions and is to the advantage of all nations. Further extension of these relations will help to create favorable conditions for achieving a more rapid growth of productive forces and will promote the non-socialist nations' efforts to improve their living standards.

This has a direct bearing on the many-sided economic aid rendered by the socialist states to the underdeveloped countries. It is the socialist states' policy to extend to the utmost the amount of this aid. The peoples of the former colonies and dependent countries which do not form part of the world socialist system are given every opportunity of making use of that system's economic achievements for furthering their struggle for national independence. And as the socialist system grows in strength these opportunities will steadily increase. This is another manifestation of the indissoluble ties and close alliance necessarily linking the national-liberation and world proletarian movements in the era of transition from capitalism to socialism on a global scale.

It is quite obvious that the economic aid rendered by the socialist countries strengthens the position of the new sovereign states of the East in their struggle against imperialist monopoly capital. This is an important objective factor conducive to the extension and strengthening of economic relations between the socialist states and the countries which have entered on the road of independent capitalist development in the era of the two systems' coexistence.

Long before the world socialist system came into being, the founders of Marxism-Leninism who were working out a proletarian international policy clearly stated that any attempt on the part of the victorious working class to take advantage of the backward nations' need for foreign help by imposing on them from the outside a new advanced social order, would ultimately only damage the cause of the world socialist revolution and undermine the friendly relations among peoples which are essential for the victory of the working class. Frederick Engels pointed out in this connection how much to the advantage of the working class of the advanced countries it would be "to bring independence as rapidly as possible" to the colonial countries; and he went on to say: "One thing is unquestionable: the victorious proletariat may not force happiness upon any foreign people without undermining by the same token its own victory."

It is the international duty of the victorious working class of the socialist countries to help the underdeveloped nations to completely destroy the fetters of national and colonial subjection, and to support in every possible way their anti-imperialist struggle and their right to an independent national status which, under capitalist conditions, is inconceivable without economic independence.

For many years the peoples of the underdeveloped countries have experienced the more abhorrent aspects of capitalist "civilization." In the course of the economic competition of the two systems the logic of events will lead them to the conclusion that the socialist road to progress is unquestionably superior. Here is what N. S. Khrushchev had to say on this score: "Communism will win, but not in the sense of any conquest by the socialist countries of other countries. No, the the people of each country will themselves weigh all the facts, and when they come to understand correctly the essence of the Marxist-Leninist teaching, they will voluntarily choose the more progressive form of society."

The aid rendered by the Soviet Union and the other socialist countries is exercising more and more influence on the struggle waged by the underdeveloped countries against the dominance of foreign capital, for genuine independence. Each new victory which socialism scores in the economic competition with capitalism, leading to a shift in the relation of forces between the imperialist camp and the world socialist system, creates ever more favorable conditions for the progress of the national-liberation movement in the underdeveloped countries. This is one of the essential features of the historical period of coexistence and competition of the two opposite world social and economic systems.

The Soviet Seven-Year Plan (1959–1965) of economic development endorsed at the 21st Congress of the CPSU opens up broad new prospects for strengthening friendly cooperation between the underdeveloped countries and the world socialist system. Successful implementation of this program and of the economic plans of the other socialist countries will mark an important stage in the struggle for a better future waged not only by the socialist nations but by all the peoples of the world.

The world socialist system is laying the foundations of a new world economy in which the characteristic capitalist relations of subjection and exploitation of the weak countries by the strong ones will be abolished for all time, giving way to relations of genuine equality of rights and mutual assistance among the nations.

The ever increasing aid extended by the socialist states to the underdeveloped countries is bound to play an important part in creating this worldwide economic system.

3. SINO-SOVIET BALANCE SHEET IN THE UNDERDEVELOPED AREAS*

BY C. P. FitzGerald

If the problem of the underdeveloped areas vexes the minds of the statesmen of the West, it is no less a problem for those of the

* From the *Annals of American Academy of Political and Social Science,* Vol. 351 (January, 1964), pp. 40–49. Reprinted by permission of the author and AAPSS.

Communist camp. The Western leaders see that the continuance of so great an imbalance in parts of the non-Communist world is a very great danger and cause of tension and strife. Sooner or later, the great masses of undernourished will lose patience with aid programs which do not fill their bellies and development projects which somehow do not secure for them a higher standard of living. The time runs short; the task is vast and seems to offer unexpected and intractable difficulties. It must, therefore, be with some relief that, turning to look at the problem from the Communist side, they can see that the efforts of Russia, and those of China, even if they ever pulled together in harmony, do not seem to have made any more impression than those of their opponents.

In the past decade, almost all the colonial territories in Asia and more than two-thirds of Africa have achieved full independence. South America already had this status and has received massive aid from the United States. But not one of the recently liberated colonial countries, and only one of the backward states of South America, has taken the Communist road to modernization. Intensely nationalist, quite often very critical of capitalism, resentful of past exploitation, they none the less refrain from joining forces with the Communist states who claim to have all the cures for their trouble ready packaged for immediate use. There is, perhaps, some reason to think that, like poor voters in England in the early days of the Labour party, these states, however critical and secretly resentful of the rich, think it wiser and more practical to vote for them rather than for the champions of the poor, simply because they "have the money." It is certain that the failure of communism to make an immediate appeal and ready conquest of the newly independent underdeveloped countries has surprised and perhaps dismayed the Communist leadership; it has also sharpened the quarrel between China and Russia, because it has provided a new cause for contention.

It would seem that the Russian view of what should now be done is conditioned by their general acceptance of the policy of coexistence. The underdeveloped countries should be given aid, even if this goes to their bourgeois nationalist governments—and helps to keep them in power—so that these governments will not be forced to turn only to the United States of America and to rely entirely on her aid. Aid from the Communist camp helps to keep the neutrals unaligned, denies their territories to the United States for bases, and helps to create a kind of glacis round the Soviet Union. As for the local revolutionary parties, the hopes of the poor, the prospects of communism, these must all wait. They should be kept alive, as a pressure group upon their nationalist governments, but the expectation of their success would seem to be relegated to that still distant day when, communism having proved to be an economic system which offers far more to everyman than capitalism has ever provided, the underdeveloped will follow the lead of the developed countries and "bury capitalism."

The Chinese preach revolutionary war. To their way of thinking, the problem has already been faced and overcome, first and foremost by themselves. They argue that their revolution was essentially the model for those which must come about in all underdeveloped countries, that in fact it cannot be stopped, and that their own was not, indeed, stopped by atomic weapons in the hands of the "imperialists." In order to see all the implications of this standpoint, it is necessary to look more carefully at what the Chinese mean by saying that:

Mao Tse-tung's theory of the Chinese Revolution is a new development of Marxism-Leninism in the revolutions of the colonial and semi-colonial countries. . . . [It] has significance not only for China and Asia, it is of universal significance for the world Communist movement. It is indeed a new contribution to the treasury of Marxism-Leninism. . . . the classic type of revolution in colonial and semi-colonial countries is the Chinese Revolution.[1]

It is first of all worth noting that this claim was expressed as long ago as 1951, in a time when Stalin yet lived and much of Asia and most of Africa was still under colonial rule. But China was "liberated": she had found the way, a hard and long way, which outside disapproval had been unable to block. So, if the Chinese revolution is the classic type, it is necessary to consider it carefully. The Chinese revolution was not a *coup d'état,* a sudden seizure of power in the capital. It ended in Communist triumph only after twenty-two years of civil war, which had already been preceded by ten years of militarist disorder before the Communist party was founded. After the fall of the Manchu dynasty in 1912, an event which the Chinese see as the prototype of the ending of colonial rule in other parts of

[1] Lu Ting-yi, speech, June 25, 1951.

Asia, the government of China was for years the plaything of generals, who were in turn displaced by the leadership of the Nationalist party under Chiang Kai-shek. Neither the early republic of the militarists nor the Kuomintang succeeded in, or seriously attempted, tackling the underlying problems of the Chinese revolution, the questions of peasant poverty, landlordism, a backward technology, and the lack of basic heavy industries. Consequently, all these regimes were doomed after brief periods to collapse. Viewed in this light, the Chinese see the present leadership in almost all the newly independent countries as sharing the characteristics of the unsuccessful successors of the Manchu emperors. Military dictatorships, nationalist parties controlled by big business, pseudo democracies dominated by leaders who are supported by a combination of military officers and professional politicians—it is all to the Chinese very reminiscent of the warlord period and the rule of the Kuomintang. . . .

Taking this rather long-term view of the prospects of revolution in Asia, and perhaps in Africa also, the Chinese consider that the Russian view which envisages aid to nationalist governments, such as that of the Congress party in India, is mistaken and a betrayal of the real interests of the working class. Such regimes must be left to get into the difficulties which their inherently "incorrect" structure and policies will inevitably produce. They will then turn to the imperialists for aid, but this will at best postpone, more probably aggravate, their problem, and the moment of revolution will approach. Anything which hinders this progression is mischievous and mistaken. The Russians, in the Open Letter of July 14th,[2] make the charge that the Chinese "claiming that the real struggle dividing the world was being waged between imperialism and the national liberation movement were thereby seeking the favour of the three continents"—Asia, Africa, and South America. This is a strange charge for one Communist party to make against another and seems to substantiate rather than to disprove the Chinese case. It would seem to imply that, for the Russians, this is not the real struggle, but, however important the battle to win a higher standard of living may be for the Communist worker in France or Italy, the Asian and the

[2] The text of this passage in *The New York Times* of July 15th differs in some words from that given in *Asian Almanac*, Vol. 1, No. 3 (July 14–20, 1963). The latter text appears to be translated from a Chinese text of the Open Letter.

African will not easily be convinced that it should take precedence over the struggle for liberation and modernization in the under-developed countries.

It would seem that, in the ideological field, the Chinese have a certain advantage: their revolution did take place in a country where conditions much resembled those now prevailing in most of Asia and in Africa. In some respects, seeing that China was also an independent but decrepit and underdeveloped state, her condition had points of similarity with many of the countries of South America. There can be little doubt that wars such as that of the Viet Cong in South Vietnam or that waged by Castro against Batista have much more in common with Chinese experience than any aspect of the Russian revolution. The three continents, whose favor the Chinese are accused of seeking, are indeed the areas where underdevelopment is most widely spread, where the contrast between rich and poor is most stark, where government is least competent and the rule of military dictators most prevalent. Most Western observers and statesmen are already disillusioned about the viability of policies and systems of government suitable to advanced countries when applied to these areas: the Russian belief that coexistence and the steady advance of Socialist economies will cure their ills must seem to the Chinese as remote from the facts as the earlier belief, dear to Western liberals, that the establishment of republics and parliamentary forms of government would lead to rapid, peaceful, and lasting progress.

If the Chinese may be right in thinking that their program is more in tune with the aspirations of the people of the underdeveloped countries, their capacity to promote this program is obviously seriously limited by many factors and attended by real dangers which, as the Russians forcefully point out, the Chinese seem to ignore. China may be seeking the "favour of the three continents," but two of these are very remote from China herself and most of the one in which she is situated, Asia, is under the control or influence of states with which Chinese relations are bad. The possibilities of giving either military aid to revolutionary wars in Africa and South America or material aid of a peaceful character to these distant regions are slight. China can only reach these countries by long sea communications, which she does not control and which can be used only by the toleration of her opponents. Hitherto, China has had relatively direct access to Africa and Western Asia by air, through the territory of the

Soviet Union, but it must be assumed that, if the policies China wishes to pursue in such countries are considered hostile or even undesirable by Russia, these facilities could be terminated.

In practice, therefore, the scope of Chinese aid, whether military or material, is confined to those regions which adjoin her own frontiers or can be reached across the territory of friendly neighbors. These countries are Korea, Vietnam, Laos, Burma, Cambodia, Thailand, Nepal, and India. North Korea is an ally and has aligned herself with China in the present dispute, but the power of the United States guards South Korea and the scope for Chinese activity in that part of the peninsula is slight. In South Vietnam there is at present what the Chinese can surely identify as a revolutionary war deserving of their support, Communist led, and in contact by North Vietnam with China herself. It does not yet appear, however, that Chinese participation in this conflict has been proved in any positive manner. Encouragement, perhaps financial support and training facilities, can easily be given, but no Chinese armed force has taken part in operations. The same situation applies in Laos, directly in touch with China, although only through a very rugged terrain. Chinese activity in road building has been observed here, but not even the Laotian political right has claimed that Chinese forces have appeared in the areas controlled by Pathet Lao. China has normal diplomatic relations with Burma and has recently concluded a boundary agreement with Burma rather in favor of Burmese claims. There would appear to be a wide gap between the theories propounded in the Peking press and the practice of the Chinese government in its relations with these countries.

Thailand, a state hostile to China and to communism, has often declared its fears of Chinese aggression and has supported the Southeast Asia Treaty Organization (SEATO) with more enthusiasm than any other Asian member of that organization. Yet Thailand has no common frontier with China, and, in spite of the alarmist tone of much Thai comment, no specific acts of Chinese aggression or overt hostility have been cited. The needs of trade appear to be more imperative than the demands of ideology: when Malaya, still under British rule, lifted the embargo on sales of rubber to China, Thailand hastened to follow suit, fearful of losing a share in a valuable market. It is at least possible that Thailand finds it convenient to parade the Chinese bogey at frequent intervals to make sure that American interest will continue to be engaged in the area and that the flow of American aid and military equipment will continue unabated. It would appear that, in these regions to which China has ready access, the principle of not exporting armed revolution is observed, whether due to fear of escalation into general war or because Marxist teaching is opposed to such action. The Chinese may be simply ready to wait for the unfolding of a process which they firmly believe to be inevitable. A revolution in being needs less open support and cannot easily be openly and violently suppressed by the "imperialists." One of the principal arguments used by the Chinese to counter the accusation that they are recklessly ready to involve the world in nuclear war is that such weapons cannot in practice be used against civil disturbances or revolutionary movements confined to the country in which they break out. Experience has shown that this has so far proved true.

The Chinese have extended some material aid of a peaceful character to such states as Cambodia and Nepal with whom they have good relations even though they are ruled by non-Communist and royal governments. A relatively small expenditure, perhaps all that China can yet afford, goes some way in Cambodia and makes an impression. With Burma and Ceylon, trade agreements operate which are beneficial to all three parties. It is probable that the Chinese do not consider any of these states yet ripe for revolution. There is ample land available in Cambodia and little or no peasant unrest. Burma is a rice exporting country. Ceylon has rich resources, even if the regime in power seems hardly capable of handling them efficiently. The "imperialists" have no foothold in these neutral countries, and it does not appear that the Chinese resent the fact that they also receive aid from America. Whatever the theory, peaceful coexistence between China, Cambodia, Burma, Ceylon, and Nepal is a practical working fact. . . .

The Communist powers had high hopes of Africa: the rapid decolonization of that continent, the disorder which attended this process in the Congo, and the expectation of similar chaos in other areas inspired the belief that there might be a rapid transition to regimes either led by or relying upon Communist support. These hopes have not so far been fulfilled. Independent Africa has acquired a strongly nationalist flavor, but, although suspicious of foreign capital and fearful of renewed exploitation, the African governments have not turned to the Communists. It is clear that neither Russia nor China is yet prepared to concede a defeat. Both pursue an active propaganda seeking to win the national regimes and to frustrate the influence of the Western powers. But it is also clear that a new and acute rivalry has developed between the two Communist powers in this continent. Neither can act directly, for neither has adjoining territories. Whereas in Southeast Asia China, by her geographical position, can exercise a direct intervention if she would, in Africa she can only work through the agency of Africans won to her views. For Russia, the limitations are not so great, but the dangers of escalation if Russia directly intervenes are perhaps greater.

It is now known from the disclosures contained in the Open Letter of the Communist party of the Soviet Union and from African news sources[3] that Chinese propaganda is directed as much against the Soviets as against the "imperialists." The Chinese have, moreover, in direct conflict with one of the hitherto distinctive features of Marxism, introduced a racist note into their propaganda. As early as 1962, at the Afro-Asian Writers Conference in Cairo, the following is alleged:

In private lobbying, the Chinese are adopting an openly racist line. "These Europeans," they say, "are all the same, whether they are French, Americans, Russians or Poles: we non-whites must get together." One Chinese delegate went so far as to talk about the "importance of us blacks sticking together."[4]

More recently, in Moshi, the Chinese, citing Cuba and the policy of coexistence, declared to their African colleagues that the Russians will let them down, "whites will back whites, but we are coloureds and your blood brothers in the struggle. Only we can understand your problems."[5]

---

[3] The Open Letter of the Communist party of the Soviet Union, July 14, 1962, reveals that, at the Third Solidarity Conference of Peoples of Asian and African countries held at Moshi in Tanganyika, 1962, the Chinese opposed the attendance of representatives of the Asian-African Solidarity Committee of the European Socialist (Communist) Parties and that the leader of the Chinese delegation went so far as to say to the Russian representative, "Whites have nothing to do here."

[4] Kenya *Daily Nation.* Quoted by James Yeh, Foreign News Service, Hong Kong, August 20, 1963.

[5] Kenya *Daily Nation, op. cit.*

This development of the Chinese propaganda in Africa has perhaps not shocked or, at least, surprised the Russians as much as they claim. As long ago as 1958, it was known to foreign residents and visitors to Peking that instances of similar prejudice against Communist Europeans were occurring and had official support. Eastern European Communists who wished to marry Chinese girls found themselves thwarted and opposed and had great difficulty, even with the backing of their embassies, in gaining a grudging permission for the girls to marry. They were then required to take their wives home, out of China.

Chinese nationalism has never been very far below the surface of Chinese communism, but there is no doubt that the ordinary untraveled Chinese, townsman or peasant, would be amazed to learn that kinship with the African peoples was claimed by his countrymen. The Chinese are not without racial and color prejudices of their own, and, although few Africans were seen in China before the Communists started to bring delegations on visits to the country, even dark-skinned Indians were uncompromisingly described as "black barbarians" in ordinary common parlance. If the new line of color kinship is to be pressed in Africa, the Chinese will have to choose and indoctrinate their emissaries with some care.

The battle for Africa is not won, either by Russians or Chinese, nor yet by the West: it is probably only beginning. In this struggle, as elsewhere in the underdeveloped parts of the world, the Chinese have severe handicaps to overcome. They cannot outbid the Russians in terms of material aid, in most regions they cannot offer military aid either, and, for a party which preaches revolutionary war, this is a grave weakness. But they also have important advantages. The insistence of Russian policy on maintaining solidarity with the "system of socialist states"—by which they mean themselves and the East European countries—cannot have very much appeal to Asians or Africans, nor yet to the underprivileged Latin America. The working class of Europe, Communist or not, has never shown very practical sympathy or support for revolution in Asia or Africa. The Chinese have the force and drive of a recently triumphant revolution, and these qualities are inherent in their people as a whole. The same characteristics which made the Chinese petty trader in Southeast Asia a millionaire before he died are present in the men whom the party sends to work in similar regions. They have patience, ability, tenacity, and resilience; they believe as firmly in their doctrine as their predecessors, the traders, believed in the virtue of getting rich. It may be that, although the West has less to fear from the material power of China in these regions, there is more cause to respect her ability to rouse revolutionary zeal and teach the techniques of guerrilla warfare.

CHAPTER XII

Competition for Comradeship

> *The United States—the richest and most powerful of all peoples, a nation committed to the independence of nations and to a better life for all peoples—can no more stand aside in this climactic age of decision than we can withdraw from the community of free nations.*
>
> —JOHN F. KENNEDY

> *The Soviet Union and the other countries of the socialist camp deem it their duty to help them [underdeveloped countries], to expand by every means trade with them and other forms of economic relations.*
>
> —NIKITA S. KHRUSHCHEV

One of the most subtle aspects of the US-Soviet competition in the cold war centers on the struggle for winning the friendship of other peoples and influencing the action of other nations. Instruments of achieving this goal are varied and numerous. At the top is summit diplomacy—the personal goodwill visits by the heads of state. President Eisenhower's trip throughout many Asian countries, President Kennedy's visit to Latin American nations, Premier Khrushchev's extensive journey to Eastern Europe, Asia, and Africa, and Premier Kosygin's travel to North Vietnam and North Korea via Peking—all these are part of the cases in point.

Foreign aid of all forms is, in the long run, designed to achieve the same goal. Both the United States and the Soviet Union fully realize that the ultimate victory in their competition will depend on the stand taken by the majority of peoples of the world. In this phenomenal struggle the Peace Corps plays a unique and important role in America's relations with underdeveloped countries. Its fundamental idea is to provide dedicated and inspired American men and women with an opportunity to go voluntarily to these countries to help improve local economic and social conditions and to win the confidence and friendship of the people through grass-roots diplomacy. The successes of the Peace Corps, however, have been frequently offset in recent years by the failure of the United States to make its intentions and character clear to peoples throughout the world.

The Soviets, on their part, employ all means available—economic and military aid, revolutionary strategy, subversive tactics, cultural exchange programs, and propaganda—in order to win the "mind" of the peoples in these countries. The Soviets play heavily on the theme that the United States aid programs are merely a new disguise for the old "imperialism" designed to maintain the underdeveloped countries in a state of economic subordination. They are determined to impress these countries with their remarkable technological and industrial achievements under Communism and with their "friendly and sympathetic" attitudes accompanied by peaceful intention, good will, and racial nondiscrimination.

This chapter deals with various facets of the US-Soviet struggle for winning uncommitted and underdeveloped countries.

Clarence B. Randall, former Consultant and Special Assistant to President Eisenhower on Foreign Economic Policy, inquires into the comparative attitudes of the United States and the Soviet Union in terms of their "will to win" and their "capacity to compete" as well as the advantages and disadvantages of each side in the economic warfare waged in newly emerging nations. For further clarification, he answers several questions dealing with these issues.

Alvin Z. Rubenstein, Professor of Political Science at the University of Pennsylvania, discusses with a great thoroughness the Soviet economic offensive in the underdeveloped and uncommitted nations in Southeast Asia, the Middle East, and Africa.

Sargent Shriver, Director of the Peace Corps, scrutinizes the origin, objective, organization, and operation of the Peace Corps, and assesses its intrinsic value in the promotion of international friendship and in the construction of a peaceful world order.

1. SOVIET-AMERICAN COMPETITION IN UNCOMMITTED COUNTRIES*

BY CLARENCE B. RANDALL

No phase of our foreign policy presents more challenge to the people of the United States than the vigorous forward thrust of Soviet economic competition in the uncommitted countries, yet there is none which is so little understood.

As a nation, we are capable of deep emotional response, but only as we react to drama. Sputnik startled us, and we became fully aware of Soviet missile strength, but we are indifferent to the Russian economic advance because it is deliberately done in a quiet and unobtrusive manner.

No professional economist can measure adequately this new force, because none of the familiar data which he likes to have at hand are available. The Soviets do not publish the essential figures, and, if they did, they would be unreliable.

Take the question of interest on capital, for example. Communism does not recognize the existence of capital in the sense in which we employ that word. Yet, when interest is not included as an element of cost in the production of goods, there can be no compilation that is comparable to ours. Similarly, since communism does not permit the forces of supply and demand to operate in a free market, all values which they give to production are arbitrarily arrived at. And, finally, in Russia, the individual who submits to higher authority a report of the output for his sector has a personal incentive for making the total appear large.

In a new nation, the statistical situation is even worse. The taking of a census and the compilation of the gross national product of a country are forms of an advanced civilization. When a new country is struggling to emerge from the primitive to the modern, the cadre

* From the *Annals of American Academy of Political and Social Science*, Vol. 336 (July, 1961), pp. 12–22. Reprinted by permission of the author and AAPSS. This article is the text of a speech to the Annual Spring Meeting, First Session, Friday morning, April 14.

of trained civil servants is barely sufficient to keep the basic minimum of government service in operation. In such an area, there can
be no orderly keeping of records for the edification of an American
economist. Add to this the element of venality, which is all too
common in the new countries, and you arrive inevitably at statistical
chaos in trying to measure the effectiveness, whether of aid or trade,
in the development of an uncommitted nation. We must learn to
understand these deficiencies.

The statistical vacuum, however, merely highlights the fact that
this issue is far broader than just economics for Americans. Our
foreign policy is integral and may not be subdivided for the con-
venience of students into separable components. Military security,
political advantage, and humanitarian considerations are all added to
economics to form the mixture which we call foreign policy.

Soviet penetration of another nation, even though limited to economics, is invariably directed toward ultimate control of that nation's
total policy. It, therefore, poses a direct threat to our own national
security which is quite separate from the economic impact as such.
One has only to think of Castro to be aware of this, or the United
Nations, where the balance of political force is already so delicate.

Likewise, the economic thrust of the Soviets into a new area
invariably reflects total disregard of human values, such as poverty,
illiteracy, and starvation levels of subsistence. Nothing is to be gained,
therefore, from fumbling around with inadequate statistics. We know
now all that we need to know, which is this: World communism is
rmined to capture control of the uncommitted nations by fair
ns or foul, is attempting this vigorously through economic pene-
on, and regards this as the surest path to their objective, which
obably is. We do not need to know precisely how far the process
gone. We need rather to know what effort is required on our part
rder that it may be resisted. We need to ask ourselves squarely
her as a nation we possess the will, and the resources, to meet
alarming challenge without altering our own way of life, and
re it is too late.

submit that the way to commence such an inquiry is to compare
ttitudes and the capabilities of the United States with those of
oviet Union within a dual frame of reference: first, as to the will
n, and, second, as to economic weapons available to each side.
e will to compete and the capacity to compete are separate

questions. No one doubts our great economic potential, but, great as this may be, it will be of no avail unless we consciously throw it into the struggle.

As of now, we Americans have no adequate posture of defense in this economic area. We have learned how to face war, but not how to face peace. We understand missiles, but not trade and economic assistance.

The United States has magnificently kept the military peace for the entire free world by the striking deterrent power of our armed forces. We have made no similar response to the economic threat. We have mobilized the best minds in the country for the design and production of incredible new missiles with cosmic potential for destruction, but we have made no similar effort to mobilize our best minds for the meeting of the economic threat.

This is solely because we have not yet put our minds to it. We simply do not comprehend the danger. What is remote is negligible. Revolution in Cuba shocks us immeasurably, because we see it from our front window, but what happens in Laos or Buganda gives us barely a fleeting moment of interest.

It is precisely in such situations that the monolithic central authority of a totalitarian state gives that government a tactical advantage in a contest with a free democracy. Where a few decide and the opinion of the mass is of no importance, the entire power of the nation can be thrown against a single target, and that is exactly what the presidium is now doing with respect to the economic penetration of the uncommitted nations.

It must be recognized, therefore, that, in terms of will to win, Russia is definitely ahead of us at this time in this economic competition. Before the typical American businessman is able to locate a new country on the map, Russia has opened an embassy in that country's capital, fully staffed with trade experts and officers who possess full authority to offer economic assistance.

We have one further handicap. In Russia, the production of goods involves no distinction between public and private effort, nor does the incentive of self-interest play any part in determining the direction which effort shall take. Here in the United States, to meet the Soviet challenge, we need both public and private effort, yet there are many instances where the incentive of self-interest is not sufficient to call forth the private effort. In our intense reliance upon private initiative, we have not yet learned how fully to co-ordinate public and private effort when an over-all national purpose must be served. There are other nations in the free world who have done this better than we, and we must learn from them.

Russia has also a clear advantage with respect to decision-making in the matter of extending economic assistance to new nations. Although there is evidence that public opinion does exist as a force within Russia, it certainly has not yet reached a point where it would restrain government from taking decisions of this sort. Nor within the structure of a totalitarian government is there any division of power, such as occurs with us when the executive branch recommends a program and the Congress refuses the appropriation.

When the Soviet government decides to penetrate Afghanistan through economic assistance, the boss man acts, and it is done. With us, months pass before decisions can be taken, and we still have no proper mechanism for long-term planning.

When it comes to the social values, to which Americans are properly so sensitive, the purposes of the Soviets are found principally in their propaganda and not in their deeds. Responsive to our instincts, we undertake programs for the basic improvement of the lot of all the people. We address ourselves to the improvement of literacy, teacher training, agricultural research, the care and feeding of infants, and similar efforts that evidence our sincere human interest in the country, whether or not such programs are spectacular. They do exactly the opposite. They ignore the tedious and the long term and seek the spotlight of immediate national attention by committing their funds to projects like a dam or a hospital.

Yet, in fairness, it must be said that what they do they do well. The steel mill which the Russians built in India is first class in every way. It is staffed by able technicians who speak the local dialects and who live on terms of equality with the native population to a degree which no other Western nation has ever achieved. Throughout the length and breadth of the country, it is known as Russian, and favorably known.

Consideration of this single project will illustrate many of the difficulties which we face in our competition in this field of economic assistance.

To begin with, how would we finance a comparable steel plant? It would be difficult to persuade an American company to risk that much private capital in India, for the reason that prices would be controlled. And wherever such a private investment came under consideration for an uncommitted country, the recent massive expropriation in Cuba would give private management pause.

On the other hand, if it were suggested that the project be financed by a long-term governmental loan by the Development Loan Fund, the cry would be raised in many circles in our country that we were thereby financing socialism by contributing to the nationalization of a basic industry, thus denying our own heritage. And if, nevertheless, the government should decide to make the required loan to the government of India, we still would not be in a position to compete as to the terms. Russia is prepared to make loans at the rate of 2½ per cent interest, which is below what our Treasury must pay on its own borrowings from the American people.

And if all of these barriers were bridged, there is still another for which no good answer is apparent. Under a system of private initiative and private responsibility, it is not likely that we would be able to staff such a steel mill with American technical and management personnel throughout the long transition period that would be required before native operators could take over.

How can we obtain such skills for service overseas in a free society? Russians go where Russians are sent, but Americans go where the pay is good, the security substantial, and the living comfortable.

The only men who could measure up to such responsibility in a foreign country already have fine jobs at home. They cannot be conscripted, as would be done in war, and they will not undertake such posts voluntarily until our nation, as a whole, has reached the point of selfless dedication to national effort in time of peace comparable to what it will give in time of war. Unhappily, that day is not at hand. The stark truth is that it still remains to be proven whether, in this world of crisis, the concept of individual responsibility can be made sufficient to meet the challenge of enforced collective responsibility.

The Soviets have still another advantage. As yet they have no apparent balance of payments problem, whereas our programs of economic assistance have played an important part in swelling the outward flow of gold. Our balance of trade as such is favorable in that our exports greatly exceed our imports, but that balance is not sufficient to meet in full the requirements for the outward flow of private investment, tourist expenditures, military assistance to our allies, and economic aid. No Russian rubles are ever granted to a new country for expenditure in world markets, for the loans are always tied to purchases in Russia. It is not actually rubles that they are sending abroad, therefore, but goods. On the other hand, the humanitarian programs which we undertake and which do not involve goods at all have to be done with dollars.

Finally, the Russian economy is more nearly complementary to those of the new nations than ours when it comes to the repayment of economic assistance. Russia is short in the production of food, grains, and other products of the soil, whereas these are precisely what we have in surplus. Since these commodities are usually about all that a new country has for export, they find it easier to service a loan to Russia than one that is due to the United States.

So much for the field of economic assistance. In the field of trade and commerce, the picture is altogether different. Here the United States has overwhelming natural advantages, if only we are prepared to put forth the total national effort which the challenge requires.

At the outset, however, we must recognize that we have one initial handicap. The Soviets understand the way of life of an under-developed country better than we do, for the reason that so much of their own land mass is still underdeveloped. They do not have to leave the confines of their own territory to examine the way of life of primitive peoples, because they still have such among their own. They still have frontiers, and the goods which they produce are designed to meet the simple necessities of those whose standard of living has but recently emerged from the subsistence level.

Much of their equipment which would be used by those living under a primitive economic regime is simple in design and rugged in construction. They make but few automobiles, but those which they do produce are intended for operation in rough terrain and in areas where few mechanics will be available.

The contrary is true of the United States. We no longer understand life on the frontier. Our consumer products are those of a sophisticated civilization, and they are now so widely distributed that life in a remote village has nearly all of the amenities that would be found in the city. Our automobiles are designed never to leave the concrete, and few Americans ever look underneath the hood.

But this is about all that can be said for the Russians in this new competition. The rest is ours.

In a developing country, it is important early to establish an inflow of consumer goods, first, to create an incentive to work on the part of those who have not been putting forth their best effort, and, second, to raise the general standard of living upon which to build literacy and the capacity for self-government.

Here is where the Soviets lack versatility. They know only a sellers' market, because in Russia there are never enough goods to go round. Their best creative talent does not go into the consumer sector, and the demand always exceeds supply. Neither the manufacturer nor the seller has to make the effort required of their counterparts in the United States. This brings it to pass that in their economy there is neither an incentive to make goods attractive nor to sell them aggressively. They have no skill in market research, in advertising, or in promotion. They make no effort to arouse desire to purchase in the buyer nor to conform production to suit his needs. As a result, the life of the ordinary individual in a Communist regime is dull and graceless, and, if they should be successful in transmitting to the inhabitants of an uncommitted country the true image of the life which they have to offer, it would defeat their own purposes.

On the contrary, ours is the way of life which the new nations seek to imitate, for it is filled with gaiety and *joie de vivre*. They are certain to want our gadgets once they come to understand what richness can thus be brought into their lives and once they come to believe that to attain them is a possibility. If, with our great resources of creative talent, we could turn slightly away from the goods of sophistication and devote ourselves consciously to the production and distribution of products especially suited to peoples who are just emerging toward the modern way of life, the Soviets would be totally outclassed. They lack imaginative gifts, and, even if they did possess them, they would be foreclosed from employing them because they could hardly develop such products for sale in the new nations while at the same time denying them to their own people.

We have the further advantage that most of the new areas understand, at least in a rudimentary way, the functioning of the free market. The origin of the bazaar is lost in the oblivion of early human history, but it is found in wide areas of the world. Among such peoples, ordinary trading, where the buyer decides what he wants and the seller decides whether to part with the goods, all carried forward on an individual basis, is as old as the earliest forms of civilization. This built-in antipathy to collectivism can be made a significant working tool in our resistance to the Soviet economic competition.

Furthermore, the entire structure of the Soviet means of production lacks the flexibility and the spontaneity that give such vitality to our economy. They are being driven toward decentralization in the field of manufacturing, thus widening somewhat the number of individuals who participate in the making of the decisions, but the multiplicity of choices arrived at are still strikingly small, when compared with the operation of the free market in our country. The mere fact that their selling mechanisms are separate from those of production, with responsibility divided for those two functions, causes unwieldly accumulations of inventory, because those who produce have no incentive to distribute.

This process of decentralization toward which the Russians seem to be moving will almost certainly make foreign trade more clumsy. Human nature being what it is, central authority will surely find it more and more difficult to compel regional officers to surrender for the export trade products which are already in scarce supply among their own people.

We have the further advantage that much of the consumer merchandise that the Communist regime has to offer to a new country is shoddy. There are matches that do not light, sugar that does not dissolve, and shoes that do not wear well. The engines of the small Moskivitch automobile do not stand hot climates well.

And they make many mistakes in deliveries, due to their lack of experience and skill in the general field of distribution and transportation. There was the famous case, for example, when cement was delivered to Burma during the monsoon season and no storage had been provided in advance. The result was quite disastrous to the cement. And then there have been occasions in Guinea when large shipments of bananas have rotted on the docks, because Russian ships did not arrive at the time agreed on or because, when they did arrive, they did not have the promised capacity.

This lack of sophistication in the merchandising field abroad reflects incompetency at home. The Russians either do not understand or do not permit the withdrawal of labor and capital to improve the distribution of goods, and, as a consequence, their own retail facilities are inadequate and unattractive. Stores are small, badly out of date by our standards, poorly equipped, and arbitrarily located with respect to the consumer demand. A Russian housewife must spend much of her day standing in line. And if they lack skill in selling and in distributing at home, it is not likely that they will be adept in these important functions when long distances and remote areas are involved.

Not only is the major effort of all Russian production concentrated in heavy industry and armament and not consumer goods, but their systems of bonuses and other incentives, which are exceptionally high in a nation which began by insisting that all individuals receive the same compensation regardless of effort, tend to substitute quantity in production for quality. Innovations to please the customer are necessarily frowned upon if they tend to interrupt the current stream of production and thus reduce the level of incentives.

For the same reasons, they put more emphasis on employing known processes than upon developing new ones. There is not the slightest doubt but that they could bring great resourcefulness to research on consumer products if they made up their minds to, but, at the present time, their methods do not breed quick readjustment to changing demand.

This, in part, reflects their system of education, which places so much emphasis on technology and so little upon the liberal arts and broad intellectual development. They take it for granted that, if a man is a good engineer, he will possess management skills when he comes to a position of leadership and responsibility.

One of their great limitations in the whole field of foreign trade is that they prefer to deal on a basis of barter. This is not only because the ruble is not a freely convertible currency, but because their whole philosophy is adverse to the free market. Barter, at best, is a clumsy medium. Among other things, it operates to cause unfair dealing, because, without a fixed price, no nation can be sure that it is getting as favorable treatment as its neighbor. Furthermore, through barter, the Soviets often take in goods which they do not want, and they are quite unscrupulous about disposing of these commodities later in world markets at prices below those asked by the other nation itself when it trades with the outside world.

We have such abundant resources in this entire field of marketing and distribution that we ought to win this economic competition on trade hands down, if once we put our minds to it. American goods are the highest quality, class by class, in the world. They can be especially designed for the particular needs of any locality in the world, and we have all the skill required to make the variety and the quality of our products known everywhere.

To do this, however, we must not only have the will to compete, but we must acquire shrewd understanding of the way of life that is involved, country by country.

We must, first of all, recognize that free enterprise is not a concept which exports itself. New nations turn to statism not because they prefer communism ideologically, but because it suits their immediate needs.

First of all, they have no source of capital except through the government. They have no traditions of thrift, no media by which the savings of the many may be brought together for establishment of manufacturing units.

And it is instinctive for those who control the government, and who thus control the capital, not to want to turn it over to private hands.

Just how we bridge this gap is not clear, but it must be bridged. A way must be found for those who are committed to the concept of private initiative to work in a spirit of co-operation with those who are committed to statism, in the hope that over the long pull the values found in the free enterprise way of life make themselves so clear that they will be adopted voluntarily.

But upon any basis of comparison, it is overwhelmingly clear that the United States possesses more advantage than the Soviet Union in this great new challenge of world economic competition and that all that is needed is to bring our great resources, both human and material, to bear upon this objective.

We can win, and on our own terms, if we want to, but we must want to very earnestly.

*   *   *

Questions and Answers

Q: Twelve weeks ago today there was a change of administration in Washington to which neither of the gentlemen referred. I wonder, in view of the new approach in Washington to these problems, whether our speakers would change their opinions or analyses?

A: I would like to say, if I may, just one personal word. I had the great privilege of being on President Eisenhower's personal staff. I will have no part whatsoever in expressing criticism of the new administration. Mr. Kennedy is my President; he is your President. I shall support him. I think he has put together an admirable team, and I am deeply sensitive to the awesome responsibility which he bears. I am for him.

Q: What role, if any, does Mr. Randall think the Peace Corps might play in economic competition, in addition to the social aspects of it, particularly in connection with his remarks about the Russian capacity for merging with the national populations with whom they work?

A: I'm tremendously interested in the concept of the Peace Corps. I think it reflects great credit on America, this popular and spontaneous desire to give up youth and opportunity to perform a service of dedication for the country and the world. I think that is a magnificent concept. It will bear very little upon the economic competition, as I see it. In the first place, these people carry no capital with them; they cannot do much with the economy without capital. Their job is to improve the way of life of the people. I am delighted with the idea that they are to undertake to live in the villages. I sense great difficulties with the program, and I am sure that Mr. Schriver, who is held in high esteem in Chicago, where he was president of the schoolboard, recognizes these difficulties. How do you screen? George Allen and I have both seen people who have turned in fine performances at home put in the midst of an alien culture, in an unfavorable climate, and then develop qualities of instability which no one could have foreseen. One or two of these young people going berserk in a remote area of the world can greatly damage the image of the United States. I sense an administrative difficulty. Under our concept, the ambassador is the chief of mission in every country. It is not yet clear to me to whom the Peace Corps young people are to report, whether they are to be directed from Washington or are to

be under the guidance and direction of the ambassador. I have discussed this with no one in Washington, of course. I think it is a great
experiment; it deserves the full support of the American people. With
full recognition that it will not immediately perform miracles, it will
have to be carried out with great restraint, great self-discipline, and
great dedication on the part of all concerned.

Q: My question has to do with where our national leaders direct
their energies. I believe that all thinking, well-informed people recognize that we will have to save our future, our nation, and our
civilization by a developed, effective world government and world
law, rather than through a high development of armament—bombs,
disease-germ warfare, chemical warfare. So what I would like is an
explanation of why our government and our potential leadership sin
by omission by not pursuing that sort of thing.

A: I would like to add to Mr. Allen's remarks, if I might, just
one thought, which is this. World government can never be imposed
from the top. No one of us would want it done by force. It must, in
the last analysis, when it comes, rest, as our government does, upon
the consent of the governed. I am, therefore, tremendously interested
in trying to arrive at closer mutuality of interest among the nations.
Upon such a base, we would build the concept of better world
relations. That is why I have become such an advocate of the liberal
trade movement. I want steadily to see world trade barriers reduced,
and, I say, this has now gained such momentum that the economy of
the entire free world will ultimately become completely integrated. I
think these forces are now so great that no country can stand against
them, no political party can stand against them, certainly no American corporation can stand against them. I think there has never been
a firmer foundation upon which to build political integration in
Europe than the mutuality of interest among the nations which has
been created by the Common Market. And I look to an extension
of that principle developing a groundwork of interrelationship between nations based upon the daily living and transactions of people.
Out of this will come closer political relationships.

Q: Mr. Randall stated that we could win the economic competitive war with the Soviets hands down if we were only to mobilize
our resources. He said, at the end, that, if we could make ourselves
want to win the economic war, we could do so. I would like to know
if he has some specific ideas on how we can so mobilize our resources

in our nation within the terms of our American tradition and our democratic way of life.

A: I hold certain naive pieces of philosophy that I can't get away from. I simply have the feeling that our democracy rests upon the concept of individual responsibility. I have heard too much in my day about our rights. I have heard too little about our obligations. Freedom to me is an integral word. I do not think we have separate freedoms. I think that freedom of enterprise is exactly the same freedom as academic freedom. I think that the businessman who resents the professor when he teaches economics as he wants to is blameworthy. And I think that the professor is blameworthy when he tries to repress and control private initiative. I think that each must understand and have respect for the other. In addition to organizing civil liberties unions—with which I sympathize—I wish we would organize civil obligations unions. I think that our entire nation rests upon that noble concept of individual responsibility. And unless, as a nation, we accept this challenge as people, as individuals, and ask ourselves what each of us may do to advance this concept, we never will meet the challenge. Unless the total impulse of the voluntary action which comes from every person in the country comes into focus from the bottom up, we'll never make it.

Q: Since the long-term rate of interest at 2.5 per cent seems to be a stumbling block, I would like to pose the question whether we could not subsidize our long-term rate of interest so that if the market demands 5 per cent and we can only lend at 2.5 per cent to an underdeveloped nation, we could get the other 2.5 per cent out of our own budget and pay it over to the people lending the money to the foreign country on a year to year basis.

A: I am very much interested that the gentleman has made that suggestion. I would have to say to him with entire candor that it has often been made. There is only one answer to it and that is completely final and irrevocable. It is politics. Can you imagine our subsidizing the interest rate by borrowing at 4.5 per cent and lending at 2.5 per cent to a remote nation and refusing to lend to the rural electrification facilities of the United States at 2.5 per cent. I cannot believe that the American Congress would long endure that kind of proposal.

Q: In the course of your paper, Mr. Randall, on your most fundamental issue in meeting this challenge, you suggest we can do this without altering our own way of life. Now, it sounds to me as if you were saying that we can have our cake and eat it, too. Now, if I misunderstood you or misinterpreted you, what price do you think we will have to pay?

A: I didn't make my point clear; it's semantics. For example, Mr. Mikoyan goes everywhere; he takes in his briefcase the literature dealing with every product in his nation. He can sell anything Russia produces; he can cut the price on one article to move another. Not long ago, a group of fairly responsible businessmen suggested that the way to answer that would be to establish in the United States a vast state trading organization which would take consignments from industry at fixed prices and then fix its own prices on these commodities in world commerce, taking a deficit, if necessary, to meet, step by step, the competition of the Soviets. That is what I mean. We must not do that. We must not adopt the Soviet way in order to meet the Soviet competition. We must find a way by which, through the voluntary assumption of responsibility by business, through the exercise of private initiative, we can compete. This is a new challenge; we must find new ways to meet it and still be true to the concept of individual freedom and individual responsibility.

2. RUSSIA AND THE UNCOMMITTED NATIONS*

BY ALVIN Z. RUBENSTEIN

The major development in Soviet foreign policy since 1955 is the change in strategy from a continental to a global orientation. Nowhere has this change unfolded more dramatically than in the "gray" areas between the Soviet and Western spheres of influence— the neutralist countries of Southern Asia, the Middle East, Africa, and most recently, Latin America. There have been occasional setbacks for Moscow, but the over-all balance sheet shows strong credit accumulations, and the potential for the future extension of Soviet influence is even more promising.

* From *Current History*, Vol. 43 (October, 1962), pp. 218–223. Reprinted by permission of the author and *Current History*.

An important forum for the Soviet courtship of underdeveloped countries is the United Nations, with its regional economic commissions and special agencies. In the years before Soviet bilateral aid became widely sought after by the neutralist countries to supplement their economic and military growth, Moscow used the various international organizations to bring its offers to the attention of prospective recipients. The pattern was always the same: first, a lengthy attack on Western trading and monopolistic practices, interference with local efforts to industrialize, and persistent profit drain; then dire warnings of the danger of subordinating young economies to Western interests through the grant of military bases and economic privileges in return for foreign aid; finally, as a glowing contrast, the disinterested and generous character of Soviet aid offers. For example, at one session of the Economic and Social Council the Soviet delegate noted that:

a) . . . the Soviet Union was prepared to develop its trade with the underdeveloped countries on the basis of equality of rights and mutual advantage. It was prepared to consider the conclusion of long term contracts with the countries of Asia and the Far and Near East and other underdeveloped countries for the purchase of goods from those countries in exchange for Soviet goods, bearing in mind the possibility of agreeing on stable prices for a lengthy period and settling accounts in national currencies of the countries concerned.

b) . . . the Soviet Union, anxious to promote the economic development of the underdeveloped countries, was prepared to supply them with industrial equipment and machinery. If the necessary agreement on conditions were reached, Soviet external trade organizations might supply industrial equipment and machinery on terms providing deferred payment.

International organizations served as a convenient framework within which to gain wide publicity for Soviet proposals and propaganda.

To further its comprehensive courtship of the uncommitted nations and to encourage them in their disputes with the West, Moscow has extended almost $7 billion bilaterally in economic and military aid. It has stressed, instead of outright aid, long-term, low-interest loans repayable in local currency and commodities; expanded trade; provided military equipment; and lent diplomatic support in situations and times deemed critical by these countries.

The Soviet explanation for the economic backwardness of the underdeveloped countries, an updated variant of the Leninist theory of imperialism, finds a ready audience among the élites in Africa, the Middle East, and other areas where the Western legacy has left poverty and resentment. It has appeal because it throws the burden for their present underdeveloped condition on the West, and not on themselves. The Soviet line of argument maintains that the majority of underdeveloped countries had been subjected to colonial domination for a long time and their backwardness is the consequence. Monopolies drained the countries of their wealth in the form of exorbitant profits. They had not been permitted to develop their resources, train specialists, or build higher educational institutions. All key political and economic positions had been reserved for the foreign rulers. Is it any wonder, ask Soviet delegates rhetorically, that the underdeveloped countries are in such straits today? Coupled with this strong anti-colonialist stand are opposition to Western policies, offers of concrete assistance, and an insistence that the Soviet model for industrialization and modernization has a relevance for these countries that is lacking in the Western pattern.

A look at the Soviet record in the four key areas—Southern Asia, the Middle East, Africa, and Latin America—may help illumine the reasons for the present growing Soviet influence among the uncommitted nations and the possible future sources of discord between Moscow and neutralist leaders.

SOUTHERN ASIA

The Soviet campaign to cultivate underdeveloped countries began in Southern Asia. The prime target is India, the most populous, strategically situated, and, by virtue of its leading role among other neutralists, politically important. Soviet prestige in New Delhi is higher now than at any time in the postwar period. At a time when India is experiencing growing difficulties in its foreign relations with the West, the support of Moscow is particularly welcome. The reasons for friendly Soviet-Indian relations are rooted in the character of India's current security problems and in Moscow's political objectives.

Fifteen years after independence, India finds itself without a dependable ally on its borders: several of its neighbors are openly hostile. Pakistan is permanently alienated because of Kashmir; Nepal objects to India's big-brother, patronizing attitude, and to its tacit support for the Nepalese revolutionaries, based in northern India, who seek to overthrow the ruling King Mahendra; China is forcing India to divert precious resources to a military buildup in disputed, sparsely populated areas of the Himalayas; and Burma regards India coolly because of an unassimilable, wealthy, and influential minority.

In this situation, India has found a staunch supporter in the U.S.S.R. Friendship with Moscow rests upon a community of mutually reinforcing interests. Moscow supports New Delhi's opposition to the American-sponsored Southeast Asia Treaty Organization (SEATO), to the vestiges of Western colonialism in Africa and Asia, and to the deepening American involvement in South Vietnam and Laos. During the Goa affair of December, 1961, the Soviet Union alone among the Great Powers fully upheld India's action. On Kashmir, Moscow has long upheld India's claims against Pakistan, which is militarily allied with the United States, and has thwarted repeated efforts in the Security Council to take some effective action. Moscow's neutrality on the Sino-Indian border dispute has angered the Chinese and been much appreciated by the Indians. Even though it is linked militarily and ideologically with Peking, on this issue Moscow has maintained a discreet silence.

The economic assistance extended by the Soviet Union, and its Eastern European satellites, in the past seven years, has been an important addition to India's planned economic development. Since undertaking its foreign aid program in 1955, the Soviet government has lent India more than $800 million for various industrial projects, including the construction of the much advertised and highly successful steel plant at Bhilai, the first government-owned oil refinery, and the foundations of a pharmaceutical industry. Moscow has probably extended more economic aid to India than it has to Communist China.

Recently, there have been reports that India may purchase two squadrons of supersonic MIG 21 jet fighters from the Soviet Union. If concluded, this transaction would be the first step toward reorienting India's procurement of military equipment from British to Soviet supply sources. Both the United States and Great Britain are seeking to dissuade India from such a move, which could jeopardize the future of Western aid to India. But the United States decision to supply Pakistan with Sabre jets has occasioned new fears among Indian military leaders. The Soviet offer is particularly attractive since Moscow has expressed a willingness to build a plant in India to produce the MIG's.

Friendship with India serves the Kremlin well in its drive for influence among neutralist countries. It demonstrates to the wary Afro-Asians that closer relations with the Soviet bloc can bring them tangible economic, military, and political dividends; it encourages India to pursue its policy of non-alignment, thus forestalling the formation of a united anti-Communist coalition in Asia; it serves as a convenient, long-term hedge against an ambitious Chinese expansionism which may, in time, further split the Communist world; and it provides the Communist Party of India with a respectability which may make the C.P.I. a major force in Indian political life, if not in the near future, then within a decade.

Soviet objectives function on several planes. Moscow's ultimate goal is a Communist India which would look to Moscow, rather than Peking, for guidance in international relations. But for the moment, friendship with India, buttressed by strong diplomatic support and generous economic assistance, makes better politics and best serves Soviet interests.

Afghanistan and Indonesia are also recipients of extensive Soviet economic and military aid. In both situations, the Soviet way has been paved by the political quarrels of these countries with Western powers or with their allies. Thus, Afghanistan's feud with Pakistan, which has several times cut land-locked Afghanistan's trade route to the outside world, afforded Moscow a golden opportunity. In addition to facilitating the transit of Afghan exports through Soviet territory, the Soviet government extended economic loans and military equipment. Its commitments have exceeded $220 million. This amount is larger than that given to any other neutralist except India, Indonesia, and Egypt, whose populations are much larger.

Though Moscow extended more than $500 million in credits to Indonesia, its record there has been unimpressive. Most of the credits have been spent on military equipment by the Sukarno regime which appears more concerned with gaining control over Dutch-held West New Guinea, than with promoting the country's economic development. Potentially the richest nation in Asia because of its resources, Indonesia remains undeveloped, unstable, and beset by internal problems. Soviet bloc economic aid has done little to stimulate development: breakdowns in equipment, and tardy deliveries of spare parts have been the Indonesian experience with Soviet economic assistance. But in its buildup for a possible showdown with the Netherlands, Indonesia has found Moscow a willing supplier of military equipment; and this overshadows the disappointments with Soviet technical and economic aid.

Laos

In recent months, attention has focused on developments in Laos. The key to South Vietnam's security against the Communist Viet Cong guerillas, and the strategic highway to Southeast Asia, Laos is a pawn in the Great Power struggle. It is not a nation but a conglomeration of tribes and ethnic groups which have no interest in politics and even less understanding of their recent diplomatic importance.

Under the agreement signed in June, 1962, at Khang Khay, Laos is to be ruled by a coalition of Right-wing, neutralist, and pro-Communist factions. Prince Souvanna Phouma, the neutralist leader, is to head the coalition, assisted by two Deputy Premiers—Prince Souphanouvong, head of the pro-Communist Pathet Lao movement, and General Phoumi Nosavan, the Right-wing military leader. The durability of this coalition is highly questionable, since pro-Communist forces already control more than 60 per cent of the country.

For the time being, Moscow seems to prefer a peaceful settlement. It has been relatively moderate in its demands. Some Western observers attribute this to Moscow's desire to contain Chinese influence in the region. However, a look at a map reveals that China, which is contiguous to Laos, can easily upset a political settlement any time it so desires. It may be that, for differing reasons, Moscow and Peking prefer not to push events to a point where a full scale American military commitment might result: Moscow may be playing for time to increase its hold over local Communist movements, while Peking, beset by severe economic crises at home, is temporarily satisfied with a partial settlement which leaves the Communist Pathet Lao in a favorable position to take over all of Laos on short notice and with little effort. Should Laos fall completely under Communist control, pro-Western Thailand and South Vietnam will be faced with graver threats to their security, and the United States may be forced to escalate its military commitments in the area.

THE MIDDLE EAST

A few years ago a study published by the Library of Congress on Soviet penetration in the Middle East noted that Moscow had undertaken a three-pronged offensive aimed at undermining, and possibly replacing, Western influence in the area:

This offensive was to embrace an active good will campaign in the Arab States coupled with aloofness toward Israel, a determined purpose to participate as a principal in any future great-power political arrangements relative to the state of affairs in the Arab Middle East, and the promotion in these countries of a vigorous trade-and-aid program.

Ending Soviet isolation—the consequence of Stalin's inflexible adherence to a bipolar conception of political alignments—has proved easy; however, Moscow has not been able to accrue the influence it hoped would be forthcoming as a reward for its aid and support. The festering Egyptian-Israeli struggle led Nasser to seek modern military equipment. Moscow quickly obliged. The 1955 arms deal, coupled with Soviet support at the time of the Suez invasion of October, 1956, enhanced Moscow's status in Cairo, and gave the Soviets the opportunity they sought. Trade between the two countries expanded. In 1958, the Soviet government agreed to help finance and construct the Aswan High Dam, the grandiose project which Egypt hopes will increase its arable lands by 25 per cent and will provide the electric power to facilitate industrialization of the country.

By 1961, however, relations between the two countries were correct but not cordial. Cairo's crackdown on local Communists more than once led Khrushchev to criticize the Nasser regime. But no split is in sight. Egypt derives economic aid for its development projects and the latest military equipment for its army from the Soviet bloc. Meanwhile, the Soviet Union encourages Nasser's anti-Western policies, and binds him ever tighter to economic and military dependence, through Soviet purchases of cotton and Soviet replacements for military equipment.

But the Soviets are playing an ill-concealed game of divide-and-dominate which limits their maneuverability in the area. Egypt's rival for leadership of the Arab bloc is Iraq, which since the 1958 overthrow of the pro-Western Faisal regime has been led by General Abdul Karim Kassim. Much to the annoyance of Nasser, Moscow has extended economic and military aid to Kassim's regime. Kassim, however, has kept the Soviets at arm's length, cracking down hard on local Communists, and criticizing the prices of Soviet goods and the tardiness of deliveries and plant assemblings. Soviet technicians have been unimpressive in action and Iraq has experienced a noticeable disenchantment with Soviet assistance.

Another source of Iraqi pique has been Moscow's encouragement of Kurdish nationalism. The Kurds are a tough, militant, tribal people who have long been at odds with established authorities in Iran, Turkey, and Iraq. The Soviets have sought to use them, since the end of World War II, as a wedge against the pro-Western Iranian and Turkish regimes. Kassim believes that Moscow is not averse to inciting the Kurds to revolt against Bagdad's authority, in the hope of paving the way for a Communist takeover. For the time being, he follows a neutralist policy, and seeks to keep local Communists fragmented and weak, while accepting military and diplomatic support from the Soviet Union. In recent months, Moscow has made diligent efforts to expand trade with Iraq, and has assumed responsibility for building a steel mill.

Political circumstances frequently seemed tailored to Soviet needs. Just as Iraqi-Soviet relations were experiencing difficulties, the problem of Kuwait afforded Moscow an opportunity to demonstrate its political support by vetoing that former British protectorate's application for admission to the United Nations. Iraq contends that Kuwait, the world's second largest oil exporter, is part of its own territory, legally and historically. Egypt, on the other hand, supported Kuwait's admission for United Nations membership. On this critical issue, Moscow stood with Iraq, a matter greatly appreciated by the Kassim regime.

Soviet penetration of the Middle East has proceeded as a consequence of Arab-Western antagonism, of tangible Soviet economic, military, and political support for the Arab countries, and of the deep-seated rivalries that permeate the Middle East.

AFRICA SOUTH OF THE SAHARA

The struggle for Africa is in its initial phase. European domination is coming to an end as more and more former colonies acquire independence, the latest being Burundi and Rwanda in Central Africa (July, 1962). Moscow, realizing that it is on the threshold of unrivalled opportunity, generally is playing a cautious hand. Soviet strategy is attempting to adapt to the conditions of Africa, to formulate an organizational weapon which can strike for political power. There are no African proletariat, no well-organized Communist parties, and no divisive class antagonisms. African societies are largely agrarian and rural, rent by tribal feuds, but united in their hostility toward the white man. In such a setting, traditional Communist tactics demand revision.

An immediate Soviet objective is to exploit African resentment against the remaining possessions of the European Powers and the deep-rooted fears of Western influence. The Soviets expect African-Western relations to deteriorate, and in the ensuing crises they hope to turn developments to their advantage. Meanwhile they are trying to convince the neutralist African states that they can depend on unstinting Soviet diplomatic support and on modest amounts of economic and technical aid. They have embarked on a foreign aid program, with emphasis on Ghana and Guinea. For a while, Soviet leaders had hoped to make them Communist showcases in Africa. They extended $200 million in credits to Ghana and $100 million to Guinea. Many trade and cultural missions were sent, and Ghana's Kwame Nkrumah and Guinea's Sekou Touré visited Moscow.

Despite the anti-Western neutralist bent of Ghana and Guinea, they have not shown themselves to be easy targets for Communist penetration. Their leaders, though Marxists, have shown no inclination to replace their former Western rulers with Soviet commissars. An attempt by the previous Soviet Ambassador to Guinea to interfere in local politics led to his expulsion and occasioned a hasty visit by Anastas Mikoyan, the Kremlin's trouble-shooter, to repair the damage. The result of this incident has been a greater willingness by Guinea to consider the establishment of closer ties with the United States.

The Soviet aid record, thus far, is marred by experts who do not speak the local language, frequent breakdowns of equipment which is not suited to tropical conditions, and an inability to offer much constructive assistance in the fields of agriculture and light industry, the main areas of African need.

In the Congo, the Soviets have been effectively rebuffed and they seem resigned to waiting for another opportunity for infiltration. The United Nations has succeeded in forestalling anarchy and Communist inroads, but whether it can bring stability and a settlement of the Katanga secession remains to be seen.

Moscow places great reliance upon propaganda and education as avenues for achieving contact with African intellectuals. It finds that "socialism" exerts wide appeal among these groups, many of whom were schooled in Western institutions. But, from available evidence, it seems Moscow fails to appreciate the peculiarly *African* features of their aspirations and attitudes. The dynamic forces sweeping Africa are nationalism and a race-conscious Africanism. Where nationalist goals conflict with orthodox Communist prescriptions for political rule and modernization, as they will increasingly in the future, Moscow may find that conditions in Africa, far from being ripe for Communist pickings, are antithetical and resistant to Soviet penetration. . . .

3. TWO YEARS OF THE PEACE CORPS*

BY SARGENT SHRIVER

Oscar Wilde is said to have observed that America really was discovered by a dozen people before Columbus, but it was always successfully hushed up. I am tempted to feel that way about the Peace Corps; the idea of a national effort of this type had been proposed many times in past years. But in 1960 and 1961 for the first time the idea was joined with the power and the desire to implement it. On November 2, 1960, Senator John F. Kennedy proposed a "peace corps" in a campaign speech at the Cow Palace in San Francisco. Thirty thousand Americans wrote immediately to support the idea; thousands volunteered to join.

The early days of the Peace Corps were like the campaign days of 1960, but with no election in sight. My colleagues were volunteer workers and a few key officials loaned from other agencies. "I use not only all the brains I have, but all I can borrow," Woodrow Wilson said. So did we. Letters cascaded in from all over the country

* From *Foreign Affairs*, Vol. 41 (July, 1963), pp. 694–707. Reprinted by permission of the Council on Foreign Relations, Inc.

in what one writer described as "paper tornadoes at the Peace Corps." The elevators to our original two-room office disgorged constant sorties of interested persons, newspaper reporters, job seekers, academic figures and generous citizens offering advice. Everywhere, it seemed, were cameras, coils of cable and commentators with questions.

An organization, we know, gains life through hard decisions, so we hammered out basic policies in long, detailed discussions in which we sought to face up to the practical problems and reach specific solutions before we actually started operations. We knew that a few wrong judgments in the early hours of a new organization's life, especially a controversial government agency, can completely thwart its purposes—even as a margin of error of a thousandth of an inch in the launching of a rocket can send it thousands of miles off course. And we knew the Peace Corps would have only one chance to work. As with the parachute jumper, the chute had to open the first time. We knew, too, that a thousand suspicious eyes were peering over our shoulders. Some were the eyes of friendly critics, but many belonged to unfriendly skeptics. The youthfulness of the new Administration, particularly the President, enhanced the risk; an older leadership would have had greater immunity from charges of "sophomorism."

Even the choice of a name took on serious overtones. The phrase "Peace Corps" was used in the original San Francisco speech, but many of our advisers disliked it. "Peace," they claimed, was a word the Communists had preëmpted, and "Corps" carried undesirable military connotations. We did not want a name contrived out of initials which a public relations firm might have devised; nor did we want to restrict participation in the program by calling it a "Youth Corps." What we did want was a name which the public at large could grasp emotionally as well as intellectually. Whatever name we did choose, we would give it content by our acts and programs. We wanted it, also, to reflect the seriousness of our objectives. We studied dozens of other names and finally came back to the original. Peace is the fundamental goal of our times. We believed the Peace Corps could contribute to its attainment, for while armaments can deter war, only men can create peace.

The ambitiousness of the name, of course, was only one reason for early skepticism about the Peace Corps. Fears were voiced that it might be a "second children's crusade." I was astonished that a nation so young had become so suspicious of its youth. We had forgotten that Thomas Jefferson drafted the Declaration of Independence at age 33. Forgotten also was the fact that more than half of the world's population is under 26, the age of the average Peace Corps Volunteer. Sixteen of the nations in Africa have heads of state under 45; five have leaders in their thirties.

Of course, youthful enthusiasm and noble purposes were not enough. They had to be combined with hard-headed pragmatism and realistic administration. In the early days of the Peace Corps we were looking for a formula for practical idealism. The formula worked out by experience has "the sweet smell of success" today, but it was far less clear two years ago.

Would enough qualified Americans be willing to serve? Even if they started, would they be able to continue on the job despite frustration, dysentery and boredom? Could Americans survive overseas without special foods and privileges, special housing, automobiles, television and air conditioners? Many Americans thought not. The Washington correspondent of the respected *Times of India* agreed with them in these words:

When you have ascertained a felt local need, you would need to find an American who can exactly help in meeting it. This implies not only the wherewithal (or what you inelegantly call the "know how") but also a psychological affinity with a strange new people who may be illiterate and yet not lack Wisdom, who may live in hovels and yet dwell in spiritual splendor, who may be poor in worldly wealth and yet enjoy a wealth of intangibles and a capacity to be happy. Would an American young man be in tune with this world he has never experienced before? I doubt it. . . .

One also wonders whether American young men and tender young girls, reared in air-conditioned houses at a constant temperature, knowing little about the severities of nature (except when they pop in and out of cars or buses) will be able to suffer the Indian summer smilingly and, if they go into an Indian village, whether they will be able to sleep on unsprung beds under the canopy of the bejeweled sky or indoors in mud huts, without writing home about it.

At a time when many were saying that Americans had gone soft and were interested mainly in security, pensions and suburbia, the Peace Corps could have been timorous. Possible ways of hedging against an anticipated shortage of applicants could have included low qualification standards, generous inducements to service, cautious programming, a period of duty shorter than two years, an enforced period of enlistment such as the "hitch" in the armed forces, or draft exemption for volunteer service in the Peace Corps. We deliberately chose the risk rather than the hedge in each case and created an obstacle course. The applicant could remove himself any time he realized his motive was less than a true desire for service. This method of self-selection has by now saved us from compounded difficulties abroad.

Our optimism about sufficient recruits was justified. More than 50,000 Americans have applied for the Peace Corps. In the first three months of this year, more Americans applied for the Peace Corps than were drafted for military service. This happened notwithstanding the fact that young men who volunteer for the Peace Corps are liable to service on their return.

Selection was made rigorous. The process was fashioned to include a searchingly thorough application form, placement tests to measure useful skills, language aptitude exams, six to twelve reference inquiries, a suitability investigation and systematic observation of performance during the training program of approximately ten weeks. We invite about one in six applicants to enter training, and about five out of six trainees are finally selected for overseas service.

We debated hotly the question of age, and whether or not older people should be eligible. We listened to proposals for an age limit in the thirties and then in the sixties and finally decided to set no upper age limit at all. Our oldest volunteer today happens to be 76, and we have more grandparents than teenagers in the Peace Corps. Some older volunteers have turned out to be rigid and cantankerous in adapting to a standard of living *their* parents took for granted, but the majority of them make a lot of us in the New Frontier look like stodgy old settlers.

From the beginning we decided that effective volunteers abroad would need systematic administrative support and direction. Leaders of several developing nations, eager to have the assistance of trained manpower, warned against repeating the experiences of other highly motivated volunteer workers who had failed abroad for lack of cohesive leadership. A good program would need good people—not only as Peace Corps Volunteers but as Peace Corps staff members abroad. There was no counterpart in the U. S. Government of civilian leaders serving abroad on a volunteer basis. There was no precedent for what these men would have to do in programming, logistics and personal support for the volunteers in their charge. We needed the ablest of leaders in each position. Could we attract them even though we did not offer post differentials, cost-of-living allowances, commissary or diplomatic privileges?

Fortunately, the answer has been a continuing "yes." The Peace Corps has attracted intelligent and dedicated men to all positions on its overseas team. Ironically, the same critics who once complained that we would unleash hordes of uninstructed adolescents on the world are now complaining that we spend substantial sums to provide instruction and adequate direction.

Some of my colleagues proposed that Peace Corps Volunteers act as technical helpers to I.C.A. technicians, "extra hands" for the more experienced older men. Peace Corps practice has moved in another direction. A natural distinction between the A.I.D. adviser at a high level in government and the Peace Corps Volunteer making his contribution as a "doer" or "worker" at the grass roots soon became apparent. It also became clear that the Peace Corps Volunteer had a new and perhaps unique contribution to make as a person who entered fully into host-country life and institutions, with a host-country national working beside him, and another directing his work. This feature of the Peace Corps contributed substantially to its early support abroad.

Discussion of the possibility that the Peace Corps might be affiliated with the I.C.A. led into the question of its relationship to U. S. political and information establishments overseas. The Peace Corps in Washington is responsible to the Secretary of State. Volunteers and staff abroad are responsible to the American Ambassador. Nevertheless, the Peace Corps maintains a distinction between its functions and those of Embassies, A.I.D. and U.S.I.A. offices. There was a design to this which Secretary Rusk has aptly described: "The Peace Corps is not an instrument *of* foreign policy, because to make it so would rob it of its contribution *to* foreign policy." Peace Corps Volunteers are not trained diplomats; they are not propagandists; they are not technical experts. They represent our society by what they are, what they do and the spirit in which they do it. They steer clear of intelligence activity and stay out of local politics. Our strict adherence to these principles has been a crucial factor in the decision of politically uncommitted countries to invite American volunteers into their midst, into their homes and even into their classrooms and schoolyards to teach future generations of national leaders. In an era of sabotage and espionage, intelligence and counter-intelligence, the Peace Corps and its volunteers have earned a priceless yet simple renown: they are trustworthy.

Another contested issue in the early days of the Peace Corps concerned private organizations and universities. We were advised by many to make grants to these institutions, then to leave recruitment, selection, training and overseas programming in their hands. That road would have led to an organization operating very much like the National Science Foundation. For better or worse, the Peace Corps chose not to become a grant-making organization and those decisions which give character to our operations—selection, training, programming, field leadership and so on—are still in our possession.

Nevertheless, the involvement of private organizations and universities has been crucial to the Peace Corps' success. America is a pluralistic society and the Peace Corps expresses its diversity abroad by demonstrating that the public and private sectors can work coöperatively and effectively. We consciously seek contracts with private organizations, colleges and universities to administer our programs. We gain the advantage of expert knowledge, long experience, tested working relationships and often even private material resources. For example, CARE has contributed more than $100,000 worth of equipment to the Peace Corps in Colombia. Initially, there was suspicion by some of these agencies that the Peace Corps, with the resources of the United States taxpayer behind it, would preëmpt their own work abroad. Suspicion has turned into understanding, however, as the United States Government, through the Peace Corps, has facilitated the work of private organizations and has focused new attention on the needs and opportunities for service abroad.

In our "talent search" we went to government, academic life, business, the bar, the medical profession and every other walk of life where leadership was available. We deliberately recruited as many Negroes and representatives of other minority groups as possible for jobs in every echelon. We knew that Negroes would not ordinarily apply for high-level policy jobs, so we decided to seek them out. Today 7.4 percent of our higher echelon positions are filled by Negroes as compared to .8 percent for other government agencies in similar grades; 24 percent of our other positions are filled by Negroes, compared to a figure for government agencies in general of 5.5 percent.

How big should the Peace Corps be? Everyone was asking this question and everyone had an answer. Advice ranged from 500 to 1,000,000. There were strong voices raised in support of "tentative pilot projects," looking to a Peace Corps of less than 1,000. However, Warren W. Wiggins, an experienced foreign-aid expert, took a broader view. He pointed out that ultra-cautious programming might produce prohibitive per capita costs, fail even to engage the attention of responsible foreign officials (let alone have an impact) and fail to attract the necessary American talent and commitment. Furthermore, when the need was insatiable why should we try to meet it with a pittance?

There were also arguments in those early days about "saturation" of the foreign country, either in terms of jobs or the psychological impact of the American presence. I have since noticed that the same arguments made about a 500–1,000 man program in 1961 were also made about our plans to expand to 5,000 volunteers (March 1963), to 10,000 volunteers (March 1964) and to 13,000 (September 1964). I am not suggesting that the Peace Corps should continue to grow indefinitely. But I am proposing that much time and energy are wasted in theoretical musings, introspections and worries about the future. Peace Corps Volunteers are a new type of overseas American. Who is to say now how many of them will be welcome abroad next year, or in the next decade? Our country and our times have had plenty of experience with programs that were too little, too late.

The question of the health of the volunteers concerned us from the beginning. The Peace Corps represents the largest group of Americans who have ever tried to live abroad "up country." Even in World War II our troops were generally in organized units where safe food and water could be provided and medical care was at hand. This would not be the case for the Peace Corps. And an incapacitated volunteer would probably be worse than no volunteer at all. How could we reduce the risks to a rational level? The Surgeon General studied the problem at our request. We then worked out a solution by which preventive health measures are provided by public health doctors assigned to the Peace Corps, while much of the actual medical care is handled by doctors of the host country. Of the first

117 volunteers returned to the United States, only 20 came back for medical reasons (21 returned for compassionate reasons, 71 failed to adjust to overseas living and 5 died or were killed in accidents). Our medical division's work is already showing up in the pages of scientific and medical journals. As an example, we recently decided to use large injections of gamma globulin as a preventive for hepatitis, which has presented one of the worst health problems for Americans overseas. Since then, there has not been a single case of infectious hepatitis reported among those who received the large injection in time.

II

Many of the original doubts and criticisms of the Peace Corps have not materialized. On the other hand, substantive problems have emerged which were little discussed or expected two years ago. One of the most difficult is the provision of adequate language training. This was foreseen, but most observers thought that the exotic languages such as Thai, Urdu, Bengali and Twi would give us our main problem, while Spanish and French speakers could be easily recruited or quickly trained. The opposite has been true. The first volunteers who arrived in Thailand in January 1962 made a great impression with what observers described as "fluent" Thai. As the volunteers were the first to point out, their Thai was not actually fluent, but their modest achievement was tremendously appreciated. Since then, of course, a large proportion of the volunteers there have become truly fluent.

On the other hand, a considerable number of volunteers going to Latin America and to French Africa have been criticized for their mediocre language fluency. Expectations are high in these countries and halting Spanish or French is not enough. We have learned that America contains rather few French-speaking bus mechanics, Spanish-speaking hydrologists or math-science teachers who can exegete theorems in a Latin American classroom. Can we devise more effective and intensive language training, particularly for farmers, craftsmen, construction foremen, well drillers and other Americans who never before have needed a second language? Should we take skilled people and teach them languages, or take people with language abilities and teach them skills?

We still need more volunteers, especially those who combine

motivation and special skills. The person with a ready motivation for Peace Corps service tends to be the liberal arts student in college, the social scientist, the person with "human relations" interests. The developing countries need and want a great many Americans with this background, but they also want engineers, agronomists, lathe operators and geologists. We cannot make our maximum contribution if we turn down requests for skills which we have difficulty finding. There are presently 61 engineers in the Peace Corps, 30 geologists and 236 nurses, respectable numbers considering the ready availability of generously paying jobs in the domestic economy. But requests still far outnumber the supply.

Other industrialized countries may soon supplement our efforts by providing volunteers to developing countries with languages and skills we lack. The motivation to serve is not distinctively American, and half a dozen industrialized nations have established equivalents of the Peace Corps within the past few months. These programs grew out of an International Conference on Human Skills organized by the Peace Corps and held in Puerto Rico last October. The 43 countries represented at the meeting voted unanimously to establish an International Peace Corps Secretariat to help spread the concept of voluntarism as a tool of economic and social transformation. The response to this initiative is a reflection of the innate vitality of the Peace Corps idea.

We face increasingly difficult choices as we grow. Should we concentrate in the future on the countries where we now have programs and resist expanding to new areas? We are already committed to programs in 47 nations. Should we favor a program where there are relatively stable social conditions, good organization and effective leadership? Or should we take greater risks and commit our resources in a more fluid and disorganized situation, usually in a poorer country, where the Peace Corps might make a crucial difference or find a great opportunity? Where should we draw the line between adequate material support to the volunteers and the perils of providing them with too many material goods? Where is the equilibrium between safeguarding the volunteer's health and morale and protecting the Peace Corps' declared purpose that he should live as does his co-worker in the host country, without special luxury or advantage?

When is a particular program completed? In Nigeria the answer is relatively easy. That country's coördinated educational development plan projects a need for 815 foreign teachers in 1965, 640 in 1966, 215 in 1968 and none in 1970. By then enough Nigerians will have been trained to fill their own classrooms. Progress may not follow so fine a plan, but the Peace Corps can look ahead to a day when its academic, teaching work in Nigeria will be done.

The answer is not so simple in Colombia, where volunteers are working on community development in 92 rural towns. There is no lack of change and progress: the Colombian Government has trebled its own commitment of resources and staff to this progressive community development program. Scores of individual communities have already learned how to organize to transform their future. When volunteer John Arango organized the first town meeting in Cutaru almost two years ago, for example, not one soul showed up. Twenty months later almost every citizen turns out for these meetings. The townsmen have changed an old jail into a health clinic; they have drained the nearby swamps; they have rebuilt wharves on the river; they have cleared stumps out of the channel to make it navigable; and they are now building the first 18 of 72 do-it-yourself houses designed by the volunteer.

John Arango's Colombian co-worker is equally responsible for the results in Cutaru. In community development, particularly, the ability of the host organization to provide able counterparts is crucial to a program's success. I might also mention that host countries have in every case made voluntary contributions to the Peace Corps programs. In Africa alone, they have supported the program to the value of $2,500,000. During and after the Puerto Rico conference, three countries in Latin America announced plans to establish home-grown Peace Corps organizations; when implemented these will help solve the shortage of counterparts. We believe North American and Latin American volunteers will complement one another and increase the total effectiveness.

The first "replacement group" in the Peace Corps is about to complete training for service in Colombia. Should we send these volunteers to fill the shoes of their predecessors in the villages which are now moving ahead, albeit shakily? Or should we send the volunteers to new communities where nothing has been done? We know that more is needed than two years of work by a North American and his Colombian co-workers to effect self-perpetuating change. On the other hand, we do not want the volunteer to become a crutch in a community's life. Some of the new volunteers in Colombia will, therefore, try to follow through with their predecessor's work, but others will take on villages where no American has served. In the meantime we are planning to study what happens in those towns where volunteers are not replaced.

Earlier I mentioned there has been a change in the nature of comment and criticism about the Peace Corps. In the beginning, the doubters worried about the callowness of youth and the ability of mortals to make any good idea work. The more recent criticism is more sophisticated and more substantive. Eric Sevareid recently observed: "While the Corps has something to do with spot benefits in a few isolated places, whether in sanitizing drinking water or building culverts, its work has, and can have, very little to do with the fundamental investments, reorganizations and reforms upon which the true and long-term economic development of backward countries depends." Mr. Sevareid acknowledges that "giving frustrated American youth a sense of mission and adding to our supply of comprehension of other societies fatten the credit side of the ledger." He adds: "If fringe benefits were all the Corps' originators had in mind, then this should be made clear to the country." I do not agree with him that the second and third purposes of the Peace Corps Act—representing America abroad in the best sense and giving Americans an opportunity to learn about other societies—are "fringe benefits." Fulton Freeman, the United States Ambassador in Colombia, believes the whole Peace Corps program could be justified by its creation of a new American resource in the volunteers who are acquiring language skills and intensive understanding of a foreign society. Former volunteers will be entering government service (150 have already applied to join U.S.I.A.), United Nations agencies, academic life, international business concerns and a host of other institutions which carry on the business of the United States throughout the world. Others will return to their homes, capable of exerting an enlightened influence in the communities where they settle. Many trite euphemisms of the ignorant and ready panaceas of the uninformed will clash immediately with the harsh facts that volunteers have learned to live with abroad.

Is the second purpose of the Peace Corps Act—to be a good representative of our society—a "fringe benefit"? Peace Corps

Volunteers are reaching the people of foreign countries on an individual basis at a different level from the influence of most Americans abroad. The Peace Corps Volunteer lives under local laws, buys his supplies at local stores and makes his friends among local people. He leaves to the diplomat and the technicians the complex tools which are peculiarly their own while he sets out to work in the local environment as he finds it.

I am not suggesting that life for the volunteer is always hard. A visiting Ghanaian said: "The Peace Corps teachers in my country don't live so badly. After all, they live as well as we do." I agree that this is not so bad; nor is our objective discomfort for discomfort's sake, but rather a willingness to share the life of another people, to accept sacrifice when sacrifice is necessary and to show that material privilege has not become the central and indispensable ingredient in an American's life. It is interesting to note that the happiest volunteers are usually those with the most difficult living conditions.

Although I disagree with Mr. Sevareid's emphasis in dismissing two of the three purposes of the Peace Corps Act as "fringe benefits," he does get to the heart of an important question when he compares the direct economic impact of the Peace Corps to fundamental investments, reorganizations and economic development. The Peace Corps' contribution has been less in direct economic development than in social development—health, education, construction and community organization. We are convinced that economic development directly depends on social development. In his valedictory report this past April as head of the Economic Commission for Latin America, Raul Prebisch observed that there are *not* "grounds for expecting that economic development will take place first and be followed in the natural course of events by social development. Both social and economic development must be achieved in measures that require the exercise of rational and deliberate action. . . . There can be no speed-up in economic development without a change in the social structure." While they have their differences, Theodore W. Schultz and J. Kenneth Galbraith have no disagreement on the essential role of social development in economic progress. In contrast, some who argue from the European-North American experience overlook the vital need for social development which had already been substantially achieved in the countries of the Atlantic community. This is the basic difference between the problem of the Marshall Plan, which was concerned with economic reconstruction in societies with abundant social resources, and the problem of forced-draft economic development in much of Asia, Africa and Latin America.

Notwithstanding the Peace Corps' primary emphasis on social development, volunteers are making a direct economic contribution in a variety of situations. They are helping to organize farmers' coöperatives in Chile, Ecuador and Pakistan; credit unions and savings and loan associations in Latin America; demonstration farms in the Near East. A group of volunteers in the Punjab sparked the creation of a poultry industry of some economic significance (using ground termite mounds for protein feed). These are "grass roots" projects. More of them will someday cause us to look back and wonder why it took so long to discover that people—human hands and enthusiasms—are an essential part of the relationship of mutual assistance which we must establish with our neighbors abroad.

The Peace Corps is not a "foreign aid" agency. Two of the three purposes of the Peace Corps as defined in the Act deal with understanding, not economic assistance. Moreover, our financial investment is in the volunteer who brings his skills and knowledge home with him. Seventy-five percent of the Peace Corps' appropriated funds enters the economy of the United States; of the remaining 25 percent, more than half (57 percent) is spent on American citizens, the Peace Corps Volunteers themselves.

A Jamaican radio commentator recently asserted that "a great distance between people is the best creator of good will. Jumble people up together on a sort of temporary basis of gratitude on one side and condescension on the other, and you'll have everyone at each other's throat in no time." If I believed this were inevitable, regardless of the attitude, preparation and mode of life of volunteers, I would advocate disbanding the Peace Corps—as well as most other programs overseas. But I have greater faith in the universality of men's aspirations and of men's ability to respect each other when they know each other. It is the American who lives abroad in isolation and the thoughtless tourist who create distrust and dislike.

I believe the Peace Corps is also having more impact than we may realize on our own society and among our own people. To take an example of the Peace Corps' impact on an institution, the President of the State University of Iowa, Virgil M. Hancher, recently observed:

The Peace Corps project (training Volunteers for Indonesia) is already having salutary effects upon this University, and these seem likely to be residual. The members of our faculty are having to come together across disciplines. They are having to think through old problems of education freshly and to tackle new ones. Along with the trainees, they are learning—learning how to teach languages in the new method, how to teach new languages, how to teach area studies better, and how to adapt old and test new methods. The project is deepening the international dimension of the State University of Iowa. This international dimension is being shared, in various ways, with the people of the state, the eastern area in particular.

American schools and students may soon benefit from the Peace Corps' initiative in another fashion. Two countries, Ghana and Argentina, have expressed interest in making the Peace Corps a two-way street by sending volunteer teachers of special competence to interested American high schools or colleges. Ghana would provide experts in African history and Argentina teachers of Spanish. Other countries may follow suit.

Our own Peace Corps Volunteers are being changed in other ways in the acquisition of languages and expertise. They will be coming home more mature, with a new outlook toward life and work. Like many other Americans, I have wondered whether our contemporary society, with its emphasis on the organizational man and the easy life, can continue to produce the self-reliance, initiative and independence that we consider to be part of our heritage. We have been in danger of losing ourselves among the motorized toothbrushes, tranquilizers and television commercials. Will Durant once observed that nations are born stoic and die epicurean; we have been in danger of this happening to us. The Peace Corps is truly a new frontier in the sense that it provides the challenge to self-reliance and independent action which the vanished frontier once provided on our own continent. Sharing in the progress of other countries helps us to rediscover ourselves at home.

The influence of the Peace Corps idea might be described as a series of widening circles, like the expanding rings from a stone thrown into a pond. The inner, most sharply defined circle represents the immediate effect of the program—accomplishments abroad in social and economic development, skills, knowledge, understanding, institution-building, a framework for coöperative effort with private organizations, research and experiment in "overseas Americanship," language training and improvements in health.

The second ring moving outward on the water might be the Peace Corps' influence on our society, on institutions and people, on the creation of a new sense of participation in world events, an influence on the national sense of purpose, self-reliance and an expanded concept of volunteer service in time of peace.

There is still a wider circle and, being farthest from the splash, the hardest to make out clearly. Perhaps I can explain it by describing the relationships I see between the Peace Corps and our American Revolution. The Revolution placed on our citizens the responsibility for reordering their own social structure. It was a triumph over the idea that man is incompetent or incapable of shaping his destiny. It was our declaration of the irresistible strength of a universal idea connected with human dignity, hope, compassion and freedom. The idea was not simply American, of course, but arose from a confluence of history, geography and the genius of a resolute few at Philadelphia.

We still have our vision, but our society has been drifting away from the world's majority: the young and raw, the colored, the hungry and the oppressed. The Peace Corps is helping to put us again where we belong. It is our newest hope for rejoining the majority of the world without at the same time betraying our cultural, historic, political and spiritual ancestors and allies. As Pablo Casals, the renowned cellist and democrat, said of the Peace Corps last year: "This is new, and it is also very old. We have come from the tyranny of the enormous, awesome, discordant machine, back to a realization that the beginning and the end are man—that it is man who is important, not the machine, and that it is man who accounts for growth, not just dollars and factories. Above all, that it is man who is the object of all our efforts."

Part Four

Accommodation–Alternative to Annihilation

CHAPTER XIII

Disarmament Negotiations

The spread of nuclear weapons and weapons technology to non-nuclear nations constitutes a grave threat to the security and peace of all nations, large and small, nuclear and nonnuclear.

—WILLIAM C. FOSTER

Time flies quickly, new factors appear that intensify instead of reduce the danger, and a revision and modification of policy in the field of disarmament cannot be postponed without jeopardizing the security of the peoples and the interests of general peace.

—PRAVDA

The world of the mid-twentieth century hangs by the "single hair" of the Damocles sword. An uncontrolled arms race among nations, especially between the United States and the Soviet Union, may ultimately serve to cut that hair. President Kennedy once said: "No sane society chooses to commit national suicide. Yet that is the fate which the arms race has in store for us. . . . The price of running this race to the end is death."

The awesome reality of the possible annihilation of all humanity lends an unprecedented urgency to the quest for disarmament. World leaders must realize the virtual certainty that another world war with modern weapons will destroy all civilization. Realizing further that war as a way of resolving international disputes is obsolete and suicidal, they therefore must find a way to destroy the means of destruction.

Yet, because of the intrinsic distrust and discord in international power politics, nations of the world pursue mutually contradicting dual policies—favoring control of force on the one hand and seeking expansion of force on the other—that make a workable general disarmament impossible. As long as there is no satisfactory agreement on disarmament among nations, each country will continue to build up the armed power deemed necessary to protect the national security and to deter a would-be aggressor. The policy of deterrence, such as both the United States and the Soviet Union have been pursuing, has been able to preserve peace, but it is only a temporary "second-best" to disarmament; it has an inherent danger of becoming added provocation, accentuating the arms race and running counter to disarmament efforts.

This chapter is devoted to showing some basic problems, difficulties, and feasibilities involved in disarmament and arms control.

Edward Teller, Professor of Physics at the University of California, addresses himself to the problem of nuclear proliferation, discusses the difficulties in detecting nuclear explosions underground and in space, advocates the use of tactical nuclear weapons in limited nuclear warfare, and supports the proposition that all secrecy concerning technical and scientific information should be discarded.

The United States Arms Control and Disarmament Agency presents descriptive studies on the arms control concept, the US-Soviet joint statement of agreed principles for disarmament, the UN study on economic consequences of disarmament, and the concept and elements of the United States disarmament plan.

William C. Foster, Director of United States Arms Control and Disarmament Agency, testifying before the Senate Committee on Foreign Relations, clarifies objectives and general categories of arms control and emphasizes the importance of research to help achieve satisfactory regulation of armament.

1. THE FEASIBILITY OF ARMS CONTROL AND THE PRINCIPLE OF OPENNESS*

BY EDWARD TELLER

There are many well-known arguments both for and against arms control. Perhaps the strongest driving force toward arms control is the conviction that without it a world catastrophe of unimaginable

* From *Arms Control, Disarmament, and National Security*, Donald G. Brennan, ed. (New York: George Braziller, 1961), pp. 122–137. Copyright © 1961 by George Braziller, Inc., and the American Academy of Arts and Sciences; reprinted by their permission.

magnitude cannot be prevented. It is hoped that an arms-control agreement can prevent the further spread of the knowledge of nuclear explosives. It is argued that arms control is in the interest of both the Russians and ourselves, and therefore we can come to an agreement. It is hoped that arms control will be a first step toward increasingly friendly relations and genuine cooperation between all people in the world.

On the other hand, arms control may well lead to a change in the balance of power with the result that the Russians could gain overwhelming superiority. This can happen by reducing those categories of arms in which we enjoy an advantage. Or else it may happen that the arms-control agreement cannot be enforced; it may then be observed only by our side but not by the Communists.

Finally, it may be urged that the regulations and the policing which will have to accompany arms control will give rise to suspicions and to friction. Thus arms control would become a source of irritation rather than a first step toward peace.

There is no doubt in my mind that human contacts between all people will promote the cause of peace. This is particularly true if these human contacts lead to positive and valuable accomplishments. Joint work on medical problems or on the exploration of our globe and the oceans of air and water are cases in point.

On the other hand, it is undeniable that disarmament may lead to frustration, friction, and failure. Therefore, there is at least some doubt whether or not arms control is the proper first step in creating a peaceful atmosphere. . . .

A short time ago we were worried about the fourth-nation problem. We are now faced with the fifth-nation problem. How long or how short a time will it be before this turns into the sixth- or seventh-nation problem? It has been claimed that the cessation of nuclear testing is the only hope we have for limiting the number of nuclear powers. I wonder whether this hope is realistic.

We like to believe that to produce nuclear weapons requires great skill. We imagine that there is a secret of nuclear weapons which we can continue to guard. The fact is that every nation which obtained a sufficient amount of nuclear explosive found out within a very short time how to make nuclear bombs. The really difficult step is the production of plutonium or some equivalent substance. After one has this substance, the rest is relatively easy.

Unfortunately, the production of nuclear explosives is closely connected with the peaceful use of nuclear reactors. We have powerfully assisted in the spread of the knowledge of nuclear reactors throughout the world. We were right in doing so. Otherwise, the world would have bypassed us. But in accepting the unavoidable we have handed to the nations of the world more than peaceful nuclear power. We have also handed them the key to the atomic bomb. This is unpleasant, but it is a fact. . . .

In the long run it is impractical to limit the knowledge of nuclear weapons to the advanced democracies. The significant fact, however, is that we have some time in which to solve the urgent problem of atomic control among the democracies. Once this has been done, an example and a nucleus will have been created. On the basis of such a new experience in international cooperation we might then be in better position to find the proper way to share full knowledge of nuclear technology with additional nations.

The spread of knowledge is unavoidable. The only practical hope we can have is to find ways of directing and influencing a process which, in the long run, we shall be unable to prevent. If we fully realize that the difficulty is unavoidable, the difficulty itself may become a stimulus. The secret of the atomic bomb is vanishing. If we face this problem, we might make a great and necessary contribution toward constructing a better world. . . .

In the summer of 1958 experts from the Soviet bloc and from several Western countries, including the United States and the United Kingdom, recommended a system of controls for atmospheric testing. With the help of a moderate number of stations distributed throughout the world and within each of the bigger countries and with the further help of appropriately planned airplane flights, nuclear tests can be policed down to a strength of one kiloton. Even smaller explosions might be noticed, and violators would have to count seriously on the possibility that their acts will be detected.

A similarly favorable technical situation was reported for testing in the oceans. The acoustic signals from underwater tests can be picked up with ease and it seems possible to pick up the radioactivity deposited in the water and thereby to verify that a nuclear explosion has been detonated.

Unfortunately, the observation of underground tests encounters much more serious difficulties. One is that the crust of the earth is a noisy medium. It is hard to distinguish nuclear explosions from the normal noise caused by major or minor earthquakes.

The second is that radioactivity from an underground test is confined to a distance of about one hundred feet or at best a few hundred feet from the explosion point. On the other hand, the uncertainty in locating the event amounts to several miles. To verify by inspection becomes difficult. In the end it boils down to an intelligence operation which must be aimed at tracing the preparations for the nuclear explosion and at finding the actual shafts through which the nuclear explosive had been put into position.

The final difficulty is that nuclear explosions can be muffled. If this is done, they will emit a greatly reduced seismic signal which is exceedingly hard to distinguish from quite minor disturbances in the earth's crust. With the simplest procedures it is possible to reduce the seismic signal by a factor of 300.

The present situation is best characterized by the fact that surveillance of muffled nuclear explosions above twenty kilotons will necessitate 600 seismic stations in the Soviet Union alone. (It is quite possible that many of these stations could be unmanned.) This would have to be accompanied by an extremely high number of on-the-spot inspections. Probably many inspections per day would be required.* The only way that has been proposed to re-establish effective control is to discover by intelligence operations the activities of preparing a site for muffled nuclear explosions. It happens that these preparations are not necessarily conspicuous. Therefore we are led back all along the line to a reliance on intelligence.

The hope that purely technical means will allow us to establish easy control of nuclear tests has not proved well-founded. Big nuclear explosions—above hundreds of thousands of tons of TNT equivalent—can be noticed and identified. Below one hundred kilotons detection of underground shots is dubious, and below twenty kilotons, the detection seems at present practically impossible.

The situation is no better for testing in interplanetary space. One can send out a rocket containing a nuclear warhead and also equipment for detection and communication. The rocket should be fired in such a way as to leave the gravitational field of the earth. After

---

* The argument assumes that cavities in limestone can be constructed in a reasonably expeditious manner and that muffling is not limited by the occurrence of salt formations.

waiting until the rocket reaches a distance comparable to that between the earth and the sun, it should be separated into a portion containing the explosive and another portion containing the rest of the equipment. These two portions should be allowed to drift apart to a distance of approximately ten miles. Then the bomb would explode and the package containing the apparatus would perform its function of observation and coded reporting.

It has been established through careful discussions that this type of operation is feasible. It has also been established that by using this method and by establishing appropriate procedures of concealment nuclear explosions up to the size of five hundred kilotons or half a megaton can be carried out without chance of detection. These discussions were based on optimistic assumptions concerning the background of radiation in space and therefore concerning the possibility of detection. It is entirely possible that even bigger explosions in space can be concealed. Therefore, nuclear explosions underground and in interplanetary space could be carried out up to a considerable size even if we assume that the best possible controls known today have been established.

There is one way in which nuclear explosions in interplanetary space could be policed in an adequate manner. One could establish a limited number of stations throughout the world which will reliably detect the firing of any outgoing space vehicle. It could then be agreed that every outgoing rocket would be inspected before it is fired. In this way we could be certain that no nuclear devices will leave the earth. Unfortunately, the Russians have rejected suggestions of this type. Therefore, the only plan of policing interplanetary tests which is feasible from a technical point of view is at present excluded because of the attitude of the Soviet government.

It is not obvious to me why this point has not been emphasized more strongly both in the Geneva discussions and in the American press. The on-site inspection of underground shots has developed into a crucial issue. Yet these inspections, even if they were granted in sufficient numbers, would turn out to be difficult and possibly futile. On the other hand, another big area of possible evasion could be adequately policed by a simple and straightforward method. It is this area in which Soviet technology is known to be ahead. Why do we focus our attention almost exclusively on the prevention of underground testing and neglect the parallel issue of testing in interplanetary space?

At the present time no world-wide system of control exists, and it will be several years before such a system could be put into effect. We could start constructing seismic stations in the United States, England, and Russia as soon as an agreement is signed. To establish the right kind of stations will be a lengthy job even in these three countries. However, it is clear that the inspection system will have to be extended to China, and this will take further time. Finally, if outgoing rockets are not inspected, the policing of interplanetary shots makes it necessary to establish an expensive and intricate system of well-equipped observational satellites. At present these satellites are not even designed. . . .

It is believed that in 1945 we found the secret of the atom bomb; in the early 1950's we developed the hydrogen bomb; and this ends the story. It is important to emphasize that this picture is false. In fact, each year has added its discoveries, and it is the cumulative results which have produced the present situation. It is accurate to state that, in comparison with the nuclear weapons of 1960, those of 1950 appear completely obsolete. If the development should continue, there is no doubt that in 1970 nuclear explosives can be produced compared to which our present weapons will appear similarly outdated.

Most people believe that any such further development in nuclear weapons is of no importance. It is the general opinion that we have reached a state of saturation. We have enough weapons to destroy the world. Why should we want more? Indeed, we do have enough weapons to destroy the world if we strike the first blow. But this we do not intend to do. In fact, we should make very sure that we shall never do this nor be tempted to do it. If, on the other hand, our nuclear weapons are to survive a Soviet attack and be available for retaliation, then it is questionable whether we have the right kind of weapons to perform this task. Similarly, if nuclear weapons are to be developed into discriminating instruments of tactical warfare, much remains to be done.

The idea of massive retaliation is impractical and immoral. It has caused considerable damage to our position in the world. We have announced that an infraction of the peace, even if were not a major infraction, might give us cause to strike back at Russia with devastating weapons. Such an action, which responds to evil with much greater evil, is contrary to our sense of justice. We did not put this policy into execution. I doubt whether we ever seriously intended to do so. Today we know that an all-out attack by us will be followed by an all-out attack from the Russians, and this will devastate our own country. It is a certainty that we shall never engage in such folly. The only result of the doctrine of massive retaliation was this: it created a militaristic picture of the United States. This picture is false. It has never had any validity. Unfortunately, it has appeared credible to many people abroad.

It is my opinion that we must not use our all-out striking power except to deter a massive blow upon the United States itself. This, however, requires that we establish what is called a second-strike force—a force which can inflict upon an aggressor intolerable destruction even after we have been attacked ourselves. If we are in the possession of such a second-strike force, we need not have a nervous trigger finger. We need not unleash our retaliation prematurely because we know that our ability to retaliate will not be destroyed.

Such a second-strike force can be created with the help of our present nuclear stockpile. However, this will be exceedingly expensive. It will cost many billions of dollars. By further nuclear testing we can reduce the weight of our nuclear explosives. This will result in smaller and more mobile missiles. The final effect will be that a second-strike force will cost a fraction of what we would have to spend for it today. Thus, a test ban will not reduce the cost of armaments. It will do the opposite: it will force us into a much more expensive program.

Massive retaliation has appeared to have one justification. It provides a shield over our allies. If we drop the idea of massive retaliation, it is necessary to find another counter-move to deter Russian nibbling. Today the Communists enjoy great military advantage: central location, superiority in massive conventional weapons and in manpower, and, finally, a political orientation which permits them to assume the initiative without any moral scruples. If we do not want the free world to succumb to piecemeal aggression, we must find a way in which these advantages can be counterbalanced.

Tactical nuclear weapons could enable us to build up a counterforce which would neutralize these Soviet advantages. Nuclear warfare makes it both necessary and possible to employ widely dispersed forces. In fact, concentration of forces in a nuclear war becomes quite impractical. At the same time light tactical nuclear weapons can be carried by small commando-type forces. These small forces are therefore in possession of very great firepower and they can accomplish the same purpose for which in previous wars we had to employ numerous troops.

It is by no means claimed that the use of tactical nuclear weapons will insure victory for our side. There can be little doubt that the Russians possess such weapons also. But, it is claimed that these small nuclear weapons will neutralize the Russian advantages of central location, massive conventional manpower, and surprise. The great power and mobility of the new weapons can be used to regain an equal chance in a limited conflict.

One can go a step beyond this point. With the help of nuclear weapons we can impose the need for extreme dispersion on the armies of an aggressor. In this way the invader will become vulnerable to guerilla tactics. Thus, we give a chance to any determined people to defend themselves if they want to do so.

But, can any nuclear war remain limited? The opposite has been asserted so often that by mere repetition it has almost assumed the status of a self-evident doctrine. Once small tactical nuclear weapons are employed—so the argument goes—the way is open for the employment of progressively bigger explosions. Eventually all-out nuclear war will follow.

The natural limitation of a nuclear war does not consist in limiting the size of nuclear explosions. The main point should be to limit the aims of the conflict and also its areas. This is the classical method by which wars have been limited in the past. In a limited conflict one should use nuclear weapons of such a size as best serves the military purpose of that conflict. In most cases the targets in a limited war will not warrant the use of big nuclear explosions. It is also most doubtful that the bombing of cities will help to win a limited war. I certainly do not consider such an employment of nuclear weapons to be helpful to our side, and I doubt that it will be considered advantageous by the Russians.

I can see no clear-cut reason why a limited nuclear war should necessarily grow into an all-out war. The assertion of this necessity is merely the Russians' way of advancing the threat of a massive retaliation. They know very well that the employment of tactical nuclear weapons would be to our great advantage. They try to use every possible means of dissuading us from using them. They are doing it more subtly by stating that all-out war is a necessary result of any use of nuclear weapons rather than by stating that all-out war will be started by their side as a measure of retaliation.

All-out war will never be in our interest, and we should never start it. If the Russians should want to embark on such a desperate enterprise, they will probably pick a time when our guard is down. While a limited nuclear war is in progress, we shall be much better prepared than in times of peace. The time of a limited nuclear conflict, therefore, would be the worst time for the Russians to launch an all-out attack.

It is my belief that limited nuclear warfare can very well stay limited. In fact, during the course of such a war danger of an all-out war will be at a minimum. Preparation for limited nuclear war is desperately needed if we are to maintain the power to defend our allies.

For all of these reasons it is necessary to continue the development of light, cheap, and flexible tactical weapons. We are at the early stages of such a development. The most important nuclear experimentations which have to accompany this development are explosions below one kiloton. During our last nuclear test series such small explosions gained a rapidly increasing importance. It is precisely these small explosions which are hardest to detect. In fact, there does not exist any realistic prospect of working out reliable detection methods, no matter how far into the future we may look.

Toward the end of World War II and in the years following Hiroshima and Nagasaki, Niels Bohr suggested a method of dealing with the problem of nuclear arms. The suggestion was clear-cut and radical. Its central part was to abandon secrecy. He strongly advocated that we return to the free discussion of discoveries and ideas which were characteristic of scientific work before World War II.

It is obvious that if freedom of information were fully established throughout the world all arms-control problems would at once become much more manageable. It would be necessary to bring about the situation where the freedom to exchange information would be guaranteed by enforceable international law. Under such conditions it would become extremely difficult to keep the development of new weapons secret, whether the development were to be pursued by testing or by other procedures. The production and deployment of weapons might become known at the same time.

Of course, this proposal could not become a reality except by a very thorough change of the world as we know it today. It would effectively mean that Russia would have to cease to be a police state. Police states cannot flourish in the full light of world publicity. Thereby a reason and perhaps the major reason of world tension would have disappeared. The possibility of arms control would become only one facet of a situation that appears to us now too wonderful to be realistic.

Nevertheless, I believe that Niels Bohr's suggestion deserves serious consideration. It strikes at the root of our difficulties. It stresses that kind of openness which is natural in free countries and which has been the lifeblood of science. In this connection, Bernhard G. Bechhoefer has pointed out to me the provision contained in Article VIII B of the Statute of the International Atomic Energy Agency. Article VIII, Sections A and B read as follows:

Each member should make available such information as would, in the judgment of the member, be helpful to the Agency.

Each member shall make available to the Agency all scientific information developed as a result of assistance extended by the Agency pursuant to article XI.

Mr. Bechhoefer adds that these provisions should be interpreted in conjunction with Article VII, paragraph F, which requires that the members of the Secretariat "shall not disclose any industrial secret or other confidential information coming to their knowledge by reason of their official duties for the Agency." What this means is that any States securing assistance—material or otherwise—from the Agency have a fairly extensive obligation to disclose their entire Atomic Energy programs; States not calling for Agency assistance— which would include the United States and the Soviet Union—have a far less extensive obligation.

The background and interpretation of these provisions are set forth in the recently published volume, entitled *Atoms and the Law* (University of Michigan, 1959), pages 1375–1376. This particular section, entitled "Atoms for Peace—The New International Atomic

Energy Agency," was written by Eric Stein and Bernhard G. Bechhoefer.

At the same time there is no doubt that serious problems will be
raised. Can we abandon secrecy in the present state of affairs? Will
such a plan not endanger our military safety? It is not true that
openness will accelerate the spread of nuclear weapons among other
nations? These questions merit thought. In my opinion they point
to the fact that a sudden and sweeping abandonment of secrecy on
the part of the United States should not be proposed. But in order to
obtain a sense of balance we should investigate the possible answers
to the questions mentioned above.

Secrecy has not prevented our most powerful enemy from developing the most powerful weapons we possess. It is not even obvious
that our secrecy measures have slowed down Soviet progress. It is
quite obvious, however, that secrecy has impeded our own work.
Because of secrecy we have had to limit the number of people who
could contribute to the development of our own weapons. Due to
secrecy it has become difficult to exchange information with our
allies. This led to duplication. It has also led to a less than complete
realism in the planning of our common defense. Secrecy has also
prevented full public discussion of the possibilities of the future
development of our weapons. The fact that most of our fellow
citizens consider nuclear explosives as weapons of terror rather than
of defense may be due to a considerable extent to secrecy. This is
only one face of the more general truth that the democratic process
does not function well in an atmosphere of secrecy.

It cannot be denied that the full publication of all nuclear facts
will aid further nations in developing nuclear explosives. However,
the gradual spread of this knowledge is unavoidable. It has been
stated above that the main limitation is the absence of nuclear materials rather than the absence of knowledge. If we can guarantee a
completely open flow of information, it will become much easier to
check the production of nuclear materials. In the long run this will
more than offset the dangers introduced by publishing the facts about
nuclear explosions.

It seems to me, therefore, that we should give most serious thought
to a gradual and well-planned abandonment of all secrecy concerning
technical and scientific facts. We should at the same time exert as
much pressure as we possibly can on every nation in the world that

they likewise permit complete freedom for the flow of information. At the present time some technical facts are subject to secrecy in many nations. We should try by every means to reverse this trend toward secrecy. Every additional secret is an obstacle to the free collaboration and the eventual union of nations. A strong and widespread condemnation of all practices of secrecy may in the long run have a strong effect even on those countries which value this form of security most. Direct influence upon the Soviet government is not likely to produce quick results. Individual Russians and particularly Russian scientists are likely to be susceptible to an approach which stresses openness together with collaboration and increasing mutual confidence. In this way we shall put ourselves in the position in which the obvious advantages of a free democracy will have the greatest effect. Instead of more restrictions and more suspicions, we shall create more freedom and more trust.

If we make progress along these lines, we may well find that arms control will become feasible. It will then become an academic question whether arms control has brought about more stability or whether greater stability has made arms control possible. The two will go hand in hand and will reinforce each other.

One can look at the problem of peace from an even more general point of view. Science and technology have made the world small. Our interrelated problems can no longer be solved on a narrow national basis. The administration has stressed this fact and has tried to proceed along the road of creating a lawful family of nations.

The need for supranational organizations is most obvious when we try to find ways by which to avoid war. But it is not only through common dangers that we are closely tied to our neighbors. Big-scale enterprises like the exploitation of atomic energy, the prediction and the eventual modification of weather, the study and cultivation of the oceans are all undertakings which are best carried forward on an international scale. It is hardly possible to do otherwise.

These positive undertakings can most easily furnish the first steps toward peace. Work toward a mutually desirable aim brings about the type of collaboration whereby no secrecy or suspicion can arise. Work along such lines can lay the foundation of friendships, and success will give the feeling of a common accomplishment on which future extended cooperation can be based.

One feeble attempt in this direction was the international geophysical year. It was a wonderful undertaking. It is a pity that it was limited to a "year" which lasted for only eighteen short months.

To state that international cooperation is difficult is to state the obvious. But we should use all possible ingenuity and determination to overcome this difficulty. We may start by close and meaningful cooperation with the NATO countries. At the same time we should work together with as many further nations as possible on projects which at first may have to be limited. Would not a yearly amount of a billion dollars be well spent on such international enterprises? Every common undertaking will help in the difficult long-range task of establishing a stable world organization which commands the loyalty of all people.

Our problem is how to insure peace and how to create a lawful world. It has been argued that only arms control can bring about a rapid solution. It is true that the more ambitious developments which I am advocating here will take a longer time. It is necessary, however, to consider this question: Is the proposed quick solution a solution at all? Is it even a step in the right direction? I believe that the road through a comprehensive and responsible world organization is longer and harder; but it is the only one that is realistic and that promises eventual success.

2. TOWARD A WORLD WITHOUT WAR*

BY ARMS CONTROL AND DISARMAMENT AGENCY

All through the decade of the 1950's the deadlock on the crucial questions of nuclear disarmament and reliable verification continued. However, nuclear weapons testing was halted in 1958, when the United States, U.S.S.R., and Great Britain each unilaterally accepted a voluntary moratorium on tests. Negotiations for a treaty banning tests permanently, under international inspection, also showed promise. But in August 1961 the U.S.S.R. announced it

* From *Toward A World Without War: A Summary of United States Disarmament Efforts—Past and Present* (Washington: Government Printing Office, 1962), pp. 7–19.

would resume testing, and meaningful progress on a test ban agreement suffered a severe setback.

The failure to stop nuclear weapons tests lent even greater urgency to new efforts to reach agreement on the broader question of disarmament. Indeed only a month after the Soviet announcement, President Kennedy in September 1961 presented to the U.N. General Assembly the broad outlines of a new comprehensive U.S. disarmament plan. This plan is based not only on the best parts of earlier proposals and studies but also on a fresh reappraisal of the whole problem made after President Kennedy took office in January 1961.

The systematic review of the disarmament question was given added impetus by the establishment in 1961 of the U.S. Arms Control and Disarmament Agency. This Agency combines activities previously carried on in several different departments and has specific responsibility for developing new approaches to disarmament and related problems. As the first governmental body anywhere to concentrate exclusively on such questions, the Disarmament Agency has brought together a highly qualified staff of experts in science, international relations, economics, and weapons systems. The work of these men and women also benefits from the many private studies and investigations which have been undertaken at U.S. universities and research institutes during the past decade. Never before have so much effort and so many resources been devoted to finding ways of stopping the arms race and building a secure peace.

American scholars have been interested in disarmament for more than half a century, but their intensive efforts started toward the end of World War II with a serious exploration of ways to control the atomic bomb. A distinguished group of scholars, scientists, and Government officials headed by David Lilienthal, the former head of the Tennessee Valley public power and reclamation project, labored for months to master the complex technical problems of the bomb and set the studious pattern for all later efforts. This group's report was the basis of the Baruch plan for international ownership of all atomic facilities.

During the 1940's and 1950's articles and books on disarmament multiplied in the United States. Institutes were established, and groups of scholars from different fields conducted broad investigations of the problem. In 1960 appeared a special 1,000-page issue of *Daedalus,* the journal of the American Academy of Arts and Sciences, devoted entirely to articles on arms control and disarmament. The foreword was written by Dr. Jerome B. Wiesner, a leading physicist with a long-standing interest in disarmament and now Special Assistant to President Kennedy for Science and Technology. A listing of the 23 contributors to the volume reveals the broad variety of authorship: three physicists, two chemists, two economists, two legal scholars, one legislator, two political scientists, one military scientist, one psychologist, two journalists, two international relations experts, two mathematicians, and one diplomat.

One of the legal scholars was Professor Louis Sohn of the Harvard Law School, who originated the idea of "zonal inspection," which has been suggested in the U.S. disarmament plan as a possible method of verification.

This intensive scholarly activity developed the "arms control" concept, which has become an important element in American thinking. The idea started with the realization that everyone's agreed goal —abolishing war—cannot be reached solely through arms reduction plans, especially since such plans seem to take so long to be agreed upon and adopted. As complex modern weapons pile up, American intellectuals argued, risks of war through accident or miscalculation increase. Arms reduction—classic "disarmament"—is simply not enough. It is equally important that the major powers *do something now* to cut the risk of war, while at the same time working for agreement on arms reduction plans.

So the concept of "arms control"—controlling, in the sense of calming, the military situation—was evolved. Arms control means measures, other than arms reduction itself, which lessen the risk of war.

"Arms control" is a twin to "arms reduction"—*not* a substitute for it. Arms control measures are *not* intended to replace arms reductions but to accompany them.

But discussions of disarmament in the United States have not been confined to the scholars. Public discussions, which are occurring with increasing frequency, have involved representatives from labor, business, the professions, and Government, as well as the universities. A number of private organizations have been formed, with varying programs, devoted to the problems of peace and disarmament.

At the United Nations, too, an atmosphere of urgency developed, and, with the active encouragement of the 15th U.N. General Assembly, U.S. and Soviet representatives in private meetings from March to September 1961 explored the basis for a new and earnest effort toward disarmament.

Out of the U.S.–U.S.S.R. discussions came the present 18-nation Geneva conference on disarmament—the most important international meeting on this question in many years. Eight new nations, representing different areas of the world, were added to the five Western and five Communist nations which had taken part in the previous negotiations. The new participants are: for Asia—India and Burma; for the Middle East—United Arab Republic; for Africa—Nigeria and Ethiopia; for Latin America—Mexico and Brazil; for Europe—Sweden.

Developments in the past year indicate that the long postwar years of negotiations and study have not been entirely fruitless. Despite much disappointment and frustration the countries concerned now have a better understanding of the problems that have hindered agreement on disarmament. There has emerged the realization that disarmament is a practical and attainable goal, not a Utopian dream; that it can begin even in the absence of mutual trust and confidence if verification procedures are adequate; and that it represents a highly complex technical, political, economic, and psychological process, which needs careful and continuous planning to succeed.

Three recent developments reflect this realistic and hopeful approach to the problem: (1) the U.S.–U.S.S.R. Joint Statement of Agreed Principles for Disarmament Negotiations of September 20, 1961; (2) the U.N. study "Economic and Social Consequences of Disarmament" of April 1962; and (3) the U.S. "Outline of Basic Provisions of a Treaty on General and Complete Disarmament in a Peaceful World,"—the most detailed and comprehensive proposal so far presented.

The U.S.–U.S.S.R. Joint Statement of Principles records agreement on a number of key issues. It states, among other things, that measures for general and complete disarmament—the goal of both nations—must include:

(1) ". . . establishment of reliable procedures for the peaceful settlement of disputes . . . [and] to strengthen institutions for maintaining peace."

(2) ". . . agreed manpower for a United Nations peace force . . . [to] deter or suppress any threat or use of arms in violation of the purposes and principles of the United Nations."

(3) ". . . disarmament . . . in an agreed sequence, by stages . . . [and] balanced so that at no stage . . . could any State . . . gain military advantage."

(4) ". . . strict and effective international control . . . [to] provide firm assurance that all parties are honouring their obligations . . . the nature and extent of such control depending on the requirements for verification . . . in each stage."

(5) ". . . an International Disarmament Organization . . . assured [of] unrestricted access without veto to all places as necessary for the purpose of effective verification."

The U.S.–U.S.S.R. Joint Statement of Agreed Principles was unanimously adopted as a United Nations resolution on December 20, 1961. Thus these became United Nations principles, furnishing a world charter for all disarmament negotiations, including the 18-nation conference at Geneva, which opened in March 1962.

The significance of these principles cannot be overestimated, for if properly applied, they contain all the elements for an effective disarmament agreement and the building of a stable peace. They recognize that war and the threat of war can be eliminated only if there are effective alternatives for settling disputes among nations; that disarmament cannot be achieved overnight but must progress through stages, creating, as it progresses, an atmosphere of mutual confidence; and lastly that effective international inspection is a legitimate and essential element of any disarmament program.

The U.N. study "Economic and Social Consequences of Disarmament" represents a milestone of a different sort in the quest for a disarmament agreement. For the first time in the many years of discussion of the problem, an international group of experts has objectively and scientifically evaluated the prospects and consequences of a disarmament agreement in economic and social terms. The group, appointed by the U.N. Secretary-General, included experts from the U.S.S.R., United States, United Kingdom, Poland, Czechoslovakia, France, Sudan, India, Pakistan, and Venezuela. These distinguished scholars examined all the available evidence on the problem, including detailed studies by a number of governments undertaken in response to the Secretary-General's inquiry, and studies by specialized agencies of the United Nations.

The group unanimously agreed that, contrary to some popular misconceptions, disarmament would *not* bring about an economic depression or large-scale unemployment, if governments took proper preventive measures. "All the problems and difficulties of transition connected with disarmament could be met by appropriate national and international measures," the report states. "There should thus be no doubt that the diversion to peaceful purposes of the resources now in military use could be accomplished to the benefit of all countries. . . . No country need fear a lack of useful employment opportunities for the resources that would become available to it through disarmament."

The experts examined in detail how the vast resources freed by disarmament might best be utilized. "There are so many competing claims," they concluded, "that the real problem is to establish a scale of priorities." The experts' report went on to list these possibilities: increased personal consumption; conversion of plants producing military equipment to production of durable consumer goods; expansion of productive capacities needed for greater consumption; more investment in social improvements such as schools, housing, and hospitals; scientific research in hitherto neglected fields; international ventures for peaceful exploitation of nuclear energy; space research; exploration of the Arctic and Antarctic; climate control; and others.

The U.S. contribution to the U.N. study went into considerable detail concerning the impact disarmament would have on the American economy. It found that the U.S. economy would benefit greatly from disarmament and that any temporary dislocations could be satisfactorily overcome by cooperative efforts of Government, business, and labor. It foresaw opportunities for a substantial increase in the American people's standard of living and ability to aid other nations as a result of the diversion of defense expenditures to consumer needs and socially beneficial projects.

But before the economic and social benefits of disarmament can be enjoyed, agreement on a disarmament plan is necessary. The United States believes it has a proposal that can be put into effect quickly, that meets the objections made to earlier plans and satisfies the security needs of all participating nations.

The new U.S. "Outline of a Treaty for General and Complete Disarmament in a Peaceful World" is wholly in accord with the U.S.–U.S.S.R. Joint Statement of Principles. First outlined by President Kennedy in his address to the U.N. General Assembly in September 1961, it was fully developed by the U.S. Arms Control and Disarmament Agency and then submitted for consideration by the 18-Nation Disarmament Conference in Geneva on April 18, 1962.

The new U.S. plan represents a "total approach" to solving the problem of war on our planet. It starts from the premise that the main objective is not the destruction of arms—important as this is—but the elimination of war and the building of a secure and lasting peace. Hence arms reduction—disarmament in the classic sense—is not treated in isolation but is made part and parcel of two other equally important elements of the peacebuilding process: (1) measures to enable the United Nations to become an effective agency for keeping the peace in a disarmed world and (2) steps to reduce the risks of war through accident or miscalculation.

Many earlier disarmament efforts had foundered because they approached arms reduction as a goal in itself, without sufficient regard for the political conditions which cause international tensions. One of the few "successful" disarmament efforts of the past, the Washington Naval Conference of 1922, for example, resulted in an agreement by France, Great Britain, Japan, Italy, and the United States to reduce their respective fleets of battleships to a fixed level. Yet this agreement, while temporarily halting a naval race in battleships, had no lasting benefit for international peace, because it was unrelated to effective peacekeeping and peacebuilding measures.

In the light of such experiences and of postwar international developments, the United States proposes a realistic, not a Utopian, plan. It does not assume that disputes and distrust among nations will vanish with a stroke of a pen on a disarmament treaty; nor does it pretend that disarmament can be achieved overnight or apart from effective international measures to safeguard the security of nations. Yet, if accepted, this plan could transform our world within a short span of years into a secure and peaceful planet.

Despite the complexity of the problem, the technique of the U.S. plan is basically simple. It is to stop the present arms race and start the world immediately on the path toward a secure world without arms. As Ambassador Arthur Dean, the U.S. delegate, put it when he presented the plan to the 18-Nation Disarmament Conference, the idea is "that the nations of the world should seize a moment in time to stop the arms race, to freeze the military situation as it then appears, and to shrink it to zero . . . like a balloon—instead of permitting more and more air to be blown into the balloon until it bursts, the air is let out of the balloon, and the balloon shrinks in simple proportion until the air is all gone."

The U.S. proposal divides the process of disarmament into three stages—the first two to be carried out in estimated 3-year periods and the last stage as promptly as possible thereafter. In order to make speedy progress possible, Stage I can begin immediately after the treaty is ratified by the U.S.S.R., the United States, and such other countries as may be agreed on. Stage II would go into effect after the measures in Stage I have been implemented and verified, when preparations for Stage II are complete, and "all militarily significant states" have joined the treaty. Stage III would commence at the completion of Stage II and after all states possessing armed forces and armaments have become parties to the treaty. This staged process is intended to protect the security interests of all participants by assuring them that they will not be disarming in good faith while others lag behind or remain outside the agreement.

The U.S. plan is based on the following elements:

1. Arms Reduction. The dismantling of the military establishments of nations begins immediately in Stage I and continues until completed in Stage III. The process of dismantling is designed to reduce as speedily as practicable the capacity of nations for waging war with nuclear and other weapons of mass destruction or with major conventional weapons. The steps for reducing the military potential extend equally to all participating nations and are so organized that they do not change the relative military strength of the participants during the disarmament process. Thus nations can proceed to disarm without fear that their relative position vis-à-vis other nations may be altered to their disadvantage. The U.S. plan provides for slashing the nuclear warmaking capacity of nations by 65 percent during the first two stages—estimated 6 years—of the treaty, and eliminating it entirely in the final stage.

2. Verification. Effective verification by an international agency to make sure that nations are carrying out their obligations is essen-

tial. In the present world atmosphere of mutual distrust and suspicion it represents the only sound guarantee nations can accept for disarming. Without such effective safeguards no nation can be certain that its national security is not being jeopardized by some unscrupulous country bent on war or conquest. Soviet Foreign Minister Gromyko stated at Geneva on March 19, 1962:

"The Soviet Union wishes to have the necessary guarantees that the disarmament obligations that have been agreed upon will be strictly carried out and that there are no loopholes which will permit the clandestine production of aggressive armaments once the process of general and complete disarmament has begun.

"Our country does not intend to take anyone at his word, least of all States which have established closed military alignments, are pursuing a policy of building up armaments and have placed their military bases as close as possible to the Soviet Union. Nor do we expect others to take us at our word."

The U.S. proposals for verification by an International Disarmament Organization (IDO) are consistent with Mr. Gromyko's analysis of the problem. They call for strict but not excessive verification—the precise amount depending on the specific disarmament measure being considered. The simpler and more limited any specific step, the simpler and more limited the verification procedure suggested.

Complex disarmament steps, however, might require more comprehensive verification procedures. Thus, a ban on production of fissionable materials which could be used to produce nuclear weapons might require disclosure of the location of all production facilities, inspection by IDO, and some check that production is not continuing clandestinely in secret facilities. Reduction of existing stockpiles of such materials, on the other hand, is a far simpler measure to verify. It would require IDO simply to supervise the destruction or transfer to peaceful purposes of a specific quantity of fissionable material.

In a further attempt to comply with the notion that the amount of inspection should be commensurate with the amount of disarmament undertaken, the U.S. plan suggests a system of progressive zonal inspection. Under this system countries would divide themselves into zones and list the military facilities or activities contained therein which are subject to verification, but not initially their precise location. Actual disclosure of location and inspection would proceed step-by-step, by opening one zone after another as disarmament progresses. By the end of Stage III, verification would extend to the entire territory of countries.

Under the U.S. plan, an International Disarmament Organization would be established within the framework of the United Nations. Its staff would be international, and its verification procedures would apply equally to all parties to the treaty. Thus it would be almost impossible for any country to gain an advantage over another by controlling or otherwise distorting the work of IDO.

3. Reducing Risk of War. Control over existing armaments and armed forces can be as important initially in preserving the peace as the destruction of weapons or liquidation of forces. It constitutes a step toward the reduction and eventual elimination of the military establishments.

Under the U.S. plan practical measures are proposed to prevent surprise attack, or war through accident, failure of communications, or miscalculation. When weapons of terrible destructiveness can be triggered on short notice, nations need the protection these measures offer, even while they progress toward complete disarmament.

Such measures, which reflect the importance of the "arms control" concept as it has developed in the United States, can be put into effect immediately and independent of actual disarmament measures. They would include, for example, banning nuclear weapons tests, stopping production of fissionable material suitable for nuclear weapons, and organizing U.N. Peace Observation teams to check on possible conflict. Their goal would be to initiate a halt in the arms race and reduce the dangers of accidental war. Indeed, by increasing mutual trust and security, such arms control measures would help to speed agreement on arms reductions and make countries more willing to continue the process of disarming once it has begun.

4. Keeping the Peace. International arrangements for keeping the peace and for settling disputes among nations must keep pace with measures for slashing arms and armies and reducing the risks of war. The U.S. plan provides for the international community to develop new and effective instruments for dealing with disputes among nations. In particular, the plan proposes to expand and strengthen international peacekeeping arrangements through such new instruments as a U.N. Peace Force, a U.N. Peace Observation Corps, and a Code of International Conduct.

Such peacekeeping arrangements would advance simultaneously

and proportionately with the dismantling of national military establishments. As the warmaking power of nations declined, the peacemaking power of the international community grows.

5. Studies for the Future. The present U.S. plan is the product of hundreds of scholars, scientists, and military experts who have studied the problem for years. It is more concrete than any disarmament plan ever presented before. Yet it is only a beginning in the systematic search for the means necessary to create a society without war. The international community will have to come to grips with such problems as disposing safely of the vast quantities of nuclear weapons to be destroyed, converting nuclear material stockpiles to peaceful uses, liquidating stockpiles and halting production of chemical and biological weapons, devising measures to guard against surprise attack or accidental war, and improving the machinery for peaceful settlement of disputes.

Studying these questions and coming up with appropriate solutions is a vital element in the disarmament process. The U.S. plan identifies some of the most important problems and proposes the machinery so that man's intelligence can be applied to their solution.

3. ARMS CONTROL AND RESEARCH*

BY WILLIAM C. FOSTER

MR. FOSTER. Thank you, Mr. Chairman. I am glad to have the opportunity to appear before you and the other members of the committee today in support of S. 672, which would extend the Arms Control and Disarmament Agency's authorization for appropriations.

This legislation would authorize appropriations totaling $55 million over the 4-year period of fiscal years 1966 through 1969. Our current 2-year authorization expires next June 30.

Four American Presidents since World War II have been deeply concerned with arms control.

* From *Hearings Before the Committee on Foreign Relations, United States Senate,* 89th Cong., 1st Sess. (February 22 and 23, 1965), pp. 2–8.

They have understood that mounting stockpiles of nuclear weapons cannot alone insure our security. They have realized that military preparedness is not in itself sufficient to assure peace. They have accepted the reality that nuclear war is senseless when a single nuclear weapon can contain more explosive force than all the bombs dropped in World War II.

Perhaps there is a measure of progress in the fact that these long-held American views are being accepted by an increasing number of other governments, including, I believe, the new leaders of the Soviet Union. It is this fact which gives us realistic hope that prudent agreements to avoid catastrophe are possible.

The nature of the modern arms race is vividly shown by Secretary McNamara's testimony last week. His estimate is that, against the forces we expect the Soviets to have during the next decade, we would find it virtually impossible to provide anything like complete protection for our population no matter how large our nuclear forces were.

By spending up to 25 billion additional dollars for defense, we might, he says, reduce our fatalities from around 150 million to perhaps 80 million—assuming 1970 population and force levels. But, by increasing their offensive missile forces, the Soviets could prevent us from achieving even this level of protection. And, they could do it at far less extra expense to them for the offensive forces than the extra cost to us for the defense.

This sort of arms race would be madness. Both sides have an interest in preventing it. And, one of this Agency's immediate tasks is to do everything possible to keep it from occurring.

Arms control measures can maintain military balance at a fixed level, or on a downward plane, rather than on an upward spiral.

They can thus offer a means of correcting a situation in which a disproportionate amount of our national resources goes into armaments.

And, if they can slow down the nuclear buildup, and inhibit the further spread of nuclear weapons, they can both reduce the chances of nuclear war and the devastation such a war would bring.

With these objectives in mind, arms control and reduction measures can be generally categorized in one or more of the following ways:

First are those ways which reduce the chances that war will break out because of accident, miscalculation, or surprise attack. The hot line which improves rapid communications between Washington and Moscow fits in this category. So do proposals for observation posts at rail junctions, highway terminals, and sea or air ports.

Second are measures which would halt increases in nuclear war-making capabilities. The freeze on numbers and types of strategic aircraft and missiles for delivering nuclear weapons is such a proposal. It was suggested by President Johnson in a message to the Geneva Conference last year.

Also in this category is the proposal for a cutoff in production of fissionable material for nuclear weapons. Both this and the freeze are what we sometimes call nonarmament, in that they would reduce the armaments which would otherwise come into being in the future.

Third are measures which attempt to halt the spread of nuclear weapons. These are frequently classified as nonproliferation, but they are in a sense nonarmament as well.

The test ban treaty falls into this category because it helps inhibit the spread of nuclear weapons into the control of additional nations. The Antarctic treaty prevents their spread to that region of the world. The U.N. resolution against weapons of mass destruction in orbit helps keep them out of space.

The measures in the nonproliferation category are the most urgent before the Agency today. The problem of nuclear spread has been made more immediate by the Communist Chinese explosion and the rapidly developing capability of other countries to follow the Chinese example.

To curb nuclear spread we will seek agreement this year—

That nations which have nuclear weapons not transfer them into the national control of nations which do not, and that nations which do not have them not acquire them either by transfer or by manufacture;

That all transfers of nuclear materials and equipment for peaceful purposes take place under effective international safeguards;

That such safeguards be applied in increasing measure to the peaceful nuclear activities of all nations;

That nuclear weapon tests of every kind—below ground as well as above—be halted under verified agreements.

The last of the four categories contains measures which propose actual reductions in world armaments. Such proposals range from comprehensive plans for the reduction of all major armaments to the suggestion that equal numbers of U.S. B–47's and Soviet TU–16's be destroyed. Within this broad range there is room for a variety of proposals, some of which may well be in the mutual interests of both East and West.

I should point out, however, that the explosion of a nuclear device by Communist China reemphasizes the fact that the world is no longer bipolar. And, although they may be slow in achieving it, we cannot expect that the Chinese will not eventually acquire a delivery system for their bomb. This is a disturbing long-range prospect, particularly for our friends in Asia. Furthermore, for both ourselves and the Soviets, it puts limits upon the amount by which we can reduce arms and still protect ourselves and our friends from Chinese aggression.

Having described some of our objectives, I would like to indicate how contract and in-house research may help achieve these objectives.

Research clearly contributed to the limited nuclear test ban treaty, the "hot line" between Washington and Moscow, and the U.N. resolution against the orbiting of nuclear weapons. Research defined the scope of the measures we would propose, the verification necessary, and the impact upon our national security. Research gave us confidence in each case that what we planned was in our national interest.

Research also supported the measures proposed to the Geneva Disarmament Conference in 1964. These included some of the more far-reaching arms control measures yet to come before that body. The five-point program suggested by the President at the beginning of the year aimed directly at stopping the spread of nuclear weapons and at preventing any further East-West buildup of stockpiles of strategic delivery vehicles. A key element of it was the "freeze" on missiles and bombers.

Over 15 separate contract and "in-house" studies were undertaken in connection with this proposal. Research is continuing as increasingly complex problems arise.

The beginnings can be traced to a 1961 panel of Government and outside experts who studied various ideas for limiting the nuclear delivery vehicles arms race. In 1962, two contracts were let to examine basic questions which had arisen. These questions included: how can the production of long-range missiles and bombers be controlled by international agreement; and what inspection techniques and instruments can be used to monitor allowed production and to spot possible clandestine production?

These early contracts contributed importantly to the Agency's fund of knowledge about nuclear delivery vehicles. Both were completed in early 1963.

Other studies followed. One contract investigated controls on missile testing, essential to the development of new weapons types. Another contract sought to determine how early in the development process of missiles and space programs controls could be imposed for the most dependable verification.

These contracts were supplemented by technical studies made by the Agency's own scientific staff to seek negotiable verification procedures fully adequate to protect U.S. security. These efforts led to the idea that limitations on strategic nuclear vehicles might be possible as a separate measure, not linked to agreement on a comprehensive disarmament program. The next step was to examine the feasibility of such a separable production freeze.

Intensive work in the Agency transformed the idea of the freeze into an exploratory program. Its provisions were developed. A verification system which could preempt possibilities for cheating was conceived. The implications of the measure for U.S. security and weapons development were analyzed. In the process other increasingly complicated research needs also emerged.

By the beginning of 1964 the Committee of Principals had thoroughly considered the proposal and recommended it to the President, who in turn approved it for exploration at Geneva. During the summer the U.S. delegation was able to describe to the other members of the Conference illustrative verification concepts for the freeze.

Work related to the freeze is continuing. A contractor is studying controls on testing new developments in military missiles and space vehicles in order to design effective verification at this stage. In-house research is analyzing and refining problems of control over the characteristics of nuclear delivery vehicles. In addition, a 6-month series of field tests was initiated to prove out and perfect inspection methods on Titan and Polaris missile production plants.

Because of the urgent need to halt the spread of nuclear weapons, much Agency research effort—particularly in 1964 and 1965—has been devoted to this problem. Major emphasis has been placed on possible international agreements to prevent proliferation and on expansion of the use of well-developed international safeguards against diversion of fissionable materials to weapons use. Because space vehicles for peaceful uses will continue to develop, the possibility of such space programs being used for military purposes in violation of an agreement is under the scrutiny of a research contract.

A number of contract studies have been concerned with reducing the risk of war by miscalculation or surprise attack.

These include—

(1) An examination of the functions of observation posts;

(2) How to detect and identify indicators of military threat at such posts; and

(3) The basic processes of escalation and deescalation of conflicts.

The area of research to which the Agency has allocated the most funds is verification and inspection. Procedures to assure compliance with a variety of possible agreements have been studied. Several have already been field-tested and refined under Project Cloud Gap, a joint effort with the Department of Defense.

In the economic impact field, the Agency has engaged in a number of contract studies, some in conjunction with other Government agencies.

In these studies, we are trying to measure the distribution of defense production and employment. We seek to analyze defense labor reemployment or "mobility." And, we are attempting to determine possible impacts of reduced defense demand on specific industries, segments of the economy, and regions of the country.

The Agency has prepared plans for a study contract analyzing the actual consequences of the closing of a representative sample of the 95 defense installations announced by Secretary McNamara last November. This study would examine particularly the experience of employees with respect to subsequent employment, the use to which the physical facilities were put, and the effect on the community or area in which the installation was located. Such studies can be used in the future by both Government and private industry to minimize harmful effects of changes in defense spending whether or not they result from arms control measures.

ACDA had no connection with or responsibility for the decisions to close these installations. However, it does have responsibility for studying what the economic impact of arms control or disarmament agreements might be (sec. 31(h) of the Arms Control and Disarmament Act). While the base closings do not result from such an agreement, their impact is probably the same as if they did.

In the years immediately ahead, increased funds are planned for contract research in most of the main areas of interest I have described. Next year, for example, economic impact research would receive an increase of about a half million dollars. A similar addition would go to research on measures to reduce the risk of war by accident or design.

Next year, for the first time, the design of special monitoring instruments for the freeze and similar measures would become a major part of the Agency's program. Another increase of about one-half a million dollars would be devoted to this area.

Finally, major increases would be allocated to the field-testing of inspection plans, and to the shaping of nonproliferation and related arms control measures. . . .

The task of pursuing realistic arms control measures requires a great range of knowledge if our national interest is to be adequately protected. That knowledge must come, in large part, from the Agency's research program. We have allocated approximately two-thirds of the money requested to this program.

Through its research, the Agency seeks—

First, to evaluate the feasibility of arms control and reduction concepts in today's world and in the future;

Second, to shape realistic measures both to control and reduce arms and to lessen the risk of war by accident or design;

Third, to develop and test verification procedures to assure compliance with such measures; and

Fourth, to appraise the political, economic and military impact possible measures might have.

To provide more effectively for the conduct of this research, the President has asked Congress for a 4-year authorization.

There is nothing unusual about a long-term authorization. In fact, we are the only Agency in the State, Justice, Commerce, Judiciary, and related agencies appropriations bill which regularly needs a new authorization just to stay in business.

A 4-year authorization would, first of all, permit longer range research and planning by the Agency and its contractors.

No one believes the problems the Agency was set up to deal with will be solved in a year or so. Long-continued effort is indispensable to progress in this field. And, if the Government wishes to commit key people and important institutions to such an effort, it should itself be prepared to indicate that funds will be available for more than a year or two.

Major research concerns, both profit and nonprofit, will more readily devote their funds to setting up or continuing arms control groups to bid and work on our contracts if they know that money has been authorized for at least 4 years.

Within the Agency itself, it will be easier to get and keep key staff experts if the Agency has a longer authorization.

Secondly, a 4-year authorization would let the world know that we intend to give even greater emphasis to long-range planning for peace at a time when tensions have increased.

This committee said in recommending the creation of the Agency during the Berlin crisis in 1961:

. . . [I]ncreased tensions make it more essential than ever before for the United States to devote a substantial effort to determine conditions under which some international agreement for the control of arms might be developed.

This is as true today as it was in 1961. We must demonstrate again that, to use the President's phrase, "Our guard is up, but our hand is out."

We live in a world of recurring crises. In a world confronted by an uncontrolled arms race and the increasing threat of nuclear spread, each new crisis is more dangerous than the last.

We all know that in a general nuclear war there could be no victors. But this knowledge, of itself, does not lessen the danger. The crises of the past and of the present emphasize the need of positive measures to reduce the risk and devastation of war.

These are what we are in business to seek.

Thank you very much, Mr. Chairman.

The CHAIRMAN. Thank you, Mr. Foster.

I would like to insert in the record a very short staff memorandum giving the background of authorizations and appropriations for the Agency just for the information of the Senate.

(The document referred to follows:)

STAFF MEMORANDUM

H.R. 2998 (S. 672), "To amend the Arms Control and Disarmament Act, as amended, in order to increase the authorization for appropriations"; H.R. 2998 passed the House, February 17; S. 672 introduced by Senator Fulbright (by request), January 22, 1965.

Purpose: The purpose of H.R. 2998 is to authorize an appropriation of $40 million for fiscal years 1966–68 for the Arms Control and Disarmament Agency (ACDA). S. 672 would authorize $55 million for 4 years, as requested by the administration.

Background: Establishment of the Agency was proposed by President Kennedy and authorized by the Congress in 1961. An open-end authorization was requested then, but Congress instead authorized the appropriation of $10 million of no-year funds. These funds neared exhaustion in 1963, and again the administration requested an open-end authorization. The Congress agreed on a 2-year $20 million authorization. Congress has appropriated $1,831,000 (including a transfer from the State Department's Disarmament Administration) for fiscal year 1962; $6,500,000 for fiscal year 1963; $7,500,000 for fiscal year 1964; and $9 million for fiscal year 1965. The ACDA proposes to request for fiscal year 1966, $12,300,000; for fiscal year 1967, $12,700,000; for fiscal year 1968 and 1969 each, $15 million.

The ACDA's main functions are (1) to make policy recommendations to the President and the Secretary of State and prepare for and manage international negotiations, such as the 18-nation disarmament conference at Geneva; and (2) to conduct, support, and coordinate research in the field of arms control and disarmament. The Agency plans to devote 30 percent of its requested funds to the first function and 70 percent to the second.

CHAPTER XIV

The Test-Ban Treaty

*Never have the nations of the world had so much to lose or so much
to gain. Together we shall save our planet or together we shall
perish in its flames.*

—JOHN F. KENNEDY

*The need immediately to suspend the tests of various types of atomic
hydrogen weapons is one of the most urgent questions of current
international relations, a question deeply agitating the minds of
millions in all countries.*

—NIKITA S. KHRUSHCHEV

*On the historic day August 6, 1945, toward the end of
World War II, President Truman announced:*

Sixteen hours ago an American airplane dropped one bomb on Hiroshima. . . . That bomb had more than 20,000 tons of T.N.T. . . . It is
an atomic bomb. It is a harnessing of the basic power of the Universe.
. . . The fact that we can release atomic energy ushers in a new era in
man's understanding of nature's forces.

*This announcement was a declaration of the birth of the atomic
age. In his concluding statement the President said: "I shall give
further consideration and make further recommendations to the
Congress as to how atomic power can become a powerful and forceful influence towards the maintenance of world peace."*

*Less than a year later, the United States Government presented its
first comprehensive proposal, known as the Baruch Plan, calling for
the control of all atomic energy activities. This was the beginning
of a series of arduous negotiations with the Soviet Union in an effort
to achieve effective international control of the atom. With the advent
of the Soviet Union as a nuclear power, an uninhibited arms race was
run to the point where the maximum danger of total annihilation
threatened all mankind.*

The successful conclusion of the Test-Ban Treaty was a result of an understanding on both sides of the magnitude of this awesome reality. It came about because there exist certain basic elements of "mutuality of interest." The Treaty demonstrates that US-Soviet cooperation and accommodation can be achieved; that competitive coexistence is not only possible but necessary; and that this is but a first step toward de-icing the cold war. It will lead to the solution of other critical issues, and will further lessen tensions and minimize the danger of nuclear war. The Treaty may help solve the problems of nuclear proliferation, and will end atmospheric contamination by radioactive fallout. It will ease the burden of the national economy; and above all, it conforms to the desires and interests of all peoples of the world.

This chapter is designed to explore the significance and implications of the Test-Ban Treaty.

The Atomic Energy Commission presents estimations of the results of nuclear bomb explosions in terms of blast and thermal effect, initial radiation, electromagnetic disturbances on world communications, local and worldwide fallout, water waves, retinal burns, and other effects.

Premier Khrushchev explains Soviet views on the conclusion of a nuclear test-ban treaty and proposes a nonaggression pact between the NATO Powers and the Warsaw Pact nations.

Vice-President Humphrey (then Senator from Minnesota), in a speech to the Senate, discusses "the fundamental questions" relating to the Nuclear Test-Ban Treaty in favor of a ratification by the Senate. He also presents the text of the Treaty together with enlightening and informative questions and answers relevant thereto.

1. ESTIMATED EFFECTS OF NUCLEAR DETONATIONS OF VARIOUS MEGATON YIELDS*

BY ATOMIC ENERGY COMMISSION

The following estimates of the possible effects of nuclear detonations of various megaton yields are subject to many uncertainties. It is impossible to predict with any assurance of accuracy the effects of actual detonations of very high yields, particularly if they were to occur at a high altitude.

A. BLAST EFFECTS

The blast wave of a 5-megaton surface detonation would be capable of causing severe damage to residential-type structures up to a distance of about 6 miles from ground zero (8 miles for a 10-megaton surface burst, 10 miles from a 20-megaton surface burst, 12 miles for a 30-megaton surface burst, 14 miles for a 50-megaton surface burst, and 17 miles for a 100-megaton surface burst). A 5-megaton surface detonation would cause severe blast damage to reinforced concrete structures out to about 4 miles (5 miles for a 10-megaton, 6 miles for a 20-megaton, 7 miles for a 30-megaton, 8 miles for a 50-megaton, and 10 miles for a 100-megaton). For an optimum air burst for air blast effects these ranges of blast damage could be increased by 30 to 40 percent.

A 5-megaton detonation above about 35 miles (44 miles for a 10-megaton, 50 miles for a 20-megaton, 60 miles for a 30-megaton, 75 miles for a 50-megaton, 100 miles for a 100-megaton) would cause insignificant blast damage on ground structures.

B. THERMAL EFFECTS

A 5-megaton surface detonation or an air burst below 50,000 feet on a clear day could cause first-degree burns to exposed skin out to a slant range of about 25 miles (35 miles for a 10-megaton, 45 miles for a 20-megaton, 55 miles for a 30-megaton, 70 miles for a

* Atomic Energy Commission Press Release, October 31, 1961.

50-megaton, and 100 miles for a 100-megaton) and second-degree burns to exposed skin out to about 17 miles (25 miles for a 10-megaton, 32 miles for a 20-megaton, 40 miles for a 30-megaton, 50 miles for a 50-megaton, and 70 miles for a 100-megaton). Paper and various similar materials would ignite at distances of about 20 miles (30 miles for a 10-megaton, 39 miles for a 20-megaton, 47 miles for a 30-megaton, 60 miles for a 50-megaton, and 85 miles for a 100-megaton). Above about 50 miles the thermal effects on the earth's surface of a 20-megaton detonation would be negligible (60 miles for a 30-megaton, 75 miles for a 50-megaton, and 110 miles for a 100-megaton). These distances would apply only on clear days and would be materially lessened when the thermal radiation is attenuated, such as on cloudy or hazy days.

C. Initial Radiation

The initial gamma and neutron radiation expected from a nuclear explosion in the range of 5 to 100 megatons at or near the surface of the earth is not expected to be of significance when compared to the radius of damage from other effects such as blast damage or thermal radiation effects.

D. Electromagnetic Effects on World Communications

Communication blackouts due to low altitude, high yield explosions are probably too localized to be of interest. If the cloud stabilizes at an altitude of about 25 miles, however, the possibility exists of producing observable effects on radio waves over distances of about 100 miles from air zero.

As a result of a 50-megaton detonation at an altitude of about 50 miles, large scale high frequency communications blackouts could be expected within a region of 2,500 miles radius and for a time span of the order of a day. At 30 miles altitude the radius of effect would be about 1,000 miles.

For detonations at the same altitudes as above but with yields less than 50 megatons, the results would be similar but the radius of effect as well as the duration of blackouts would be less. Conversely, a 100-megaton detonation at the same altitudes as discussed for the 50-megaton burst would have a larger effects radius and a longer duration of communications blackout.

It is important to note that in order for a radio wave to be affected, the wave must pass through the disturbed region. Detonations in the Soviet Union of these yields at high altitudes would probably affect some North America to Europe communications. By increasing the altitude of detonation beyond 50 miles the radius of effects would be increased, but the duration of such communications blackouts should decrease. For a detonation of high yield at an altitude of 600 miles, the radius of the communications blackout effect may extend to 4,000 miles.

E. LOCAL FALLOUT

For a 20-megaton surface burst, for example, assuming 50 percent fission yield and 40-knot winds, local fallout of 450 roentgens would be expected at 360 miles downwind (higher exposures at lesser distances) for persons fully exposed for 96 hours following the start of fallout at that place. (Four hundred and fifty roentgens would be expected at 415 miles downwind for a 30-megaton detonation, at 500 miles downwind for a 50-megaton detonation, and at 620 miles downwind for a 100-megaton detonation.) It is expected that exposure to 450 roentgens would result in 50 percent deaths.

For detonations at altitudes such that the fireball does not approach near the ground there would be very little local fallout. The fireball for a 20-megaton nuclear explosion would be about 3½ miles in diameter. (About 4 miles for 30-megaton, about 5 miles for 50-megaton, and about 7 miles for 100-megaton.)

F. WORLDWIDE FALLOUT

Assuming that (a) these detonations took place in the atmosphere so that the fireball does not approach the ground and (b) the fission yield was 50 percent of the total yield, then a 20- or 30-megaton detonation would produce less fission products than the current U.S.S.R. tests to date (excluding, of course, the detonation of October 23 which is estimated to have been about 30 megatons), and the 100-megaton detonation might produce more than twice this amount.

The debris spread worldwide (as distinguished from local) from all past nuclear tests of all nations prior to resumption by Soviets of atmospheric tests on September 1, 1961, is estimated to have been the equivalent of 60 megatons of fission yield. Thus, for example, a 100-megaton detonation (50 megatons of fission) might produce almost as much worldwide radioactivity as all past tests to November 3, 1958.

The distribution of fallout from such high yield detonations is not known with certainty. However it is estimated that if they were fired in the lower atmosphere, then at most three-fourths of the worldwide fallout occur in the 30° to 60° northern latitude zone. If the detonation took place at higher altitudes (greater than 20 miles) the amount of worldwide fallout of long lived radionuclides would be more equally partitioned between the northern and southern hemispheres.

A 5-megaton detonation in the lower atmosphere fired north of 30° north latitude might deposit about 4 millicuries of strontium 90 per square mile in the United States, and the one-hundred-megaton shot might scale up to about 75 millicuries of strontium 90 per square mile. There were about 70 millicuries of strontium 90 per square mile deposited in the United States before the current U.S.S.R. tests.

It is estimated that increasing the current level of strontium 90 in the United States by manifold would still result in less strontium 90 in the bones than permitted by radiation exposure guides now in effect for the general public for normal peacetime operations.

G. WATER WAVES

Water waves produced by high yield nuclear detonations could be of appreciable magnitude hundreds of miles from a deep underwater burst. A 50-megaton burst at a depth of 2,700 feet in deep water would generate wave heights from 20 to 50 feet at a range of 100 miles and 5 to 12 feet at 400 miles. A 100-megaton burst at about 4,000 feet in deep water would generate wave heights of about 28 to 70 feet at a range of 100 miles and 3- to 7-foot waves at 1,000 miles. For lesser burst depths the waves would be of lesser magnitude.

In all cases bottom profiles, in shallow water, and shoreline characteristics could greatly affect wave heights. The increase in the water level at the shoreline from a deep underwater high yield burst could be higher than that of the deep water waves at the same distance from the detonation.

An explosion of 50 megatons at surface of ocean would produce waves of a height of about 1 to 10 feet at 100 miles and 3 inches to 2½ feet at 400 miles. For an above-surface explosion at 10,000 feet altitude it is predicted that the waves produced would be less than one-half of the surface case. For higher altitudes the waves produced would not be of significant height. All of the above figures are based on a depth of water in the area of generation of about 16,000 feet; for shallower depths the wave heights would be less. In general it is expected that the wave heights would vary as the square root of the yield.

H. RETINAL BURNS

If a person were looking at the point of burst from any of these detonations, then burns to a portion of his retina causing some visual loss might be received at ground distances up to 500 miles away on a clear day with no cloud cover for a burst occurring at a 30-mile altitude. A burst at 60-mile altitude might produce the same result at 700 miles. As the altitude of burst increases the severity of retinal damage decreases. However, the severity of retinal damage increases at night.

For a 50-megaton burst in the lower atmosphere on a clear day, for example, retinal burns may be possible out to 250 miles (out to 210 miles for a 20-megaton burst, out to 290 miles for a 100-megaton burst).

I. OTHER EFFECTS

From any of these detonations at high altitude (30 miles to 1,000 miles) widespread and spectacular aurorae could be visible at distances from ground zero to 1,000 miles and, for the larger yields, perhaps out to 2,000 miles for the higher altitudes bursts. These aurorae would not be harmful to human beings. The air glow in the ionosphere produced by the shock wave may also be visible for more than 1,000 miles.

For bursts in deep space, 50,000 miles or more, there would be one sharp pulse of light that might be noticeable only to a person looking directly at the burst. On the basis of current knowledge, it is not expected that there would be any other observable effects to the unaided eye at the earth's surface.

2. NUCLEAR TEST BAN AND PEACE*

BY NIKITA S. KHRUSHCHEV

Comrades, I should like to speak on the question of ending nuclear tests. It will be recalled that the resumption of talks has been planned for mid-July in Moscow. The thought, of course, arises everywhere—will a test ban agreement be concluded now at last? This is a legitimate interest and I should like to present our views on this subject.

The Soviet Government has expressed more than once its readiness without any delay to sign a treaty banning all nuclear tests for all time—I repeat, all nuclear tests no matter where they are staged. Many years ago we raised the question of banning nuclear weapons and banning their testing.

However, the Western Powers—above all the United States—do not accept such an agreement. They are endlessly stalling the discussions, advancing various artificial pretexts in order to evade the discontinuance of all nuclear tests. They are insisting most obstinately on international inspections.

It has been proven by science and fully confirmed by practice that there is no need whatever of any inspections to check the discontinuance of tests, including underground tests. The national facilities for detecting nuclear explosions at the disposal of states, all the more so if combined with automatic seismic stations whose installation we accept, guarantee reliable control over the discontinuance of all tests. Notwithstanding all this, the Western Powers stubbornly link a solution of the problem of ending nuclear tests with so-called international inspections.

This means that the demands of the Western Powers on inspection have another explanation. What is it? We have long realized that the Western Powers need international inspection not to control the discontinuance of tests, but to penetrate by any means various regions

* Khrushchev's speech, July 2, 1963, in East Berlin. Reprinted from *Nuclear Test Ban Treaty: Hearings Before the Senate Committee on Foreign Relations,* 88th Cong., 1st Sess. (Washington: Government Printing Office, 1963), pp. 1000–1001.

of the Soviet Union for intelligence purposes. Thus, it is not an issue of control over the discontinuance of tests but, essentially, the legalization of espionage.

If earlier some people still could have doubts over the real purposes of the Western Powers when they called for inspection, there are now no longer any foundations for this. It is common knowledge that the Soviet Government late last year made a big concession to the Western Powers accepting two or three inspections annually. What was the Western Powers' reply to this manifestation of good will? Far from properly appreciating this step of ours, they tried to force us to bargain over the number of inspections and the conditions of holding them. After this it has become still clearer that our Western partners are not interested in concluding an equal agreement but want to obtain the opportunity of flying over Soviet territory, engaging in aerial surveys and other things which are not at all linked with the discontinuance of tests but answer the requirements of NATO military headquarters.

However, it is time for the imperialist gentlemen to know that the Soviet Government will never abandon the security interests of its country and of all the Socialist countries and will not open its doors to NATO intelligence agents. This is no subject for bargaining. Our stand in this respect is clear and unshaken.

The Soviet Government is convinced that the early conclusion of an agreement banning all nuclear tests—in the atmosphere, in outer space, underwater, and underground—is in the interests of the peoples. However, this is now obviously impossible in view of the position of the Western Powers. Carefully analyzing the obtaining situation, the Soviet Government, prompted by the sentiment of high responsibility for the destinies of the peoples, declares that since the Western Powers obstruct the conclusion of an agreement banning all nuclear tests, the Soviet Government expresses its willingness to conclude an agreement banning nuclear tests in the atmosphere, in outer space, and underwater. We have made this proposal before but the Western Powers frustrated an agreement by advancing supplementary conditions which envisaged large-scale inspection of our territory.

If the Western Powers now agree to this proposal, the question of inspection no longer arises, for the Western Powers declare that no inspections whatever are needed to check the fulfillment by the states of their commitments to stop nuclear tests in the atmosphere, in outer space, and underwater. Hence, the road to a solution of the problem is open. The Soviet Government expresses the hope that the Western Powers, heeding the aspirations of the peoples, will take a positive attitude on this Soviet Government proposal.

The conclusion of a test ban agreement will eliminate the hazards of radioactive contamination of the atmosphere and will remove the threat to the health of present and future generations. The conclusion of such an agreement, undoubtedly, will also help to improve the international climate, ease tension and, hence, may facilitate mutually acceptable solutions of other international problems as well.

Of course, an agreement on the ending of nuclear tests, notwithstanding all the importance of this major act, cannot stop the arms race, and cannot avert or even substantially weaken the danger of thermonuclear war. That is why the Soviet Government believes that now, at the conclusion of a test ban agreement, it is necessary to also take another big step toward easing international tension and strengthening confidence between states—to sign a nonagression pact between the two main military groups of states—the NATO countries and the Warsaw Pact states. The Soviet Union and other Socialist countries have been proposing such a pact for a number of years. We note with satisfaction that this proposal is enlisting increasing international support, including support in some NATO countries. The time has now come to implement this proposal.

A test ban agreement combined with the simultaneous signing of a nonagression pact between the two groups of states will create a fresh international climate more favorable for a solution of major problems of our time, including disarmament. These problems affect the interests of the broadest masses of the people. That is precisely why the Communists urge all peoples, all sections of the population, irrespective of their political views and convictions, to rally in the common struggle to avert another world war, and to maintain an enduring peace between states.

violation of this treaty with the almost certain risks of a continued and unrestricted arms race. On balance, it is clear that the national security interests of the United States are protected far more by adhering to the treaty than by rejecting it.

The overwhelming response of the American people in favor of this treaty is most heartening. Over the past week there have been literally hundreds of favorable editorials appearing in papers from coast to coast.

I shall introduce many of these editorials in the RECORD this afternoon.

On July 8, 1963, the Louis Harris poll reported that 73 percent of the American public supports a limited test-ban agreement and only 17 percent were in outright opposition. This confirms the 77 percent in favor as reported by the Gallup Poll several years ago.

Dozens of the Nation's leading businessmen, religious leaders, scientists and civic leaders have recently demonstrated their support of the test-ban treaty through newspaper advertisements and official pronouncements. Executives of such companies as Inland Steel, Eastman Kodak, the Pennsylvania Railroad, the R. J. Reynolds Tobacco Co., the Illinois Central Railroad have publicly endorsed the treaty. The Federation of American Scientists recently issued a statement urging ratification by the Senate. Many individual scientists, including three Nobel laureates, have indicated their support. Clearly there is a large body of informed scientific opinion in favor of the test ban.

The issue of U.S. ratification transcends considerations of party or politics. Republicans and Democrats alike have joined in active support of the treaty. Such Republican statesmen as Ambassador James Wadsworth, former U.S. test-ban negotiator, and former Secretary of Health, Education, and Welfare Arthur Flemming are prominent members of the Eisenhower administration who are urging an overwhelming vote for ratification by the Senate.

Many reasons can be advanced as to why it was possible to reach agreement with the Soviet Union on a nuclear test ban. I believe the most important reason is the careful, prudent, persistent effort of the United States toward this objective during the past 7 years. What prompted the Soviet Union now to agree to the treaty? It is not my purpose today to examine Soviet motives, but I am convinced that the Soviet Union is serious about this treaty, that it is in the mutual interests of the Soviet Union and the United States to adhere to it, and that the Soviet Union is aware of the international commitment and responsibility included in its provisions.

What is important today is the fact that we have an agreement. It has been carefully negotiated, initialed, and is about to be signed by representatives of the United States, along with those of Great Britain and the Soviet Union. This agreement is the first major breakthrough in the area of arms control since World War II.

As such, it is a first, practical step for the cause of peace and control of the massive weapons of destruction which man has developed.

The Senate soon faces the process of ratifying the nuclear test-ban treaty. A careful and responsible discussion is needed, both for the Senate and for public understanding. I am confident that this treaty—in a sense initiated by the United States—is in the interest of the United States and consistent with our national security policy. And there can be no doubt that this treaty is in the interest of mankind and an imperative for the safety of our children and all future generations.

Mr. President, I ask unanimous consent that the full text of the treaty itself be printed in the RECORD at the conclusion of my remarks.

I also have had prepared a comprehensive series of questions and answers relating to the treaty, and I ask unanimous consent to have them printed in the RECORD following the text of the treaty itself. In the coming debate on the question of whether the Senate will advise and consent to the treaty banning these tests, I believe it essential that fundamental questions relating to this decision be kept in clear and accurate focus. It is for this reason that these questions and answers are being placed in the RECORD.

There being no objection, the text of the treaty and the questions and answers were ordered to be printed in the RECORD, as follows:

TEXT OF TEST-BAN TREATY INITIATED JULY 25

Following is the text of the test-ban treaty initiated in Moscow July 25:

TITLE

Treaty Banning Nuclear Weapons Tests in Atmosphere, in Outer Space and Underwater

The Governments of the United States of America, the United Kingdom of Great Britain and Northern Ireland, and the Union of Soviet Socialist Republics, hereinafter referred to as the "Original Parties",

Proclaiming as their principal aim the speediest possible achievement of an agreement on general and complete disarmament under strict international control in accordance with the objectives of the United Nations which would put an end to the armaments race and eliminate the incentive to the production and testing of all kinds of weapons, including nuclear weapons,

Seeking to achieve the discontinuance of all test explosions of nuclear weapons for all time, determined to continue negotiations to this end, and desiring to put an end to the contamination of man's environment by radio-active substances.

Have agreed as follows:

ARTICLE I

1. Each of the parties to this Treaty undertakes to prohibit, to prevent, and not to carry out any nuclear weapon test explosion, or any other nuclear explosion at any place under its jurisdiction or control:

a. in the atmosphere, beyond its limits, including outer space, or underwater, including territorial waters or high seas; or

b. in any other environment if such explosion causes radioactive debris to be present outside the territorial limits of the state under whose jurisdiction or control such explosion is conducted. It is understood in this connection that the provisions of this subparagraph are without prejudice to the conclusion of a treaty resulting in the permanent banning of all nuclear test explosions, including all such explosions underground, the conclusions of which, as the Parties have stated in the preamble to this Treaty, they seek to achieve.

2. Each of the Parties to this Treaty undertakes furthermore to refrain from causing, encouraging, or in any way participating in, the carrying out of any nuclear weapon test explosion, or any other nuclear explosion, anywhere which would take place in any of the environments described, or have the effect referred to in paragraph 1 of this article.

ARTICLE II

1. Any party may propose amendments to this Treaty. The text of any proposed amendment shall be submitted to the Depository Governments which shall circulate it to all Parties to this Treaty. Thereafter, if requested to do so by one-third or more of the Parties, the Depository

Governments shall convene a conference, to which they shall invite all the Parties, to consider such amendment.

2. Any amendment to this Treaty must be approved by a majority of the votes of all the Parties to this Treaty, including the votes of all of the original Parties. The amendment shall enter into force for all Parties upon the deposit of instruments of ratification by a majority of all the Parties, including the instruments of ratification of all the original Parties.

ARTICLE III

1. This Treaty shall be open to all States for signature. Any State which does not sign this Treaty before its entry into force in accordance with paragraph 3 of this article may accede to it at any time.

2. This Treaty shall be subject to ratification by signatory States. Instruments of ratification and instruments of accession shall be deposited with the Governments of the original Parties—the United States of America, the United Kingdom of Great Britain and Northern Ireland, and the Union of Soviet Socialist Republics—which are hereby designated the Depository Governments.

3. This Treaty shall enter into force after its ratification by all the original Parties and the deposit of their instruments of ratification.

4. For States whose instruments of ratification or accession are deposited subsequent to the entry into force of this Treaty, it shall enter into force on the date of the deposit of their instruments of ratification or accession.

5. The Depository Governments shall promptly inform all signatory and acceding States of the date of each signature, the date of deposit of each instrument of ratification of and accession to this Treaty, the date of its entry into force, and the date of receipt of any requests for conferences or other notices.

6. This Treaty shall be registered by the Depository Governments pursuant to Article 102 of the Charter of the United Nations.

ARTICLE IV

This Treaty shall be of unlimited duration.

Each Party shall in exercising its national sovereignty have the right to withdraw from the Treaty if it decides that extraordinary events, related to the subject matter of this Treaty, have jeopardized the supreme interests of its country. It shall give notice of such withdrawal to all other Parties to the Treaty three months in advance.

ARTICLE V

This Treaty, of which the English and Russian texts are equally authentic, shall be deposited in the archives of the Depository Governments. Duly certified copies of this Treaty shall be transmitted by the

Depository Governments to the Governments of the signatory and acceding States.

In witness whereof the undersigned, duly authorized, have signed this Treaty.

Done in triplicate at Moscow, this ———— day of ————, one thousand nine-hundred and sixty-three.

TEST-BAN TREATY—QUESTIONS AND ANSWERS

1. What kind of tests are banned by the agreement?

Tests in the atmosphere, underwater, including territorial waters or high seas, and in space are banned, but not underground tests.

2. Why are underground tests not included in the agreement?

This is the most difficult testing environment to police, because it is not always possible to distinguish seismic waves produced by earthquakes from those caused by nuclear explosions. In these cases it is necessary to conduct onsite inspections. This means going directly to the location where the event occurred to determine the cause of the tremor. The Soviet Union will accept only a token number of these inspections. Moreover, the Soviet representatives have refused to discuss ways in which these inspections could be most effectively conducted.

3. Are there any restrictions on underground testing?

Any number, any size, and any type nuclear explosion, for peaceful or military purposes, may be conducted in the underground environment as long as such explosion does not cause radioactive debris to be present outside the territorial limits of the country conducting the explosion. This means that testing of peaceful uses of atomic energy may continue.

This limitation takes into consideration a certain amount of venting of nuclear debris in an underground explosion. It is not unusual for some radioactive material to reach the surface of the earth through cracks or fissures in the ground following a subsurface test. However, such debris generally remains within a local area near the point of detonation. Under the terms of the treaty, there would be no violation of the treaty if venting occurs and the debris remains within national borders.

4. The agreement refers to a ban on underwater tests including territorial waters or high seas. What does this mean?

It means that underwater nuclear explosions cannot be conducted in the oceans up to the shoreline nor can they be conducted in rivers or inland lakes.

5. Is it true that the treaty in no way restricts our use of nuclear weapons in time of war?

Yes. The treaty is designed to limit the testing of nuclear weapons, not their use in time of war.

6. Is any party to the treaty precluded from giving information or technical assistance on nuclear matters to other countries?

The treaty simply prevents signatory states from causing, encouraging, or participating in any way in a nuclear explosion in the three prohibited environments. This does not mean that a party to the treaty could not provide technical assistance and information to another state on nuclear matters. However, if, for example, this same information contributed materially to a programed series of atmospheric tests, it would not be in keeping with the treaty obligations.

7. Does the Soviet Union have a veto power over amendments to the treaty?

The three original parties to the treaty—the United States, United Kingdom, and U.S.S.R. have the power to veto treaty amendments. Any amendments to be adopted must be approved by a majority of all the signatory nations including the affirmative votes of these three nations. Any amendment that varied the rights of the United States under the treaty would, of course, require Senate approval.

8. As a depository government, would the United States be compelled to recognize all regimes which adhere to the treaty?

No. The fundamental factor in determining recognition is intent. If we do not intend to recognize a regime, the rule of international law is that such an intent cannot be deduced merely because we are party to a multilateral treaty by which the unrecognized regime is also bound. Multilateral treaties often have a great many parties not all of which recognize the governments of all of the others, such as the armistice negotiations in Korea.

9. Is provision made in the treaty for a party to withdraw if it believes its security interests are being threatened?

The treaty does contain a withdrawal clause. This provides that a party can withdraw if it feels that extraordinary events, related to the subject matter of the treaty, have jeopardized its supreme interests. The decision as to whether a State's supreme interests were being jeopardized by a test or a series of tests is for that State alone to make. If it believes this to be the case, it gives 3 months' notice of its intention to withdraw. No further obligations are entailed.

The 3-month notice would not apply if the Soviet Union were to test in plain violation of the treaty. In such circumstances we would proceed to test immediately if this was considered necessary.

10. Why is this limited test-ban agreement in our national interest?

There are a number of reasons. This treaty can: Act as a deterrent to the spread of nuclear weapons to many additional countries, thereby lessening the danger of nuclear war; drastically reduce or end the hazards of radioactive fallout; have the practical effect of slowing down the pace of the arms race; be a first step toward reduced world tensions and broader areas of agreement on the control of nuclear weapons.

11. What are the risks of secret testing and sudden withdrawal?

Actually, the danger of clandestine testing in the prohibited environments, the atmosphere, space, and underwater, is minimal. In addition to the fact that we have good verification capabilities in these environments, there would be little value in attempting to carry out types of tests in these environments that could be freely conducted underground.

The risk of a nation suddenly breaking off the treaty and testing is also small. We will maintain on a standby basis those testing facilities affected by the ban. This is a strong deterrent to any nation which might contemplate gaining the upper hand in this way.

12. How do we know if a state violates the agreement?

The system for policing the agreement is really a "reciprocal inspection system"—you police me, I police you. The United States has a national detection network that permits detection and identification of nuclear tests in the atmosphere, underwater, and in space. Since we own and operate our own monitoring system we can make any changes we wish in the system to increase its effectiveness.

13. Is it possible to detect tests if they are conducted in far outer space?

Since fairly large tests can be conducted underground, the primary concern centers on space tests of several megatons or more.

Our verification capability for such tests is good. A 1-megaton test detonated about 1 million miles from the earth will be picked up by our present national detection system. This ability could be increased to a hundred million miles or more, if necessary, by establishing a satellite detection system around the earth or the sun.

But a party contemplating clandestine tests in space has more to reckon with than the possibilities of being caught. Not only is it an extremely expensive undertaking but it is time consuming. To obtain results from a test millions of miles away could take weeks or months. This is further compounded by any number of technical difficulties that would have to be overcome to gain even limited knowledge from the explosion.

14. The Soviet Union has tested large megaton weapons. We haven't. From a military standpoint, aren't we going into this treaty at a disadvantage?

We have in our stockpile a large number of nuclear weapons with different amounts of explosive power. These can be used for a variety of strategic or tactical purposes. Complementing this is a sophisticated system of delivery vehicles. This mix in our nuclear arsenal permits us to respond in an infinite number of ways to any overt aggressive act.

The possession of 50 to 100-megaton bombs would not increase, to any significant degree, the deterrent we now possess. By choice, we have concentrated on mobile and efficient weapons with, not a large, but rather a sufficient yield. This we have done by choice. Should we wish to possess larger weapons than we now have in our stockpile, this could well be done under the treaty by techniques we have used successfully in the past.

In these circumstances it certainly cannot be said we are at a disadvantage in terms of nuclear weapons development.

15. What about development of an antiballistic missile? Don't we need further tests in the atmosphere to test out this system?

The development of an antiballistic missile is proceeding. However, to date there has been no decision as to whether we should attempt to deploy such a system. In part, this is due to the fact that the effectiveness of the ABM is questionable. Any ABM defense is susceptible to saturation—incoming missiles launched in such quantities as to overwhelm the defensive missiles, or decoys—launching of dummy missiles along with the real McCoy to lead defensive missiles astray. These are real problems. In any case, it is quite unlikely that tests connected with this problem would further materially advance our security.

16. We are evidently ahead of the Soviet Union in the development of tactical nuclear weapons. Under the terms of this treaty testing can be conducted in the underground environment where such weapons are proven out without violating the treaty. Doesn't this afford the Soviet Union an opportunity to catch up in this important area?

Testing is legal in this environment for the United States, United Kingdom, and the U.S.S.R. We can match the U.S.S.R. test for test in this area if need be. But, without such agreement the rate at which the Soviet Union could catch up with us would certainly be greater since in the absence of an agreement it could test in all environments.

17. Suppose France or Communist China tests in the prohibited environments. How would this affect the agreement?

Initially, it is well to recognize that with this treaty in effect, there would certainly be greater pressures on these two countries to desist in any testing program than would exist in the absence of an agreement. But even with continued testing by France or the initiation of tests by Communist China, there are a dozen or so other technically able countries which, in light of this action by the three nuclear powers, may well forego development of an individual nuclear capability. This alone is a significant gain in efforts to halt the spread of nuclear weapons to many countries.

In any event, should a signatory state consider its national security seriously jeopardized by testing by others, it would be free to withdraw from the agreement.

18. Isn't there a real danger that with this agreement in hand we may now feel we can relax our guard against further attempts by the Communists to encroach on free world nations?

This may be the greatest danger we face.

It would be a great mistake to assume that because the Soviet Union is a party to this limited test-ban agreement the millennium has arrived.

The Communists have in no way given up their avowed objective of world domination even though the Soviet Union may use means other than nuclear war to achieve it. While we must continue earnestly to seek further arrangements designed to reduce international tensions and limit and control armaments, we must not so relax our guard as to invite aggression.

19. Does the treaty in any way inhibit the Atomic Energy Commission's plowshare program—the peaceful uses of atomic energy?

AEC officials have said that this agreement will not seriously inhibit their plowshare program.

A few projects may be affected. But most of the experiments—underground excavations, mining and resource development—and certain other experiments in pure science would not be disrupted.

20. What are some of the reasons the Soviet Union might believe this agreement to be in its interest?

Some of the advantages of such an agreement that would accrue to us would accrue to the Soviet Union as well. Continuation of radioactive fallout is, in the long run, as serious a hazard to the Soviet people as it is to Americans. The danger that other countries, some of which may act in an irresponsible fashion, might acquire nuclear weapons poses as great a threat to the security of U.S.S.R. as to the security of the United States.

Then there's the matter of economics. An unrestricted testing program is very costly.

There is reason to believe the Soviet Union is aware of these points, just as there is reason to believe that it sees the agreement serving its interests in the ideological dispute which now plagues the Communist camp.

WIDESPREAD EDITORIAL SUPPORT FOR TEST-BAN TREATY

I wish to call to the attention of the Senate a number of articles and editorials—which recently have been appearing in the press—concerning the proposed nuclear test-ban treaty.

As the U.S. delegation embarks for Moscow, to sign the historic treaty banning nuclear tests in the atmosphere, underwater, and in outer space, it is reassuring and heartening to note this widespread editorial support for the treaty that has been appearing in all sections of the country.

In his address to the Nation on Friday evening, President Kennedy urged every American to participate in the debate related to whether the Senate will advise and consent to this treaty. I am sure that each one of us recognizes the importance of this debate, and also recognizes that it will be far reaching in its effect upon our Nation in terms of public opinion and public education on the all-important issue of American foreign policy.

The editorial notice accorded the question of treaty ratification demonstrates that this is, indeed, a matter of great concern to a large majority of our citizens. How heartening and refreshing it is, Mr. President, that the American people are demonstrating this keen interest in a matter of such importance, which is so complex and so intricate in its provisions.

As a Senator who has publicly indicated his support for the treaty, it is particularly heartening to read the editorial support coming from such newspapers as the Houston Chronicle, the Dallas Times-Herald, the Little Rock (Ark.) Gazette, the Des Moines Register, the Atlanta Constitution, the Cleveland Plain Dealer, the Denver Post, the New York Journal-American, the Miami News, the Milwaukee Journal, the Portland Oregonian, the Charlotte News, the Salt Lake City Tribune, the Omaha World-Herald, the Greensboro News, the San Francisco Chronicle, the Nashville Tennessean, the Louisville Courier-Journal, and the Dayton Journal Herald—to mention only a few of the hundreds of newspapers throughout America that are editorializing favorably on this most important issue of foreign policy and peace.

These newspapers are only a small percentage of those carrying editorials generally in favor of the test-ban treaty. But this selection serves to indicate the strong support that exists in all sections of the country—North, South, East, West, and the central portions of our Nation—that such support is nonpartisan in nature, that it is voiced by papers of both liberal and conservative persuasions, and that a sensible and realistic appraisal of the treaty exists among these editors.

Let me note briefly certain of the principal themes running through these editorials:

First, that the treaty represents a minimum first step on the road to peace. It does nothing to limit the size or effectiveness of the U.S. Military Establishment; that point needs to be underscored. I can hear the critics of the treaty now saying that it would limit our military effectiveness and national security. Fortunately, thoughtful editors and commentators are setting that bit of fiction at rest.

The editorials continue to point out that the treaty would merely bring about a halt of the unrestricted and unlimited testing of nuclear weapons in the three environments that are noted in the treaty. Furthermore, the treaty does not signal an end to the cold war but, rather, is at least an opening toward further negotiation.

Then the editors note that the increasing danger of radioactive fallout will be controlled. Clearly no American family is immune from the rising dangers of radioactivity resulting from atmospheric tests; therefore, the entire Nation should rejoice at the opportunity to bring such atmospheric testing to a halt.

I paraphrase what editors are saying.

Third, that the technical risks relating to Soviet cheating are far outweighed by the certain grave risks of continuing the testing, development, and proliferation of nuclear weapons. That is, on balance, the security of the United States is protected far more effectively by ratifying the treaty than by not ratifying.

The Senate will weigh these opinions and arguments with care and objectivity in the weeks ahead.

I wish to underscore the importance of a detailed, deliberate, great debate on the entire subject of our relationships with the Soviet Union, and particularly the test-ban treaty. Those persons voicing doubts and reservations about the treaty should be given, and will be given, full and complete opportunity to make their case, first before the Senate committees that will hear the testimony, and particularly the Senate Committee on Foreign Relations, and then before the Senate itself. But I am confident—and this outpouring of favorable editorials bolsters this confidence—that when all the evidence is in, that when all facts have been carefully weighed, the Senate will vote overwhelmingly in favor of this first small step toward a more peaceful world.

CHAPTER XV

Common Interests in Survival

Perseverance in the pursuit of peace is not cowardice, but courage; restraint in the use of force is not weakness, but wisdom.
—HUBERT H. HUMPHREY

Our successes convince all mankind that the forces of peace and reason are growing stronger, that the Soviet people are paving a true road to the triumph of universal peace and progress.
—LEONID I. BREZHNEV

A quarter of a century ago, one of the great statesmen of our time, Sir Winston Churchill, then Prime Minister of Great Britain, delivered his famous "finest hour" speech before the House of Commons, in which he pointed out that the survival of Christian civilization depended upon the outcome of the imminent Battle of Britain. By analogy, we might say that the Nazi's intended invasion was to Britain in those days what the nuclear "balance of terror" is to the world today. If we extend the analogy further and paraphrase Sir Winston's speech to describe the moment of present danger for the peoples of the world, the paraphrase might read as follows:

If we can muster our sanity the world may be free and the life of the world may move forward into broad, sunlit uplands; but if we fail, then the whole world, and all that we have known and cared for, will sink into the abyss of a new dark age made more sinister, and perhaps more prolonged, by the lights of a perverted science, Let us, therefore, brace ourselves to our duty and so bear ourselves that if the world civilization lasts for a thousand years men will still say, "This was their finest hour."

Peace is precious and precarious. The survival of mankind depends not on war but on peace. The US-Soviet competition on the ground of peace is productive and healthy; on the field of battle, destructive and suicidal. In the thinking of both the United States and the Soviet Union, there has been a fundamental fallacy that anything which promotes the interests of one side is ipso facto *detrimental to the interests of the other. On the contrary, the two nations must share the common interests in peace, in disarmament, and in survival. For Americans, the quest and choice must be not "better dead than red" or "better red than dead," but* neither dead nor red; *and for the Soviets,* neither will we bury you, nor you us.

This chapter focuses on an inquiry into the attitudes of the leaders of the United States and the Soviet Union toward the problem of mutual survival in the nuclear age.

President Kennedy urges every American to reexamine his own attitude toward peace, toward the Soviet Union, toward the cold war, and toward freedom and peace at home.

Premier Khrushchev explains the nature, scope, and significance of "peaceful coexistence," which enables the nations of the world to maintain a stable balance of world order and to achieve permanent relaxation of tensions.

President Johnson pledges that he will spare neither his office nor himself in the quest for peace. Then he enumerates and explains several goals of peace: restraint in the use of power, search for practical solutions to particular problems, respect for the rights and fears of others, cooperation in solving greater problems than immediate conflicts, and the ability to adjust disputes by peaceful means.

1. TOWARD A STRATEGY OF PEACE*

BY JOHN F. KENNEDY

"There are few earthly things more beautiful than a University," wrote John Masefield, in his tribute to the English universities—and his words are equally true here. He did not refer to spires and towers, to campus greens and ivied walls. He admired the splendid beauty of the university, he said, because it was "a place where those who hate ignorance may strive to know, where those who perceive truth may strive to make others see."

I have, therefore, chosen this time and this place to discuss a topic

* Commencement address at the American University, Washington, D.C., June 10, 1963.

on which ignorance too often abounds and the truth is too rarely perceived—yet it is the most important topic on earth: world peace.

What kind of peace do I mean? What kind of peace do we seek? Not a *Pax Americana* enforced on the world by American weapons of war. Not the peace of the grave or the security of the slave. I am talking about genuine peace, the kind of peace that makes life on earth worth living, the kind that enables men and nations to grow and to hope and to build a better life for their children—not merely peace for Americans but peace for all men and women, not merely peace in our time but peace for all time.

I speak of peace because of the new face of war. Total war makes no sense in an age when great powers can maintain large and relatively invulnerable nuclear forces and refuse to surrender without resort to those forces. It makes no sense in an age when a single nuclear weapon contains almost 10 times the explosive force delivered by all of the Allied air forces in the Second World War. It makes no sense in an age when the deadly poisons produced by a nuclear exchange would be carried by the wind and water and soil and seed to the far corners of the globe and to generations yet unborn.

Today the expenditure of billions of dollars every year on weapons acquired for the purpose of making sure we never need to use them is essential to keeping the peace. But surely the acquisition of such idle stockpiles—which can only destroy and never create—is not the only, much less the most efficient, means of assuring peace.

I speak of peace, therefore, as the necessary rational end of rational men. I realize that the pursuit of peace is not as dramatic as the pursuit of war, and frequently the words of the pursuer fall on deaf ears. But we have no more urgent task.

Some say that it is useless to speak of world peace or world law or world disarmament—and that it will be useless until the leaders of the Soviet Union adopt a more enlightened attitude. I hope they do. I believe we can help them do it. But I also believe that we must reexamine our own attitude, as individuals and as a nation, for our attitude is as essential as theirs. And every graduate of this school, every thoughtful citizen who despairs of war and wishes to bring peace, should begin by looking inward—by examining his own attitude toward the possibilities of peace, toward the Soviet Union, toward the course of the cold war, and toward freedom and peace here at home.

First: Let us examine our attitude toward peace itself. Too many of us think it is impossible. Too many think it unreal. But that is a dangerous, defeatist belief. It leads to the conclusion that war is inevitable, that mankind is doomed, that we are gripped by forces we cannot control.

We need not accept that view. Our problems are manmade; therefore they can be solved by man. And man can be as big as he wants. No problem of human destiny is beyond human beings. Man's reason and spirit have often solved the seemingly unsolvable, and we believe they can do it again.

I am not referring to the absolute, infinite concept of universal peace and good will of which some fantasies and fanatics dream. I do not deny the values of hopes and dreams, but we merely invite discouragement and incredulity by making that our only and immediate goal.

Let us focus instead on a more practical, more attainable peace, based not on a sudden revolution in human nature but on a gradual evolution in human institutions—on a series of concrete actions and effective agreements which are in the interest of all concerned. There is no single, simple key to this peace, no grand or magic formula to be adopted by one or two powers. Genuine peace must be the product of many nations, the sum of many acts. It must be dynamic, not static, changing to meet the challenge of each new generation. For peace is a process, a way of solving problems.

With such a peace there will still be quarrels and conflicting interests, as there are within families and nations. World peace, like community peace, does not require that each man love his neighbor; it requires only that they live together in mutual tolerance, submitting their disputes to a just and peaceful settlement. And history teaches us that enmities between nations, as between individuals, do not last forever. However fixed our likes and dislikes may seem, the tide of time and events will often bring surprising changes in the relations between nations and neighbors.

So let us persevere. Peace need not be impracticable, and war need not be inevitable. By defining our goal more clearly, by making it seem more manageable and less remote, we can help all peoples to see it, to draw hope from it, and to move irresistibly toward it.

Second: Let us reexamine our attitude toward the Soviet Union. It is discouraging to think that their leaders may actually believe what their propagandists write. It is discouraging to read a recent authoritative Soviet text on military strategy and find, on page after page, wholly baseless and incredible claims—such as the allegation that "American imperialist circles are preparing to unleash different types of wars . . . that there is a very real threat of a preventive war being unleashed by American imperialists against the Soviet Union . . . [and that] the political aims of the American imperialists are to enslave economically and politically the European and other capitalist countries . . . [and] to achieve world domination . . . by means of aggressive wars."

Truly as it was written long ago: "The wicked flee when no man pursueth." Yet it is sad to read these Soviet statements—to realize the extent of the gulf between us. But it is also a warning—a warning to the American people not to fall into the same trap as the Soviets, not to see only a distorted and desperate view of the other side, not to see conflict as inevitable, accommodation as impossible, and communication as nothing more than an exchange of threats.

No government or social system is so evil that its people must be considered as lacking in virtue. As Americans we find communism profoundly repugnant as a negation of personal freedom and dignity. But we can still hail the Russian people for their many achievements—in science and space, in economic and industrial growth, in culture and in acts of courage.

Among the many traits the peoples of our two countries have in common, none is stronger than our mutual abhorrence of war. Almost unique among the major world powers, we have never been at war with each other. And no nation in the history of battle ever suffered more than the Soviet Union suffered in the course of the Second World War. At least 20 million lost their lives. Countless millions of homes and farms were burned or sacked. A third of the nation's territory, including nearly two-thirds of its industrial base, was turned into a wasteland—a loss equivalent to the devastation of this country east of Chicago.

Today, should total war ever break out again—no matter how—our two countries would become the primary targets. It is an ironical but accurate fact that the two strongest powers are the two in the most danger of devastation. All we have built, all we have worked for, would be destroyed in the first 24 hours. And even in the cold war, which brings burdens and dangers to so many countries—including this nation's closest allies—our two countries bear the heaviest burdens. For we are both devoting massive sums of money to weapons that could be better devoted to combating ignorance, poverty, and disease. We are both caught up in a vicious and dangerous cycle in which suspicion on one side breeds suspicion on the other and new weapons beget counterweapons.

In short, both the United States and its allies, and the Soviet Union and its allies, have a mutually deep interest in a just and genuine peace and in halting the arms race. Agreements to this end are in the interests of the Soviet Union as well as ours, and even the most hostile nations can be relied upon to accept and keep those treaty obligations, and only those treaty obligations, which are in their own interest.

So let us not be blind to our differences, but let us also direct attention to our common interests and to the means by which those differences can be resolved. And if we cannot end now our differences, at least we can help make the world safe for diversity. For in the final analysis our most basic common link is that we all inhabit this planet. We all breathe the same air. We all cherish our children's future. And we are all mortal.

Third: Let us reexamine our attitude toward the cold war, remembering that we are not engaged in a debate, seeking to pile up debating points. We are not here distributing blame or pointing the finger of judgment. We must deal with the world as it is and not as it might have been had the history of the last 18 years been different.

We must, therefore, persevere in the search for peace in the hope that constructive changes within the Communist bloc might bring within reach solutions which now seem beyond us. We must conduct our affairs in such a way that it becomes in the Communists' interest to agree on a genuine peace. Above all, while defending our own vital interests, nuclear powers must avert those confrontations which bring an adversary to a choice of either a humiliating retreat or a nuclear war. To adopt that kind of course in the nuclear age would be evidence only of the bankruptcy of our policy—or of a collective death wish for the world.

To secure these ends, America's weapons are nonprovocative, carefully controlled, designed to deter, and capable of selective use.

Our military forces are committed to peace and disciplined in self-restraint. Our diplomats are instructed to avoid unnecessary irritants and purely rhetorical hostility.

For we can seek a relaxation of tensions without relaxing our guard. And, for our part, we do not need to use threats to prove that we are resolute. We do not need to jam foreign broadcasts out of fear our faith will be eroded. We are unwilling to impose our system on any unwilling people, but we are willing and able to engage in peaceful competition with any people on earth.

Meanwhile we seek to strengthen the United Nations, to help solve its financial problems, to make it a more effective instrument of peace, to develop it into a genuine world security system—a system capable of resolving disputes on the basis of law, of insuring the security of the large and the small, and of creating conditions under which arms can finally be abolished.

At the same time we seek to keep peace inside the non-Communist world, where many nations, all of them our friends, are divided over issues which weaken Western unity, which invite Communist intervention, or which threaten to erupt into war. Our efforts in West New Guinea, in the Congo, in the Middle East, and in the Indian subcontinent have been persistent and patient despite criticism from both sides. We have also tried to set an example for others—by seeking to adjust small but significant differences with our own closest neighbors in Mexico and in Canada.

Speaking of other nations, I wish to make one point clear. We are bound to many nations by alliances. Those alliances exist because our concern and theirs substantially overlap. Our commitment to defend Western Europe and West Berlin, for example, stands undiminished because of the identity of our vital interests. The United States will make no deal with the Soviet Union at the expense of other nations and other peoples, not merely because they are our partners but also because their interests and ours converge.

Our interests converge, however, not only in defending the frontiers of freedom but in pursuing the paths of peace. It is our hope —and the purpose of Allied policies—to convince the Soviet Union that she, too, should let each nation choose its own future, so long as that choice does not interfere with the choices of others. The Communist drive to impose their political and economic system on others is the primary cause of world tension today. For there can be no doubt that, if all nations could refrain from interfering in the self-determination of others, the peace would be much more assured.

This will require a new effort to achieve world law, a new context for world discussions. It will require increased understanding between the Soviets and ourselves. And increased understanding will require increased contact and communication. One step in this direction is the proposed arrangement for a direct line between Moscow and Washington, to avoid on each side the dangerous delays, misunderstandings, and misreadings of the other's actions which might occur at a time of crisis.

We have also been talking in Geneva about other first-step measures of arms control, designed to limit the intensity of the arms race and to reduce the risks of accidental war. Our primary long-range interest in Geneva, however, is general and complete disarmament, designed to take place by stages, permitting parallel political developments to build the new institutions of peace which would take the place of arms. The pursuit of disarmament has been an effort of this Government since the 1920's. It has been urgently sought by the past three administrations. And however dim the prospects may be today, we intend to continue this effort—to continue it in order that all countries, including our own, can better grasp what the problems and possibilities of disarmament are.

The one major area of these negotiations where the end is in sight, yet where a fresh start is badly needed, is in a treaty to outlaw nuclear tests. The conclusion of such a treaty—so near and yet so far— would check the spiraling arms race in one of its most dangerous areas. It would place the nuclear powers in a position to deal more effectively with one of the greatest hazards which man faces in 1963, the further spread of nuclear arms. It would increase our security; it would decrease the prospects of war. Surely this goal is sufficiently important to require our steady pursuit, yielding neither to the temptation to give up the whole effort nor the temptation to give up our insistence on vital and responsible safeguards.

I am taking this opportunity, therefore, to announce two important decisions in this regard.

First: Chairman Khrushchev, Prime Minister Macmillan, and I have agreed that high-level discussions will shortly begin in Moscow looking toward early agreement on a comprehensive test ban treaty. Our hopes must be tempered with the caution of history, but with our hopes go the hopes of all mankind.

Second: To make clear our good faith and solemn convictions on the matter, I now declare that the United States does not propose to conduct nuclear tests in the atmosphere so long as other states do not do so. We will not be the first to resume. Such a declaration is no substitute for a formal binding treaty, but I hope it will help us achieve one. Nor would such a treaty be a substitute for disarmament, but I hope it will help us achieve it.

Finally, my fellow Americans, let us examine our attitude toward peace and freedom here at home. The quality and spirit of our own society must justify and support our efforts abroad. We must show it in the dedication of our own lives, as many of you who are graduating today will have a unique opportunity to do, by serving without pay in the Peace Corps abroad or in the proposed National Service Corps here at home.

But wherever we are, we must all, in our daily lives, live up to the age-old faith that peace and freedom walk together. In too many of our cities today the peace is not secure because freedom is incomplete.

It is the responsibility of the executive branch at all levels of government—local, State, and national—to provide and protect that freedom for all of our citizens by all means within their authority. It is the responsibility of the legislative branch at all levels, wherever that authority is not now adequate, to make it adequate. And it is the responsibility of all citizens in all sections of this country to respect the rights of all others and to respect the law of the land.

All this is not unrelated to world peace. "When a man's ways please the Lord," the Scriptures tell us, "he maketh even his enemies to be at peace with him." And is not peace, in the last analysis, basically a matter of human rights—the right to live out our lives without fear of devastation, the right to breathe air as nature provided it, the right of future generations to a healthy existence?

While we proceed to safeguard our national interests, let us also safeguard human interests. And the elimination of war and arms is clearly in the interest of both. No treaty, however much it may be to the advantage of all, however tightly it may be worded, can provide absolute security against the risks of deception and evasion. But it can, if it is sufficiently effective in its enforcement and if it is sufficiently in the interests of its signers, offer far more security and far fewer risks than an unabated, uncontrolled, unpredictable arms race.

The United States, as the world knows, will never start a war. We do not want a war. We do not now expect a war. This generation of Americans has already had enough—more than enough—of war and hate and oppression. We shall be prepared if others wish it. We shall be alert to try to stop it. But we shall also do our part to build a world of peace where the weak are safe and the strong are just. We are not helpless before that task or hopeless of its success. Confident and unafraid, we labor on—not toward a strategy of annihilation but toward a strategy of peace.

2. ON PEACEFUL COEXISTENCE*

by Nikita S. Khrushchev

I have been told that the question of peaceful coexistence of states with different social systems is uppermost today in the minds of many Americans—and not only Americans. The question of coexistence, particularly in our day, interests literally every man and woman on the globe.

We all of us well know that tremendous changes have taken place in the world. Gone, indeed, are the days when it took weeks to cross the ocean from one continent to the other or when a trip from Europe to America, or from Asia to Africa, seemed a very complicated undertaking. The progress of modern technology has reduced our planet to a rather small place; it has even become, in this sense, quite congested. And if in our daily life it is a matter of considerable importance to establish normal relations with our neighbors in a densely inhabited settlement, this is so much the more necessary in the relations between states, in particular states belonging to different social systems.

You may like your neighbor or dislike him. You are not obliged to be friends with him or visit him. But you live side by side, and what can you do if neither you nor he has any desire to quit the old home and move to another town? All the more so in relations between states. It would be unreasonable to assume that you can make it so hot for your undesirable neighbor that he will decide to move to Mars or Venus. And vice versa, of course.

What, then, remains to be done? There may be two ways out: either war—and war in the rocket and H-bomb age is fraught with the most dire consequences for all nations—or peaceful coexistence. Whether you like your neighbor or not, nothing can be done about it, you have to find some way of getting on with him, for you both live on one and the same planet.

But the very concept of peaceful coexistence, it is said, by its alleged complexity frightens certain people who have become unaccustomed to trusting their neighbors and who see a double bottom in each suitcase. People of this kind, on hearing the word "coexistence," begin to play around with it in one way and another, sizing it up and applying various yardsticks to it. Isn't it a fraud? Isn't it a trap? Does not coexistence signify the division of the world into areas separated by high fences, which do not communicate with each other? And what is going to happen behind those fences?

The more such questions are piled up artificially by the cold-war mongers, the more difficult it is for the ordinary man to make head or tail of them. It would therefore be timely to rid the essence of this question of all superfluous elements and to attempt to look soberly at the most pressing problem of our day—the problem of peaceful competition.

II

One does not need to delve deeply into history to appreciate how important it is for mankind to ensure peaceful coexistence. And here it may be said parenthetically that the Europeans might have benefited a great deal in their day if, instead of organizing senseless crusades which invariably ended in failure, they had established peaceful relations with the differently-minded peoples of the Moslem East.

But let us turn to facts concerning the relatively recent past when the watershed between states no longer consisted of different religious creeds and customs, but of much deeper differences of principle relating to the choice of social systems. This new situation arose on the threshold of the 1920s when, to the booming of the guns of the Russian cruiser *Aurora* which had joined the rebellious workers and peasants, a new and unprecedented social system, a state of workers and peasants, came into the world.

Its appearance was met with the disgruntled outcries of those who naïvely believed the capitalist system to be eternal and immutable. Some people even made an attempt to strangle the unwanted infant in the cradle. Everybody knows how this ended: our people voted with their arms for Soviet power, and it came to stay. And even then, in 1920, V. I. Lenin, replying to the question of an American correspondent as to what basis there could be for peace between Soviet Russia and America, said: "Let the American imperialists not touch us. We won't touch them."

From its very inception the Soviet state proclaimed peaceful coexistence as the basic principle of its foreign policy. It was no accident that the very first state act of the Soviet power was the decree on peace, the decree on the cessation of the bloody war.

What, then, is the policy of peaceful coexistence?

In its simplest expression it signifies the repudiation of war as a means of solving controversial issues. However, this does not cover the entire concept of peaceful coexistence. Apart from the commitment to nonaggression, it also presupposes an obligation on the part of all states to desist from violating each other's territorial integrity and sovereignty in any form and under any pretext whatsoever. The principle of peaceful coexistence signifies a renunciation of interference in the internal affairs of other countries with the object of altering their system of government or mode of life or for any other motives. The doctrine of peaceful coexistence also presupposes that political and economic relations between countries are to be based upon complete equality of the parties concerned, and on mutual benefit.

It is often said in the West that peaceful coexistence is nothing else than a tactical method of the socialist states. There is not a grain of truth in such allegations. Our desire for peace and peaceful coexistence is not conditioned by any time-serving or tactical considerations. It springs from the very nature of socialist society in which there are no classes or social groups interested in profiting by war or seizing and enslaving other people's territories. The Soviet Union and the other socialist countries, thanks to their socialist system, have an unlimited home market and for this reason they have no need to pursue an expansionist policy of conquest and an effort to subordinate other countries to their influence.

It is the people who determine the destinies of the socialist states. The socialist states are ruled by the working people themselves, the workers and peasants, the people who themselves create all the material and spiritual values of society. And people of labor cannot want war. For to them war spells grief and tears, death, devastation and misery. Ordinary people have no need for war.

Contrary to what certain propagandists hostile to us say, the coexistence of states with different social systems does not mean that they will only fence themselves off from one another by a high wall and undertake the mutual obligation not to throw stones over the wall or pour dirt upon each other. No! Peaceful coexistence does not mean merely living side by side in the absence of war but with the constantly remaining threat of its breaking out in the future. *Peaceful coexistence can and should develop into peaceful competition for the purpose of satisfying man's needs in the best possible way.*

We say to the leaders of the capitalist states: Let us try out in practice whose system is better, let us compete without war. This is much better than competing in who will produce more arms and who will smash whom. We stand and always will stand for such competition as will help to raise the well-being of the people to a higher level.

The principle of peaceful competition does not at all demand that one or another state abandon the system and ideology adopted by it. It goes without saying that the acceptance of this principle cannot lead to the immediate end of disputes and contradictions which are inevitable between countries adhering to different social systems. But the main thing is ensured: the states which decided to adopt the path of peaceful coexistence repudiate the use of force in any form and agree on a peaceful settlement of possible disputes and conflicts, bearing in mind the mutual interests of the parties concerned. In our age of the H-bomb and atomic techniques this is the main thing of interest to every man.

Displaying skepticism about the idea of peaceful competition, Vice President Nixon, in his speech over the Soviet radio and television in August, 1959, attempted to find a contradiction between the Soviet people's professions of their readiness to coexist peacefully with the capitalist states and the slogans posted in the shops of our factories calling for higher labor productivity in order to ensure the speediest victory of Communism.

This was not the first time we heard representatives of the bourgeois countries reason in this manner. They say: The Soviet leaders argue that they are for peaceful coexistence. At the same time they declare that they are fighting for Communism and they even say that Communism will be victorious in all countries. How can there be peaceful coexistence with the Soviet Union if it fights for Communism?

People who treat the question in this way confuse matters, willfully or not, by confusing the problems of ideological struggle with the question of relations between states. Those indulging in this sort of confusion are most probably guided by a desire to cast aspersions upon the Communists of the Soviet Union and to represent them as the advocates of aggressive actions. This, however, is very unwise.

The Communist Party of the Soviet Union at its Twentieth Congress made it perfectly clear and obvious that the allegations that the Soviet Union intends to overthrow capitalism in other countries by means of "exporting" revolution are absolutely unfounded. I cannot refrain from reminding you of my words at the Twentieth Congress: "It goes without saying that among us Communists there are no adherents of capitalism. But this does not mean that we have interfered or plan to interfere in the internal affairs of countries where capitalism still exists. Romain Rolland was right when he said that 'freedom is not brought in from abroad in baggage trains like Bourbons.' It is ridiculous to think that revolutions are made to order."

We Communists believe that the idea of Communism will ultimately be victorious throughout the world, just as it has been victorious in our country, in China and in many other states. Many readers of FOREIGN AFFAIRS will probably disagree with us. Perhaps they think that the idea of capitalism will ultimately triumph. It is their right to think so. We may argue, we may disagree with one another. *The main thing is to keep to the positions of ideological struggle, without resorting to arms in order to prove that one is right.* The point is that with military techniques what they are today, there are no inaccessible places in the world. Should a world war break out, no country will be able to shut itself off from a crushing blow.

We believe that ultimately that system will be victorious on the globe which will offer the nations greater opportunities for improving their material and spiritual life. It is precisely socialism that creates unprecedentedly great prospects for the inexhaustible creative enthusiasm of the masses, for a genuine flourishing of science and culture, for the realization of man's dream of a happy life, a life without destitute and unemployed people, of a happy childhood and tranquil old age, of the realization of the most audacious and ambitious human projects, of man's right to create in a truly free manner in the interests of the people.

But when we say that in the competition between the two systems, the capitalist and the socialist, our system will win, this does not mean, of course, that we shall achieve victory by interfering in the internal affairs of the capitalist countries. Our confidence in the victory of Communism is of a different kind. It is based on a knowledge of the laws governing the development of society. Just as in its time capitalism, as the more progressive system, took the place of feudalism, so will capitalism be inevitably superseded by Communism—the more progressive and more equitable social system. We are confident of the victory of the socialist system because it is a more progressive system than the capitalist system. Soviet power has been in existence for only a little more than 40 years, and during these years we have gone through two of the worst wars, repulsing the attacks of enemies who attempted to strangle us. Capitalism in the United States has been in existence for more than a century and a half, and the history of the United States has developed in such a way that never once have enemies landed on American territory.

Yet the dynamics of the development of the U.S.S.R. and the U.S.A. are such that the 42-year-old land of the Soviets is already able to challenge the 150-year-old capitalist state to economic competition; and the most farsighted American leaders are admitting that the Soviet Union is fast catching up with the United States and will ultimately outstrip it. Watching the progress of this competition, anyone can judge which is the better system, and we believe that in the long run all the peoples will embark on the path of struggle for the building of socialist societies.

You disagree with us? Prove by facts that your system is superior and more efficacious, that it is capable of ensuring a higher degree of prosperity for the people than the socialist system, that under capitalism man can be happier than under socialism. It is impossible to prove this. I have no other explanation for the fact that talk of violently "rolling back" Communism never ceases in the West. Not long ago the U.S. Senate and House of Representatives deemed it proper to pass a resolution calling for the "liberation" of the socialist countries allegedly enslaved by Communism and, moreover, of a number of union republics constituting part of the Soviet Union. The authors of the resolution call for the "liberation" of the Ukraine, Byelorussia, Lithuania, Latvia, Estonia, Armenia, Azerbaijan, Georgia, Kazakhstan, Turkmenistan and even a certain "Ural Area."

I would not be telling the full truth if I did not say that the adoption of this ill-starred resolution was regarded by the Soviet people as an act of provocation. Personally I agree with this appraisal.

It would be interesting to see, incidentally, how the authors of this resolution would have reacted if the parliament of Mexico, for instance, had passed a resolution demanding that Texas, Arizona and California be "liberated from American slavery." Apparently they have never pondered such a question, which is very regrettable. Sometimes comparisons help to understand the essence of a matter.

Traveling through the Soviet Union, leading American statesmen and public figures have had full opportunity to convince themselves that there is no hope of sowing strife between the Soviet people and the Communist Party and the Soviet Government, and of influencing them to rebel against Communism. How, then are we to explain the unceasing attempts to revive the policy of "rolling back" Communism? What do they have in mind? Armed intervention in the internal affairs of the socialist countries? But in the West as well as in the East people are fully aware that under the conditions of modern military technique such actions are fraught with immediate and relentless retaliation.

So we come back to what we started with. In our day there are only two ways: peaceful coexistence or the most destructive war in history. There is no third choice.

III

The problem of peaceful coexistence between states with different social systems has become particularly pressing in view of the fact that since the Second World War the development of relations between states has entered a new stage, that now we have approached a period in the life of mankind when there is a real chance of excluding war once and for all from the life of society. The new alignment of international forces which has developed since the Second World War offers ground for the assertion that a new world war is no longer a fatal inevitability, that it can be averted.

First, today not only all the socialist states, but many countries in Asia and Africa which have embarked upon the road of independent national statehood, and many other states outside the aggressive military groupings, are actively fighting for peace.

Secondly, the peace policy enjoys the powerful support of the broad masses of the people all over the world.

Thirdly, the peaceful socialist states are in possession of very potent material means, which cannot but have a deterring effect upon the aggressors.

Prior to the Second World War the U.S.S.R. was the only socialist country, with not more than 17 percent of the territory, 3 percent of the population, and about 10 percent of the output of the world. At present, the socialist countries cover about one-fourth of the territory of the globe, have one-third of its population, and their industrial output accounts for about one-third of the total world output.

This is precisely the explanation of the indisputable fact that throughout the past years, hotbeds of war breaking out now in one and now in another part of the globe—in the Near East and in Europe, in the Far East and in Southeast Asia—have been extinguished at the very outset.

What does the future hold in store for us?

As a result of the fulfillment and overfulfillment of the present Seven Year Plan of economic development of the U.S.S.R., as well as of the plans of the other socialist countries of Europe and Asia, the countries of the socialist system will then account for a little more than half of the world output. Their economic power will grow immeasurably, and this will help to an even greater extent to consolidate world peace: the material might and moral influence of the peace-loving states will be so great that any bellicose militarist will have to think ten times before risking going to war. It is the good fortune of mankind that a community of socialist states which are not interested in new war has been set up, because to build socialism and Communism the socialist countries need peace. Today the community of socialist countries which has sprung up on the basis of complete equality holds such a position in the development of all branches of economy, science and culture as to be able to exert an influence towards preventing the outbreak of new world wars.

Hence we are already in a practical sense near to that stage in the life of humanity when nothing will prevent people from devoting themselves wholly to peaceful labor, when war will be wholly excluded from the life of society.

But if we say that there is no fatal inevitability of war at present, this by no means signifies that we can rest on our laurels, fold our arms and bask in the sun in the hope that an end has been put to wars once and for all. Those in the West who believe that war is to their benefit have not yet abandoned their schemes. They control considerable material forces, as well as military and political levers, and there is no guarantee that some tragic day they will not attempt to set them in motion. That is why it is so much the more necessary to continue an active struggle in order that the policy of peaceful coexistence may triumph throughout the world not in words but in deeds.

Of much importance, of course, is the fact that this policy has in our day merited not only the widest moral approval but also international legal recognition. The countries of the socialist camp in their relations with the capitalist states are guided precisely by this policy. The principles of peaceful coexistence are reflected in the decisions of the Bandung Conference of Asian and African countries. Furthermore, many countries of Europe, Asia and Africa have solemnly proclaimed this principle as the basis of their foreign policy. Finally, the idea of peaceful coexistence has found unanimous support in the decisions of the twelfth and thirteenth sessions of the United Nations General Assembly.

In our view, peaceful coexistence can become lasting only if the good declarations in favor of peace are supported by active measures on the part of the governments and peoples of all countries. As far as the Soviet Union is concerned, it has already done a good deal in this respect, and I am able to share some experiences with you.

As far back as March 12, 1951, the Supreme Soviet of the U.S.S.R. adopted a "Law on the Defense of Peace," stating:

(1) Propaganda for war, in whatever form it may be conducted, undermines the cause of peace, creates the menace of a new war and therefore constitutes the gravest crime against humanity.

(2) Persons guilty of war propaganda should be brought to court and tried as heinous criminals.

Further, the Soviet Union has in recent years unilaterally reduced its armed forces by more than 2,000,000 men. The funds released as a result have been used to develop the economy and further raise the material and cultural living standards of the Soviet people.

The Soviet Union has liquidated its bases on the territories of other states.

The Soviet Union unilaterally discontinued the tests of atomic weapons and refrained from conducting them further until it became finally clear that the Western powers refused to follow our example and were continuing the explosions.

The Soviet Union has repeatedly submitted detailed and perfectly realistic proposals for disarmament, meeting the positions of the Western powers halfway. But to solve the disarmament problem it is necessary for our Western partners to agree and desire to meet us halfway too. This is just what is lacking.

When it became clear that it was very difficult under these conditions to solve the complex disarmament problem immediately, we proposed another concrete idea to our partners: Let us concentrate our attention on those problems which lend themselves most easily to a solution. Let us undertake initial partial steps on matters concerning which the views of the different parties have been brought closer together.

It is perfectly clear that one of these questions today is the question of discontinuing atomic and hydrogen weapon tests. The progress achieved in this matter justifies the hope that an agreement on the discontinuation of nuclear weapon tests will shortly be reached. Implementation of this measure will, of course, be an important step on the way to the solution of the disarmament problem and the banning of nuclear weapons in general.

Attributing much importance to contacts and intercourse between statesmen of all countries, the Soviet Government a few years ago proposed that an East-West heads of government conference be convened in order to come to terms—taking into account present-day realities and guided by the spirit of mutual understanding—on concrete measures, the realization of which would help to relax international tension.

We also proposed that this conference consider those international questions for the settlement of which realistic prerequisites already existed. As a first step toward such a settlement, we proposed to the powers concerned that a peace treaty be concluded with Germany and that West Berlin be granted the status of a demilitarized free city. I want to emphasize particularly that we were guided primarily by the desire to put a final end to the aftermath of the Second World War. We regard the liquidation of the consequences of the Second World War and the conclusion of a peace treaty with the two German states—the German Democratic Republic and the German Federal Republic—as the question of questions.

Indeed, 14 years have already passed since the war ended, but the German people are still without a peace treaty. The delay has afforded wide scope for renewed activities of the West German militarists and revanchists. They have already proclaimed their aggressive plans, laying claim, for instance, to lands in Poland and Czechoslovakia. Of course, the German revanchists are thinking not only of a march to the East; they also know the way to the West. In the Second World War the Hitlerites occupied Western Europe before advancing against the Soviet Union.

Will the direction chosen by the modern German revanchists for their aggression be any consolation to the peoples of Europe if a global war breaks out on that continent? The lessons of history should not be ignored. To do so often ends in tragedy.

Some say: The Soviet people are unduly sensitive. Can one assume that Western Germany is now in a position to precipitate another world war? Those who put the question thus forget that Western Germany is at present acting in the world arena not alone but within the military North Atlantic bloc. She plays a paramount rôle in this bloc. And more than that, life has shown that the North Atlantic Alliance is being gradually converted into an instrument of the German militarists, which makes it easier for them to carry out aggressive plans. It is not at all impossible, therefore, that Western Germany, taking advantage of her position in the North Atlantic Alliance, might provoke hostilities in order to draw her allies into it and plunge the whole world into the chasm of a devastating war.

All this indicates how timely and realistic are the proposals of the Soviet Government for the conclusion of a peace treaty with Germany and for bringing the situation in West Berlin back to normal.

And yet, some of the Western opponents of the Soviet proposals say that if the Soviet Union really stands for peaceful coexistence it should even be asked to commit itself to the preservation of the existing status quo. Others argue that if the Western powers agree to the conclusion of a peace treaty with the two German states that would amount to a retreat on their part, and the Soviet Union should make some compensation for this "retreat."

There are no grounds whatever for these assertions, in our opinion. The task before us is to do away with the aftermath of the Second World War and to conclude a peace treaty. And any possibility of someone gaining and others losing, of someone acquiring and others making concessions, is out of the question here. All the parties concerned acquire a stronger foundation for the maintenance of peace in Europe and throughout the world in the shape of a peace treaty. Does this not accord with the interests of all the peoples?

At times, and of late especially, some spokesmen in the West have gone so far as to say that the abolition of the aftermath of the Second World War is a step which would allegedly intensify rather than ease international tension. It is hard to believe that there are no secret designs behind allegations of this kind, especially when attempts are made to present in a distorted light the policy of the U.S.S.R., which is intended to secure a lasting and stable peace, by alleging that it all but leads to war. It seems to us, on the contrary, that the Soviet position on the German question corresponds most of all to the present-day reality.

It now seems that no sober-minded leader in the West is inclined any longer to advance the unrealistic demand for the so-called reunion of Germany before the conclusion of a peace treaty, in as much as more and more political leaders are becoming aware of the fact that reunion in the conditions now obtaining is a process which depends upon the Germans themselves and not upon any outside interference. We should start from the obvious fact that two German states exist, and that the Germans themselves must decide how they want to live. In as much as these two states, the German Democratic Republic and the German Federal Republic, do exist, the peace treaty should be concluded with them, because any further delay and postponement of this exceptionally important act tends not only to sustain the abnormal situation in Europe but also to aggravate it still further.

As for Germany's unity, I am convinced that Germany will be

united sooner or later. However, before this moment comes—and no one can foretell when it will come—no attempts should be made to interfere from outside in this internal process, to sustain the state of war which is fraught with many grave dangers and surprises for peace in Europe and throughout the world. The desire to preserve the peace and to prevent another war should outweigh all other considerations of statesmen, irrespective of their mode of thinking. The Gordian knot must be cut: the peace treaty must be achieved if we do not want to play with fire—with the destinies of millions upon millions of people.

IV

In this connection it is impossible to ignore also the question of West Berlin. It is commonly known that the German revanchists have made West Berlin the base for their constant undermining and subversive activity directed towards the provoking of war. We resolutely reject any attempts to ascribe to the Soviet Union the intention of seizing West Berlin and infringing upon the right of the population in this part of the city to preserve its present way of life. On the contrary, in demanding the normalization of the situation in West Berlin, we have proposed to convert it into a free city and to guarantee, jointly with the Western states, the preservation there of the way of life and of the social order which suits the West Berlin inhabitants best of all. This shows that the positions of the Government of the Soviet Union and the Governments of the Western states, judging by their statements, coincide on this question. We, and so do they, stand for the independence of West Berlin and for the preservation of the existing way of life there.

It is, therefore, only necessary to overcome the difficulties born of the cold war in order to find the way to an agreement on West Berlin and on the wider question of the conclusion of a peace treaty with the two German states. This is the way to ease international tensions and to promote peaceful coexistence. It would strengthen confidence between states and assist in the gradual abolition of ·unfriendliness and suspicion in international relations.

Implementation of the Soviet proposals would not injure the interests of the Western powers and would not give any one-sided advantages to anybody. At the same time, the settlement of the German question would prevent a dangerous development of events in Europe, remove one of the main causes of international tension and create favorable prospects for a settlement of other international issues.

The proposals of the Soviet Union were discussed at the Foreign Ministers' Conference in Geneva. The Ministers did not succeed in reaching an agreement, but the Geneva Conference did accomplish a great deal of useful work. The positions of the two sides were positively brought closer together and the possibility of an agreement on some questions has become apparent.

At the same time, we still have substantial differences on a number of questions. I am deeply convinced that they are not fundamental differences on which agreement is impossible. And if we still have differences and have not reached agreement on certain important questions, it is, as we believe, with adequate grounds—a result of the concessions made by the Western powers to Chancellor Adenauer, who is pursuing a military policy, the policy of the German revanchists. This is a case of the United States, Britain and France dangerously abetting Chancellor Adenauer. It would have been far better if the NATO allies of Western Germany would persuade Chancellor Adenauer, in the interest of the maintenace of peace, that his policy imperils the cause of peace and that it may ultimately end in irreparable disaster for Western Germany. All this emphasizes again that the representatives of the states concerned must do some more work in order to find mutually acceptable decisions.

I believe that my trip to the United States and the subsequent visit of President Eisenhower to the Soviet Union will afford the possibility for a useful exchange of opinions, for finding a common tongue and a common understanding of the questions that should be settled.

V

We are prepared now as before to do everything we possible can in order that the relations between the Soviet Union and other countries, and, in particular, the relations between the U.S.S.R. and the U.S.A., should be built upon the foundation of friendship and that they should fully correspond to the principles of peaceful coexistence.

I should like to repeat what I said at my recent press conference in Moscow: "Should Soviet-American relations become brighter, that will not fail to bring about an improvement in the relations with other states and will help to scatter the gloomy clouds in other parts of the globe also. Naturally, we want friendship not only with the U.S.A., but also with the friends of the U.S.A. At the same time we want to see the U.S.A. maintain good relations not only with us, but with our friends as well."

What, then, is preventing us from making the principles of peaceful coexistence an unshakable international standard and daily practice in the relations between the West and East?

Of course, different answers may be given to this question. But in order to be frank to the end, we should also say the following: *It is necessary that everybody should understand the irrevocable fact that the historic process is irreversible.* It is impossible to bring back yesterday. It is high time to understand that the world of the twentieth century is not the world of the nineteenth century, that two diametrically opposed social and economic systems exist in the world today side by side, and that the socialist system, in spite of all the attacks upon it, has grown so strong, has developed into such a force, as to make any return to the past impossible.

Real facts of life in the last ten years have shown convincingly that the policy of "rolling back" Communism can only poison the international atmosphere, heighten the tension between states and work in favor of the cold war. Neither its inspirers nor those who conduct it can turn back the course of history and restore capitalism in the socialist countries.

We have always considered the Americans realistic people. All the more are we astonished to find that leading representatives of the United States still number in their midst individuals who insist on their own way in the face of the obvious failure of the policy of "rolling back" Communism. But is it not high time to take a sober view of things and to draw conclusions from the lessons of the last 15 years? Is it not yet clear to everybody that consistent adherence to the policy of peaceful coexistence would make it possible to improve the international situation, to bring about a drastic cut in military expenditures and to release vast material resources for wiser purposes?

The well known British scientist, J. Bernal, recently cited figures to show that average annual expenditures for military purposes throughout the world between 1950 and the end of 1957 were expressed in the huge sum of about 90 billion dollars. How many factories, apartment houses, schools, hospitals and libraries could have been built everywhere with the funds now spent on the preparation of another war! And how fast could economic progress have been advanced in the underdeveloped countries if we had converted to these purposes at least some of the means which are now being spent on war purposes!

VI

It is readily seen that the policy of peaceful coexistence receives a firm foundation only with increase in extensive and absolutely unrestricted international trade. It can be said without fear of exaggeration that there is no good basis for improvement of relations between our countries other than development of international trade.

If the principle of peaceful coexistence of states is to be adhered to, not in words, but in deeds, it is perfectly obvious that no ideological differences should be an obstacle to the development and extension of mutually advantageous economic contacts, to the exchange of everything produced by human genius in the sphere of peaceful branches of material production.

In this connection it may be recalled that soon after the birth of the Soviet state, back in the early 1920s, the Western countries, proceeding from considerations of economic interest, agreed to establish trade relations with our country despite the acutest ideological differences. Since then, discounting comparatively short periods, trade between the Soviet Union and capitalist states has been developing steadily. No ideological differences prevented, for instance, a considerable extension of trade relations between the Soviet Union and Britain and other Western states in recent years. We make no secret of our desire to establish normal commercial and business contacts with the United States as well, without any restrictions, without any discriminations.

In June of last year the Soviet Government addressed itself to the Government of the United States with the proposal to develop economic and trade contacts between our two countries. We proposed an extensive and concrete program of developing Soviet-American trade on a mutually advantageous basis. The adoption of our proposals would undoubtedly accord with the interests of both states and peoples. However, these proposals have not been developed so far.

Striving for the restoration of normal trade relations with the United States, the Soviet Union does not pursue any special interests. In our economic development we rely wholly on the internal forces of our country, on our own resources and possibilities. All our plans for further economic development are drawn up taking into consideration the possibilities available here. As in the past, when we outline these plans we proceed only from the basis of our own possibilities and forces. Irrespective of whether or not we shall trade with Western countries, the United States included, the implementation of our economic plans of peaceful construction will not in the least be impeded.

However, if both sides want to improve relations, all barriers in international trade must be removed. Those who want peaceful coexistence cannot but favor the development of trade, economic and business contacts. Only on this basis can international life develop normally.

VII

Peaceful coexistence is the only way which is in keeping with the interests of all nations. To reject it would mean under existing conditions to doom the whole world to a terrible and destructive war at a time when it is fully possible to avoid it.

Is it possible that when mankind has advanced to a plane where it has proved capable of the greatest discoveries and of making its first steps into outer space, it should not be able to use the colossal achievements of its genius for the establishment of a stable peace, for the good of man, rather than for the preparation of another war and for the destruction of all that has been created by its labor over many millenniums? Reason refuses to believe this. It protests.

The Soviet people have stated and declare again that they do not want war. If the Soviet Union and the countries friendly to it are not attacked, we shall never use any weapons either against the United States or against any other countries. We do not want any horrors of war, destruction, suffering and death for ourselves or for any other peoples. We say this not because we fear anyone. Together with our friends, we are united and stronger than ever. But precisely because of that do we say that war can and should be prevented. Precisely because we want to rid mankind of war, we urge the Western powers to peaceful and lofty competition. We say to all: Let us prove to each other the advantages of one's own system not with fists, not by war, but by peaceful economic competition in conditions of peaceful coexistence.

As for the social system in some state or other, that is the domestic affair of the people of each country. We always have stood and we stand today for non-interference in the internal affairs of other countries. We have always abided, and we shall abide, by these positions. The question, for example, what system will exist in the United States or in other capitalist countries cannot be decided by other peoples or states. This question can and will be decided only by the American people themselves, only by the people of each country.

The existence of the Soviet Union and of the other socialist countries is a real fact. It is also a real fact that the United States of America and the other capitalist countries live in different social conditions, in the conditions of capitalism. Then let us recognize this real situation and proceed from it in order not to go against reality, against life itself. Let us not try to change this situation by inter-ferences from without, by means of war on the part of some states against other states.

I repeat, there is only one way to peace, one way out of the existing tension: peaceful coexistence.

3. THE SINGLE GOAL OF PEACE*

BY LYNDON B. JOHNSON

Following are the foreign policy portions of an address made by President Johnson at a Swedish celebration at Minneapolis, Minn., on June 28, 1964.

The Bible counsels us: "To everything there is a season, and a time to every purpose under the heaven . . . a time of war, and a time of peace."

* From *Department of State Bulletin*, Vol. 51 (July 20, 1964), pp. 79–81.

So I come today to speak to you in the hope that, after decades of war and threats of war, we may be nearing a time of peace. Today, as always, if a nation is to keep its freedom it must be prepared to risk war. When necessary, we will take that risk. But as long as I am President, I will spare neither my office nor myself in the quest for peace. That peace is much more than the absence of war. In fact, peace is much the same thing in our world community as it is here in your community, or in the small community of Johnson City, Texas, where I grew up.

If, in your town, every morning brings fear that the serenity of the streets will be shattered by the sounds of violence, then there is no peace. If one man can compel others, unjustly and unlawfully, to do what he commands them to do, then your community is not a place of peace. If we have neither the will nor a way to settle disputes among neighbors without force and violence, then none of us can live in peace. If we do not work together to help others fulfill their fair desires, then peace is insecure. For in a community, as in the world, if the strong and the wealthy ignore the needs of the poor and the oppressed, frustrations will result in force. Peace, therefore, is a world where no nation fears another, or no nation can force another to follow its command. It is a world where differences are solved without destruction and common effort is directed at common problems.

Such a peace will not come by a single act or a single moment. It will take decades and generations of persistent and patient effort. That great son of Sweden, Dag Hammarskjold, once said:

> The qualities it requires are just those which I feel we all need today— perseverance and patience, a firm grip on realities, careful but imaginative planning, a clear awareness of the dangers—but also of the fact that fate is what we make it. . . .

With these qualities as our foundation, we follow several goals to the single goal of peace. And what are those goals? First is restraint in the use of power. We must be, and we are, strong enough to protect ourselves and our allies. But it was a great historian who reminded us that: "No aspect of power more impresses men than its exercise with restraint."

We do not advance the cause of freedom by calling on the full might of our military to solve every problem. We won a great victory in Cuba because we stood there for many days, firm without using force. In Viet-Nam we are engaged in a brutal and a bitter struggle trying to help a friend. There, too, we will stand firm to help maintain their own freedom and to give them counsel and advice and help as necessary.

Second is the search for practical solutions to particular problems. Agreements will not flow from a sudden trust among nations. Trust comes from a slow series of agreements. Each agreement must be fashioned as the products of your famous craftsmanship are fashioned, with attention to detail, with practical skills, with faith in the importance of the result.

And so, even while we are caught in conflict in one part of the world, we labor to build the structure of agreement which can bring peace to all the rest of the world. In this way we have signed a treaty already ending nuclear tests in the atmosphere. Already we have cut back our production of atomic fuel and weapons. Already we have established a "hot line" between Washington and Moscow. Already we are meeting with the Soviets to pool our efforts in making fresh water from the oceans. These agreements, by themselves, have not ended tensions or they have not ended war. But because of them we have moved much closer to peace.

And the third point that I want to bring up is respect for the rights and fears of others. We can never compromise the cause of freedom. But as we work in our world community we must always remember that differences with others do not always flow from a desire for domination. They can come from honest clash of honest beliefs of goals. And in such cases our strength does not entitle us to impose our interest. Rather, our desire for peace compels us to seek just compromise. And we must also recognize, although this is very hard to do, that other nations may honestly fear our intentions or the intensions of our allies. There is no need for such fear. For we in America seek neither dominion or conquest. But where it exists, we must work to dispel that fear.

The fourth point that I want to make is cooperation in solving the problems which are greater than immediate conflicts. Most of our neighbors in the world live in the midst of hunger and poverty. Most of our neighbors live in the midst of disease and ignorance. We are proud of the fact that here in America, across the world, American workers and American food and American capital are building industry and are expanding farms, are educating the young and are caring for the sick and are feeding the hungry.

We will continue to seek such cooperation. No peace and no power is strong enough to stand for long against the restless discontent of millions who are without hope. For peace to last, all must have a stake in its benefits.

Fifth is the ability to adjust disputes without the use of force. It is, in short, the pursuit of justice. We can find guidance here in our own country's historic pledge to the rule of law. That is a pledge to abide by the law and to accept its settlements. It is a pledge to submit to courts and to be satisfied by court decisions. It is a pledge to respect, uphold, and always obey the law of the land. For if any take grievances and disputes into their own hands, the safety and the freedom of all is in peril. "Due process" is the safeguard of our civilization. As a President of the United States and as an individual citizen, I stand totally committed to the integrity of justice and the enforcement of the law. But legal government depends upon law-loving and law-abiding citizens. Today the key to peace in our own land is obedience to the great moral command that no man should deny to another the liberties the Constitution creates, as the law defines those liberties. And it rests on the even more hallowed rule that, whatever our disagreements, we treat others with the peaceful respect that we reserve and desire for ourselves. So, too, we seek a world community in which answers can win acceptance without the use of force. For this purpose, all the machinery of international justice is useless unless it is infused with the good faith of nations. On a worldwide basis, we place much hope in the United Nations.

Twenty years after World War I the League of Nations was discredited. Twenty years after World War II the United Nations is, thank God, a stronger force for peace than ever before. Our support —the steadfast support of nations like Sweden—has made that possible. And let any of those who might choose to criticize the United Nations always remember that where the United Nations has gone, from Iran to the Congo, the Communists have not conquered. This is not because the United Nations supports our cause or because it exists just to help us against our enemies. It is because the United Nations is on the side of national independence, on the side of peaceful justice, of self-determination, of human freedom; and that is the side that we are on, too.

These are the several tasks—these are the several paths that we take to peace. At times in the solitude of my office, peace seems discouragingly distant. My days are often filled with crisis and conflict. Yet each time that I come here among the people of my country I feel new hope and renewed faith. There was a legendary figure who, each time his feet touched the earth, redoubled his strength. Your friendship and your warmth and your wishes are equally the source of my strength.

    .   .   .   .   .

I want to remind you finally, as I finish, that it is with the people and not with their leaders that the final question whether the liberties and the life of this land shall be "preserved to the latest generations." If you can do this, if you do do this, then our children's children will gladly remember us in the ancient phrase: "Blessed are the peace-makers, for they shall be called the children of God."

CHAPTER XVI

The Thaw and Thorn
in American-Soviet Relations

With the Soviet Union we seek peaceful understanding that can lessen the danger to freedom. . . . If we are to live together in peace, we must come to know each other better.
—LYNDON B. JOHNSON

The USSR Government is firmly and consistently pursuing a Leninist line in its foreign policy aimed at ensuring the peaceful coexistence of states with different social systems.
—ALEKSEI N. KOSYGIN

With the advent of the cold war, which has been intensified by the production of thermonuclear weapons of mass destruction and by the complexity of US-Soviet competition in every conceivable field of international politics, the peoples of the two nations and the world as a whole have been walking on a psychological "tightrope." In the words of Erich Fromm: "To live for any length of time under the constant threat of destruction creates certain psychological effects in most human beings—fright, hostility, callousness, a hardening of the heart, and a resulting indifference to all the values we cherish. Such conditions will transform us into barbarians—though barbarians equipped with the most complicated machines."

Although Fromm's description may not be a totally accurate prediction, the existence of disquieting symptoms in our societies to substantiate his pessimism is undeniable. In this sense, any kind of thaw in US-Soviet relations, no matter how insignificant it may appear, will contribute to the relaxation of world tensions and to the improvement of the international atmosphere. For this reason the successful conclusion of the Nuclear Test-Ban Treaty was of historic importance.

449

Both sides may regard the occasion as a steppingstone toward further détente in their relations. There is no evidence to indicate that the Johnson-Humphrey Administration in Washington and the Kosygin-Brezhnev collective leadership in Moscow are any less interested in détentes than the late President Kennedy and former Premier Khrushchev. The new leaders on both sides are not averse to fresh efforts at accommodation with each other now that they have firmly established themselves in their respective governments.

This chapter deals with some areas of accommodation and détente between the United States and the Soviet Union.

President Johnson emphasizes the importance of the US-Soviet Consular Convention as a step forward in developing understanding between the two countries. The President's statement is followed by a complete text of the Convention.

Business Week *speculates on future policies of the new Brezhnev-Kosygin regime in Moscow, presents brief biographical backgrounds of the two new leaders, and describes the circumstances surrounding the ouster of Khrushchev.*

Richard Lowenthal, Professor of International Relations at the Free University of Berlin, analyzes the direction of the Kremlin's new leadership to show that it has sought to temporize the rift with Peking by shifting emphasis from direct confrontation to indirect competition for influence in the newly emerging nations; he also shows that, at the same time, Soviet policy toward the West has changed "from direct approaches to the United States aiming at a major détente to indirect maneuvers for exploiting the disagreements within the Western alliance."

1. A STATEMENT ON AMERICAN-SOVIET CONSULAR CONVENTION, WITH TEXT OF CONVENTION*

BY LYNDON B. JOHNSON

We have just concluded negotiations with the Soviet Union on a consular convention. The agreement will be signed in Moscow on June 1. I have authorized Ambassador [Foy D.] Kohler to sign for the United States. I understand Soviet Foreign Minister [Andrei A.] Gromyko will be signing for the Soviet Union.

This treaty, which I will submit to the Senate for its advice and consent, is a significant step in our continuing efforts to increase contacts and understanding between the American people and the peoples of the Soviet Union. It will make possible improved consular services in both countries. American citizens visiting the Soviet Union, either as tourists or for business reasons, will have available to them a greater degree of consular protection than ever before. For example, Americans detained in the Soviet Union for any reasons will be assured of access without delay to American consular officials. American businessmen and shipping companies will be able to call on U.S. consular services to assist in representing their interests. And the mechanics for dealing with a whole range of legal problems from complicated questions of inheritance to simple notary services will be considerably eased.

It is my hope that this treaty—the first bilateral treaty between the United States and the Soviet Union—will be a step forward in developing understanding between our two countries, which is so important in the continuing struggle for peace.

TEXT OF CONVENTION, SIGNED JUNE 1

Press release 262 dated June 1, as corrected.

* From *Department of State Bulletin,* Vol. 50 (June 22, 1964), pp. 979–985. White House press release dated May 27.

CONSULAR CONVENTION

BETWEEN THE GOVERNMENT OF THE UNITED STATES OF AMERICA AND THE GOVERNMENT OF THE UNION OF SOVIET SOCIALIST REPUBLICS

The Government of the United States of America and the Government of the Union of Soviet Socialist Republics,

Desiring to cooperate in strengthening friendly relations and to regulate consular relations between both states,

Have decided to conclude a consular convention and for this purpose have agreed on the following:

DEFINITIONS

ARTICLE 1

For the purpose of the present Convention, the terms introduced hereunder have the following meaning:

1) "Consular establishment"—means any consulate general, consulate, vice consulate or consular agency;

2) "Consular district"—means the area assigned to a consular establishment for the exercise of consular functions;

3) "Head of consular establishment"—means a consul general, consul, vice consul, or consular agent directing the consular establishment;

4) "Consular officer"—means any person, including the head of the consular establishment, entrusted with the exercise of consular functions. Also included in the definition of "consular officer" are persons assigned to the consular establishment for training in the consular service.

5) "Employee of the consular establishment"—means any person performing administrative, technical, or service functions in a consular establishment.

OPENING OF CONSULAR ESTABLISHMENTS, APPOINTMENT OF CONSULAR OFFICERS AND EMPLOYEES

ARTICLE 2

1. A consular establishment may be opened in the territory of the receiving state only with that state's consent.

2. The location of a consular establishment and the limits of its consular district will be determined by agreement between the sending and receiving states.

3. Prior to the appointment of a head of a consular establishment, the

sending state shall obtain the approval of the receiving state to such an appointment through diplomatic channels.

4. The diplomatic mission of the sending state shall transmit to the foreign affairs ministry of the receiving state a consular commission which shall contain the full name of the head of the consular establishment, his citizenship, his class, the consular district assigned to him, and the seat of the consular establishment.

5. A head of a consular establishment may enter upon the exercise of his duties only after having been recognized in this capacity by the receiving state. Such recognition after the presentation of the commission shall be in the form of an exequatur or in another form and shall be free of charge.

6. The full name, function and class of all consular officers other than the head of a consular establishment, and the full name and function of employees of the consular establishment shall be notified in advance by the sending state to the receiving state.

The receiving state shall issue to each consular officer an appropriate document confirming his right to carry out consular functions in the territory of the receiving state.

7. The receiving state may at any time, and without having to explain its decision, notify the sending state through diplomatic channels that any consular officer is persona non grata or that any employee of the consular establishment is unacceptable. In such a case the sending state shall accordingly recall such officer or employee of the consular establishment. If the sending state refuses or fails within a reasonable time to carry out its obligations under the present paragraph, the receiving state may refuse to recognize the officer or employee concerned as a member of the consular establishment.

8. With the exception of members of the staff of the diplomatic mission of the sending state, as defined in paragraph c of Article 1 of the Vienna Convention on Diplomatic Relations, no national of the sending state already present in the receiving state or in transit thereto may be appointed as a consular officer or employee of the consular establishment.

ARTICLE 3

Consular officers may be nationals only of the sending state.

ARTICLE 4

The receiving state shall take the necessary measures in order that a consular officer may carry out his duties and enjoy the rights, privileges, and immunities provided for in the present Convention and by the laws of the receiving state.

ARTICLE 5

1. The receiving state shall either facilitate the acquisition on its territory, in accordance with its laws and regulations, by the sending state of premises necessary for its consular establishment or assist the latter in obtaining accommodation in some other way.

2. It shall also, where necessary, assist the sending state in obtaining suitable accommodation for the personnel of its consular establishment.

ARTICLE 6

1. If the head of the consular establishment cannot carry out his functions or if the position of head of a consular establishment is vacant, the sending state may empower a consular officer of the same or another consular establishment, or one of the members of the diplomatic staff of its diplomatic mission in the receiving state, to act temporarily as head of the consular establishment. The full name of this person must be transmitted in advance to the foreign affairs ministry of the receiving state.

2. A person empowered to act as temporary head of the consular establishment shall enjoy the rights, privileges and immunities of the head of the consular establishment.

3. When, in accordance with the provisions of paragraph 1 of the present Article, a member of the diplomatic staff of the diplomatic mission of the sending state in the receiving state is designated by the sending state as an acting head of the consular establishment, he shall continue to enjoy diplomatic privileges and immunities.

CONSULAR FUNCTIONS

ARTICLE 7

A consular officer shall be entitled within his consular district to perform the following functions, and for this purpose may apply orally or in writing to the competent authorities of the consular district:

1) To protect the rights and interests of the sending state and its nationals, both individuals and bodies corporate;

2) To further the development of commercial, economic, cultural and scientific relations between the sending state and the receiving state and otherwise promote the development of friendly relations between them;

3) To register nationals of the sending state, to issue or amend passports and other certificates of identity, and also to issue entry, exit, and transit visas;

4) To draw up and record certificates of birth and death of citizens of the sending state taking place in the receiving state, to record marriages and divorces, if both persons entering into marriage or divorce are citizens

of the sending state, and also to receive such declarations pertaining to family relationships of a national of the sending state as may be required under the law of the sending state, unless prohibited by the laws of the receiving state;

5) To draw up, certify, attest, authenticate, legalize and take other actions which might be necessary to validate any act or document of a legal character, as well as copies thereof, including commercial documents, declarations, registrations, testamentary dispositions, and contracts, upon the application of a national of the sending state, when such document is intended for use outside the territory of the receiving state, and also for any person, when such document is intended for use in the territory of the sending state;

6) To translate any acts and documents into the English and Russian languages and to certify to the accuracy of the translations;

7) To perform other official consular functions entrusted to him by the sending state if they are not contrary to the laws of the receiving state.

Article 8

1. The acts and documents specified in paragraph 5 of Article 7 of the present Convention which are drawn up or certified by the consular officer with his official seal affixed, as well as copies, extracts, and translations of such acts and documents certified by him with his official seal affixed, shall be receivable in evidence in the receiving state as official or officially certified acts, documents, copies, translations, or extracts, and shall have the same force and effect as though they were drawn up or certified by the competent authorities or officials of the receiving state; provided that such documents shall have been drawn and executed in conformity with the laws and regulations of the country where they are designed to take effect.

2. The acts, documents, copies, translations, or extracts, enumerated in paragraph 1 of the present Article shall be authenticated if required by the laws of the receiving state when they are presented to the authorities of the receiving state.

Article 9

If the relevant information is available to the competent authorities of the receiving state, such authorities shall inform the consular establishment of the death of a national of the sending state.

Article 10

1. In the case of the death of a national of the sending state in the territory of the receiving state, without leaving in the territory of his

decease any known heir or testamentary executor, the appropriate local authorities of the receiving state shall as promptly as possible inform a consular officer of the sending state.

2. A consular officer of the sending state may, within the discretion of the appropriate judicial authorities and if permissible under then existing applicable local law in the receiving state:

a) take provisional custody of the personal property left by a deceased national of the sending state, provided that the decedent shall have left in the receiving state no heir or testamentary executor appointed by the decedent to take care of his personal estate; provided that such provisional custody shall be relinquished to a duly appointed administrator;

b) administer the estate of a deceased national of the sending state who is not a resident of the receiving state at the time of his death, who leaves no testamentary executor, and who leaves in the receiving state no heir, provided that if authorized to administer the estate, the consular officer shall relinquish such administration upon the appointment of another administrator;

c) represent the interests of a national of the sending state in an estate in the receiving state, provided that such national is not a resident of the receiving state, unless or until such national is otherwise represented: provided, however, that nothing herein shall authorize a consular officer to act as an attorney at law.

3. Unless prohibited by law, a consular officer may, within the discretion of the court, agency, or person making distribution, receive for transmission to a national of the sending state who is not a resident of the receiving state any money or property to which such national is entitled as a consequence of the death of another person, including shares in an estate, payments made pursuant to workmen's compensation laws, pension and social benefits systems in general, and proceeds of insurance policies.

The court, agency, or person making distribution may require that a consular officer comply with conditions laid down with regard to: (a) presenting a power of attorney or other authorization from such non-resident national, (b) furnishing reasonable evidence of the receipt of such money or property by such national, and (c) returning the money or property in the event he is unable to furnish such evidence.

4. Whenever a consular officer shall perform the functions referred to in paragraphs 2 and 3 of this Article, he shall be subject, with respect to the exercise of such functions, to the laws of the receiving state and to the civil jurisdiction of the judicial and administrative authorities of the receiving state in the same manner and to the same extent as a national of the receiving state.

ARTICLE 11

A consular officer may recommend to the courts or to other competent authorities of the receiving state appropriate persons to act in the capacity of guardians or trustees for citizens of the sending state or for the property of such citizens when this property is left without supervision.

In the event that the court or competent authorities consider that the recommended candidate is for some reason unacceptable, the consular officer may propose a new candidate.

ARTICLE 12

1. A consular officer shall have the right within his district to meet with, communicate with, assist, and advise any national of the sending state and, where necessary, arrange for legal assistance for him. The receiving state shall in no way restrict the access of nationals of the sending state to its consular establishments.

2. The appropriate authorities of the receiving state shall immediately inform a consular officer of the sending state about the arrest or detention in other form of a national of the sending state.

3. A consular officer of the sending state shall have the right without delay to visit and communicate with a national of the sending state who is under arrest or otherwise detained in custody or is serving a sentence of imprisonment. The rights referred to in this paragraph shall be exercised in conformity with the laws and regulations of the receiving state, subject to the proviso, however, that the said laws and regulations must not nullify these rights.

ARTICLE 13

1. A consular officer may provide aid and assistance to vessels sailing under the flag of the sending state which have entered a port in his consular district.

2. Without prejudice to the powers of the receiving state, a consular officer may conduct investigations into any incidents which occurred during the voyage on vessels sailing under the flag of the sending state, and may settle disputes of any kind between the master, the officers and the seamen insofar as this may be authorized by the laws of the sending state. A consular officer may request the assistance of the competent authorities of the receiving state in the performance of such duties.

3. In the event that the courts or other competent authorities of the receiving state intend to take any coercive action on vessels sailing under the flag of the sending state while they are located in the waters of the

receiving state, the competent authorities of the receiving state shall, unless it is impractical to do so in view of the urgency of the matter, inform a consular officer of the sending state prior to initiating such action so that the consular officer may be present when the action is taken. Whenever it is impractical to notify a consular officer in advance, the competent authorities of the receiving state shall inform him as soon as possible thereafter of the action taken.

4. Paragraph 3 of this Article shall not apply to customs, passport, and sanitary inspections, or to action taken at the request or with the approval of the master of the vessel.

5. The term "vessel," as used in the present Convention, does not include warships.

ARTICLE 14

If a vessel sailing under the flag of the sending state suffers shipwreck, runs aground, is swept ashore, or suffers any other accident whatever within the territorial limits of the receiving state, the competent authorities of the receiving state shall immediately inform a consular officer and advise him of the measures which they have taken to rescue persons, vessel, and cargo.

The consular officer may provide all kinds of assistance to such a vessel, the members of its crew, and its passengers, as well as take measures in connection with the preservation of the cargo and repair of the ship, or may request the authorities of the receiving state to take such measures.

The competent authorities of the receiving state shall render the necessary assistance to the consular officer in measures taken by him in connection with the accident to the vessel.

No customs duties shall be levied against a wrecked vessel, its cargo or stores, in the territory of the receiving state, unless they are delivered for use in that state.

If the owner or anyone authorized to act for him is unable to make necessary arrangements in connection with the vessel or its cargo, the consular officer may make such arrangements. The consular officer may under similar circumstances make arrangements in connection with cargo owned by the sending state or any of its nationals and found or brought into port from a wrecked vessel sailing under the flag of any state except a vessel of the receiving state.

ARTICLE 15

Articles 13 and 14, respectively, shall also apply to aircraft.

RIGHTS, PRIVILEGES AND IMMUNITIES

ARTICLE 16

The national flag of the sending state and the consular flag may be flown at the consular establishment, at the residence of the head of the consular establishment, and on his means of transport used by him in the performance of his official duties. The shield with the national coat-of-arms of the sending state and the name of the establishment may also be affixed on the building in which the consular establishment is located.

ARTICLE 17

The consular archives shall be inviolable at all times and wherever they may be. Unofficial papers shall not be kept in the consular archives.

The buildings or parts of buildings and the land ancillary thereto, used for the purposes of the consular establishment and the residence of the head of the consular establishment, shall be inviolable.

The police and other authorities of the receiving state may not enter the building or that part of the building which is used for the purposes of the consular establishment or the residence of the head of the consular establishment without the consent of the head thereof, persons appointed by him, or the head of the diplomatic mission of the sending state.

ARTICLE 18

1. The consular establishment shall have the right to communicate with its Government, with the diplomatic mission and the consular establishments of the sending state in the receiving state, or with other diplomatic missions and consular establishments of the sending state, making use of all ordinary means of communication. In such communications, the consular establishment shall have the right to use code, diplomatic couriers, and the diplomatic pouch. The same fees shall apply to consular establishments in the use of ordinary means of communication as apply to the diplomatic mission of the sending state.

2. The official correspondence of a consular establishment, regardless of what means of communication are used, and the sealed diplomatic pouch bearing visible external marks of its official character, shall be inviolable and not subject to examination or detention by the authorities of the receiving state.

ARTICLE 19

1. Consular officers shall not be subject to the jurisdiction of the receiving state in matters relating to their official activity. The same

applies to employees of the consular establishment, if they are nationals of the sending state.

2. Consular officers and employees of the consular establishment who are nationals of the sending state shall enjoy immunity from the criminal jurisdiction of the receiving state.

3. This immunity from the criminal jurisdiction of the receiving state of consular officers and employees of the consular establishment of the sending state may be waived by the sending state. Waiver must always be express.

ARTICLE 20

1. Consular officers and employees of the consular establishment, on the invitation of a court of the receiving state, shall appear in court for witness testimony. Taking measures to compel a consular officer or an employee of the consular establishment who is a national of the sending state to appear in court as a witness and to give witness testimony is not permissible.

2. If a consular officer or an employee of the consular establishment who is a national of the sending state for official reasons or for reasons considered valid according to the laws of the receiving state cannot appear in court, he shall inform the court thereof and give witness testimony on the premises of the consular establishment or in his own abode.

3. Whenever under the laws of the receiving state an oath is required to be taken in court by consular officers and employees of the consular establishment, an affirmation shall be accepted in lieu thereof.

4. Consular officers and employees of the consular establishment may refuse to give witness testimony on facts relating to their official activity.

5. The provisions of paragraphs 1, 2, 3, and 4 shall also apply to proceedings conducted by administrative authorities.

ARTICLE 21

1. Immovable property, situated in the territory of the receiving state, of which the sending state or one or more persons acting in its behalf is the owner or lessee and which is used for diplomatic or consular purposes, including residences for personnel attached to the diplomatic and consular establishments, shall be exempt from taxation of any kind imposed by the receiving state or any of its states or local governments other than such as represent payments for specific services rendered.

2. The exemption from taxation referred to in paragraph 1 of this Article shall not apply to such charges, duties, and taxes if, under the law of the receiving state, they are payable by the person who contracted with the sending state or with the person acting on its behalf.

ARTICLE 22

A consular officer or employee of a consular establishment, who is not a national of the receiving state and who does not have the status in the receiving state of an alien lawfully admitted for permanent residence, shall be exempt from the payment of all taxes or similar charges of any kind imposed by the receiving state or any of its states or local governments on official emoluments, salaries, wages, or allowances received by such officer or employee from the sending state in connection with the discharge of his official functions.

ARTICLE 23

1. A consular officer or employee of a consular establishment who is not a national of the receiving state and who does not have the status in the receiving state of an alien lawfully admitted for permanent residence, shall, except as provided in paragraph 2 of this Article, be exempt from the payment of all taxes or similar charges of any kind imposed by the receiving state or any of its states or local governments, for the payment of which the officer or employee of the consular establishment would otherwise be legally liable.

2. The exemption from taxes or charges provided in paragraph 1 of this Article does not apply in respect to taxes or charges upon:

a) The acquisition or possession of private immovable property located in the receiving state if the persons referred to in paragraph 1 of this Article do not own or lease this property on the behalf of the sending state for the purposes of the consular establishment;

b) Income received from sources in the receiving state other than as described in Article 22 of the present Convention;

c) The transfer by gift of property in the receiving state;

d) The transfer at death, including by inheritance, of property in the receiving state.

3. However, the exemption from taxes or similar charges provided in paragraph 1 of this Article, applies in respect to movable inherited property left after the death of a consular officer or employee of the consular establishment or a member of his family residing with him if they are not nationals of the receiving state or aliens lawfully admitted for permanent residence, and if the property was located in the receiving state exclusively in connection with the sojourn in this state of the deceased as a consular officer or employee of the consular establishment or member of his family residing with him.

ARTICLE 24

A consular officer or employee of a consular establishment and members of his family residing with him who are not nationals of the receiving state and who do not have the status in the receiving state of aliens lawfully admitted for permanent residence, shall be exempt in the receiving state from service in the armed forces and from all other types of compulsory service.

ARTICLE 25

A consular officer or employee of a consular establishment and members of his family residing with him who do not have the status in the receiving state of aliens lawfully admitted for permanent residence, shall be exempt from all obligations under the laws and regulations of the receiving state with regard to the registration of aliens, and obtaining permission to reside, and from compliance with other similar requirements applicable to aliens.

ARTICLE 26

1. The same full exemption from customs duties and internal revenue or other taxes imposed upon or by reason of importation shall apply in the receiving state to all articles, including motor vehicles, imported exclusively for the official use of a consular establishment, as applies to articles imported for the official use of the diplomatic mission of the sending state.

2. Consular officers, and employees of the consular establishment, and members of their families residing with them, who are not nationals of the receiving state, and who do not have the status in the receiving state of aliens lawfully admitted for permanent residence, shall be granted, on the basis of reciprocity, the same exemptions from customs duties and internal revenue or other taxes imposed upon or by reason of importation, as are granted to corresponding personnel of the diplomatic mission of the sending state.

3. For the purpose of paragraph 2 of this Article the term "corresponding personnel of the diplomatic mission" refers to members of the diplomatic staff in the case of consular officers, and to members of the administrative and technical staff in the case of employees of a consular establishment.

ARTICLE 27

Subject to the laws and regulations of the receiving state concerning zones entry into which is prohibited or regulated for reasons of national security, a consular officer shall be permitted to travel freely within the limits of his consular district to carry out his official duties.

ARTICLE 28

Without prejudice to their privileges and immunities, it is the duty of all persons enjoying such privileges and immunities to respect the laws and regulations of the receiving state, including traffic regulations.

ARTICLE 29

1. The rights and obligations of consular officers provided for in the present Convention also apply to members of the diplomatic staff of the diplomatic mission of the Contracting Parties charged with the performance of consular functions in the diplomatic mission and who have been notified in a consular capacity to the foreign affairs ministry of the receiving state by the diplomatic mission.

2. Except as provided in paragraph 4 of Article 10 of the present Convention, the performance of consular functions by the persons referred to in paragraph 1 of this Article shall not affect the diplomatic privileges and immunities granted to them as members of the diplomatic mission.

FINAL PROVISIONS

ARTICLE 30

1. The present Convention shall be subject to ratification and shall enter into force on the thirtieth day following the exchange of instruments of ratification, which shall take place in Washington as soon as possible.

2. The Convention shall remain in force until six months from the date on which one of the Contracting Parties informs the other Contracting Party of its desire to terminate its validity.

In witness whereof the Plenipotentiaries of the two Contracting Parties have signed the present Convention and affixed their seals thereto.

Done in Moscow on June 1, 1964 in two copies, each in the English and the Russian language, both texts being equally authentic.

For the Government of the	For the Government of the
United States of America	Union of Soviet Socialist
Foy D. Kohler	Republics
Ambassador of the United States	A. Gromyko
of America to the USSR	Minister for Foreign Affairs of
	the Union of Soviet Socialist
	Republics

PROTOCOL

To the Consular Convention Between the Government of the United States of America and the Government of the Union of Soviet Socialist Republics

1. It is agreed between the Contracting Parties that the notification of a consular officer of the arrest or detention in other form of a national of the sending state specified in paragraph 2 of Article 12 of the Consular Convention between the Government of the United States of America and the Government of the Union of Soviet Socialist Republics of June 1, 1964, shall take place within one to three days from the time of arrest or detention depending on conditions of communication.

2. It is agreed between the Contracting Parties that the rights specified in paragraph 3 of Article 12 of the Consular Convention of a consular officer to visit and communicate with a national of the sending state who is under arrest or otherwise detained in custody shall be accorded within two to four days of the arrest or detention of such national depending upon his location.

3. It is agreed between the Contracting Parties that the rights specified in paragraph 3 of Article 12 of the Consular Convention of a consular officer to visit and communicate with a national of the sending state who is under arrest or otherwise detained in custody or is serving a sentence of imprisonment shall be accorded on a continuing basis.

The present Protocol constitutes an integral part of the Consular Convention between the Government of the United States of America and the Government of the Union of Soviet Socialist Republics of June 1, 1964.

Done at Moscow on June 1, 1964 in two copies, each in the English and the Russian language, both texts being equally authentic.

For the Government of the United States of America
FOY D. KOHLER
Ambassador of the United States of America to the USSR

For the Government of the Union of Soviet Socialist Republics
A. GROMYKO
Minister for Foreign Affairs of the Union of Soviet Socialist Republics

2. THE KREMLIN'S NEW LEADERSHIP*

BY *Business Week*

The new Communist bosses—Leonid I. Brezhnev and Aleksei N. Kosygin—began this week the process of splitting the power of the Soviet Union between them. Last week, they had revealed their surgical efficiency in the skill with which they cut Nikita Khrushchev out.

At midweek, though Khrushchev hadn't yet been seen in public, his successors were professing allegiance to the deposed premier's policies of peaceful coexistence and higher living standards at home. Yet, last week Brezhnev, 57, grabbed Khrushchev's chief position of power —the job of Communist Party First Secretary—and Kosygin, 60, became premier, as the world heard in astonishment that the spectacular 11-year-long Khrushchev era of Russian history had ended.

Much of what happened remains cloaked in mystery. But one thing seems clear: Khrushchev's Communist Party colleagues had grown increasingly impatient of his one-man show, his "hare-brained scheming," his boasting, and his hasty decision-making. When it paid off, as in the first years of his regime, they kept silent; but when his failures mounted—in agriculture, in slow economic growth, in the widening rift with Red China, and in the steady factionalization of the Communist world empire—they plotted his downfall.

The end came, notably, just before major decisions had to be made on allocation of resources for future long-term plans, before December's Moscow meeting scheduled to take some action against Red China, and before Khrushchev's trips to West Germany and the United Nations planned for next year.

I. NEW ROAD

Now, for the third time in its turbulent 47-year history, Soviet Russia is turning into a new—and unknown—road. While few signposts were yet visible, it appeared the new regime would:

* From *Business Week* (October 24, 1964), pp. 30–33. Reprinted by permission of McGraw-Hill, Inc.

▪ Mark time, initially at least, in its relations with the West while the new leaders consolidate their power and reassess the nation's goals. Such pauses are traditional during a period of inner stress in Russia. Thus, while no important moves toward a detente may be in the works for the immediate future, neither are rash moves to heighten tensions likely.

▪ Try to find some basis for better relations with Red China, particularly since Peking has heightened its prestige with its nuclear ability. While no real rapprochement would seem likely between the competing Communist giants, moves may be made to postpone or reshape the Dec. 12 meeting of 26 Communist parties. The preparations have been badly bungled, with only 12 foreign parties so far agreeing to attend.

▪ Further "de-Stalinize" internally, and establish a more consistent ideological framework—though not necessarily a more liberal one—for intellectuals and artists, and 225-million Russian people to live and work in. Neither Brezhnev nor Kosygin was a member of Stalin's inner group, as was Khrushchev, and they can go further in exposing the brutal dictator's crimes.

▪ Push reforms in the industrial sector and in agriculture to spur a higher growth rate. One move may be to stress the concept of profitability as a major success indicator in industry. This controversial measure was much discussed under Khrushchev, but never moved out of the experimental stage. This week, the new leadership took its first step toward reform by ordering one third of Russia's garment and footwear industries to operate on a consumer-oriented basis, rather than total central planning. In agriculture, the scientific approach to farm productivity, now being emphasized, will be pushed harder.

▪ Trim new Soviet foreign aid commitments, which this year have been running at a higher rate (about $900-million) than at any time since 1958, or significantly turn the emphasis of the program more toward smaller Communist countries or those where political results can be expected. On the basis of Kosygin's past remarks to Westerners about the high cost of the space race, some pruning of the Soviet aerospace program wouldn't be surprising.

▪ Shake up personnel in key ministries and party posts, to remove any Khrushchev stalwarts. There also could be a military shakeup in which some of the older marshals would be replaced by younger men.

The newcomers might seek to play a more powerful role in the Soviet leadership, and to place more emphasis on conventional forces than did Khrushchev. The death this week in an airplane crash of Sergei Biryuzov, Soviet chief of staff, may hasten the process. Removal of Khrushchev's son-in-law, Aleksei Adzhubei, as editor of the government newspaper Izvestia could prompt further shakeups in propaganda organs.

II. ORGANIZATION MEN

Certainly, it's true that the style of the new Soviet leadership will be vastly different from that of Khrushchev. While Brezhnev and Kosygin are not colorless men, they do not possess Khrushchev's ebullience, his mercurial temper, his peasant earthiness. There's little indication they will conduct foreign policy by shoe-banging, or at diplomatic cocktail parties, or in interviews with Western newsmen.

Essentially, Brezhnev and Kosygin are products of post-revolutionary Russia; they are basically technocrats and organization men, not revolutionaries; both men were spotted by Khrushchev's keen eye as capable men and comers.

Brezhnev, as Party First Secretary, will play the key role in the new regime. A black-haired Ukrainian, he has an outward poise and air of self-confidence reminiscent of a top Western industrial manager. Indeed, he was trained as a metallurgical engineer, and his first job was in an iron and steel works. He entered party work in 1937, apparently catching Khrushchev's eye around that time. He may have strengthened his relationship with Khrushchev during World War II, when both did political work with the Red Army in the Ukraine.

Postwar, Brezhnev's star rose rapidly. In 1952, he became a member of the party's Central Committee and an alternate on the policymaking Presidium. After a second political post with the armed forces, he was tabbed by Khrushchev to supervise development of the giant Virgin Lands grain growing area. Then, he moved up to the largely ceremonial job of President of the U.S.S.R., which enabled him to meet many foreign dignitaries and to travel abroad.

Last July, Khrushchev—or the top party policymakers—seemingly pointed to Brezhnev as Khrushchev's heir-apparent by appointing him to full-time party secretarial duties.

A disturbing note, for some Westerners, is Brezhnev's past and present connections with the Soviet military establishment. He reportedly is close to several marshals, and himself holds the rank of lieutenant-general.

Kosygin, even more than Brezhnev, is a proven industrial organizer and planner, and his role largely will be that of running the Soviet economy. A sandy-haired man with a lined face, he is agreeable to talk to and is regarded as less ideologically "musclebound" than some of his colleagues. Kosygin first worked in the textile industry, then became commissar of it in 1939, and later commissar of all consumer industries.

As his abilities became known, he moved ahead in party circles. In 1946, Kosygin was named a candidate member of the party Presidium (then known as the Politburo). After a term as finance minister, he apparently fell into Stalin's disfavor, was stripped of his Presidium membership and relegated to economic-planning chores. In a few years, he again emerged in the Presidium, and was appointed a deputy premier in the Soviet government with primary duties as chief economic planner. During Khrushchev's recent trips abroad, Kosygin ran the government.

III. TIME TO PLAN

If Russia's two new leaders are better equipped to run a country that has changed much since Khrushchev came on the scene in 1953, they will have little more room for maneuver than he did. As Communists, they have ideological commitments that limit their flexibility internally, and pretensions to lead the world Communist movement that limit their freedom of action abroad.

They are faced, as Khrushchev was, with parceling out Russia's limited resources to a host of powerful claimants. Meantime, Russia's population has grown by 35-million in the past 10 years, the agriculture problem has remained unsolved, weaponry and the aerospace industry have grown vastly more costly and complex, and Russia's consumers are clamoring for more consumer goods. Abroad, Russia's East European satellites are agitating for still more independence.

Obviously, with these problems, Brezhnev and Kosygin want no quick confrontations, either with the U.S. abroad or with a disgruntled populace at home. Thus, they were quick to pledge continuance of Khrushchev's over-all policies. Indeed, not long after they engineered the anti-Khrushchev coup, Brezhnev and Kosygin sent the Soviet ambassador in Washington, Anatoly Dobrynin, to reassure Pres. Johnson personally that Khrushchev's policies would be continued. In private conversations, Soviet functionaries in the U.S. quickly spread the word that the new regime was—if anything—more anxious than ever to trade with the U. S. This week, a number of U. S. businessmen received visas for a November trip to Moscow. It was pointed out that Kosygin has extensive experience in dealing with Western industrialists.

In their first public appearance this week, the Brezhnev-Kosygin duo told the Russian people of their intentions to continue Khrushchev's foreign and domestic policies—while saying nothing about their attitude toward Red China. The occasion was Monday's big Red Square demonstration for the three new Soviet cosmonauts. Brezhnev, in an apparent bid for popular support, also appealed for a "high level of organization, unity, and cohesion" around the new Communist leadership. He didn't mention Russia's feud with China.

But for thousands of anxious Russian citizens, the Red Square show was notable mainly for the absence, for the first time in years, of the rotund figure of Khrushchev. Few accepted the official press explanation that Khrushchev had asked to be relieved of his duties because of his 70 years and "deteriorating" health. If the old man was being honorably retired, they asked, why was it necessary to expel him completely from the Presidium—the party's inner circle of policymakers? Glumly, they watched Khrushchev's portraits being methodically removed from the city center outward. Many privately remembered that truly "collective" leadership has never worked for a long period in Soviet Russia.

Thus, in the aftermath of the coup, Moscow was swept with rumors that the gaunt, mysterious 62-year-old party theoretician, Mikhail Suslov, had played the key role in ousting Khrushchev and was running the new show from behind the scenes; and that Nikolai Podgorny, a tough Ukrainian, was waiting in the wings as Khrushchev once did.

But a heartening sign, during Khrushchev's overthrow, was the absence of tanks or unusually large number of security police on Moscow's streets.

If the details of the coup were murky, the picture that emerged this week was of a long-growing dissatisfaction with Khrushchev within the Communist hierarchy. The resentment may have been building since the 1962 Cuban missile crisis, and been heightened by the steadily worsening relations with the Chinese and by last year's farm disasters. But there probably was one—as yet obscure—cause for the crisis point last week.

In any case, it seems clear that Khrushchev had in recent times tried to run roughshod over the party's top policymakers, plunging ahead with schemes they opposed or assuming he could bypass them by appealing directly to the Russian people. On Oct. 2, for example, Khrushchev was quoted briefly as saying Soviet economic specialists had been told to draw up a new economic plan that would give first priority to "satisfying the growing material and spiritual needs" of the people. This switch to consumer goods, if carried out, would be a revolutionary departure for the Soviets who always have placed their greatest emphasis on heavy industry and defense. But the full text of Khrushchev's remarks never was published.

The experts reason that this may have generated a fierce argument in which all the various claimants on resources, and particularly the military, fought to keep from being cut back, and possibly joined forces to halt Khrushchev's plans. Most analysts lean to the view that such an internal dispute more likely forced the crisis than the handling of the Sino-Soviet quarrel, though the break with China and the rapid disintegration of the Communist world that has accompanied it no doubt weighed heavily in the anti-Khrushchev dossier.

Early last week, apparently unaware of the storm-clouds, Khrushchev went about his business with his customary exuberance. At his vacation villa on the Black Sea on Monday, he talked by radio-telephone with the three orbiting cosmonauts.

Meanwhile, in his absence, the Communist Party's 10-man Presidium met in Moscow. A vote was taken, and a majority was found to favor Khrushchev's ouster. Shortly after, the Central Committee convened quickly in Moscow and Khrushchev, who had by now returned, evidently made a fiery speech in his own defense.

But the members turned thumbs down. Khrushchev's fabled ability to survive had finally failed him.

There are many ironies in Khrushchev's downfall. Brezhnev and Kosygin were, of course, his proteges. Suslov, who may have engineered the coup, once helped to save Khrushchev in a battle for control with the old Stalinist group. The Central Committee contains many men put there by Khrushchev.

Furthermore, Khrushchev had been concerned that, when he finally left the Russian scene, an orderly transition of power should take place. Only a few months ago, he chaired a meeting of the Constitutional Commission of the Supreme Soviet. At that meeting, one of the subjects presumably discussed was the defining of a better means for the transfer of power.

Most of all, the one thing that could have kept Khrushchev in power would have been a personal secret police, similar to Stalin's. But his dismantling of a large part of the terror apparatus after Stalin's death may have been Khrushchev's greatest legacy to the Russian people.

3. THE SOVIETS CHANGE THEIR FOREIGN POLICY*

BY RICHARD LOWENTHAL

Is it true that Soviet foreign policy is still continuing along the same lines as in Nikita Khrushchev's time? Last October, when this overconfident and willful leader was suddenly overthrown, not a few people in the West were worried: Would not his successors seek to restore Communist unity by adopting Peking's militant anti-Western strategy? Now, half a year later, it is obvious to all that the gulf between the two major Communist powers cannot be bridged; hence the Western public has settled back in the comfortable assumption that nothing important has changed in Soviet foreign policy. But that assumption is wrong.

In fact, there has been a marked shift both in the immediate priorities and in the style of Soviet relations with the outside world. It has not been announced or explained: On the contrary, the new men have reacted against the Khrushchevian style of basing Soviet diplomacy on grandiose, comprehensive concepts, and have preferred to make their adjustments quietly and with a minimum of verbal fuss. But in substance, they have shifted the emphasis of their relations with Communist China from direct opposition, in terms of ideology and

* From *The New York Times Magazine* (April 4, 1965), p. 30 ff. Reprinted by permission of *The New York Times* and the author.

power-politics, to indirect competition for influence on the anti-Western, revolutionary-nationalist governments and movements of the underdeveloped world. At the same time, in their relations with the West, they have transferred their main effort from direct approaches to the United States aiming at a major *détente* to indirect maneuvers for exploiting the disagreements within the Western alliance. In the latest resolution of the Central Committee approving the communiqué of the March conference of 19 Communist parties, this shift of priorities is hinted at by mentioning the struggle against imperialism and for national liberation ahead of the struggle for peace.

The change is clearly to our disadvantage: The Soviets have become more active in probing the weak spots of the Western position, both in Europe and among the new nations, than they were during the last two years of Khrushchev's rule. But while they have abandoned, for the time being, the latter-day Khrushchev's urgent search for an all-embracing dialogue with the United States, they have not returned to the equally urgent and all-embracing offensive against the Western alliance which the early Khrushchev pursued, at mounting expense and risk, from the launching of the sputniks in 1957 to its final debacle in the Cuban missile crisis of 1962. Rather, they seem to have concluded that they can obtain a breathing spell in the arms race without paying the price that a negotiated over-all *détente* would require, and that they can go on patiently undermining Western positions in various parts of the world without incurring the heavy costs of a dramatic over-all offensive.

Similarly, the new rulers of the Soviet Union have not been tempted for a moment to submit to Mao Tse-tung's ideological authority, or to allow Russia's foreign policy to be dictated by Peking. But they did make a serious attempt—the first one since the Communist world conference of 1960—to see whether the ideological conflict could be kept within bounds, and a modicum of cooperation be restored between the two major Communist states, by more limited concessions. While these have not been sufficient to reactivate the Sino-Soviet alliance, or even to end Chinese ideological attacks and efforts to split the Communist movement, they have eased the Soviets' international position: For a time at least, the two powers have stopped moving along an actual "collision course."

Few of those who use this term are aware of the degree of military tension that was apparently reached along the border of Sinkiang in the last months of Khrushchev's reign. Though territorial differences had always been an element in the background of the dispute, the Chinese, conscious of the disparity of military power, had long deliberately refrained from pressing their claims. Yet in an interview granted to visiting Japanese Socialists last July, Mao accused the Soviets of having grabbed foreign lands at the expense of Poland, Rumania, Finland and Germany as well as of Japan and China, of harboring further claims on Chinese territory in Sinkiang and the Amur River region, and of backing them up by troop concentrations.

In August, Aleksei Adzhubei, Khrushchev's son-in-law, told a German weekly that "not only our entire military might but the heart of all our people" was guarding the Soviet frontiers, "in the West and in the East." Finally, on Sept. 2, Pravda reprinted the Mao interview, explaining that the Soviets had vainly asked for an official denial and rejecting Mao's views—but not his statement about Soviet troop concentrations.

All this suggests that the military build-up of both sides must have increased considerably above the "normal" needs of closing the border against refugees—precisely during the last few months before the Chinese nuclear test explosion in Sinkiang. We are entitled to wonder whether the increase of tension was not connected with the approach of that event. Possibly, Mao feared Soviet military action to prevent his test.

It seems clear, at any rate, that when the bomb had exploded and Khrushchev had fallen, border tension dropped quickly to the normal level of the preceding years. Moreover, the new Soviet leaders, by supporting the Chinese proposal for a meeting of the five nuclear powers to ban the use of atomic weapons, indicated their acceptance of China's membership in the "nuclear club."

When a Chinese delegation headed by Chou En-lai went to the Moscow November celebrations to explore the attitude of the new leaders, the Soviets refused to disavow their major policies and doctrines, but offered to resume aid to China and to stop public ideological polemics. Subsequently, the preparatory conference of 26 Communist parties, which Khrushchev had called for mid-December in the hope of getting a condemnation of Chinese views, was postponed until March amid assurances that no "showdown" or "excommunication" was intended; and when it finally met, it adopted a communiqué plainly intended to offer the Chinese a platform on which they could step if they were willing to try to heal the split.

Finally, as the guerrilla war in Vietnam began to approach a crucial stage, a Soviet delegation headed by Premier Kosygin was dispatched to Hanoi, and subsequently to Korea. The mission had the double purpose of demonstrating Soviet solidarity with Communist parties and governments within the Chinese power sphere, and of seeking to regain some influence over those parties—yet without any attacks on the Chinese and in a framework of at least formal cooperation with them.

It is now clear that the new Soviet tactics have failed either to restore a facade of Sino-Soviet cooperation, or to improve the Soviets' ideological position in the struggle for influence over the Communist parties. But they have reduced direct, physical tension on Russia's Far Eastern border, and they have enabled the Soviets to regain at least some foothold of political influence in Vietnam, a foothold the Chinese are now trying to eliminate by increasingly bitter attacks.

While seeking to take the heat out of the confrontation with their Chinese allies and rivals, the new Soviet leaders have also allowed their zeal for major bilateral negotiations with the United States to cool down.

The American Presidential campaign had imposed the usual pause on the dialogue, yet even when the election was over the men who had taken over from Khrushchev showed little eagerness for resuming. They took friendly, if hesitant, note of President Johnson's offer for an exchange of visits, but they showed no sense of urgency and offered no new proposals for negotiation. Instead, they began to exploit and encourage President de Gaulle's illusion that the major problems of Europe might one day be solved without the United States.

In this respect, at least, the attitude of the new Soviet rulers is closer to that of Stalin than to that of Khrushchev. It was the most fundamental maxim of Stalinist foreign policy that every resource of Soviet diplomacy should be employed to keep the "imperialists" divided—to play one potentially hostile power group against another. When Stalin finally found that his postwar conquests had united his opponents in a single camp under American leadership, he was profoundly worried; the last years of his life were spent in vain but persistent attempts to revive nationalist opposition to American "domination" in Western Europe, particularly over the issue of West German rearmament.

Khrushchev, on the other hand, took American leadership of the West for granted to a much greater extent. As long as he believed he could break up the alliance, he relied not so much on baits to the separate interests of its major partners as on threats against its most exposed members—combined with efforts to persuade the United States to reduce its commitments. When the attempt at a break-through by blackmail had clearly failed, the effort at reaching a *détente* by negotiation was even more concentrated on the "direct wire" to Washington.

In particular, it is remarkable how little use Khrushchevian diplo-macy made of President de Gaulle's ambition to build up an inde-pendent world power based on a French-led Western Europe: The general was seen as a minor obstacle to the nuclear test ban and a major potential source of backing for the West German "mili-tarists," rather than as a hopeful force for the disruption of the Western alliance.

The new team in the Kremlin has changed all that. It operates on the assumption that a *détente* with the United States over Europe is safe enough without further negotiations, and that any pressure for either German reunification or West German nuclear participa-tion can be most easily frustrated by playing Paris against Washing-ton.

Thus, the new men have deliberately helped de Gaulle to turn the granting of French long-term credits to the Soviet Union into a major political gesture. They have relied on de Gaulle to stop the M.L.F. without their having to pay any diplomatic price for its prevention, and to veto the West German proposal for a standing four-power conference on the German problem before they them-selves could be put into the embarrassing position of having to reject it. They have encouraged the French Communists in a policy that amounts to tactical support of de Gaulle against the center parties led by Gaston Defferre, the Socialist Mayor of Marseilles, because those parties are the main supporters of Western unity. They have eagerly welcomed de Gaulle's suggestion for a settlement of the German question "among Europeans"—a term meant to include

Russia, but not the United States—and have applauded his proposals for a reconstruction of the U.N. that would destroy any chances of future executive action, as well as for a "return to the gold standard" which would result in a drastic slowdown of the growth rate of the Western economies. And they have even begun to turn around the Western tactics of increased contact with the East European states by advising the most loyal among their Communist governments—notably Hungary and Bulgaria—to send delegations to Paris and support Gaullist hopes for an "independent" Europe "from the Atlantic to the Urals."

Nor is the new Soviet attitude to de Gaulle the only example of a more active exploitation of conflicts of interest and outlook within the Western alliance. Moscow's former reticence in dealing with the Cyprus problem has now given way to a major campaign for weaning Turkey away from NATO.

The revival of Soviet interest in probing the weak spots of the West is not confined to Europe. In Africa, the unending troubles of the Congo have furnished Khrushchev's successors with an opportunity to kill two birds with one stone—to turn a number of nationalist governments against the West, and to outbid the Chinese in their support.

The tribal rebellions against the Adoula Government in Leopoldville had been protracted and troublesome, but had enjoyed little outside support, except from China. Then, following the withdrawal of the United Nations, Adoula was replaced by Tshombe, who proceeded to fight the rebels with the help of white mercenaries. At that point, many African nationalist governments began to express sympathy for the rebels, and, as Tshombe received American logistic support, they came to hold the West in general and the United States in particular responsible for his return to power.

An atmosphere was thus created in which even the action taken to rescue the rebel-held white hostages was regarded by most Africans as an act of Western intervention in an African civil war—one in which a number of Arab and African governments were willing to intervene on the other side by supplying arms and instructors to the rebels. At that moment, the Soviet Government offered to replace any arms which these countries—Egypt and Algeria in the first place—would dispatch in the cause of "African solidarity." Thus, without incurring the slightest risk on the spot, the Soviets both ensured the involvement of these "nonaligned" powers in anti-Western action and proved themselves superior to the Chinese in the effectiveness of their aid for "national liberation."

Soviet political gains from this maneuver have been all the greater because of a more flexible ideological attitude toward revolutionary-nationalist regimes which Russia had begun to adopt in the last year of Khrushchev's reign, and which the new men took over and developed. During the Moscow visit of "Comrade" Ben Bella and Khrushchev's own visit to Nasser last spring, the Soviets officially admitted for the first time that some of the new nationalist regimes might embark on the road of "socialist development" without the leadership, or even the separate existence, of local Communist parties. Last December, two months after Khrushchev's fall, Pravda reported that a meeting of representatives of Communists—not of Communist parties—from the Arab countries had approved the principle that work inside the ruling nationalist-revolutionary parties was the best contribution Communists in some of those countries could make, as indeed they have been doing quite openly in Algeria at least since the beginning of 1964. By turning the local Communists of those countries from potential rivals of the nationalist leaders into valued but noncompetitive advisers, the Soviets have considerably strengthened their own chances of influencing government policies there.

Clearly, the new tactics of Khrushchev's successors have been much more successful against the West than against Communist China. In Europe, the divided West has been unable to follow up the advantage it enjoyed after the Cuban missile crisis and still held at the time of the test-ban agreement. In Africa and Asia, the decline of Western influence has been marked; it can be measured in the willingness of the bulk of the excolonial nations, despite their vital interest in an effective United Nations machinery, to yield to Soviet blackmail designed to paralyze that machinery on the issue of contributions.

But the Soviet attempt to regain influence in Vietnam, as both a supporter of local Communists and as a potential mediator, has come up against intransigent Chinese opposition (and has received little encouragement from the United States). The Soviet offer of a truce in ideological polemics has drawn nothing but ridicule from Peking. Worst of all, from Moscow's point of view, the attempt to strengthen the Soviet ideological position by calling an international "unity conference" has ended in humiliating political defeat, with the Soviets forced to acknowledge that they lack the authority to bring about a representative conference, even of their own supporters, without the consent and participation of their Chinese opponents.

In part, of course, this difference in results may be due to the difference in the continuity, determination and over-all vision with which the new Soviet tactics have been met, respectively, by Western and by Chinese policy. But in part it probably reflects the peculiar aptitudes and weaknesses of the men who have shaped the new tactics. Neither First Secretary Brezhnev, nor Premier Kosygin, nor even President Mikoyan is noted for a particular concern with the intricacies of Communist doctrine. Indeed, they seem to have left the handling of the disastrous international conference to the ailing Suslov and his specialist collaborators without even putting in an appearance.

Both Mikoyan, who has by far the greatest international experience among them, and Kosygin, on whom the main burden for presenting Soviet foreign policy seems to have devolved, have spent the main part of their careers in positions of primarily economic responsibility, and the new style of Soviet foreign policy suggests that, like good economists, they are seeking to obtain a maximum of tangible results with a minimum of outlay. That is, perhaps, a natural reaction for the leaders of a country that is still suffering from the strains produced by a period of excessive commitments in multiple directions—leaders who must be highly conscious of the close interconnection between foreign policy and the allocation of national resources. But it is hardly adequate for offering new inspiration to those armies of former believers who have lost their faith in the unique mission of the Soviet fatherland.

The evidence for a change in Soviet foreign policy has been presented here with no intention to suggest that the new leaders have worked out a new "master plan." What it does suggest is that they have changed their priorities and have developed a new attitude that is more skillfully "opportunist" than under Khrushchev—in the literal sense of exploiting the opportunities offered to them by the weaknesses of the West.

In recent months, that Soviet "opportunism" has done effective harm to our cause; yet it has been based on openings created not by the Soviet leaders but by the West's own errors and disunities. There is, of course, no way in which the leaders of an alliance consisting of sovereign states with different interests and internal problems could avoid *all* such weaknesses. But at least a few general lessons may perhaps be drawn from the story that has been told here.

The first is that the Soviets are still opponents, and indeed the main opponents, of the United States and of the West in general. Their conflict with China is not of a kind that would threaten their physical security and force them into our arms—not for a long time to come. Internal change may gradually reduce Soviet hostility to the West, but this will not occur quickly, nor be independent of our own actions. But so long as Soviet resources are applied to the detriment of the West, Russia remains our main opponent, for— again, for a long time to come—Russia's resources are incomparably more powerful than those of China.

The second lesson concerns the primacy of Europe among the contested areas of the world. For all the growth—often tragically slow—in the development of other world regions, the small subcontinent from which Western civilization has sprung still outranks them all in the importance of its human and material potential. It is not by the control of Southeast Asia that the world balance of power can be shifted—not in our lifetime.

The final point is the importance of continuity and initiative in world affairs, and particularly in dealing with new men in control of a great power. The statesman who wishes to influence the conduct of new opponents must actively create conditions that will deter them from one course and induce them to another. He cannot afford to wait for them to make up their minds before he makes up his.

Bibliography

Acheson, Dean. *Power and Diplomacy.* New York, Atheneum, 1962.

Adler, Selig. *The Isolationist Impulse, Its 20th Century Reaction.* New York, Collier, 1961.

Almond, Gabriel A., and James S. Coleman, eds. *The Politics of the Developing Areas.* Princeton, Princeton University Press, 1960.

Armstrong, John A. *The Politics of Totalitarianism: The Communist Party of the Soviet Union from 1934 to the Present.* New York, Random House, 1961.

Barnett, A. D. *Communist China and Asia.* New York, Harper, 1960.

Berdyaw, Nicolas. *The Origin of Russian Communism.* Translation by R. M. French. Ann Arbor, Michigan, University of Michigan Press, 1960.

Bergson, Abram. *The Real National Income of Soviet Russia Since 1928.* Cambridge, Mass., Harvard University Press, 1961.

Boyd, R. G. *Communist China's Foreign Policy.* New York, Praeger, 1962.

Brzezioski, Z. K. *The Soviet Bloc: Unity and Conflict.* Cambridge, Mass., Harvard University Press, 1960.

Buchan, Alastair. *NATO in the 1960's.* New York, Praeger, 1960.

Buss, C. A. *The People's Republic of China.* Princeton, New Jersey, Van Nostrand, 1962.

Butwell, Richard. *Southeast Asia Today and Tomorrow, A Political Analysis.* New York, Praeger, 1961.

Campaigne, J. G. *American Might and Soviet Myth.* Chicago, Regnery, 1960.

Campbell, Robert W. *Soviet Economic Power.* Cambridge, Mass., Riverside Press, 1960.

Cerf, J. H. and Pozen Walker. *Strategy for the 60's.* New York, Praeger, 1961.

Clark, Grenville and L. B. Sohn. *World Peace Through World Law.* 2nd ed. Cambridge, Mass., Harvard University Press, 1960.

Conquest, Robert. *Power and Policy in the U.S.S.R.: The Study of Soviet Dynastics.* New York, St. Martin's Press, 1961.

481

482 SELECTED BIBLIOGRAPHY

Cook, F. J. *The Warfare State.* New York, Macmillan, 1962.

Dallin, Alexander. *Soviet Conduct in World Affairs.* New York, Columbia University Press, 1960.

Dallin, David J. *Soviet Foreign Affairs After Stalin.* Philadelphia, Lippincott, 1961.

Daniels, Robert V. ed. *A Documentary History of Communism.* New York, Random House, 1960.

Davids, Jules. *America and the World of Our Time: United States Diplomacy in the 20th Century.* New York, Random House, 1960.

Deutschen, Isaac. *The Great Conflict: Russia and the West.* New York, Oxford University Press, 1960.

Edwardes, Michael. *Asia in the Balance.* Baltimore, Penguin, 1962.

Emerson, Rupert. *From Empire to Nation: The Rise of Self-Assertion of Asian and African Peoples.* Cambridge, Harvard University Press, 1960.

Garthoff, R. L. *Soviet Strategy in the Nuclear Age.* New York, Praeger, 1962.

Graebuer, N. A. *Cold War Diplomacy.* Princeton, New Jersey, Van Nostrand, 1962.

Gross, E. A. *The United Nations: Structure for Peace.* New York, Harper, 1962.

Heilbroner, R. L. *The Making of Economic Society.* Englewood Cliffs, New Jersey, Prentice-Hall, 1962.

Hsieh, A. L. *Communist China's Strategy in the Nuclear Age.* Englewood Cliffs, New Jersey, Prentice-Hall, 1962.

Hudson, G. F., *et al.* eds. *The Sino-Soviet Dispute.* New York, 1961.

Jackson, W. A. D. *Russo-Chinese Borderlands.* Princeton, New Jersey, Van Nostrand, 1962.

Kahn, Herman. *On Thermonuclear War.* Princeton, New Jersey, Princeton University Press, 1960.

Kennan, G. F. *Soviet Foreign Policy, 1919–1941.* Princeton, New Jersey, Van Nostrand, 1960.

Kennan, George F. *Russia and the West under Lenin and Stalin.* Boston, Little, Brown, and Co., 1960.

Kissinger, H. A. *The Necessity for Choice: Prospects of American Foreign Policy.* New York, Harper, 1961.

Knorr, Klaus and W. J. Baumal, eds. *What Price Economic Growth?* Englewood Cliffs, New Jersey, Prentice-Hall, 1961.

Liska, George. *The New Statecraft: Foreign Aid in American Foreign Policy.* Chicago, University of Chicago Press, 1960.

Lerner, Max. *The Age of Overkill: A Preface to World Politics.* New York, Simon and Schuster, 1962.

Lukacs, John. *A History of the Cold War.* Garden City, New York, Doubleday, 1961.

Martin, Laurence W. *Neutralism and Nonalignment.* New York, Praeger, 1962.

Marguard, Leo. *People and Policies of South Africa,* 3rd ed. London, Oxford University Press, 1962.

Massachusetts Institute of Technology. Center for International Studies, *Economic, Social, and Political Change in the Underdeveloped Countries.* U. S. Senate Committee on Foreign Relations, March 30, 1960.

McKay, Vernon. *Africa in World Politics.* New York, Harper, 1962.

Millis, Walter, Reinhold Niebuhr, Harrison Brown, James Real, and W. D. Douglas. *A World Without War.* New York, Washington Square Press, 1961.

Montgomery, J. D. *The Politics of Foreign Aid.* New York, Praeger, 1962.

Mosely, P. E. *The Kremlin and World Politics.* New York, Vintage, 1960.

Myrdal, Gunner. *Beyond the Welfare State: Economic Planning and Its International Implications.* New Haven, University Press, 1960.

Neal, F. W. *United States Foreign Policy and the Soviet Union.* Fund for the Republic, Center for the Study of Democratic Institutions, Santa Barbara, California, 1961.

Peretz, Don. *The Middle East Today.* New York, Holt, Rinehart, Winston, 1963.

Rivkin, Arnold. *Africa and the West: Elements of Free World Policy.* New York, Praeger, 1961.

Rossiter, Clinton. *Conservatism in America.* New York, Vintage, 1962.

Rostov, W. W. *The Process of Economic Growth.* New York, Norton, 1962.

———— *The Stages of Economic Growth: A Non-Communist Manifesto.* Cambridge, Mass., Harvard University Press, 1960.

———— *The United States in the World Arena.* New York, Harper, 1960.

Schilling, T. C. and M. H. Halperin. *Strategy and Arms Control.* New York, Twentieth Century Fund, 1961.

Schuman, F. S. *The Cold War: Retrospect and Prospect.* Baton Rouge, Louisiana State University Press, 1962.

Seton-Watson, Hugh. *From Lenin to Khrushchev: The History of World Communism.* New York, Praeger, 1960.

Seton-Watson, Hugh. *Neither War Nor Peace: The Struggle for Power in the Postwar World.* New York, Praeger, 1960.

Sharaki, H. B. *Governments and Politics in the Middle East in the 20th Century.* Princeton, New Jersey, Van Nostrand, 1962.

Shepherd, G. W., Jr. *The Politics of African Nationalism*. New York, Praeger, 1962.

Sievers, A. M. *Revolution, Evolution, and the Economic Order*. Englewood Cliffs, New Jersey, Prentice-Hall, 1962.

Spanier, J. W. and J. L. Nogee, *The Politics of Disarmament*. New York, Praeger, 1962.

Spiro, H. J. *Politics in Africa*. Englewood Cliffs, New Jersey, Prentice-Hall, 1962.

Stillman, Edmund and William Pfaff. *The New Politics: America and the End of the Post War World*. New York, Harper, 1962.

Stoessinger, J. G. *The Might of Nations, World Politics in Our Time*. New York, Random House, 1961.

Strausze-Hupe, Robert, *et al. A Forward Strategy for America*. New York, Harper, 1961.

Thompson, K. W. *Political Realism and the Crisis of World Politics*. Princeton, New Jersey, Princeton University Press, 1960.

Thompson, K. W. *American Diplomacy and Emergent Patterns*. New York, New York University Press, 1962.

Thorp, W. L. ed. *The United States and the Far East*. Englewood Cliffs, New Jersey, Prentice-Hall, 1962.

Turner, G. B. and R. D. Challenger, eds. *National Security in the Nuclear Age*. New York, Praeger, 1960.

Ulam, A. B. *The Unfinished Revolution*. New York, Random House, 1960.

Wallerstein, Immanuel. *Africa: The Politics of Independence*. New York, Vintage, 1961.

Ward, Barbara. *The Rich Nations and the Poor Nations*. New York, Norton, 1962.

Whitaker, U. G., Jr. *Propaganda and International Relations*. San Francisco, Chandler Publishing Co., 1962.

Wiens, H. J. *Pacific Islands: Bastions of the United States*. Princeton, New Jersey, Van Nostrand, 1962.

Williams, W. A. *The Tragedy of American Diplomacy*. New York, Delta, 1962.

Wolf, Charles, Jr. *Foreign Aid: Theory and Practice in Southern Asia*. Princeton, New Jersey, Princeton University Press, 1960.

Wolfers, Arnold. *Discord and Collaboration: Essays in International Politics*. Baltimore, Johns Hopkins, 1962.

Zagoria, D. S. *The Sino-Soviet Conflict 1956–1961*. Princeton, New Jersey, Princeton University Press, 1962.